Introduction to Adaptive Sport and Recreation

Robin Hardin, PhD

University of Tennessee

Joshua R. Pate, PhD

Lees-McRae College

EDITORS

HUMAN KINETICS

Library of Congress Cataloging-in-Publication Data

Names: Hardin, Robin L., 1970- editor. | Pate, Joshua R., editor.
Title: Introduction to adaptive sport and recreation / Robin Hardin, Joshua
  R. Pate, editors.
Description: Champaign, IL : Human Kinetics, 2025. | Includes
  bibliographical references and index.
Identifiers: LCCN 2024016680 (print) | LCCN 2024016681 (ebook) | ISBN
  9781718214538 (paperback) | ISBN 9781718214545 (epub) | ISBN
  9781718214552 (pdf)
Subjects: LCSH: Sports for people with disabilities. | Physical fitness for
  people with disabilities. | People with disabilities–Recreation. |
  BISAC: SPORTS & RECREATION / Disability Sports | SPORTS & RECREATION /
  Olympics & Paralympics
Classification: LCC GV709.3 .I67 2025 (print) | LCC GV709.3 (ebook) | DDC
  796.04/56–dc23/eng/20240509
LC record available at https://lccn.loc.gov/2024016680
LC ebook record available at https://lccn.loc.gov/2024016681

ISBN: 978-1-7182-1453-8 (print)

Copyright © 2025 by Robin Hardin and Joshua R. Pate

Human Kinetics supports copyright. Copyright fuels scientific and artistic endeavor, encourages authors to create new works, and promotes free speech. Thank you for buying an authorized edition of this work and for complying with copyright laws by not reproducing, scanning, or distributing any part of it in any form without written permission from the publisher. You are supporting authors and allowing Human Kinetics to continue to publish works that increase the knowledge, enhance the performance, and improve the lives of people all over the world.

To report suspected copyright infringement of content published by Human Kinetics, contact us at **permissions@hkusa. com**. To request permission to legally reuse content published by Human Kinetics, please refer to the information at **https:// US.HumanKinetics.com/pages/permissions-translations-faqs**.

The web addresses cited in this text were current as of February 2024, unless otherwise noted.

Acquisitions Editor: Andrew L. Tyler; **Developmental Editor:** Jacqueline Eaton Blakley; **Managing Editor:** Chital Mehta; **Copyeditor:** Michelle Horn; **Proofreader:** Joyce Li; **Indexer:** Ferreira Indexing; **Permissions Manager:** Laurel Mitchell; **Graphic Designer:** Nancy Rasmus; **Layout:** MPS Limited; **Cover Designer:** Keri Evans; **Cover Design Specialist:** Susan Rothermel Allen; **Photograph (cover):** David Berding/Getty Images; **Photographs (interior):** © Human Kinetics, unless otherwise noted; **Photo Asset Manager:** Laura Fitch; **Photo Production Manager:** Jason Allen; **Senior Art Manager:** Kelly Hendren; **Illustrations:** © Human Kinetics; **Printer:** Color House Graphics, Inc.

Printed in the United States of America   10   9   8   7   6   5   4   3   2   1

The paper in this book is certified under a sustainable forestry program.

Human Kinetics
1607 N. Market Street
Champaign, IL 61820
USA

United States and International
Website: **US.HumanKinetics.com**
Email: info@hkusa.com
Phone: 1-800-747-4457

Canada
Website: **Canada.HumanKinetics.com**
Email: info@hkcanada.com

E8717

CONTENTS

PREFACE   vii

CHAPTER 1   Theoretical and Social Considerations of Adaptive Sport and Recreation **1**

Justin A. Haegele, PhD, and Cathy McKay, EdD

What Is a Disability?   2
Ableism   6
Inclusion Versus Integration   7
Theoretical Considerations   9
Summary   12

CHAPTER 2   Barriers and Opportunities for Access and Inclusion **15**

Kathleen McCarty, PhD; Laurin Bixby, PhD; and Winston Kennedy, PT, DPT, MPH, PhD

Models of Disability Perception   17
Understanding Barriers   20
Attempts to Mitigate Disparities   23
Social-Ecological Model   27
Summary   30

CHAPTER 3   Innovation in Disability Sport and Recreation **33**

David Legg, PhD, and Simon Darcy, PhD

What Is Innovation?   33
Examples of Innovation   35
Approaches to Innovation   39
How to Share an Innovation   41
Summary   41

CHAPTER 4   History and Development of the Paralympic Games **43**

Ian Brittain, PhD

Early History of Disability Sport   43
The Stoke Mandeville Games   45
The Start of the Paralympic Games   48
Development of the Paralympic Games   51
Impact of the Paralympic Games Linking to the Olympic Movement   52
How the Term *Paralympic* Has Changed Over Time   52

Impairment Groups That Participate in the Paralympic Games   52
Current Governance Structure for the Paralympic Movement   55
Aims of the Paralympic Games Beyond Sport   58
Summary   60

CHAPTER 5   Legal Aspects of Disability Sport and Recreation   63

Anita Moorman, JD

History of the Disability Rights Movement   64
International Legal and Policy Efforts on Disability Rights   64
United States Legal Framework for Disability Rights   67
Impact of Disability Rights Laws on Athletic Participation   73
Impact of Disability Rights Laws on Sports Venues   76
Summary   86

CHAPTER 6   Media and Disability Sport   89

Erin Pearson, MA, and Laura Misener, PhD

Introduction   89
Media Representation of Disability   90
Media Representation of Disability Sport and the Paralympic Games   91
Competing Perspectives of Disability Sports Coverage   96
The Future of Disability Sports Coverage   100
Summary   102

CHAPTER 7   Elite Adaptive Sport   103

Jeff Ward, PhD, and Mary Hums, PhD

Major Games Featuring Disability Sport   103
Current Issues in Disability Sport Competition   117
Summary   119

CHAPTER 8   Sport for Athletes With Intellectual Impairment   121

Abby Fines, PhD, and Christina Mehrtens, PhD

Special Olympics Versus Paralympics   121
Contextualizing Intellectual Disability Within Sport   122
Intellectual Disability and Special Olympics   128
Intellectual Impairment and the Paralympics   137
Summary   141

CHAPTER 9   Para-Athlete Development   143

Darda Sales, PhD, PLY, and Laura Misener, PhD

Long-Term Development Model   144
American Development Model   145
Foundation, Talent, Elite, Mastery Model   146
Application of the Long-Term Development Model to Para-Athletes   148
Considerations for the Development of Para-Athletes   148
What's Next?   159
Summary   160

CONTENTS   **v**

CHAPTER 10   **Adaptive Sports and Recreation for Military Populations**   **161**

Jasmine Townsend, PhD, CTRS, FDRT, CARSS-II, and Derek Whaley, MS, CTRS, CARSS-I

Common Health Conditions Among Service Members and Veterans   163
Veteran-Focused Treatment Options   163
Adaptive Sports and Recreation for Military Service Members   165
Characteristics of Community-Based Adaptive Sports and Recreation Programs   171
Benefits of Adaptive Sports for Military Populations   172
Summary   175

CHAPTER 11   **Adaptive Youth Sports**   **177**

Anthony G. Delli Paoli, PhD, and Javier Robles, JD

Adaptive Youth Sports Settings   177
Adaptive Youth Sports Participation   179
Summary   184

CHAPTER 12   **Funding Disability Sport**   **187**

Michael Cottingham, PhD; Tiao Hu, MS; Don Lee, PhD; and Oluwaferanmi Okanlami, MD

Costs and Expenses Related to Disability Sport   188
Sources of Funding   193
Collegiate Programs   200
Funding Personnel: Disability Sport Promoters   202
Future Trends in Disability Sport Funding   204
Summary   204

CASE STUDY   **University of Alabama Adapted Athletics**   **205**

Margaret Stran, PhD, and Brent Hardin, PhD

Starting the Program   206
Sports   208
Organization   210
People   210
Facilities   212
Funding   215
Sport for All   217
Outreach   219
Change   219
Advice   220
Summary   221

GLOSSARY   222
REFERENCES   229
INDEX   252
ABOUT THE EDITORS   261
ABOUT THE CONTRIBUTORS   262

PREFACE

We were collecting data for a research study focused on sport management faculty members' use of disability-related content in the classroom when interview after interview kept revealing the same message: *There are no resources for this area.* One after another, faculty who did include disability content in their sport management courses kept saying they used search engines to find content or relied on personal information for building class assignments and reading materials. Each participant in the study mentioned the need for a textbook—a resource that collected and synthesized foundational content that could be used to educate students studying sport management and issues related to disability.

More concerning was the low number of responses to our study. We asked more than 700 sport management faculty members if they included disability-related content within their classes; fewer than 20 responded that they did. Perhaps the invitation was just deleted, or perhaps those to whom we reached out did not have time to opt into a qualitative interview about their classes. However, based on those who did participate and respond, it became clear that (1) a foundational academic resource was an essential need for faculty, and (2) such a resource did not exist.

We hope it does now.

The aim of this book is to provide a foundation for knowledge in adaptive sport and recreation—through a management lens. This book is targeted toward undergraduate and graduate students and can be used in courses within sport management programs and related disciplines. Alternatively, it may be used by faculty or professionals as a resource of key knowledge in adaptive sport and recreation management. Our hope for this textbook is that it serves sport management programs, students, and faculty by introducing the major areas of adaptive sport and recreation that can be further explored.

Disability is multilayered and complicated, and disability within a sport or recreational setting is even more complex. In sport management programs across the world, students enter their professional careers with foundational knowledge in sport communication, events, facilities, finance, and marketing. The industry itself would never ignore the impact of major population segments when it comes to buying power, brand loyalty, or customer service. Estimates vary, but most sources suggest that between 19 and 25 percent of the global population is living with some form of disability. For sport to not embrace that population as participants, spectators, and consumers is not good business. There is a need to educate students in the area of adaptive sport and recreation so they can be professionally prepared to serve all populations as sport managers.

Organization

The chapters in this book have been written by an accomplished and well-respected group of contributors who have dedicated their professional and personal lives to researching and advocating for disability to be more inclusive in sport management. A short biography of each contributor is featured at the conclusion of the book. With trust in their expertise, we gave them the freedom to shape their chapters in the manner they saw fit.

Academics and practitioners in this field have a wide array of perspectives and approaches, and each of these chapters therefore reflects the uniqueness of the contributors' experience and knowledge. At the same time, all chapters reflect foundational understandings that are critical to a modern understanding of adaptive sport and recreation.

The book opens with chapters covering theoretical foundations as well as social issues surrounding adaptive sport and recreation. Chapter 1 focuses on the key elements of theoretical and social considerations related to adaptive sport and recreation, including contact theory, isolation theory, the social model of disability, and the medical model of disability. Chapter 2 moves to examine the barriers and facilitators for sport and recreation opportunities for people with disabilities. Chapter 3 provides an overview of how innovation has been used to facilitate adaptive sport and recreation opportunities.

In chapter 4, the book moves into the history of the Paralympic Games, from its beginnings following World War II to the modern Paralympic Games. Chapter 5 follows with an examination of key legal principles related to the rights of people with disabilities, including the Americans with Disabilities Act and Section 504 of the Rehabilitation Act of 1973. The presentation of adaptive sport and recreation in the media is encompassed in chapter 6, along with a discussion of the dominant frames and narratives of the media coverage. These contributions are by some of the top scholars in the field, and we are grateful for their willingness to contribute to this book.

The next part of the book describes different types of adaptive sport and recreation participation opportunities. Chapter 7 examines opportunities in elite adaptive sport and provides an overview of international competitions for athletes with disabilities. Chapter 8 examines adaptive sport and recreation for individuals with intellectual disabilities, with a focus on the Special Olympics and Virtus. Chapter 9 discusses principles of athlete development as well as an overview of models used in athlete development, with a focus on para-athletes. Chapter 10 covers the role of adaptive sports and recreation in the military setting, with a focus on the benefits of adaptive sports and recreation for military members. Chapter 11 shifts to adaptive youth sports, examining the barriers as well as providing guidance on how to negotiate those barriers.

The book concludes with the practical application of many of the concepts discussed in the other chapters. In chapter 12, Dr. Michael Cottingham and colleagues offer guidance on funding adaptive sport and recreation programs as well as providing a funding model for such programs. The book concludes with a case study of University of Alabama Adapted Athletics by Dr. Margaret Stran and Dr. Brent Hardin. This chapter details the history of the growth of the program at Alabama, the funding model, the programming, and the operation of the program. It is a blueprint for success that can be used by students in the classroom or individuals looking to start a program. References to other chapters throughout the case study remind readers where to find further exploration of key topics covered.

Use of Language

Language use can be a confusing aspect of disability. What should I say? What should I not say? What is the proper term? We posit that the debate around language within the disability rights movement is one aspect that is holding the movement back. There are several terms that can be used in relation to sport and disability:

- adapted
- adaptive
- disability sport
- disabled sport
- parasport

Language choices around disability can be polarizing because different groups prefer to use different terms and phrases. Different geographic regions have preferences, as do different disciplines within disability and sport or physical education. They all make good points supporting their preferences. Two terms that are often used interchangeably are *disability* and *impairment*. For clarity, *impairment* refers to the medical diagnosis for an individual in relation to their physical, intellectual, or cognitive condition. *Disability*, however, is socially constructed and relates to decisions that may limit or prevent access. Again, these terms and their definitions may be debated by scholars and advocates. That debate can be saved for another setting since the focus of this publication is foundational knowledge for students, many of whom may have never been in scholarly settings critically examining disability and sport.

Two distinct differences in language approach in this area are person-first language and identity-first language. Person-first language focuses on recognizing the person above any identity or characteristic (e.g., *person with a disability*) and shifts emphasis away from disability (e.g., *accessible seating*). Identity-first language focuses on embracing the disability characteristic as part of the human identity because it cannot be separated from the individual (e.g., *disabled person*, *disabled seating*). These two are the most widely practiced approaches, but they are not the only ones. The language debate, again, is not the focus of this textbook, but it is an aspect we felt compelled to clarify. We asked each chapter's contributors to use the language approaches that they feel comfortable with using, so you will notice variation from chapter to chapter.

We chose to use the term *adaptive* in this book's title for specific reasons. First, the United Nations recommends the use of person-first language, and *adaptive* was a term that we felt aligned best. Second, a good friend, mentor, and disability rights advocate strongly encouraged *adaptive* rather than *disability* or *para* for the book's title. The late Eli Wolff was a major influence on this book; his voice is the foundation of many of our

decisions, and he recommended many possible contributors. His influence is sprinkled throughout these pages—if not directly, then certainly indirectly. When we had a conversation inviting him to contribute in some way and asked questions about his opinions on decisions, he recommended using *adaptive* as a more encompassing term. Anyone who ever worked alongside Eli knows that when he recommends something, it is with a great deal of thought for the greater good of the disability community. We went with *adaptive*.

Dr. Pate's Point of View

I was born with cerebral palsy and walk with forearm crutches as I live my daily life. I spent nearly 30 years of my life ignoring that characteristic, which worked well as an adolescent. I played football after church with my friends, "catching" the pass by hitting the ball with my crutch before it landed. I played pickup basketball at the West End park in my hometown by being a defensive specialist, swiping the ball away with my crutch for steals and smacking blocked shots. I was a referee and umpire in school activities. I kept statistics for my high school basketball team and announced for the baseball team. But I did not really participate in sport until I stopped ignoring my disability and started accepting it, agreeing to try adaptive snow skiing in Snowmass, Colorado. It changed my life.

After that first experience on the snow of Colorado, I went again the following year. I quit my job and went back to school to earn a doctorate so I could research disability and sport. I started adaptive water skiing in Georgia and Tennessee. I purchased a handcycle and regularly trained with a national champion cyclist. I was not going to be an elite athlete; I just wanted to show it could be done and learn for myself.

Disability (which is the term I use rather than *impairment*), to me, is a characteristic just like eye color, hair color, skin tone, height, weight, and so on. Sometimes we may not be in control of the impairment, but we certainly have control over the impact of disability and how it may be a barrier or not for our lives. I credit my faith and my family for establishing my lens through which I view disability's impact on my life and others. I know that I was created in a perfectly made image and that my daily living may look different from others and may operate at a different speed.

My goal is to take disability into the world where it typically is not seen. I am a husband with a disability. I'm a father with a disability. I coach youth sport teams, teach sport management, serve on boards, drive Jeeps, and still ski when I can—all things any other person may choose to do. That approach often leads to some stares and some questions and some private conversations, and all of that is good. That means people are learning how to process someone who may look or move or act differently, which positions us to be more accepting of a broader range of ideas and knowledge.

One thing I always aimed to do with friends and relationships is to develop such a deep relationship with someone that they forget about my disability. My longtime college roommate reached that level when he asked me to go play tennis with him one afternoon without even thinking about how we might do that. My coeditor, Dr. Hardin, has reached that level because the vast majority of our dialogue and work are not about personal barriers in my life but more about daily life, work, or other water cooler topics. My family is at that level because they depend on me to achieve certain tasks, I have my household chores, and we have our family fun and family disagreements. Others have made it to that level, and they know who they are. It follows a continuum that Eli Wolff spoke often about, where disability progresses from invisible (when it is not present in a space) to visible (when it is present in a space but treated differently) and back to invisible (when it is present in a space and not treated differently because we are simply used to its presence). Let's hope this book will help us get there.

Dr. Hardin's Point of View

My familiarity with adaptive sports and recreation is primarily due to my relationship with my coeditor, Dr. Pate, who was a student in the sport management program at the University of Tennessee earning his bachelor's degree in May 2002. I began my faculty position in the sport management program in August 2001, but I had limited interaction with Dr. Pate during that time of overlap. I did interact with him while he earned his master's degree in communications at Tennessee while also working in Tennessee athletics in the sports information department. I was also working in that department after beginning my faculty position, providing content for athletic department publications (e.g., media guides, press relations) as well as the athletic department website. Our interactions and conversations during those two years were mostly centered on general sports topics and Tennessee athletics.

Dr. Pate joined the staff of the president's office at Georgia State University after he earned his master's degree, and he eventually transitioned to a position with Turner Sports as an interactive producer focusing on coverage of NASCAR. He had spent three years at Turner Sports when he reached out to me in the spring of 2008 about pursuing a doctorate specializing in sport management. Those conversations continued for the next year. The pieces began to fall into place for Dr. Pate to join our program in the fall of 2009 as a graduate teaching associate. He was assigned to teach foundational sport management courses as well as serve as the graduate assistant for the sport management student association. His office was across the hall from my office. My introduction to adaptive sport and recreation as well as issues facing people with disabilities truly began in August 2009.

The building that houses sport management faculty offices was built in the early 1970s, so it is certainly not the most ADA-friendly building on campus. An issue quickly arose when Dr. Pate was assigned to teach a class in a room located three floors away from his office. He had to take one elevator down two floors, then walk down a lengthy hallway to a set of double-doors that did not have an automatic opener to get to another elevator to get to the floor where his class was being held. This was obviously an untenable situation. I worked with our department room scheduler and other faculty to have Dr. Pate's class moved to a more accessible location for him. Another issue that quickly became evident was the door egresses and openings throughout the building. Many doors did not have automatic openers, nor did they provide enough clearance for him to enter and exit rooms without hindrance. The elevators in the buildings were also subject to regular maintenance due to their age, which at times forced Dr. Pate to ascend more than 20 steps to get to his office. This is quite challenging for someone who uses forearm crutches for walking. In less than a week, I was exposed to the daily life challenges that Dr. Pate faced for many of the everyday tasks that I simply took for granted.

One of the reason Dr. Pate chose to pursue a PhD was his belief that he could make an impact on the disability community by becoming an advocate as well as by increasing awareness. He had an immediate impact on increasing awareness for me and other faculty in our department. This also happened rather quickly in the research realm when Dr. Pate's first research endeavor was to examine accessible parking practices at football games of members of the Southeastern Conference (SEC). We discovered that policies and practices throughout the conference were inconsistent and generally lacked understanding of ADA parking requirements. This led to other research projects involving disability issues as well as adaptive sports and recreation during the next three years, culminating with his dissertation examining service quality at the Lakeshore Foundation, an Olympic and Paralympic training facility in Birmingham, Alabama. I was fortunate to accompany Dr. Pate on a visit to Lakeshore Foundation

and was able to learn more about the facility and the Paralympic training programs housed there. My awareness of adaptive sports and recreation and issues within the disability community increased exponentially during those three years of Dr. Pate's doctoral studies.

Dr. Pate finished the requirements of his doctorate in the spring of 2012 and accepted a faculty position at James Madison University beginning that fall. We have continued to conduct research together on a variety of disability-related topics, with one of the areas of interest being how those topics are introduced to students in sport management programs across North America. We realized that the topic is covered mostly on a superficial level—if at all—in most programs. My knowledge of these topics has increased tremendously during my time with Dr. Pate, through formal and information interactions. We have traveled throughout the United States and Canada together and discussed these topics at length, and I have become much more informed because of these interactions. My hope is this book will also increase awareness about creating opportunities and providing services for those participating in adaptive sports and recreation as well as provide a resource for sport management professionals and administrators working in this area of sport management.

Conclusion

This book can be used in both undergraduate- and graduate-level courses within sport management programs and related disciplines. The book can certainly serve as stand-alone resource for a class focused on adaptive sport and recreation. However, we encourage educators to consider how adaptive sport and recreation content can be infused throughout the curriculum and how specific chapters can be used as a resource in other classes. A sport communication class can use the chapter on the media coverage of the Paralympics to demonstrate how consumer perceptions are influenced by the media. Chapter 5 provides an excellent resource for a class on legal aspects of sports or facilities management. Chapter 4 can be used in a class on sport history or sociocultural aspects of sport. The book can serve as a resource for faculty to use to incorporate adaptive sport and recreation content within the curriculum.

The infusion of adaptive sport and recreation content is essential if sport management programs are to offer a comprehensive education to prepare future professionals for the industry. But this book should not be limited to sport management curriculum and faculty. Coaching education programs can use the book as a resource for developing strategies for working with athletes with disabilities—not only at the elite level but also at the recreational level. Hospitality, tourism, and physical education programs, among others, could use the book as a valuable resource for their curriculum as well. Training and education should be provided to any type of professional who will be interacting with athletes or consumers with physical or intellectual disabilities in the pursuit of physical activity or leisure activities. This book can help meet that goal.

CHAPTER 1

Theoretical and Social Considerations of Adaptive Sport and Recreation

Justin A. Haegele, PhD, and Cathy McKay, EdD

LEARNING OBJECTIVES

After reading this chapter, you will be able to do the following:

- Explain the concept of ableism and its role in adaptive sport and recreation.
- Identify examples of inspiration porn in adaptive sport and recreation.
- Identify and describe characteristics specific to social and medical models of disability.
- Describe inclusion as a subjective experience and identify the implications for this definition within adaptive sport and recreation settings.
- Describe the key elements of contact theory and social isolation theory.

This chapter addresses social and theoretical considerations found within the fields of adaptive sport and recreation. After a brief introduction, we consider the question, What is a disability? We address this question through the lens of both the medical and social models of disability. Next, we discuss ableism and its role in adaptive sport and recreation. Then, we explore the well-known concepts of inclusion and explain the distinctions between inclusion and integration. Finally, we introduce two key theoretical frameworks commonly applied to adaptive sport and recreation.

A cross-disciplinary body of practical, social, and theoretical knowledge influences how decisions are made about providing services for disabled persons, as well as which services are provided and why. This chapter briefly reviews several social and theoretical considerations that adaptive sport and recreation practitioners should be mindful of when deciding practices. These considerations cover different understandings of what disability is, ableism and inspiration porn, integration and inclusion, and theoretical frameworks that drive practice. This chapter is not meant to encompass all social and theoretical considerations that might influence practice. Rather, it provides important, recent considerations that may be helpful when constructing and implementing adaptive sport and recreation programs.

What Is a Disability?

Before engaging in meaningful conversations about social and theoretical considerations associated with adaptive sport or recreational activities for disabled persons, we must first discuss what the term *disability* means and what a disability is. Over the years, disability has been understood in a variety of ways, largely influenced by those considered the **cognitive authority**. A cognitive authority is a professional organization or collection of people who have the social capital to establish definitions and are key gatekeepers in particular fields. As authority over knowledge and understanding shifts, the thinking of those acting within a social context shifts along with it. For example, early notions of disability were framed in Western Judeo-Christian societies' religious discourses, where impairments of the body were thought to be a product of a higher being (Fitzgerald, 2006; Haslett & Smith, 2020). This perspective toward disability was largely supplanted as doctors and scientists replaced religious leaders as the cognitive authority in developing societal perceptions toward disabled people (Humpage, 2007).

Disability is conceptualized in different ways, and each viewpoint has implications for disabled people, service providers, and society in general (Barton, 2009; Haegele & Hodge, 2016). Among other implications, these ideas provide frameworks for understanding how service providers in adaptive sport and recreation spaces think about, interact with, and value disabled persons. For example, one's orientation toward disability is likely to influence decisions about (1) the focus of activities or lessons, (2) the type and quality of instruction or opportunities, (3) the language used when speaking with or about disabled individuals, and (4) what it means to be competent or successful in an adaptive sport or recreation environment (Barton, 2009; Haslett & Smith, 2020). In this section, we will outline two of the most dominant international models, the medical model and the social model. We will explain each model thoroughly, compare and contrast the models, and demonstrate the implications of each model within adaptive sport or recreation contexts. We are not endorsing either model specifically but are sharing perspectives on both models to help readers shape their own thinking toward disability. In addition, readers should recognize that while these two models are discussed often, they are two of the many models through which to view disability overall. Readers may consider extending their knowledge of ways to understand and view disability by engaging with other prominent models, such as the social relational model, the global south model, or the international classification of functioning, disability, and health (ICF) model.

The Medical Model of Disability Discourse

When medical professionals replaced religious leaders as the cognitive authority in society, it opened the door for a medical understanding of disability, particularly given the medical field's ability to define, heal, and cure illness and injuries (Brittain, 2004). The **medical model of disability** defines disability as a medical problem that resides in the individual as a defect in or failure of a bodily system that is abnormal and pathological (Goodley, 2016).

> The medical model defines disability as a medical issue: a defect in or failure of the body that society views as a problem.

Given the focus on the body, it is unsurprising that the medical model conceptualizes disability as a biological product and as an individual phenomenon that results in limited functioning that is viewed as a problem (Goodley, 2016). This can include structural or functional deficiencies caused by physical, sensory, affective, or cognitive issues (Haegele & Hodge, 2016). According to the medical model of disability discourse, limitations associated with having a disability are considered a product of an impairment. Those ascribing to this model believe that something is inherently disabling about impairments, and the challenges disabled people face are independent of wider sociocultural or political environments (Goodley, 2016).

Within this model, disability is viewed as being inherently negative and is therefore something that the medical community should intervene to help remediate or "fix" using psychological or medical interventions (Haegele & Hodge, 2016; Mitra, 2006). In this way, disability is conflated with the "sick role," similar to illness, where medical personnel should help cure individuals' disabilities so that they can function "normally" within society. Thus, to reduce disability and therefore gain independence, the medical community must help eradicate the cause of and "fix" impairments. Within this model, access to treatment or medical services to reduce disability is available only via referral by diagnosis, placing medical professionals and medical diagnoses in critical roles for disabled people. When disabilities cannot be eliminated or "fixed," disabled people are often viewed as pitiful or in need of help or charity (Roush & Sharby, 2011).

Historically, the medical model has underpinned many aspects of research and practice in adaptive sport and recreation contexts. For example, many adaptive sport or recreation opportunities are restricted to those who have specific diagnoses, making medical professionals important gatekeepers to individuals' involvement within sport or recreational opportunities. Classification systems within adaptive sport, which tend to group participants based on impairment severity, are also largely medically informed. In addition, medical model understandings of disability have influenced the language that we use when we talk about disabled people within these, and all, contexts. Medical model language generally centers on specific diagnoses (e.g., a person with cerebral palsy) and revolves around differences based on what is considered normal, acceptable, and valued compared to what is viewed as abnormal or devalued (Spencer et al., 2020) and is largely present in most adaptive sport and recreation research and practice. This language is well aligned with the normative nature of disability as conceptualized within discourse in the medical model of disability.

Another aspect is the persistent negative disability stereotypes common to the medical model and the way these beliefs can influence how disabled people experience sport and recreation. In this model, disability is discussed as a deficit, which focuses on a biophysical assumption of normality and creates a problematic normal and abnormal dichotomy (Haslett & Smith, 2020). This language can influence how people interact with and talk about disabled people, including in sport and recreation contexts, and can reinforce harmful and stigmatizing ideals about disability being undesirable (Spencer et al., 2020). For example, disabled athletes may find themselves being mocked or disregarded by others when expressing interests in exploring higher-level sport because of understandings that disabled people are limited and that high-level competition is not possible. These ideas can be attributed to the deficit-based definitions, language, and perceptions the medical model of disability discourse has established.

The Social Model of Disability Discourse

The **social model of disability**, sometimes considered a reaction to the medical model of disability discourse, has gained popularity among academics in adaptive sport and recreation contexts. According to Mitra (2006), there are at least nine versions of the social model of disability discourse. Many of these models share common assumptions of disability, and this chapter will discuss these similarities as conceptualized with the phrase *the social model*.

In the social model, disabled academics and advocates, as well as allies, supplant medical professionals as the cognitive authority. Social model advocates suggest that society imposes disability on individuals with impairments. That is, rather than impairments being inherently disabling, social model advocates suggest that the behaviors of those within society who do not take into account people who have impairments and exclude them from various aspects of community life are what disable them. Importantly, the terms **impairment** and **disability** are different concepts in the social model of disability, where the former refers to a biological phenomenon (e.g., physical, social, cognitive, emotional) and the latter refers to disadvantages or restrictions of activities caused by societal organizations or structures (Goodley, 2016; Haegele & Hodge, 2016). This is a critical distinction. Unlike the medical model's stance that disabilities are inherently negative, it suggests that one's body function does not limit their activities or abilities; society does (Roush & Sharby, 2011). Therefore, there is nothing inherently disabling about impairments, and impairments are considered neither positive nor negative. This distinction is important to remember. Exclusion and social isolation can both be a product of society's inability, unwillingness, or failure to remove the barriers disabled people encounter or the perceptions toward them as being less able.

> The social model suggests that society imposes disability on individuals who have impairments.

Unlike the deficit thinking medical model language perpetuates, the social model of disability suggests that impairment be considered a form of diversity, like gender, sexual orientation, race, or ethnicity, that offers a unique perspective that should be valued and celebrated (Goodley, 2016). Therefore, rather than attempting to "fix" disabled individuals, advocates of the social model suggest that solutions should be focused on societal change. Social model thinkers suggest that societal change, and the associated change in attitude toward disabled people, could be the impetus to reduce many problems typically associated with disability. The overarching

message of the social model is a call to move society from one that discriminates against those with impairments to one of social inclusion.

The social model of disability also has language considerations that influence the way in which we talk about disability. Rather than using a person-first language model (such as *person with a disability*), social model thinkers tend to use an identity-first language model (such as *disabled person*) to refer to persons who are oppressed, or disabled, by society. As noted earlier, in the social model, people do not *have* disabilities but rather are actively *disabled* by society. Given conceptual differences between impairment and disability, social model thinkers may also use alternative language such as *person with an impairment* or *person experiencing disability*; however, these terms are much less commonplace than the phrase *disabled person*. Persons interacting with disabled people should also be mindful of the language preferences of those within specific disability communities. For example, communities of autistic or neurodivergent people have recently reclaimed their impairment-related language and tend to present in ways that are consistent with social model thinking. According to Spencer and colleagues (2020), "such terms frame the ways their minds work as neutral or positive human variations and frame their social and medical treatment as forms of oppression, eugenics, and genocide" (p. 137). That is, the reclamation of autism-related terminology is aligned with the idea that autism should not be considered a detrimental feature of the human experience. Rather, differences associated with autism are considered positive or neutral features. These beliefs and preferences appear well aligned with social model thinking and, unsurprisingly, social model language.

While social model thinking may represent progressive thinking in several ways, it is not without its criticisms. One notable criticism is related to attempts to separate impairment from disability completely, which does not fully account for the lived experiences of

The Charlottesville Cardinals: Wheelchair Basketball Team and Disability Sport Advocates

The Charlottesville Cardinals wheelchair basketball team was formed in early 1980 by six local athletes in the Charlottesville, VA, area. Our team was created to provide disabled athletes an opportunity for exercise and competitive recreation and to educate the general public concerning the capabilities of individuals with disabilities. Since our formation, over 700 disabled athletes have participated with the Cardinals, and we have played in front of over 175,000 people across the United States, Canada, and Puerto Rico. In addition to competitive recreation, we are proud to have a reputation of developing highly skilled athletes. We have been perennially ranked among the top 20 teams in the country for over 20 years and are very proud of our commitment to skill development and high-level competition. Our team was initially sponsored by the Therapeutic Recreation Program of the City of Charlottesville. Later, a local center for independent living, the Independence Resource Center, became our key sponsor.

As an organization and team, we strive to advocate for societal change related to approaching disability as one of the many forms of diversity. Our players identify not only as disabled but also as White, Black, and Brown; as he, she, and their; and as adolescent, adult, and older adult. We work tirelessly to advance social inclusion through community and school engagement efforts, hoping that our stories and experiences will allow those with whom we engage to better understand and value our diverse abilities. Our engagement includes school presentations where we demonstrate wheelchair basketball and play against a faculty or student team; school visits where we teach and lead lessons on the skills of wheelchair basketball; and community demonstrations at parades and festivals. We also partner with a variety of universities in Virginia, as well as up and down the East Coast, to advance programming related to disability sport and disability etiquette. Our hope is that our community and school-based advocacy efforts allow for students and community members to broaden their perspectives on disability. This broadening includes learning and growing as inclusive members of organizations and schools, coming to know and understand the power that sport can play in changing our communities and our society, and advancing attitudes toward disability.

Photo and sidebar used with permission from JMU University Marketing and Branding.

disabled people. This thought has led some to propose the social relational model of disability, which suggests that disability is imposed on top of restrictions that are caused by one's impairment (Reindal, 2008, 2009), therefore taking into consideration both the biomedical restrictions of impairment and societal restrictions of disability. The social model has also been criticized as being idealistic and monolithic, in that it considers only one form of an individual's identity (i.e., their disability) without exploring the implications of other oppression they may face associated with additional identity markers (e.g., racism, sexism, transphobia). To better understand how these identities interact to inform experiences, readers may consider exploring research and scholarship associated with **intersectionality**, which provides a lens through which we can understand how differences among disabled people (e.g., racial, cultural, ethnic differences) interact to influence experiences within society.

Ableism

Ableism, like sexism, racism, or heterosexism, is a form of prejudice; it views disabled people as inferior, abnormal, or "less than" nondisabled people (Smith et al., 2021). Given the overview in the prior section, it may be unsurprising that ableism is generally linked to the medical model of disability in that disabled people are viewed as needing to be changed or fixed to fit into society and therefore are inferior to nondisabled people until that fixing occurs. Like other forms of discrimination, ableism supports the social demotion of those who do not fit into idealized or normative ideologies (Campbell, 2009). Ableism is inherent to legal, educational, ethical, and political practices and is represented in society where nondisabled people are viewed as the standard (Campbell, 2009). This results in public spaces and opportunities, including recreation spaces or opportunities, being constructed to serve standard people and exclude those who do not fit into standard ideologies, like disabled people.

> Ableism is a form of prejudice that views disabled people as inferior or abnormal.

Like other forms of oppression, ableism can take on a variety of different forms, including systemic ableism, direct ableism, and indirect ableism. **Systemic ableism**, often unnoticed or unquestioned by nondisabled people, is a form of ableism that includes physical barriers, laws, and practices that restrict freedom and equality for disabled people. Also included within this definition is an ongoing failure to help remediate these issues. This form of ableism is deeply rooted in our social structure as a result of long-held beliefs and active discrimination against disabled people. **Direct ableism** encompasses purposeful conscious, aggressive, and oppressive acts. Some common examples of direct ableism can include asking unnecessarily invasive questions about one's personal life or medical history or restricting participation in certain activities because of a disability diagnosis. More extreme examples, where nondisabled people purposely and maliciously humiliate and dehumanize disabled people, can include (1) suspecting that disabled people "fake" needs to get special attention, (2) feeling like and expressing that it is an inconvenience to "deal with" disabled people and their "special privileges," or (3) overprotecting or sheltering disabled people from activities deemed to be too dangerous by nondisabled others. Finally, **indirect ableism**, sometimes considered to be ignorance or well-meaning ableism, is unconscious behavior that is not intended but still is harmful. This may include people using expressions such as "you are acting bipolar" or "you are so retarded" that use disability as an insult and represent disability as a negative problem that needs to be fixed.

One form of indirect ableism that has appeared often in adaptive sport and recreation settings is **inspiration porn**. Inspiration porn, a concept typically credited to the late comedian and former teacher Stella

Young, is a meme, image, video, or feel-good article that sensationalizes disabled people to inspire audiences of nondisabled people (Darrow & Hairston, 2016). This type of media is generally characterized by sentimentality or pity, disabled people being anonymously objectified, and an uplifting moral message, primarily targeted at nondisabled viewers.

Despite the well-meaning intentions of these inspirational images, they depict disabled people in ways that objectify them, devalue their experiences, and mystify their place in the world (Grue, 2016). As Martin (2019) noted, disabled people see these images as co-opting a disabled persons' impairment; they are objectifying because the person is equated to their disability. In addition, the "positive" messages rely on an assumption that disability is, by default, tragic, and that without this tragedy, there would be no uplifting effect of disabled people being portrayed as brave or accomplished. Inspiration porn is disproportionately common in physical activity and sport contexts and often leverages and exploits disabled athletes. Images of these athletes with quotes like "The only disability in life is a bad attitude" or "So . . . what's your excuse again?" are intended to motivate nondisabled persons to exercise and train harder by objectifying and materializing disabled people in images where they are "overcoming" their disability. Service providers in adaptive sport and recreation spaces must not convey this form of indirect ableism and must understand that these depictions have hidden consequences for disabled people. Providers should not use images like these as motivational tools because, as Stella Young noted, "I'm not your inspiration, thank you very much."

> Inspiration porn sensationalizes disabled people for audiences of nondisabled people to inspire them and is generally characterized by sentimentality, pity, or an uplifting moral message.

Inclusion Versus Integration

In adaptive sport and recreation literature, conversations about inclusion are omnipresent. These conversations use the term *inclusion* in a variety of ways, often without explicit or clear definitions, so it may have several different meanings (Haegele, 2019; Spencer-Cavaliere et al., 2017). The term has been described as a "semantic chameleon," its meaning changing depending on which context it is being used (Liasidou, 2012; Petrie et al., 2018). This is problematic, because without a clear understanding of the term's meaning, the different ways inclusion is interpreted can ultimately influence how practitioners decide to provide services and the adaptive sport and recreation activities for disabled people. This section will clarify the meaning of the term *inclusion* and juxtapose the concept of inclusion as a subjective experience with the concept of *integration*.

First, we turn our attention to the term *inclusion* being used to represent a physical space. We view this use of the term as a dangerous misinterpretation of what inclusion is and should be. When *inclusion* is used to represent a physical space or location, it assumes that spaces where disabled and nondisabled people are all together are inclusive. If this logic were true, experiences that are challenging or negative within those spaces—something disabled people in various sport and physical activity contexts experience—would also be considered inclusive (Haegele & Sutherland, 2015). This is paradoxical to the notion that inclusion is a positive attribute or "the right thing to do" (Yell, 1995, p. 398). Additionally, when one physical space is highly valued (in this case, where disabled and nondisabled people are together), it devalues other spaces. Adaptive sport contexts specifically designed for disabled athletes (e.g., the Paralympics) would hold lesser societal value than integrated settings do. Finally, if the only threshold to being inclusive is for people to exist together in one space, then there is little motivation for service providers to engage disabled and nondisabled athletes in meaningful experiences. Many recreation (and educational) programs are advertised as being "inclusive" and merely pay lip service to the prospect of inclusion while simply enrolling disabled and nondisabled people in the same setting.

To reduce concerns about the misinterpretation of inclusion as a physical space or setting, we suggest using the term **integration**. Integration should describe a physical space in which disabled and nondisabled people receive services together (Haegele, 2019). **Inclusion** must extend beyond materiality and individuals' physical existence within a space and center on the subjective experiences of the person being included—in this case, disabled persons (Haegele, 2019). We adopt Stainback and Stainback's (1996) interpretation of the hallmark of inclusive experiences as the subjective experience of a sense of belonging, acceptance, and value understood from the perspective of the person being included. This is aligned with the position that the feelings and opinions of disabled persons themselves are central to interpretations of the inclusiveness of experiences (Haegele, 2019; Spencer-Cavaliere & Watkinson, 2010) and supports distinctions between being integrated into a setting and feeling included in that setting (Slee, 2018). This is important because disabled and nondisabled people experience various recreation and sport settings quite differently, even though they may be integrated into the same spaces (Haegele et al., 2021).

There are important implications for understanding this definition of inclusion for adaptive sport and recreation service providers. First is that service providers must center the voices of disabled persons when attempting to understand the quality, meaning, and inclusiveness of the opportunities that they provide. By engaging with disabled persons, service providers can gain important insight into how spaces are experienced and what can be done to enhance experiences within these spaces. We argue that this is, generally, a departure from the stakeholder-centric decision making that permeates throughout adaptive sport and recreation. This disallows "inclusion checklists" or "inclusive strategies" as a barometer for or guarantee of inclusive experiences. Stakeholders construct these tools to make themselves feel as though they are providing adequate service, but the tools are seldom co-constructed with disabled people or grounded in any reflective thinking. Rather, we would encourage service providers to engage in meaningful conversations about adaptive sport and recreation experiences with disabled consumers of the services to better understand the experiences. Said another way, we suggest that service providers focus more on whether their service recipients *feel included* and less on whether the providers *feel like they are including* disabled people.

> Service providers must center the voices of disabled persons when attempting to understand the quality, meaning, and inclusiveness of the opportunities that they provide.

This has implications for considerations around the setting, and the context of the setting, in decision making about inclusive practices. First, this idea allows practitioners to question the inclusiveness of integrated settings. Rather than assuming that integrated placements provide inclusive experiences, practitioners can reflect on whether these settings truly are inclusive. Second, since inclusion is a subjective experience and not a specific physical space, understanding inclusion this way also allows inclusive experiences to exist in settings outside those that are typically considered inclusive. With that, subjective experiences in self-contained settings, such as Paralympic sport settings specifically designed for disabled athletes only, can be explored to see whether participants feel included—that is, accepted, belonging, and valued—within that setting. This also opens the door for a reconstruction of the value hierarchy of physical settings where adaptive sport and recreation opportunities are offered. Settings may be selected based on the availability of the participants feeling included within a setting, rather than a priori assumptions that integrated contexts are "better" because disabled and nondisabled people are together.

Theoretical Considerations

Thus far, this chapter has focused largely on exploring social considerations that influence how we engage with and discuss adaptive sport and recreation. In addition to these factors, we must be mindful of theoretical considerations that influence our work in this area. While the word *theory* is used frequently in scholarship about adaptive sport and recreation settings, it is often met with anxiety by practitioners. However, theories are useful to guide practice. Theories are like maps that help researchers and practitioners decide what to do, how to do it, and why to do it (Maher & Coates, 2020). Theories can provide a convenient way to ensure decisions and program implementation are conceptually aligned with one another. In this section, we will describe two theories, contact theory and social isolation theory, that can contribute to our thinking in adaptive sport and recreation contexts and inevitably influence the way we construct and implement programs.

Contact Theory

Allport's (1954) contact theory states that contact with people different from oneself will lead to attitude change if presented under the right conditions. The theory was first proposed when considering how to improve relationships between groups and has been used to explain human relations in terms of prejudice and difference. Allport theorized that when people encounter others, their prejudiced ideas diminish as they come to understand the other person.

> Contact theory states that contact with people different from oneself will lead to attitude change if presented under the right conditions.

Contact theory is relevant to adaptive sport and recreation literature because it is the basis for many awareness and education programs that provide an avenue to influence perceptions of and biases regarding disability (McKay et al., 2015, 2019, 2022a, 2022b). Allport's (1954) contact theory sought to understand the nature of contact that will produce positive attitude change. Allport specified four necessary conditions for contact to improve negative attitudes: (1) equal status, (2) cooperation toward common goals, (3) meaningful personal interactions, and (4) identification and acceptance of social norms provided by authority. All four have been interpreted in a variety of ways in contact theory research (McKay, 2018).

Equal status contact is one of the main conditions of favorable contact in that group members must be seen as, and behave as, equals. If members of a group have inferior or superior roles or behave with status that places them into superior or inferior conditions, existing stereotypes will be reinforced.

Cooperation toward common goals reveals how interactions allow group members to work together and collaborate, as opposed to them working competitively or in isolation.

Meaningful personal interactions support a connection level that is necessary in bringing contact theory to life. Allport (1954) asserted that meaningful personal interactions allow group members to get to know one another as individuals, connecting personalities and life experiences.

Finally, support from authority brings to light a norm of acceptance (McKay, 2018), where socially accepted contact will bring more positive results. From a practical standpoint, adaptive sport awareness programs often meet this component because they are sponsored by a governing body, planning committee, or grant funding, all of which are support from authority.

Contact theory is well supported in the literature, with comprehensive literature reviews by Pettigrew (1998) and Dovidio and colleagues (2003) that showcase its extensive use. Contact theory has improved attitudes toward intellectually disabled people (McManus et al., 2011), physically disabled people (Kalymon et al., 2010; McKay et al., 2015; McKay & Park, 2019), racial and ethnic groups (Pettigrew, 1971; Sigelman & Welch, 1993), and elderly people (Schwartz & Simmons, 2001) when the four components (equal status, cooperation, common goals, and support from authority) are present. Pettigrew and Tropp (2006) indicated in their contact theory meta-analysis that when all four contact conditions were present and functioning together, a significantly higher mean effect size was achieved, and intergroup outcomes were best met.

Contact theory considerations related to adaptive sport and recreation are realized through experiences that bring disabled and nondisabled people together in sport and recreation settings to accomplish common goals and break down biases. The components of contact theory are incorporated when university recreation centers offer sitting volleyball and wheelchair basketball clinics where local disability sport club members facilitate instruction on the skills of the game and then play alongside the participants. Similarly, when community organizations offer Paralympic School Day experiences that go beyond simulations and bring together disabled and nondisabled participants to learn about and experience parasport in a collaborative and team-oriented fashion with many meaningful interactions, the components of contact theory are manifested. The well-researched parasport education and awareness program, the Paralympic School Day (PSD) program of the International Paralympic Committee (2006), is rooted in contact theory and has been used in a variety of research and practical settings to indicate the power of contact in changing attitudes and perceptions toward disability (Liu et al., 2010; McKay et al., 2015, 2019, 2022a, 2022b; Panagiotou et al., 2008).

Social Isolation Theory

Social isolation theory describes what occurs when an individual is distanced psychologically or physically from their network of desired or needed relationships. It is typically accompanied by feelings related to loss or marginality (Biordi & Nicholson, 2013). Social isolation, which is contradictory to the subjective feelings of inclusion described previously in this chapter (Haegele, 2019), can occur when people struggle to connect with others. When marginalized groups are isolated from the beneficial social values of other groups (Harding, 2009), social isolation theory can make this seem like the norm. Research indicates that disabled people are at high risk for social isolation because they may struggle to establish intimate relationships with others and face barriers related to integration (Cacioppo & Patrick, 2008; Macdonald et al., 2018; Warner & Kelley-Moore, 2010). Research for the social model of disability has moved to exploring the barriers that seem to result in disabled people being overrepresented in the population who are lonely and isolated (Macdonald et al., 2018). Social isolation has been further defined as involving the number, frequency, and quality of contacts; the longevity or durability of contacts; and the negativism attributed to the isolation felt by the individual involved (Biordi & Nicholson, 2013).

> Social isolation is the distancing of an individual, psychologically or physically, from their network of desired or needed relationships with other persons and is typically accompanied by feelings related to loss or marginality.

Meaningful social contact has been explored in sport, leisure, and education

Paralympic School Day

The International Paralympic Committee's open-source Paralympic School Day program is based on contact theory and provides an example of bringing theory to practice in the parasport field. The program aims to educate about the lives and abilities of Paralympians to increase awareness and understanding through a realistic and holistic portrayal of parasport and the athletes who participate. Contact with the athletes during this program brings the four components of contact theory together because the program is created to be collaborative, equal in status, inclusive of multiple meaningful interactions, and supported by authority. Paralympic School Day engages learners through many activities, encouraging participants to challenge and find meaning in their own beliefs and experiences and supporting a shift in the paradigm through which participants view disability. Accessed through the International Paralympic Committee's website, the program has 19 activity cards divided into four categories: respect for sporting achievement, acceptance of individual differences, sport as a human right, and empowerment and social support in sport. The program has been well researched during the past decade, with studies focusing on changing perceptions toward disability and parasport. Modifications to the program exist for learners of all ages (including adults), the overall goal being to use the dimensions of contact theory to break down biases and address the societal norms that often govern perceptions of disability.

Photo and sidebar used with permission from JMU University Marketing and Branding.

research and appears in topics related to aging, the immigrant experience, poverty, disability, sporting event experiences, motherhood, inner-city youth, physical education experiences, and women in prison (Dacombe, 2013; Glover, 2018; Pate et al., 2014; Spencer-Cavaliere & Rintoul, 2012; Tarvainen, 2021). Glover (2018) calls for an increased focus on social isolation and meaningful social contact, sharing that social isolation is a societal problem that may be the by-product of modernity. Contributing to this idea, Dacombe (2013) shares that social isolation is split between isolation on the individual level and isolation at the community level. He introduced the concept of social capital in the form of bridging capital, when social connections encompass people from a broad social network, and bonding capital, when social connections remain within homogeneous social groupings. Understanding these social structures and issues allows organizational and societal changes to foster connections and provide social resources to combat isolation. In the school setting, Spencer-Cavaliere and Rintoul (2012) explored feelings of alienation in physical education, examining three constructs of alienation: powerlessness, meaninglessness, and social isolation. In this study, social isolation connected to a feeling of separateness from a group, with social factors being identified as representative of the children's perspectives.

Disabled people face social isolation when personal, physical, social, and systemic barriers prevent integration with society, and they may lack the feelings associated with inclusion (Pate et al., 2014). For example, a systemic barrier that leads to isolation because a disabled person cannot be a sport spectator is an inaccessible physical and social environment for parking and seating that prevents disabled people from being able to connect and integrate (Darcy, 2012). Social barriers were explored by Tarvainen (2021), who documented social isolation through the stories of individuals with disabilities. Within this project, stories related to feeling bodily difference, social isolation, and emotional loneliness were shared in physical activity settings such as dance halls, where nondisabled people expressed that disabled people were in their way (Tarvainen, 2021). In addition, stories were shared that related to being underrepresented in the workplace, where social relations are not extended to disabled people, and to alienation and stigmatization of being disabled, due to the person not embodying the symbols of society that are promoted through ableist norms and claims (Tarvainen, 2021). Ableism promotes conditions of social isolation and leads to alienation and negative attitudes toward disability. These examples of personal, social, physical, and systemic barriers ultimately affect one's sense of belonging and social interactions, creating social isolation and providing potential avenues for critical thought related to social isolation theory.

Summary

A variety of social and theoretical considerations influence adaptive sport and recreation fields. These considerations can inform the decisions practitioners make, such as what activities are valued, the physical settings in which these activities take place, and how best to understand the meaning and value of these activities. In this chapter, we provided detailed overviews of several considerations, including those related to concepts of disability as seen through the medical and social models, ableism and the role it plays in practice, the conceptual distinctions between inclusion and integration, and various theoretical frameworks that may influence practice. Readers are encouraged to continue to engage with additional readings that explore these social and theoretical concepts to deepen their knowledge and, importantly, enhance their practice.

CRITICAL THINKING EXERCISES

1. To start a discussion about disability and adaptive sport, write the word *disability* on a piece of paper. Then create a mind map to brainstorm all the words that come to mind that connect with disability. This mind mapping allows connections and relationships to form.

2. Write down (a) three key facts about the Olympic movement, (b) your five favorite Olympians, and (c) a highlight from the recent Olympic Games. Next,

repeat this process with the Paralympic movement: (a) three key facts about the movement, (b) your five favorite Paralympians, and (c) a highlight from the recent Paralympic Games.

3. What is the difference between being called inspirational and actually inspiring others? Read the article written by Alex Azzi for NBC Sports, discussing inspiration with Paralympian Mallory Weggemann (https://www.nbcsports.com/on-her-turf/news/paralympian-mallory-weggemann-limitless-memoir). Does this article make you want to change your answer to the initial question?

4. List the four components of contact theory on a piece of paper (equal status, collaborative, meaningful interactions, support from authority). Next, list examples and nonexamples of each under the component. An example of equal status would be that all students can select their seats in a classroom. A nonexample would be that first-year students are required to sit in the front row, thus creating an "othering" of the first-year students. Next, take a few minutes to write down your own experiences with each component.

CHAPTER 2

Barriers and Opportunities for Access and Inclusion

Kathleen McCarty, PhD; Laurin Bixby, PhD; and Winston Kennedy, PT, DPT, MPH, PhD

LEARNING OBJECTIVES

After reading this chapter, you will be able to do the following:

- Identify current models for understanding disability and health.
- Demonstrate knowledge of barriers and facilitators to health and physical activity opportunities for people with disabilities as grounded by the social-ecological model.
- Design elements of a recreation or physical activity specifically for or inclusive of people with disabilities.

This chapter examines the **barriers** to sport and physical activity participation for people with disabilities and describes design elements of programs with their best interests at the center. Words such as *physical activity*, *sport*, *parasport*, *adaptive sport*, *inclusive fitness*, *exercise*, and *recreation* are used interchangeably. However, it is important, first, to be reflexive about the ways disability and people with disabilities are viewed.

To further the understanding of barriers to physical activity and sport participation for people with disabilities, the structure of **ableism** in society and how that contributes to perspectives, or paradigms, that inform views of disability needs to be acknowledged. The **Americans with Disabilities Act (ADA)** was passed in 1990 to protect the civil rights of disabled people. It defines disability as "a physical or mental impairment that substantially limits one or more major life activities of such individual" (Americans with Disabilities Act of 1990, n.d.). Therefore, *ableism is a prejudice against disabled individuals*, often resulting from a belief that nondisabled people are superior, such as believing someone with a disability needs "fixing" or a cure to be fulfilled or to be considered "fully human," a perspective deeply rooted in medical culture (McCarty et al., 2021). This also feeds into a deeply rooted narrative of people with disabilities being upheld as an inspiration simply for existing or with the assumption that they have "overcome" something great (i.e., their disability).

In a highlighted excerpt from his book, *Exile and Pride*, Eli Clare (2012) went on to discuss inspiration:

> The nondisabled world is saturated with these stories: stories about gimps who engage in activities as grand as walking 2,500 miles or as mundane as learning to drive. They focus on disabled people "overcoming" our disabilities. They reinforce the superiority of the nondisabled body and mind. They turn individual disabled people, who are simply leading their lives, into symbols of inspiration. The dominant story about disability should be about ableism, not the inspirational supercrip crap, the believe-it-or-not disability story. (para. 4)

The term **supercrip** describes another problematic ableist stereotyping process heroizing anyone with a disability (Silva & Howe, 2012). Martin (2017) further defines the problems with supercrip.

> The supercrip identity presents a person with a disability as living a normal existence as a result of overcoming or defeating their disability via heroic efforts. Berger (2008) asserts that the supercrip identity promotes unrealistic expectations about what individuals with disabilities should and can achieve provided they put forth enough effort. (p. 141)

Martin deftly identifies, in his final sentence, the importance of looking at ableism through an intersectional lens, which will be discussed in this chapter as well. Intersecting social identities with disabled athletes may mean different capability levels based on the privileges afforded to them. Historically, White people in power have upheld White supremacist ideals by using the ableist viewpoint of disability to disproportionately assign disability labels to Black, Indigenous, and Latino individuals to keep them out of positions of power (Annamma et al., 2013).

Talila Lewis (2022), who works in community with Black and other negatively racialized disabled people, created a working definition of ableism:

> A system of assigning value to people's bodies and minds based on societally constructed ideas of normalcy, productivity, desirability, intelligence, excellence, and fitness. These constructed ideas are deeply rooted in eugenics, anti-Blackness, misogyny, colonialism, imperialism, and capitalism. This systemic oppression that leads to people and society determining people's value based on their culture, age, language, appearance, religion, birth or living place, "health/wellness," and/or their ability to satisfactorily re/produce, "excel," and "behave." You do not have to be disabled to experience ableism. (para. 4-6)

A critique within adaptive sport spaces is a failure to acknowledge disability as an intersectional experience with other marginalized social groups. The field, perhaps unintentionally, tends to highlight affluent White disability experiences, and suggestions for change come from the same lens. Therefore, practitioners should build cultural competence and be sensitive enough to ask difficult questions of themselves and the field.

Practitioners must be aware of the social identities present in coalitions, on teams, and in the leadership structure, noticing which groups are missing and what strategies can be used to intentionally include missing groups. Ableism may show up or affect people differently based on several factors, as Lewis points out in their definition. Building a sensitivity around this intersectional perspective of ableism will help build a truly equitable and inclusive space.

> Practitioners must be aware of the social identities present in coalitions, on teams, and in the leadership structure, noticing which groups are missing and what strategies can be used to intentionally include missing groups.

Models of Disability Perception

There are several different approaches, definitions, or perspectives when it comes to understanding disability. There are various ways to frame disability, but certain models have become more common. These models of disability perception are systems of beliefs that help illuminate societal attitudes about disability and actions toward disabled people. While some models help further disability justice and the inclusion of people with disabilities, other models perpetuate ableism and the exclusion of people with disabilities. Understanding different models of disability can help you identify how disability is viewed in various spaces and clarify the barriers to inclusion that people with disabilities in physical activity and adaptive sport face.

Medical Model

The underlying assumption of the medical model is that a disability is a health condition in need of a cure. For example, an athlete injured with a broken ankle may temporarily experience disability until the injury is healed or cured through rehabilitation. The medical model of disability suggests that a person who acquires a disability is in the same situation and is expected to cure or resolve any impairment and return to "normal" rather than anticipating an adjustment to their environment for their new reality. If an environmental barrier, such as stairs, exists, the medical model suggests that a disabled person should strive toward being able to climb the stairs rather than society addressing the environmental barrier by adding a ramp.

Within this model, the power of defining a person's health is invariably put in the hands of medical professionals (e.g., doctors; Iezzoni & Freedman, 2008; Sartorius, 2006; Shakespeare et al., 2009). Through this approach, the focus of any intervention for hardship is on a person's disability. This approach can be problematic in that it can encourage perceptions of remorse or failure if the disability cannot be cured or "overcome" and contributes to perceptions that a person is unable to live a full life, or any life at all, with the presence of their disability. This can lead to reduced societal expectations of people with disabilities or believing that a disabled person's only course is that of a hospice patient who is made comfortable while awaiting death.

Although that last statement is hyperbole, the medical model of disability has hurt the disability community in several ways. There are procedures like forced sterilization for people with disabilities and prenatal testing for a selection of pregnancy based on "risk" for disability (Hubbard, 1986). Researchers like Shakespeare (1998) have warned that these practices are **eugenics**, which is "the science of improving the population by control of inherited qualities" (p. 668). Eugenics is steeped in White supremacy and a desire to weed out what is considered genetically inferior (Keisch & Scott, 2015). It, therefore, means prejudice against race, sex, religion, and other categories deemed inferior to the nondisabled White majority. This prejudice can lead to pity or charity models of viewing disability, where people with disabilities are seen merely as victims of unfortunate circumstances whose nondisabled supporters are doing them a favor by being involved in their lives (Retief & Letšosa, 2018).

However, the medical model should not be disregarded entirely. Being able to identify a condition leading to disability can be empowering in the right circumstance. For example, a person experiencing chronic pain and fatigue may go years without a clear diagnosis, which can be emotionally distressing and can exacerbate the physical condition. Accessing a diagnosis is often a frustrating and expensive process. Once obtained, however, a clear diagnosis can validate a person's experience, provide access to care and resources, and lead to opportunities for social support from others with the same condition or diagnosis. In this way, using the medical model and identifying the disabling condition can be a huge relief, even if there is no cure or treatment for the condition.

> Obtaining a clear diagnosis can be empowering because it can validate a person's experience, provide access to care and resources, and lead to opportunities for social support from others with the same condition or diagnosis.

There is power in identifying a disability because it can lead to disability pride and involvement in the disability community. Many visibly (and invisibly) disabled people do not want the people around them to ignore their disability. Rather, they often desire others to recognize and celebrate difference. This parallels the experience of people of color who do not want others to claim that they "do not see race" but instead want others to recognize and embrace differences. However, recognizing and embracing difference does not mean that nondisabled people should casually comment on or inquire about someone's disability. To recognize and celebrate disability, nondisabled people can ensure that disabled people's access needs are met, view disability as a neutral or positive identity, and help promote equity and inclusion.

Social Model

Another common lens used to view disability is the social model. Whereas the medical model views disability as an individual concern, the social model asserts that disability is the result of physical environments and social structures that privilege some bodies and minds over others. Essentially, a person is disabled by buildings and spaces designed without consideration for people with disabilities (e.g., including only stairs, high curbs, and nonautomatic doors) as well as by sociopolitical landscapes that systemically privilege nondisabled people (e.g., negative attitudes and beliefs toward disability and legislation that neglects or harms people with

disabilities). In a lecture, Eli Clare (2013) observed, "We have defined disability as a matter of social justice—disability residing not in paralysis but in stairs without an accompanying ramp, not in blindness but in the lack of Braille and audio-recorded books" (para. 7).

If an athlete who uses a wheelchair encounters stairs, the social model perspective suggests reconsidering the construction of the stairs and building a ramp or elevator. This approach has led to **Universal Design**, where buildings, parks, homes, and city centers are built from the ground up, taking into consideration the needs of all, regardless of their ability or disability. This can include ramps, wider entryways, automatic doors, wheelchair-accessible gym equipment, and sensory corner getaways. This social model approach, though, can also be problematic in that it can lead to a hero narrative for people with disabilities, where others focus solely on the outside world being to blame for any hardship they experience or others assume what those hardships are with no regard for their embodied disability. The medical and social models of disability can be bridged to account for both the body or mind and environmental factors that shapes the lived experience of being disabled.

Critical and Justice Models

Shakespeare (1998) defined equality for people with disabilities as "the political principle that people should be treated equally, should be included rather than excluded from society, and should have the right to be heard, regardless of physical or intellectual endowment" (p. 665). In medical and social models of disability an inherent hierarchy is present. Within the medical model, the absence of disability is still viewed as preferential to the presence of a disability. Even in the social model, a person may be viewed as more or less disabled (i.e., more or less capable) in any given environment, with increased capabilities being more favorable. In both models, there is still a negative connotation to disability.

Perspectives from critical and justice models such as critical disability theory (Hosking, 2008), critical disability studies (Meekosha & Shuttleworth, 2009), DisCrit (Annamma et al., 2013), and disability justice (Invalid, 2017) view disability as a neutral part of the human condition. This understanding of disability comes from a systems-level perspective, in which the devaluation of disability is built into structures or systems, such as health care, education, employment, and the legal system. From this perspective, the systemic barriers are negative, not the disability itself. Ableism is the problem, not disability.

Critical and justice models center the voices of people with disabilities. These models emphasize the importance of recognizing everyone's humanity and allowing for individual interpretation of experienced disability. For instance, some people prefer person-first language (i.e., "person with a disability" or "person with autism"), whereas others prefer identity-first language (i.e., "disabled person" or "autistic"). Identity-first language is well-established in the deaf and autistic communities and is also common in the broader disability community (Ladau, 2021). In fact, some in the disability community argue that person-first language is problematic because it implies that being disabled somehow masks one's humanity, so it is necessary to recognize the person first. However, this ultimately implies that disability is negative when disability is neutral and can have a positive meaning when embraced as an identity. While person-first language has origins in the disability rights movement as an effort to promote respect for disabled people, the push to exclusively use person-first language by many nondisabled people in academic, government, and medical organizations has accentuated the stigmatization of disability as something negative. For many people involved in the disability community, being disabled is part of one's personhood, and disability thus cannot be separated from the person. Therefore, identity-first language views disability as neutral or positive and being a part of

disabled culture brings with it a sense of community and pride. In a blog article, Lydia X.Z. Brown (2011) wrote:

> When people say "person with autism," it does have an attitudinal nuance. It suggests that the person can be separated from autism, which simply is not true. It is impossible to separate a person from autism, just as it is impossible to separate a person from the color of his or her skin. (para. 8)

Critical disability models highlight that there is no one right answer when it comes to disability language. This chapter uses identity-first and person-first language interchangeably, but deference should be given to what the group or individual prefers. Listen to disabled people and not organizations led by nondisabled people when it comes to determining what language to use.

> For many people involved in the disability community, being disabled is part of their personhood and disability thus cannot be separated from the person.

There is also evidence that programs or interventions that center disabled people's perspectives and adopt critical and justice models of disability are more successful. A disability movement motto is "Nothing about us, without us," which emphasizes that disabled people must be fully included in guiding policies, programs, and perspectives that relate to disability (Charlton, 2000). The experience of the disabled population should guide the development of a plan to ease physical pain and adapt environments to meet their access needs. The focus is not on a return to normalcy or on ignoring the experience of living with a disability. Rather, the focus is on recognizing both the lived experience and environmental barriers in the context of a world designed by and for nondisabled people. Hosking (2008) wrote:

> CDT is based on a social model of disability which recognizes disability not as the inevitable consequence of impairment but as a complex socially constructed interrelationship between impairment, individual response to impairment, and the social environment and that the social disadvantage experienced by disabled people is caused by a social environment which fails to meet the needs of people who do not match a society's expectation of "normalcy." (pp. 16-17)

Ultimately, these critical and justice models disrupt preconceived notions of what it means to be human and call for self-reflexivity on what social conditions allow for full integration of people with disabilities into society. Centering the voices of the disability community and allowing space for a neutral or positive understanding of disability can advance a movement for disability autonomy and ameliorate barriers to participation in sports and physical activities.

Understanding Barriers

Adaptive sports and recreation are categorized as physical activities that are modified or created to meet the unique needs of people (Winnick & Porretta, 2016). Adaptive sports and recreation were first introduced for veterans with disabilities following World War II. Soldiers who had been injured during the war would participate in physical rehabilitation that, eventually, resulted in developing parasport competition and led to what we now know as the **Paralympics**. Since the creation of adaptive sports, limited opportunities exist for people with disabilities to participate in adaptive sport and physical activity. Barriers to participation are well-documented (Barr & Shields, 2011; Fitzgerald, 2018; Martin, 2013; Rimmer et al., 2004, 2005; Shields & Synnot, 2016) and more intentional communication and engaging the disabled community in health and fitness is warranted (Smith & Wightman, 2021).

The work of many researchers, most notably Dr. Jim Rimmer, have contributed to understanding the current landscape for exercise and physical activity participation for people with disabilities. Barriers to physical activity and recreation are often categorized into two categories: personal barriers and environmental barriers.

Personal Barriers

While many external or environmental barriers prevent disabled people from participating in sports or other physical activities, it is also important to recognize the embodied experience of living with a disability. Recognizing this disability experience illuminates personal barriers to participation in adaptive sports or recreation. For example, many disabled people experience physical pain. While sometimes movement can help reduce pain, it can exacerbate pain or cause new pain or injury. Gentle movement can often help people with rheumatoid arthritis keep their joints moving and reduce pain, but someone with a connective tissue disorder like Ehlers-Danlos syndrome may find that the same movements end up exacerbating pain and risk injury or dislocation. It is important to find movements that do not cause more pain. Often, low-impact exercises like swimming and strengthening the muscles around joints can be beneficial for people with chronic pain.

Another common personal barrier is fatigue or lack of energy. Similar to pain, exercise can sometimes help build energy for those who experience chronic fatigue, but in other instances, exercise can deplete energy to the point that people with disabilities end up having to stay in bed and rest rather than participating in other necessary activities or work. In the field of adaptive sport and recreation, it is important to validate and understand disabled people's experiences and not push an individual when it is not appropriate.

There are also personal barriers to participation in adaptive sport or recreation that result from fears of encountering interpersonal

Low-impact exercises like swimming can be beneficial for people with chronic pain.
Tempura/E+/Getty Images

ableism. Disabled people are often bombarded with people staring or strangers asking intrusive questions or making comments, such as the infamous "What's wrong with you?" "What happened to you?" or "Why are you in a wheelchair or use a cane?" Many disabled people have also encountered comments such as "You are too young or pretty to be disabled," or "I don't know how you even get out of bed each day. I wouldn't if I were you." Most visibly disabled people can relate to the moment when a passerby tilts their head and gives an expression of pity or when people dramatically pull a child out of the way or show signs of fear or disgust. Another common experience is the "overly helpful" person who assumes a disabled person is not capable and ends up insisting on helping even when it is not necessary or helpful. For example, a nondisabled person may rush to hold the door open for a wheelchair user who can open the door, and the nondisabled person gets in the way, making things more difficult. The stigma around disability also leads to people being shocked or amazed when disabled people participate in physical activities, perpetuating the **inspiration porn** or supercrip narratives. People with disabilities may also be hesitant to exercise in public. Disabled bodies may look or move differently than nondisabled bodies, and disabled people may feel self-conscious about exercising in front of nondisabled people out of fear of being stared at, interrupted, pitied, offered unnecessary help, or given demeaning "praise."

> In the adaptive sport and recreation field, it is important to validate and understand disabled people's experiences and not push an individual when it is not appropriate.

Another personal barrier may be having low motivation to participate in physical activities or sports due to environmental factors. Knowing or fearing that the exercise equipment at a gym is inaccessible may make a disabled person reluctant to go to the gym. Even factors such as weather can lead people to have low motivation to work out. For example, many electric wheelchairs cannot be out in the rain without risking damage to the motor or computer that powers the chair, so an electric wheelchair user may be less likely to participate in physical activities when it is raining. Extreme heat or cold may cause a flare of pain or fatigue for an individual with inflammatory arthritis, making it more challenging to exercise. Gym staff may not be properly trained to work with people with disabilities, or the gym may not offer adaptive fitness programs, reducing a disabled individual's motivation to participate in sports, recreation, or other physical activities. These personal barriers are often related to or exacerbated by barriers in the environment.

Environmental Barriers

It is crucial to identify and ameliorate environmental barriers to participation in adaptive sport and recreation. This can include physical barriers, such as a lack of curb cuts or automatic door openers, but it can also include transportation barriers, steep costs, lack of adaptive equipment, staff not trained in adaptive fitness, discriminatory policies, or lack of compliance with the Americans with Disabilities Act of 1990 (ADA). If neighborhoods lack smooth sidewalks or adequate curb cuts, it may be unsafe for a disabled person to get outside or travel to a fitness center. A wheelchair user or others with mobility-related disabilities may be unable to access a fitness program or gym if the center is on a steep hill. Even if an individual can physically access an adaptive fitness space, it is important to remember that access does not guarantee inclusion. Disabled people need to play an integral part in the design and operation of adaptive fitness or adaptive sport programs to ensure policies and practices promote both access *and* inclusion.

Environmental barriers continue to affect people with disabilities at multiple levels, including contributing to exacerbated health inequities. Individuals with disabilities are a known but often overlooked **health disparities** group, meaning that there is a gap in health outcomes between disabled and nondisabled people based on social, economic, or environmental disadvantages (Krahn et al., 2015). Adults with disabilities experience greater risk for chronic health conditions such as coronary heart disease, cancer, diabetes, and hypertension and report access and societal barriers to physical activity (Krahn et al., 2015). Furthermore, characteristics that intersect with disability (e.g., gender, age, race, ethnicity, education level, country of origin) can mean different access, barriers, and risk levels.

Intersectionality is a term Dr. Kimberlé Crenshaw used in the late 1980s. In an interview with Columbia Law School, Crenshaw (2017) described intersectionality as:

> A lens through which you can see where power comes and collides, where it interlocks and intersects. It's not simply that there's a race problem here, a gender problem here, and a class or LBGTQ problem there. Many times, that framework erases what happens to people who are subject to these things. (para. 4)

Disability has historically been an underexplored intersection (Meekosha, 1998), but more researchers are beginning to examine it. Maroto et al. (2019) highlighted the importance of including disability within intersectional work and introduced a "hierarchy of disadvantage." People who experienced the highest rates of poverty and lowest levels of education were those who claim multiple identities that are systemically marginalized, namely disabled women of color (Maroto et al., 2019). Socially constructed identities such as race or ethnicity and gender identity are considered fundamental determinants of opportunity structures, defining access to both the resources that promote health and exposure to the risks that undermine health (Dill & Zambrana, 2009). They influence health outcomes (Shavers et al., 2012; Warner & Brown, 2011) and physical activity engagement (Belcher et al., 2010; Saffer et al., 2013); therefore, it is important to promote the investigation of intersectional experiences, especially within the disability community. Separation of identities may obscure important differences in how health is produced and maintained, undermining efforts to eliminate health disparities.

Effects of Barriers

Overall, barriers also affect societal participation. High school students with disabilities are matriculating to college at a much lower rate than their nondisabled peers (Wagner et al., 2005), are at a greater risk of dropping out of college upon arrival (Wessel et al., 2009), and are experiencing higher rates of unemployment (Janus, 2009). This may not seem connected until understanding that sport and fitness participation has been shown to combat these hardships, particularly for people with disabilities (Groff et al., 2009; Lastuka & Cottingham, 2016; Yazicioglu et al., 2012). However, if opportunities are limited, participation will be low and people with disabilities will not experience the benefits of participating in sports and fitness. Carroll et al. (2014) found that adults with disabilities reported being inactive at a higher prevalence than their nondisabled peers (47% compared to 26%, respectively), leading to greater risk of comorbidities and disease.

Attempts to Mitigate Disparities

To develop solutions that promote inclusivity and mitigate health disparities between disabled and nondisabled people, it is important to acknowledge different perspectives or paradigms that inform people's views of disability and understand the personal and environmental barriers to participation in adaptive sport and recreation. This section will discuss initiatives and legislation designed to mitigate these disparities and improve participation in sports, recreation, and physical activity among disabled people in the United States. Previous attempts at mitigating health disparities for people with disabilities have had mixed success.

Healthy People (1979)

Recognizing the gap in actively targeting people with disabilities in health-promoting efforts, national initiatives, such as the Healthy People program through the U.S. Office of Health and Human Services have intentional objectives to mitigate the disparities between disabled and nondisabled people. Every 10 years, the surgeon general publishes a Healthy People initiative with specific aims on how to guide the country into more healthful practices. Healthy People 2020, published in 2010, was the first Healthy People report to include an entire section targeting people with disabilities; note that it took three decades for people with disabilities to be an intentionally targeted group. Further, the most recent report, Healthy People 2030, has little reference to physical activity, sport, or recreation for people with disabilities. Unfortunately, ableism continues to be present in health fields due in part to people with disabilities not being viewed as people who can or should aim to stay fit. This deficit in perspective also leads to a lack of inclusion or employment of disabled people in the health field (Meeks et al., 2018). The lack of representation of people with disabilities means that nondisabled people are often creating individual health goals or policies about disabled people, which can cause more harm than good (Lorenc et al., 2013).

> Ableism persists in health fields due in part to people with disabilities not being viewed as people who can or should aim to stay fit.

Section 504 of the Rehabilitation Act (1973)

Section 504 of the Rehabilitation Act of 1973 is a federal law that protects people from discrimination based on a disability. It is enforced by the U.S. Department of Health and Human Services Office for Civil Rights. Section 504 applies to any employer or organization that receives federal funding, so it includes students attending public elementary and secondary schools. Section 504 of the Rehabilitation Act (1973) states:

> No otherwise qualified individual with a disability in the United States shall, solely by reason of her or his disability, be excluded from the participation in, be denied the benefits of, or be subjected to discrimination under any program or activity receiving Federal financial assistance.

Interestingly, it passed just a year after Title IX of the Educational Amendments Act (1972), which states:

> No person in the United States shall, on the basis of sex, be excluded from participation in, be denied the benefits of, or be subjected to discrimination under any education program or activity receiving Federal financial assistance.

When considering the impact Title IX had on women's participation in higher education and collegiate sports, one can only wonder why the disabled community did not experience the same effects from an almost identical law.

Individuals With Disabilities Education Act (1975)

The Individuals With Disabilities Education Act (IDEA) is a law that ensures special education and related services are available to eligible children. This law ensures students with disabilities are entitled to a "free appropriate public education" (FAPE), meaning that schools are required to provide specialized schooling to meet the needs of every student with a disability. Though this law does not pertain specifically to sports or physical activity, physical education arguably fits under the purview of IDEA and therefore is relevant in this context.

The Americans With Disabilities Act of 1990

The Americans with Disabilities Act of 1990 (ADA) is a civil rights law designed to prohibit discrimination against people with disabilities. This includes intentional and unintentional discrimination in places of employment, schooling, transportation, and any spaces that are available for the public. The passing of the ADA has made a critical impact on the accessibility of buildings and other physical structures. Curb cuts, ramps, more elevators, accessible parking, door buttons, and chirping intersections are all examples of efforts resulting from the ADA. The term *reasonable accommodation* is a result of the ADA. For instance, a reasonable accommodation may be for an employer to create a desk space that is accessible to a wheelchair user or a quiet space for an employee with a sensory processing disability.

The Olympic and Amateur Sports Act (1998)

Previously the Amateur Sports Act of 1978, the newly titled Olympic and Amateur Sport Act was brought about by Senator Ted Stevens of Alaska. This act changed the landscape of governance for the Paralympics, officially recognizing the United States Olympic Committee (USOC) as the governing body for the Paralympics. Further, Hums and colleagues (2003) noted that, with updated language and inclusion of the Paralympic alongside mentions of Pan American and Olympic Games, the amendment "reflects equal status for athletes with disabilities" (p. 264). The amendment brought greater attention to the rights and needs of Paralympic athletes in parallel to their Olympic counterparts.

IDEA ensures that students with disabilities are entitled to a free appropriate public education, including physical education.

Convention on the Rights of Persons With Disabilities (2006)

In 2006, the United Nations drafted the human rights treaty, Convention on the Rights of Persons with Disabilities (CRPD; 2006). This treaty states:

> The Convention is intended as a human rights instrument with an explicit, social development dimension. It adopts a broad categorization of persons with disabilities and reaffirms that all persons with all types of disabilities must enjoy all human rights and fundamental freedoms. It clarifies and qualifies how all categories of rights apply to persons with disabilities and identifies areas where adaptations have to be made for persons with disabilities to effectively exercise their rights and areas where their rights have been violated, and where protection of rights must be reinforced. (para. 3)

Though this definition is broad, it encompasses many areas in its articles, including Article 30, which is explicit to participation in cultural life, recreation, leisure, and sport. The article points to access points and participation to both integrated sport opportunities (e.g., providing a deaf swimmer with a light cue to start their race alongside hearing swimmers) and segregated sport opportunities (e.g., sitting volleyball). Unfortunately, though the U.S. government has signed the agreement, it has yet to ratify this treaty. This means that the United States agrees with the statements made but has not committed to taking any action such as creating laws that would see these ideals realized.

Dear Colleague Letter (2013)

In 2013, a Dear Colleague Letter was released by the Office of Civil Rights. A Dear Colleague Letter is sent by congressional offices to colleagues in other offices to garner support or opposition, request funding, demand action, or provide concrete updates about the status of a piece of legislation.

The goal of this letter was to clarify existing legislation—Section 504—which mandates equitable programming access for people with disabilities. This clarification was a reminder that publicly funded K-12 schools and, though only briefly mentioned, institutions of higher education are required to provide equitable access to some form of adaptive activity or athletic extracurricular opportunity for students with disabilities. One of the specifications in Section 504 was that no student should be denied *extracurricular activity* involvement. The Dear Colleague Letter specified further that sports and physical activity should be included in those extracurricular activities and urged more action on the creation and integration of programs.

Cottingham et al. (2015) found later that, within the United States, roughly 750 K-12 institutions were offering adaptive athletic programs for students, while McCarty et al. (2023) found that there are only 16 collegiate adaptive sports programs in the entire country. This is still not adequate to provide for all disabled students. For reference, there are thousands of K-12 schools and more than 1,000 universities that provide athletic programs for nondisabled students.

Parasport Movement

Considered a flagship for adaptive sports, the parasport movement represents a coalition of like-minded partners from the community, up to the national level. Operating concurrently with the disability rights movement, the goal of the parasport movement is to provide more playtime and airtime for adaptive sports and to eradicate stigma for people with disabilities in all levels of sport, particularly the elite level (Howe, 2008). Based on its grassroots nature, the movement is advanced by creating more adaptive sport opportunities. These efforts have resulted in significant changes and a continued pressure on leadership to treat disabled athletes as equals to nondisabled athletes.

While the parasport movement has been integral to expanding adaptive sport opportunities, disabled athletes still face many barriers at the highest level of competition. The International Paralympic Committee (IPC) sometimes serves as a barrier for accessing and competing in adaptive sports. There are several examples of elite athletes with disabilities who have trained for the Paralympics but have been deemed ineligible to compete by IPC **classifications**. IPC classifications are used to determine eligibility for competing in a parasport and to determine the way athletes are divided into groups for competition. In this way, the IPC operates as a gatekeeper of who can participate. Many ambulatory wheelchair users with connective tissue disorders or complex regional pain syndrome who have trained in elite wheelchair basketball have been barred from competing in the Paralympics because they are deemed "not the right kind of disabled" by IPC classifications (*Wheelchair Basketball Player "wrong kind of disabled" after Rule Change*, 2020, para. 3).

Another barrier to participation in the Paralympics is the denial of reasonable and essential accommodations. For example, swimmer Becca Meyers, a six-time Paralympic medalist, was forced to withdraw from the 2021 Tokyo Paralympic Games because the U.S. Olympic & Paralympic Committee (USOPC) denied her accommodation request of bringing her own personal care assistant (PCA). The USOPC argued that Meyers did not need to bring a trusted PCA because there would be a single PCA provided for all Paralympic swimmers. While the USOPC was aiming to ensure COVID-19 safety with this provision, its denial of a consistently available and trusted PCA ultimately served as an insurmountable barrier for Meyers to be able to compete (MacDonald, 2021). The parasport movement is still up against many barriers at the highest levels and needs to prioritize inclusion of all elite athletes with disabilities, whether by pushing for a re-examination of IPC classifications or ensuring that all athletes' access needs are fully met.

Organizations and Coalitions

Many sports organizations give invaluable efforts to the parasport movement and continue to open opportunities and change the lives of people with disabilities. Organizations such as the National Center on Health, Physical Activity and Disability (NCHPAD), Lakeshore Foundation, Move United, Challenged Athletes Foundation, Endeavor Games, the American Association of Adapted Sports Programs (AAASP), International Federation of Adapted Physical Activity (IFAPA), Inclusive Fitness Coalition (IFC), and many others lead the way on adaptive sport, fitness, and recreation at all levels. Even traditional sport groups, such as the National Intramural and Recreational Sports Association (NIRSA), are beginning to examine their adaptive offerings and work for increased inclusion.

Still Work to Be Done

There have been decades of effort toward creating more inclusive fitness and sport spaces that can contribute to better health outcomes for people with disabilities. However, barriers are still present, leading to continued health disparities. These barriers come from places that can be difficult to detect. Understanding ableism and where it comes from; recognizing the different models of disability and how various perspectives can contribute to barriers; and knowing the history of previous initiatives, movements, and legislation aimed at promoting disability rights and adaptive sport opportunities helps eliminate the barriers to participation in adaptive sport, recreation, and physical activity that disabled people experience.

Social-Ecological Model

The **social-ecological model (SEM)** is a way of examining a problem or phenomenon at many levels (Martin Ginis et al., 2016). The SEM has five levels: (1) individual, (2) interpersonal, (3) organizational, (4) community, and (5) atmosphere policy (see figure 2.1). The relationship of these levels can be described like matryoshka, or Russian nesting dolls with the individual level as the smallest doll and each other level stacking on top with the policy level as the largest, most overarching doll. However, all levels are interdependent and should be considered when

FIGURE 2.1 The five levels of the social-ecological model.

integrating and using the SEM (Kennedy et al., 2021). This section provides a description of the five levels of the SEM and details how these levels fit into our discussion on models of disability, barriers, and parasport.

Individual Level

The individual level concerns experience, attitudes, knowledge, and competencies directly related to the individual. These are generally personal and bodily factors that affect the experience of the individual. This could be an individual's experience of disability, diagnosis, social identities (e.g., race, gender identity and expression, sexuality, nationality, class), pain, fatigue, motivation, skills, and other co-occurring conditions. This also includes an individual's attitudes, self-confidence, values, and beliefs. The individual level also captures an individual's level of risk taking.

Adaptive athletes are capable and work just as hard as nondisabled athletes and should therefore be treated as such. Disabled athletes are not more fragile in mind or body and deserve to be challenged. When creating programs and working within already established organizations, encourage the adoption of a critical or justice model of disability so that athletes' embodied experience of disability and structural barriers are both recognized and addressed. Athletes' lived experiences and access needs will be different depending on an individual's disability type and intersecting social identities; this perspective applies when working with any athlete or group of athletes. Listen to people's experiences and expertise and build programs together.

> Athletes' lived experiences and access needs will be different depending on an individual's disability type and intersecting social identities; this perspective applies when working with any athlete or group of athletes.

Interpersonal Level

The interpersonal level concerns relationships and interactions within an individual's network. This includes primary exchanges, such as with family, caregivers, and close friends, as well as secondary groups that are larger and broader, such as peer groups in school, work, or sports teams. The interpersonal level may include the groups that are within a person's rehabilitation setting or even the physical therapists and doctors, giving special attention to the relationship between the person and provider, not the organization or hospital system. Any contact a person has with another individual or group and the competencies, attitudes, and beliefs that encompass that relationship can be considered part of the interpersonal level.

There are several recommendations for addressing barriers at the interpersonal level. Knowing the level of supports that surround athletes and programs is key to a program's success. Building the morale of the team is paramount. Many elite disabled athletes discuss how team members become family and how those bonds mean everything by building a sense of support, love, and belonging. It is important that coaches, nondisabled peers, and anyone else interfacing with the adaptive sport world do not adopt an assumption of charity. People with disabilities do not want to be demeaned or be seen as victims of some terrible or negative circumstance. Disabled people who participate in adaptive sports resist being objects of pity, charity, or inspiration. Further, nondisabled people working in adaptive sport alongside disabled athletes are not there to "help" disabled people. Rather, applying a critical disability lens can ensure priorities that center disabled people's voices in all aspects of the program by treating disabled athletes with respect and dignity—just as nondisabled athletes would be treated—hiring disabled coaches and ensuring that people with disabilities are in leadership positions at all levels of the organization.

Organizational Level

The organizational level relates to institutions where people gather and which serve an established purpose. This can include places like church or recreation communities, schools, governing bodies, municipalities, hospital or health care systems, or places of work. The organizational level captures institutions that have some form of structure and purpose for a specific community along with the attitudes and values that are embedded in these institutions. This level is often interwoven with the community level, so many of the examples or barriers will overlap across the organizational and community levels.

Included in the organization level, national governing bodies, such as the American Association of Adapted Sports Programs (AAASP), National Wheelchair Basketball Association (NWBA), U.S. Tennis Association (USTA), and global governance units, such as the International Paralympic Committee (IPC) and **Special Olympics**, dictate much of adaptive sport opportunities within the United States. Since the United States supports most sports growth within schools, individual schools, whether K-12 or universities, and a school's willingness to support adaptive sport programs can be a barrier or facilitator to the development and growth of adaptive sport programs. Further, local organizations like the YMCA or other gym systems open the potential for partnerships for adaptive fitness initiatives. Individual factors at any one of these institutions can make or break an adaptive sport opportunity. If a university is willing to support a sitting volleyball team but there is no league for the team to participate in, the athletes may not have the same opportunities or potential for play, limiting the sustainability of the program.

Community Level

The community level includes relationships that populations or organizations form between one another. This often includes coalitions of like-minded partners, associations of businesses, and built spaces meant for gathering, such as a local park. The community level is where customs thrive, and values inform the overall culture. The community level may capture the presence or absence of green spaces, sidewalks, streetlights, and bike lanes, all of which contribute to the overall feel and nature of the community.

Organizations such as those listed in the Organizations and Coalitions section (e.g., Move United, NCHPAD; see p. 27) have built communities of like-minded partners all over the nation. These organizational partnerships connect disabled and nondisabled people, provide resources, offer trade secrets, and post job opportunities. Similarly, many parks and recreation departments in local cities have hired staff and partnered with nonprofit organizations to provide more adaptive movement opportunities at levels ranging from recreational to elite. Though these opportunities are still sparse in some places and vary widely, more are emerging that help create a more truly inclusive environment for disabled community members.

The physical and attitudinal environment within any community can determine the type of engagement an individual can have with adaptive sport or recreation opportunities as well as with the broader community. There are varied understandings of what disability is and who disabled people are, and this will be reflected in the community spaces people occupy (e.g., the presence of well-paved sidewalks or chirping crosswalk signs). Different community partners are more than prepared to support and promote physical activity for people with disabilities, but not every organization is prepared to support adaptive sport and physical activity (Ross et al., 2021). There is also the opportunity to share perspectives that support physical activity engagement for disabled people with community partners to help shift cultural and attitudinal environments to be more inclusive. To address barriers at the community level, bring together the disabled community and interested partners to build a coalition with a common goal of attending city planning meetings to understand current initiatives relating to disability and sport.

> Different community partners are more than prepared to support and promote physical activity for people with disabilities, but not every organization is prepared to support adaptive sport and physical activity.

Policy Level

Last is the policy level, which pertains to all laws and governance, from local to federal levels, that exist within and around a population. The policy level may include a university's inclusion policy, a municipal park and recreation department's codes on park maintenance, or national laws surrounding adaptive sport or recreation opportunities, for example. This level also accounts for how these policies are governed, disseminated, and adhered to (or not).

Section 504 of the Rehabilitation Act, IDEA, and the ADA are examples of national laws that have been passed to support people with disabilities and disability rights. However, given the need for the Dear Colleague Letter in 2013 and continued efforts by the parasport movement, the outcomes of these acts have come up short. Further, there is little guidance or policy on mandating either segregated or integrated sport opportunities at any educational level. Poor enforcement of disability rights legislation could contribute to the lack of sports pipeline for disabled athletes and a stagnation in the number of adaptive sport programs.

The ableism that is often embedded in policies and practices that influence disabled individuals' ability to participate in sports and recreation activities must be addressed. For example, disability activists are currently pushing for an increase in Social Security Disability Insurance asset limits to allow for more financial security. Further, disability-related legal protections need to be reinforced so that people with disabilities have equal access to participate in the labor force and other aspects of society. Recently, there have been attempts to undermine disability rights by dismantling the protection of disparate impact discrimination under ADA and Section 504. For example, in March 2022, the Los Angeles Community College District was set to petition the Supreme Court (*Payan v. LACCD Explainer—Disability Rights Education & Defense Fund*, 2021), arguing that disparate impact or "unintentional" discrimination should no longer be protected under ADA or Section 504. Disability discrimination may be unintentional but leads to vast inequalities and the exclusion of disabled people. It is incredibly challenging to prove that discrimination is intentional. A similar case was almost brought to the Supreme Court by CVS in December 2021; however, both LACCD and CVS withdrew prior to their petition date in part due to the successful mobilization of the disability community (Diament, 2021). These attempts to undermine disability rights may not be the last. Thus, people need to mobilize to protect existing disability rights and ensure that ADA and Section 504 are widely enforced, ensuring the inclusion of people with disabilities in all aspects of life, including participation in sports and physical activities.

Summary

There are many ways to view disability that affect the dismantling or perpetuation of ableism. Disability models discussed in this chapter include the medical, social, critical, and justice models. Understanding these models of viewing health and disability helps to make barriers to physical activity apparent. When these barriers are made clear, they can be studied, interrogated, and mitigated with the help with of disabled individuals' voices at the center. This is necessary work because people with disabilities face many barriers to sports and physical activity, leading to poor health outcomes. Many efforts have been tried to mitigate these effects, but barriers persist, leading to an even greater need to keep exploring options. The social-ecological model (SEM) is a helpful framework for acknowledging barriers and working on solutions. When investigating issues, going through each level (i.e., individual, interpersonal, organizational, community, and policy) can be a helpful exercise for identifying systems of ableism. Within this process, to build or expand a sport or physical activity program for people with disabilities, center the voices of disabled people and make space for disabled experts in leadership.

CRITICAL THINKING EXERCISES

1. Let's start with some questions:
   - What is your experience or connection with disability?
   - Have you ever participated in or around parasport and recreation?
   - What is your goal in supporting others engaging in parasport and recreation?

   Hold on to these. Perhaps write them down in a notebook or keep them in mind.

2. Stella Young called an overcelebration of disabled normalcy "inspiration porn" and produced a TED Talk titled, "I'm Not Your Inspiration, Thank You Very Much." Find the video by entering "Stella Young TED Talk" into your preferred Internet search engine or visit TED.com and search for it. Watch the video and consider the following questions:
   - How does Young's talk fit into our discussion on ableism?
   - Young talked about an objectification of disabled people's lives. Where have you seen examples of that? Can you think of health and fitness examples?
   - What are your thoughts on Young's dream to "live in a world where we don't have such low expectations of disabled people that we are congratulated for getting out of bed and remembering our own names in the morning"? Do we live in that world? Could we?

3. Review the working definition of ableism from Talila Lewis (p. 16).
   - What did you understand from Lewis' definition?
   - What didn't you understand from Lewis' definition?
   - What thoughts or feelings came up as you read it?
   - What questions do you still have?

4. If it is not the individual person and not the environment, then what is it? We would like to challenge you to think what *isn't* it? Dr. Tobin Siebers, in his book *Disability Theory* (2008), suggests a "complex embodiment" that allows both realities to coexist. Siebers argues that disability stems from both bodily and environmental factors.
   - How can both things be true?
   - Can we hold multiple perspectives as both potentially helpful and harmful?
   - What do we do with this information, and how do we hold both truths?

5. Why do you think such a low number of adults with disabilities meet physical activity guidelines? The following statements each represent an answer to why participation in physical activity is low among disabled people. Read each statement and indicate which model of disability is being applied (medical, social, or critical):
   - There are no local adaptive sports programs in their area.
   - People with disabilities are lazy and do not know how to care for themselves.

- The closest gym is up a steep hill from the bus stop.
- People with disabilities are not being targeted for fitness initiatives because there is an assumption that they can never be healthy or practitioners don't know how to work with them.

  Why do these perspectives make a difference, and why is it important to know the differences? How might solutions or interventions vary depending on the model of disability applied?

6. Based on what has been covered in this chapter, it is evident that people with disabilities face many barriers to participation in physical activity and sport. Let's see how your school stacks up to disability inclusion and ways it could be better. Create a goal for a physical activity or sport program on your campus. This could be something that needs to be created (e.g., adaptive training for recreation center staff) or a continuation of an offering already in existence (e.g., find practice space for wheelchair basketball team). Envision a goal, hypothesize barriers, and imagine some solutions. Discuss the process and what questions come up for you. Does your goal seem possible at your university? Can you reimagine ways it could be better? An example is provided for your reference:

TABLE 2.1   **Program Goal *(Example: Build an affordable program for all participants)***

	Barriers	Possible solutions
Individual	Cost is still too high	Include a sliding scale
Interpersonal	No fundraising personnel	Hire grant writer or send staff to grant writing course
Organizational	No affordable transportation	Brainstorm ride shares
Community	Lack of community support or interest in the mission	Find one partnering business to share in cost and effort
Policy	Inflation and rising costs	Price lock guarantees

CHAPTER 3

Innovation in Disability Sport and Recreation

David Legg, PhD, and Simon Darcy, PhD

LEARNING OBJECTIVES

After reading this chapter, you will be able to do the following:

- Identify how innovation has shaped and been shaped by disability sport.
- Understand the innovation process.
- Know how to take an innovative idea into practice.

This chapter explores the nexus of disability, sport, and innovation. As with other areas of disability, a great deal of innovation is user-led, where people with a disability identify opportunities to improve performance and set about the process of innovation to address the needs of themselves and others with disabilities. Other innovations in disability sport come about as a complementary outcome from innovations more generally. For example, improvements in materials may lead to innovations in nondisabled cycling and then in cycling for people with disabilities before being adapted for use in wheelchair racing. This chapter explores examples of innovation in disability sport and recommends processes to follow for budding innovators and entrepreneurs as well as opportunities to showcase these innovations.

Disability itself is complex with no simple, black-and-white considerations when it comes to sport or any other areas of an individual's life. Ableist practices tend to overlook, omit, or "other" people with disabilities, as if they do not exist. Hence, people with disabilities become "necessity entrepreneurs" (Darcy et al., 2020) who see an unmet need as an opportunity to innovate and take the idea to market through creating their own business. They innovate transformative solutions to barriers in their lives simply because they must, and disability sport and recreation is no different from other areas of social participation. Innovation is thus a cornerstone of adaptive sport, and perhaps a cause and an effect of the evolution of it, but it is unquestioningly what makes it exciting and confounding.

What Is Innovation?

Innovation can be defined as any change that creates value. As commonly used, the term implies newness, but innovation does not necessarily refer only to creating new products. It can also describe a process of recycling products and using them in different ways. More recently the term *circular economy* has been used to describe "sharing, leasing, reusing, repairing, refurbishing, and recycling" materials and products (US EPA, 2021).

Innovators create value by solving problems through products or services, companies or social enterprises, or nonprofit organizations. Innovators can also address challenges by looking at processes inside an organization or marketing approaches. Wherever they occur, innovations enable people with disability to be more active, more often, and perhaps more proficiently throughout the entire athlete pathway.

Innovation in Business

The term *innovation* has frequently been used in a business context to describe an important driver of economic progress for nations, companies, and individuals (SRI, 2019, p. 1). McKinsey, a global management consulting firm that has written a great deal on innovation, has identified eight essentials of innovation, emerging from

> a multiyear study comprising in-depth interviews, workshops, and surveys of more than 2,500 executives in over 300 companies, including both performance leaders and laggards, in a broad set of industries and countries. What the authors found were the set of eight essential attributes that are present, either in part or in full, at every big company that's a high performer in product, process, or business-model innovation. (de Jong et al., 2015, p. 2)

The eight essential attributes are aspire, choose, discover, evolve, accelerate, scale, extend, and mobilize (de Jong et al., 2015):

- *Aspire*. How can the innovation change the lives of people with impairments? Can innovating be quantified and evaluated?
- *Choose*. Which innovation will make the greatest impact based on available resources such as time, capacity, or money?
- *Discover*. What potential innovations are available? McKinsey suggests this

answer often lies at the intersection of the problem itself, technology, and a business model. Can a change or unique way of positioning any of these three lead to innovations in adapted physical activity?

- *Evolve*. Stay connected to changing contexts, constantly challenge assumptions, and pay attention to changes outside of your own experience. For instance, how can innovations in fashion be applied in sport and recreation?
- *Accelerate*. Support and reward risk taking, testing, and innovative approaches. Address the barriers that thwart innovative ideas from percolating throughout the organization.
- *Scale*. How can innovations for one impairment group be applied to others or within the able-bodied population? Are there ways to take innovations for a specific disability and apply them for a larger audience?
- *Extend*. What partners should or could be brought into the process? The adage of "It's incredible what can be accomplished when nobody cares who gets the credit" is appropriate here.
- *Mobilize*. There are often thinkers and doers, and it is important to have both involved in the innovation process.

Innovation is not just for business students or entrepreneurs. Employers are looking for employees who can think innovatively and entrepreneurially or intra-entrepreneurially (from within an organization) by identifying new ways of generating revenue. Innovation does not always result in a viable product; rather value can be found in the *process* of learning and **ideating**. Innovating requires identifying a problem and exploring a solution, calling on such skills as problem solving, critical thinking, customer or user discovery, design thinking, and pitching, all of which can benefit one's career, regardless of whether that means starting a business or joining an established organization (Maurya, 2016).

Innovation in Sport, Disability, and Disability Sport

For those studying sport and recreation, understanding innovation may be even more relevant. The International Council of Sport Science and Physical Education (ICSSPE) noted that "sport is sometimes seen as a sector which lags behind the corporate sector in terms of innovative thinking, technology and reinventing itself to stay relevant with new generations" (ICSSPE, 2020, p. 1). Innovation in disability sport and disability culture is far-reaching, and there are literally hundreds of examples (i.e., disabilityinnovation.com). An innovative and entrepreneurial spirit and mindset is built out of necessity for people experiencing disability due to discrimination and a lack of opportunity (Darcy et al., 2020). There has also been an economic incentive to innovate in disability spaces. Using innovation to access and sell to persons with a disability is becoming more common and companies are recognizing the importance of diversity, accessibility, and inclusion because it is both the right and potentially profitable thing to do. As one example, a Global Investor Group representing US$2.8 trillion is appealing to companies to be more inclusive as "Fortune 1000 companies realize environmental, social, and governance factors impact their management, culture, brand, and financial well-being" (Disability:IN, 2022, p. 2).

> Why are people left to innovate for themselves rather than have mainstream companies innovating new products and services for all customers?

An example of a profitable innovation is the "ThisAbles" project, which was conceived to allow people with disability to better use IKEA products. IKEA's vision is to "create a better everyday life for as many people as possible" (IKEA, 2022, p. 1). Here, IKEA partnered with several nonprofit organizations including Access Israel (Sabina-Aouf, 2019; Slefo, 2019; ThisAbles, 2022). Another example is Johnny Matheny, who lost his arm due to cancer and now uses a mind-controlled prosthetic limb attached directly to his skeleton using Bluetooth technology (Bloomberg, 2015). Yet another example is Roy Allela, a Kenyan engineer and innovator who created a set of gloves that can translate signed hand movements into audible speech, allowing those who are deaf and hard of hearing but who do not know sign language to communicate more easily (Because of them we can, 2019). All these innovators recognize that more customers using a company's products is better for the company's bottom line. This population segment has been overlooked for too long, and if it is served properly, it could dramatically change the financial success of any company (Harris Prager, 1999).

Examples of Innovation

There are many opportunities for innovation to occur when it is recognized that people with a disability may not be able to participate equitably in everyday life.

Clothing

It has been noted that there are more clothing lines for dogs than for people living with disabilities (Jordan, 2021; Ryan, 2018). In response, the 2022 Sydney Fashion Show integrated clothing designed for people with disabilities within their mainstream programs showing adaptive clothing for all different embodiments (Cassidy, 2022).

Another innovation is the T-Glove, which two Canadian college students created to assist persons with quadriplegia in grasping. According to Halpenny (2020):

> The T-Glove has low-friction cords on the fingertips of the glove which runs down the hand, mimicking tendons in the fingers. A separate chord is attached to the thumb, keeping it away from the rest of the fingers and putting it in the position required to grasp onto objects. The tips of the fingers, thumb, and palm consist of special pads that increase friction which help the individual to hold on to what they have grasped. (p. 8)

Jackson (2021) noted that "for many disabled people, off-the-peg clothes are inaccessible and cause discomfort, from fiddly buttons to seams that chafe in a wheelchair. Clothing plays an important part in living well," and "due to restricted mobility, clothing choices can impact whether people with disabilities can operate functionally" (p. 2). Nike responded to this barrier and need by developing the Nike Go FlyEase shoe (Nike, 2021). The innovation was motivated by an American teenager, Matthew Walzer, who contacted Nike in 2012. Walzer has cerebral palsy and wanted a shoe that he could put on and take off by himself. He wrote a letter to Nike:

> My dream is to go to the college of my choice without having to worry about someone coming to tie my shoes every day. I've worn Nike basketball shoes all my life. I can only wear this type of shoe because I need ankle support to walk. At 16 years old, I can completely dress myself, but my parents still have to tie my shoes. As a teenager who is striving to become totally self-sufficient, I find this extremely frustrating and, at times, embarrassing. (Fleming, 2021, p. 5)

The Go style was an innovation from the original FlyEase shoe series, which incorporated zippers and straps instead of laces. The Go series then took the inclusive approach a step further by allowing "wearers to step into their shoes without a single adjustment or closure point" (Huber, 2021, p. 1).

Clothing brand Tommy Hilfiger has also taken an innovative approach and created a clothing line for children with disabilities in 2016. This was then expanded in 2018 when they unveiled a full line of clothing and accessories titled Tommy Adaptive (Tommy Hilfiger, 2022).

"Modifications such as adjustable hems, one-handed zippers, side-seam openings, bungee cord closure systems, adjustable waists, and magnetic buttons and Velcro make the fashionable designs much more disability friendly. Some shirts are even made with easy-open necklines and expanded back openings" (Gallucci, 2018, p. 4).

Similarly, Zappos launched Zappos Adaptive in 2017 to provide shoppers with disabilities "fashionable and functional footwear options" (Zappos, 2022, p. 1). An example was a partnership between Zappos and Sorel where they "added dual zippers and enlarged heel pull loops for an easier on/off experience" (Zappos, 2022, p. 1).

> How might innovations affect the ability of those with disabilities to compete directly against those without disabilities?

Gaming

Gaming and esport is another sector that is becoming a beacon for innovation with disability. The gaming sectors and physical activity sectors (in the form of the New York City Marathon) intersected to develop a wheelchair-accessible interactive video game (Booten, 2018). The innovation here is enabling "people, including those in wheelchairs, to race one another in place using a Dance Revolution–like touchpad" (Booten, 2018, p. 1). Microsoft's Xbox has also taken an inclusive approach to recent designs to their game consoles so that those with limited finger dexterity can use adapted joy sticks and touchpads that enable them to compete equitably against those with full finger function (Spencer, 2018; Takahashi, 2018). In his blog, Hamilton (2017) talked about the changing trends in gaming, suggesting these adaptations are not frivolous:

> A good deal of accessibility elsewhere is aimed at the basics, making sure that people can access buildings, cross a road, use a government website, and so on. But life is not about existing on those basics. Games mean access to recreation, culture, socialising. These are all critically important; they mean the difference between existing and living. (p. 1)

CHRISTIAN BAGG

Canadian Christian Bagg is an entrepreneur and the inventor of the Bowhead Reach. Bagg was profiled in *Men's Journal* and *Canadian Cycling Magazine* for his innovations relating to mountain biking for persons with spinal cord injuries and the Bowhead Reach. This is unlike anything built previously. "It's not a mountain bike or an electric bike or an ATV or a wheelchair," says Bagg, the founder and inventor of Bowhead Corp. "I don't know what it is, but I do know there's nothing else like it" (Stuart, 2022, p. 1). He further explains that his development came about due his own desire to return to his pre-injury outdoor activities. "I was a mountain biker before I was injured and wanted to be a mountain biker after I was injured. But the technology just wasn't there," says Bagg (McKall, 2022, p. 6).

Riders using Bowhead Reach bikes.

Rob Perry

In 1996, at age 20, Bagg had a spinal cord injury from a snowboarding accident resulting in paraplegia. Bagg found it difficult to find properly fitting equipment due to his large frame. This led to him using his engineering and machinery skills to build a custom chair, and he then went on to develop further adaptive equipment that would allow him to continue his outdoor lifestyle (Jones, 2021). One of his most successful innovations came as "he was searching for a way to keep his cross-country skis edging on a sidehill, and he came up with the idea for an articulating joint" (Stuart, 2022, p. 5). He was then able to adapt this for an adapted mountain bike with "the articulating parallelogram-shaped front axle becoming the key link in the Reach, allowing the front end to follow the terrain, while the rest of the machine stays flat. What's unique about this is that the leaning and steering are not connected," explains Bagg. "I can be on a 30-degree side slope and still be level. No other adaptive bike or vehicle does it" (Stuart, 2022, p. 6). Learn more about Christian and Bowhead Corp by visiting their corporate website at www.bowheadcorp.com.

Others are being innovative with wheelchair designs that can be both functional and style conscious. Wong (2015) described wheelchairs as "horrible medical devices" and could not "understand why companies didn't advance their wheelchairs in the same way bike companies did with their products." *The Guardian* also profiled a variety of wheelchair adaptation options, including a tank-chair designed by a combat veteran that is "capable of conquering sand, snow, gravel, rocks, and mud;" a mountain trike; and the Whill, which looks like "what you might get if Apple turned its sleek, minimalist hand to wheelchair design" (Wainright, 2014, p. 1). Another example is Dave Lee and the Signal Snowboard team, who built a hybrid adaptive snowboard as part of their program Every Third Thursday so that they could go boarding with their friends (Network A, 2012). They merged "Signal Snowboard's technology and Crankbrothers' mountain bike component technology to create a new next-level custom adaptive snowboard customized to get a new crew of shredders on the hill" (Network A, 2012, p. 1). With equipment innovation comes organizational innovation to deliver sport and recreation opportunities for all in alpine and beach environments so these experiences can be offered to all people with disability after trailblazing individuals have forged the initial pathways (see Dickson et al., 2021; Darcy et al., 2023; Patterson et al., 2015).

Equipment

Innovation that enables persons with disabilities to be more active is also being seen in equipment development. The Sierra Club, as but one example, profiled eight pieces of adapted outdoor gear, including a swim fin that attaches to a prosthetic and can either rotate depending on the stroke or be fixed for when treading water (Davidson, 2011).

There have also been numerous innovations specifically around the development of wheelchairs. Christian Bagg is an excellent example of this. His Bowhead Reach mimics the capabilities of a downhill mountain bike (Stuart, 2022) and looks like the "badass lovechild of a dune buggy and electric mountain bike. It makes it possible for paraplegics to reach around banked corners, huck it off 15-feet jumps in bike parks, roll off-camber rock drops, and navigate just about any trail" (Stuart, 2022, p. 3).

Facilities

Sporting facilities are also becoming far more innovative with their designs to ensure that they can welcome *all* guests (Darcy, 2017; Dickson et al., 2016; Kitchin et al., 2022). At the Pro Sports Assembly, "Rocket Mortgage Fieldhouse and Kulture City shared their inspiration and activation that led to the first sensory space built-in a professional sports arena for persons with autism" (Pro Sports Assembly, 2021, p. 1). Different embodiments require different inclusive practices, and quiet spaces or places for families to be able to enjoy an experience without having to worry about their family member with autism are gaining momentum. The creation of quiet spaces is a good example of how facilities are acknowledging the need to be innovative to best serve the diversity of their fans.

Travel and Tourism

Travel and tourism have benefited greatly from innovative thinking as it relates to disability. For example, the Freedom Seat provides passengers who have a disability an opportunity to use their own wheelchairs on an airplane, giving more comfort for the person flying *and* minimizing the chances of the wheelchair being damaged or lost during transit. The innovation is relatively simple in that the seat used for a nondisabled person slides over top of the other seat beside it, leaving an open space and locking system on the ground that attaches to the wheelchair (Molon Labe, 2022). The wheelchair is then placed and locked in place where the seat that slid sideways used to be located. While perhaps a simple innovation, the potential upside for the individual and industry is massive. A market study completed by Open Doors suggested that "27 million U.S. travelers with disabilities took 81 million trips and spent US$58.7 billion on travel in 2018-19, up from US$34.6 billion in the prior 2015 study" (Munoz, 2021, p. 3). This innovation makes travel easier and could increase the comfort level of wheelchair users, thus increasing the willingness to travel as has been outlined through developing accessible tourism as a conceptual framework (Buhalis & Darcy, 2011; Darcy et al., 2020).

Marketing

Sport marketing is also increasingly aware of this confluence of innovation and disability. Procter & Gamble and Toyota, both companies being worldwide partners of the Olympic and Paralympic Games, have "embraced the opportunity to showcase and push their own boundaries as innovators through disability, technology, inclusion, and sport" (IOC Media, 2021, p. 1). Procter & Gamble, for instance, recognized that even the most mundane activities that relate to sport may be barriers if they are inconvenient or challenging. Putting on deodorant after a practice may be something many take for granted, but not all have the luxury of being able to do so. Recognizing this, Unilever launched Degree Inclusive, the world's first deodorant designed specifically for people with a disability. The product features a hooked design for use with one hand and magnetic closures on the cap that is easier for someone with limited grip strength to manage. The deodorant also includes a braille label and instructions for persons with a visual impairment (Caciatorre, 2021). Similarly, Procter & Gamble North America has launched an easy-open lid for their Olay cosmetics. It features a winged cap that is simpler to grip along with high-contrast labeling and braille text (Heasley, 2021). Purdys Chocolatier has also used braille labeling on their packaging with a box co-created with the visually impairment community. The 18-piece gift box features "braille orientation tabs, a braille chocolate legend, as well as a QR code that brings users to an accessible screen-reader version of the legend" (Purdy's, 2021, p. 2).

These examples are but a few of the many that exist, and you are encouraged to look around and identify other best practices. By doing this, you start your journey as an innovator in the disability sport sector.

People should not become intimidated by thinking they will never envision something as remarkable as what has been described. The process of innovation can seem overwhelming, but when it is approached as a process, it can be quite manageable. We will now examine four approaches that may help identify a problem that innovation can solve and then design the thinking innovation process to create that solution.

> The process of innovation can seem overwhelming, but when it is approached as a process, it can be quite manageable.

Approaches to Innovation

Now that we have reviewed various examples of innovation within an adapted context, it is important to consider the various approaches to pursuing this. There are many approaches, but this chapter examines four particular approaches for facilitating innovation.

The first approach is advocated by Mount Royal University's Institute for Innovation and Entrepreneurship (DePaul, 2022). It encourages potential innovators to ask themselves five questions when considering or searching for an innovative approach:

- What existing innovations support persons with disabilities? Are there any gaps?
- Can an innovation from somewhere else be applied to a different activity?
- What are the various areas in which the innovation can assist persons with disabilities to participate in sport and recreation?
- Are some innovations inexpensive and easy to implement?
- Are there innovations for those beyond technology or access that we should consider?

An example could be creating a button-up baseball jersey with magnetic buttons. Perhaps a fan with poor finger dexterity wanted to wear the team jersey, but putting it on and taking it off was challenging. Magnetic buttons are used in other realms but could be applied to clothing and would be relatively inexpensive and easy to add to an existing shirt.

A second approach also advocated by Mount Royal's Institute for Innovation and Entrepreneurship is to use "how might we" questions, such as the following:

- How might we encourage a person with visual impairment to participate in a specific physical activity?
- How might we enhance the experience of going to the gym for a person with a spinal cord injury?
- How might we encourage a person with visual impairment to participate in ice hockey?
- How might we enhance the experience of a person with learning disabilities going to the gym?

Using the last example, we could then start to consider ways in which to enhance the gym experience, including signage in the parking lot, the welcoming nature of the entrance with regard to staff training, the ease of purchasing food and beverages through a prepaid or subscription service, or the ability to use the equipment independently.

A third approach, also known as SCAMPER, suggests seven strategies:

1. *Substitute.* What would happen if we did X instead of Y?
2. *Combine.* What would happen if we combined elements?
3. *Adapt.* What changes are needed to adapt to a different context?
4. *Modify/Magnify/Minimize.* What could we modify by increasing or decreasing that creates more value?
5. *Put to another use.* How else could this be used?
6. *Eliminate.* What could be taken away that makes it simpler or different?
7. *Reverse or rearrange.* What would happen if the order was changed? (Faust, 2020)

An example could be using skateboarding for a person with a spinal cord injury. Here we could *substitute* the skateboard with an adapted wheelchair and *combine* the elements from sport chairs used in wheelchair rugby with more traditional skateboard designs. The entrances and parking lots to the skateboard parks might need to be *adapted*, and signage could indicate that those using wheelchairs were welcome at the park. The adaptations to the wheelchair and design changes might then be appealing to a younger audience that uses wheelchairs. Other barriers that would hinder the participation from a structural perspective around the skatepark such as gravel paths could be changed, and finally all future skateparks could be developed with the inclusion of persons using wheelchairs being front of mind.

A fourth approach is design thinking (Brown, 2008; Razzouk & Shute, 2012), which is defined as

a methodology that imbues the full spectrum of innovation activities with a human-centered design ethos. By this, I mean that innovation is powered by a thorough understanding, through direct observation, of what people want and need in their lives and what they like or dislike about the way particular products are made, packaged, marketed, sold, and supported. (Brown, 2008, p. 1)

The Stanford University School of Design described this way of thinking in five steps (Hasso Plattner Institute of Design at Stanford University, 2022):

1. Empathize with the potential user. This can be enhanced through interviews and shadowing that encourages the innovator to be nonjudgmental. Instead, the goal is seeking to understand the potential user's true experience.
2. Define the problem that the user faces.
3. Ideate, which means sharing ideas with others and brainstorming various iterations of the idea.
4. Create a prototype.
5. Test the innovation and then circle back to step one in a process of refinement.

Joachim et al. (2020, 2021) provides a review of design thinking elements within a sport management context with an example of how design thinking was incorporated into the hybrid commercial franchise of a not-for-profit sport organization. The approach fostered the engagement of all stakeholders (players, spectators, sponsors, franchise governance, volunteers, etc.) in identifying challenges and seeking transformative solutions and innovation for value creation across this relatively new organization for a professional sport for women. There was an advantage in understanding and creating holistic sport experiences across stakeholders and identifying competing organizational challenges to frame solutions. The same skills and processes could be used in adaptive sport organizations given the challenges they face in having a sustainable business model (see Dickson et al., 2021). This forms part of the wider research process in sport (Veal & Darcy, 2014).

Developing an Entrepreneurial Mindset

With the knowledge of various innovation approaches, one has a framework for thinking about innovations in disability sport and recreation. Anyone who is ambitious can take this to "the next level" and consider becoming even more entrepreneurial. To do this, a potential innovator should consider mapping out the innovation using a lean canvas (DePaul, 2022). With a lean canvas, an innovator would start with the problem to be solved and the existing options on how this problem is being addressed. Second, solutions could be listed with key metrics that could tell the innovator how the business, related to the innovation, is doing. A third step is to identify the unique value proposition. Why is the innovation unique and worthy of another person's attention? Ultimately, and perhaps most importantly, the innovator would then have to identify customer segments and the market need. Not doing this step is by far the most common reason start-ups fail (DePaul, 2022; Skok, 2012).

Several considerations should be made to avoid failure of the innovation. Innovators should meet with persons with disabilities to understand the problems or challenges they face. Listening and reflecting is crucial. Cultivate your own empathy, which inspires innovation and recognizes that problems exist because no one has spent the time to truly understand the problem and identify a solution. Sample statements could be: "Tell me about the last time you did X," "What was good about that experience?" "What was challenging?" "How did it make you feel?" and "Have you sought other ways to accomplish X?" (DePaul, 2022).

With all these suggestions, the key is to spend the time at the front end. As Albert Einstein noted, "If I had one hour to save the world, I would spend 55 minutes trying to understand the problem and 5 minutes trying to devise a solution" (Spradlin, 2012, p. 1).

How to Share an Innovation

After learning about several innovations and the processes by which to create them, innovators should start the process of developing the innovation, and once created, ensure that it is shared. There are several launchpads, incubators, and other innovation hubs available. Contact them and ask about opportunities to be mentored or enter competitions or what further development opportunities might exist. There are also impairment specific innovation opportunities such as Praxis, which, in association with the Ideation Clinic at the University of Toronto, launched a six-month kickstart program designed to help participants develop ideas for those living with spinal cord injuries. Examples include the Comcast NBCUniversal SportsTech Accelerator (2022) (www.comcastsportstech.com), the Global Disability Innovation Hub in the UK (www.disabilityinnovation.com/), the MaRS (2022) launchpad for start-ups in Canada (www.marsdd.com/our-sectors/health/), and the Ideation Clinic (www.ideation .clinic/2022-praxis-ideation-challenge).

Summary

Innovation has been described as what drives advocacy, so innovations must occur for persons with a disability to be more active more often. In this chapter, you have learned about innovation and explored examples of where this has occurred in disability sport. The processes by which someone can be innovative and how this can be enhanced to become shareable have also been reviewed. The goal is to get everyone thinking more innovatively so persons with a disability can be more active, more often.

CRITICAL THINKING EXERCISES

1. What are some general barriers that people experiencing disability face to participating in disability sport? What are the barriers that an individual with a specific impairment might face? Barriers, also known as constraints, can be broken into intrapersonal, interpersonal, and structural components and have been shown to be interdependent and overlapping with disability type and the level of support needs, creating complexity to understand what affects an individual with a disability to undertake sport (see Darcy et al., 2017).

2. After identifying these barriers, what are some options in which innovations could enable greater participation in a specific sport and recreational activity for persons experiencing disability?

3. What are some ways in which you as a student could better understand the needs of persons experiencing disability?

CHAPTER 4

History and Development of the Paralympic Games

Ian Brittain, PhD

LEARNING OBJECTIVES

After reading this chapter, you will be able to do the following:

- Explain the origins of the Paralympic Games.
- Outline the potential role of sport and physical activity in the lives of disabled people.
- Explain the links between the International Olympic and International Paralympic Committees.
- Explain the development and various meanings of the term *Paralympic*.
- Indicate the various impairment groups that participate in the Paralympic Games.
- Name the sports currently on the Summer and Winter Paralympic Games programs.

This chapter explains the history and origins of the **Paralympic Games**, including the development and meanings of the term *Paralympic*, and outlines the impairment groups that participate in the Paralympic Games. We will also explore the link between the International Olympic and International Paralympic Committees, how they try to ensure fair competition, and the goals of the Paralympic Games beyond sport. The chapter concludes by describing how, in some countries, various organizations are using Paralympic history and heritage to highlight not only the aims of the Paralympic Games and movement in sporting terms but also the issues disabled people face in the wider society and the potential role of the Paralympic Games in tackling these issues.

Early History of Disability Sport

One of the earliest mentions regarding any kind of sport for disabled people is in *The Badminton Library of Sports and Pastimes* that was published in 1889. It refers to a "cripples race" on Newmarket Heath in England in the early 1660s, apparently in the presence of King Charles II (Shearman, 1889). There is,

This chapter is partly adapted from *The Paralympic Games Explained: Second Edition* by Ian Brittain, 2016, Routledge.

however, little evidence of sport for disabled people after that until the mid- to late 19th century because in most societies, disabled people were more likely to be institutionalized to keep them out of sight (Dunn & Sherrill, 1996; for an interesting explanation of the rise of sport as a rehabilitative tool for disabled people, see Peers, 2012). Sainsbury (1998) cites several examples of sports and leisure clubs for disabled people in the early part of the 20th century, including the British Society of One-Armed Golfers (1932) and the "Disabled Drivers" Motor Club (1922). The first international organization responsible for a particular impairment group and its involvement in sport—Comité International des Sports des Sourds (CISS)—was set up in 1924 by a deaf Frenchman, Eugène Rubens-Alcais, with the support of six national sports federations for the deaf. In August 1924, the first International Silent Games were held in Paris with athletes from nine countries in attendance (DePauw & Gavron, 2005). Now called the Deaflympics, there are summer and winter versions that occur in the year following their Olympic and Paralympic counterparts.

The Influence of World War II on Disability Sport

Before World War II, the likelihood of surviving a spinal cord injury was small, with most dying within three years following their injury (Legg et al., 2002). This first came to the attention of Ludwig Guttmann, the universally accepted founder of the Paralympic movement, when training as a doctor in Germany in the 1930s. He apparently encountered a coal miner with a broken back and was shocked to learn from the consultant that such cases were considered a waste of time because the patient would likely be dead in a couple of weeks (Craven, 2006). Death was usually a result of sepsis or kidney failure, or both (Brandmeyer & McBee, 1986). However, things changed after World War II with the introduction of sulfa drugs that increased the chances of survival for those with spinal cord injuries.

Given the low survival rates before World War II and the negative attitudes toward people with visible disabilities within the wider society, another major issue for people with spinal injuries was the high levels of depression as a result of their impairment (Anderson, 2003).

As stated previously, before World War II, there is scant evidence of competitive sport being used in the rehabilitation or day-to-day lives of people with physical disabilities such as spinal cord injuries. However, it appears that Guttmann, recognizing the physiological and psychological values of sport, introduced it as part of the overall treatment program for patients in the spinal unit (McCann, 1996). Guttmann's aim was to not only give his patients a sense of self-worth and hope but also demonstrate to the wider nondisabled society that individuals with spinal injuries could still be active and contributing members of society (Anderson, 2003).

Guttmann introduced sport to the rehabilitation program cautiously with sports such as darts, snooker, punchball, and skittles (Guttmann, 1952). Guttmann then briefly introduced the sport of wheelchair polo, but this was quickly deemed too rough and was replaced with wheelchair netball (Scruton, 1968), which later developed into what we now know as wheelchair basketball. The next sport to be introduced was archery, which played a key role in what was to follow. Archery was an excellent way to strengthen the muscles of the upper limbs, shoulders, and trunk on which a wheelchair user's well-balanced, upright position depends (Guttman, 1952). It also allowed the individual, once proficient, to compete on equal terms with their nondisabled counterparts. These experiments were the beginning of a systematic development of competitive sport for people with spinal cord injuries as an essential part of their medical rehabilitation and social reintegration in the community of a country like Great Britain, where sport in one form or another plays such an essential part in the life of so many people (Guttmann, 1976).

SIR LUDWIG GUTTMANN, CBE, FRS

Ludwig Guttmann was a German-Jewish neurologist born in the small town of Tost in Upper Silesia (now Toszek, Poland) on July 3, 1899. He fled Nazi Germany with his family in 1939 and eventually settled in Oxford, where he found work at Oxford University. In September 1943, the British government commissioned Guttmann as the director of the National Spinal Injuries Centre at the Ministry of Pensions Hospital, Stoke Mandeville, Aylesbury (Scruton, 1998). His main role at Stoke Mandeville was to treat the large number of military personnel and civilians who had received spinal cord injuries during the war. Guttmann only accepted the role with the understanding that he would be totally autonomous in deciding his treatment methods (Goodman, 1986). Guttmann is famous for introducing sport as part of the rehabilitation process for his patients, and that eventually led to the Stoke Mandeville Games, one of the largest multisport events after the Olympic Games. Guttmann was president of the International Stoke Mandeville Games Federation and the International Sports Organization for the Disabled (ISOD), meaning he was responsible for developing sport for four different impairment groups (amputees and les autres, blind and visually impaired, cerebral palsied, and spinal cord injuries). Queen Elizabeth II knighted him in 1966 for his services to disabled people, and he passed away aged 80 on March 18, 1980.

© World Abilitysport - www.worldabilitysport.org

> Improvements in medical knowledge, new drugs, and the introduction of sport to the rehabilitation process all came together to improve the life expectancy and opportunities for spinal cord–injured patients.

The Stoke Mandeville Games

The Stoke Mandeville Games, which would eventually become what is now the Paralympic Games, began life rather simply as an archery demonstration between two teams of paraplegics from the Ministry of Pensions Hospital at Stoke Mandeville and the Star and Garter Home for Injured War Veterans at Richmond in Surrey. The event was held to mark the donation of an adapted bus for the patients at Stoke Mandeville. The bus would not only allow patients to travel around the country to various activities and events but also allow them to get back out into the community and enter more into the life of the town (Brittain, 2014). The choice of date for this event is perhaps more interesting—Thursday, July 29, 1948, the same day as the opening ceremony for the Games of the 14th Olympiad at Wembley in London less than 35 miles away. This link between what was happening at Stoke Mandeville and the Olympic movement is one that Guttmann would regularly cultivate (Brittain, 2016).

The following year, the archery demonstration event of 1948 became the Grand Festival of Paraplegic Sport and was held on Wednesday, July 27, 1949. Following all the work Guttmann and his staff did at Stoke Mandeville and several of his patients moving to rehabilitation centers nearer to their own homes and taking their enthusiasm for sport with them, the number of teams at the Games in 1949 rose to six, and wheelchair netball was added as a new sport (Stoke Mandeville calling, 1949). Over the next three years, the number of competitors and teams entering

Archers demonstrate their skill in the 1948 Stoke Mandeville Games.
© World Abilitysport - www.worldabilitysport.org

the Games at Stoke Mandeville slowly rose, and one new sport was added to the program each year. Guttmann's dream, however, was to take the Games to an international footing, something he finally achieved in 1952, when a team of four paraplegics from the Aardenburg Military Rehabilitation Centre in Doorn in the Netherlands became the first truly international competitors at the Games. During the next four years, the international nature of the Games rose dramatically so that in 1956, 18 nations were represented at the Games and 21 different nations had competed since 1952 (Scruton, 1956). Except for 1956, they continued to add one new sport to the program each year so that by 1959 there were 11 sports. A chronology of these early Stoke Mandeville Games can be seen in table 4.1.

It may appear surprising that an event starting out as a demonstration with just two teams and 16 athletes could grow in just 12 years to a competition boasting more than 300 competitors and more than 20 international teams. During that period, the organizers were also forced to make several extensions to the accommodation at Stoke Mandeville to house all the athletes. They also introduced a National Stoke Mandeville Games in 1958 to select the British team to compete in the International Games (Scruton, 1957). There are five possible mechanisms by which Guttmann and his team managed to achieve this expansion:

1. As already mentioned, when Guttmann's patients left Stoke Mandeville and were transferred to rehabilitation centers closer to where they lived, they took their newfound enthusiasm for sport as a rehabilitation tool with them. Many of them returned year after year to take part in the Games. Similarly, doctors and surgeons from around the world visited Stoke Mandeville to train under Guttmann, and they then returned home to their own countries and introduced sport as a rehabilitative tool at their own

TABLE 4.1 **A Chronology of the Early Stoke Mandeville Games (1948-1959)**

Year	Days	Teams	Competitors	Sports	New sport
1948	1	2 SU	16	1	Archery
1949	1	7 SU	37	2	"Netball"
1950	1	11 SU	61	3	Javelin
1951	1	11 SU	121	4	Snooker
1952	1	1 NT+12 SU	130	5	Table tennis
1953	2	5 NT+13 SU	200	6	Swimming
1954	2	12 NT+13 SU	250	7	Dartchery
1955	2	13 NT+15SU	280	8	Fencing, basketball replaced netball
1956	2	17 NT+19 SU	300	8	-
1957	3	23 SU+22 SU	360	9	Shot put
1958	3	20 NT	350	10	Throwing the club
1959	3	17 NT	360	11	Pentathlon

Adapted by permission from I. Brittain, "Key Points in the History and Development of the Paralympic Games," in *The Palgrave Handbook of Paralympic Studies,* edited by I. Brittain, & A. Beacom (London: Palgrave-MacMillan, 2018), 11. Reproduced by permission of Taylor and Francis Group, LLC, a division of Informa plc.

hospitals or rehabilitation centers. One example was Dr. Ralph Spira from Israel (Brittain & Hutzler, 2009).

2. In 1947, the team at Stoke Mandeville started publishing a magazine called *The Cord* that contained articles and advice for paraplegics and would often contain articles on Guttmann's use of sport as a rehabilitation tool as well as reports on the Stoke Mandeville Games. Because practical information for paraplegics was in short supply at the time, the magazine was sent around the world, raising awareness of the Games in the process. It continued to be published up until 1983.

3. Guttmann would often travel internationally to give lectures or provide training in his methods for other doctors and would always take these opportunities to challenge key people in other countries to bring a team to the Games the following year, as was the case with Sir George Bedbrook at the Royal Perth Hospital on a visit

in 1956. Australia sent its first team to Stoke Mandeville the following year (Lockwood & Lockwood, 2007).

4. Guttmann was also good at attracting media attention for the Games by inviting high-ranking politicians and celebrities to attend the Games and give out prizes. For example, in 1955, Roger Bannister, who had become the first man to run under four minutes for the mile the previous year, was invited to give out the prizes at the Games (International Games Stoke Mandeville, 1955). This then ensured a good media presence at the Games and good publicity for them through first national and later international news outlets.

5. The final mechanism Guttmann used to cement the importance of the Games in people's minds, despite the lukewarm response it received when he first suggested it, was his constant comparisons to the Olympic Games. Its effect and design appeared to have

been twofold: First, to give his patients something tangible to aim for and to give them a feeling of self-worth, and second, to catch the attention of the media and people and organizations involved with paraplegics worldwide.

The Start of the Paralympic Games

Guttmann's consistent linking of the Stoke Mandeville Games with the Olympic Games moved to another level following the annual meeting of the World Veterans Federation in Rome in May 1959. A meeting with various people from the National Institute for Insurance Against Accidents at Work (INAIL) and Dr. Maglio of the Spinal Unit, Ostia, Rome, was held. The decision was made for the 1960 Stoke Mandeville Games to be held in Rome a few weeks after the Olympic Games were to take place in the same city (The 1960 International Stoke Mandeville Games for the Paralysed in Rome, 1960).

Following a reasonably successful event in Rome where 21 nations participated, the idea of hosting a 1964 Games in Tokyo, which had already been selected to host the Olympic Games, was raised. An invitation to the Japanese hosts led to Japan sending its first team to the Stoke Mandeville Games in 1962 and, ultimately, its acceptance to host the Games in Tokyo in 1964. Twenty-one nations again attended. The 1968 Olympic Games were due to be held in Mexico City and, despite initial interest from Instituto Nacional de Rehabilitación to host the Games of 1968, the director of the rehabilitation center in Mexico City ultimately concluded that financial constraints and accessibility issues with facilities in Mexico City meant they would be unable to host the Games. Following offers from both New York and Tel Aviv, it was decided that the 1968 Games would be held in Israel (Brittain, 2014).

It was hoped that the Games would be held by the Olympic host city in 1972, which was to be Munich. However, the Munich Olympic Organizing Committee declined to host on the basis that the Olympic village was to be converted into housing immediately after the Games, and it was, apparently, too late to change this. The Germans did, however, offer the alternative of Heidelberg University, which was accepted. In 1976, with the Olympic Games due to be held in Montreal, Canada, the Organizing Committee once again declined to host the Games, which were now to be a much larger combined International Stoke Mandeville Games Federation (ISMGF) and International Sports Organization for the Disabled (ISOD) Games consisting of paraplegics, blind, and amputee athletes, which added to both the size and the complexity of the Games. The Games were eventually held in Toronto, Canada, instead. The 1980 Paralympic Games were awarded to Arnhem in the Netherlands following a lack of response from the Olympic organizers in Moscow (Brittain, 2014).

No evidence can be found that any attempt was made by ISMGF or ISOD to secure the use of the Los Angeles Olympic venues in 1984 for their own Games, although the Games were awarded to the United States to host. However, following political moves by the National Wheelchair Athletics Association, the decision was taken to split them into ISMGF Games, to be organized by NWAA at the University of Illinois, and ISOD Games, to be organized by ISOD in Nassau County, New York, at around the same time. However, political and fundraising problems around the wheelchair Games forced the University of Illinois to withdraw their support for the Games in early 1984, and the wheelchair Games were transferred at short notice to Stoke Mandeville (Brittain, 2014).

From 1988 onward, the Summer Paralympic Games have been held in the same host city as the Olympic Games beginning about two weeks after the Olympic closing ceremony. The only exception to this was the Paralympic Games for Intellectually Disabled Athletes that was held in Madrid in 1992 as a precursor to intellectually disabled athletes being added to the program with the other four impairment groups in Atlanta four years later (Brittain, 2016). See table 4.2 for details of how the Games have developed between 1960 and 2022.

CHAPTER 4 | History and Development of the Paralympic Games   49

TABLE 4.2   A Chronology of the Summer and Winter Paralympic Games

Year	Location	No. of countries	Americas	Africa	Asia	Europe	Oceania	No. of athletes	No. of sports	Impairment groups included
1960	Rome, Italy	21	2	1	1	16	1	~328	9	SCI
1964	Tokyo, Japan	21	2	2	3	12	2	~378	10	SCI
1968	Tel Aviv, Israel	28	4	3	3	16	2	~730	11	SCI
1972	Heidelberg, West Germany	42	7	5	5	23	2	~984	11	SCI
1976	**Örnsköldsvik, Sweden**	**16**	**2**	**1**	**1**	**12**	**0**	**198**	**2**	**A, BVI, SCI**
1976	Toronto, Canada	40	10	3	5	19	3	~1369	14	A, BVI, SCI
1980	**Geilo, Norway**	**18**	**2**	**1**	**1**	**12**	**2**	**299**	**3**	**A, BVI, SCI**
1980	Arnhem, the Netherlands	42	8	5	5	22	2	~1973	14	A, BVI, CP, SCI
1984	**Innsbruck, Austria**	**21**	**2**	**0**	**1**	**16**	**2**	**419**	**3**	**ALA, BVI, CP, SCI**
1984	Stoke Mandeville, UK &	41	10	3	6	19	3	~1097	10	SCI
	New York, USA	45	6	3	9	25	2	~1750	15	ALA, BVI, CP
1988	**Innsbruck, Austria**	**22**	**2**	**0**	**1**	**17**	**2**	**377**	**4**	**ALA, BVI, CP, SCI**
1988	Seoul, South Korea	60	11	4	16	27	2	3059	17 + 1 Demo	ALA, BVI, CP, SCI
1992	**Tignes-Albertville, France**	**24**	**2**	**0**	**2**	**18**	**2**	**365**	**3**	**ALA, BVI, CP, SCI**
1992	Barcelona, Spain &	83*	16	11	20	33	2	3001	16	ALA, BVI, CP, SCI
	Madrid, Spain	75	22	13	11	28	1	~1600	5	ID
1994	**Lillehammer, Norway**	**31**	**2**	**0**	**3**	**24**	**2**	**471**	**5**	**ALA, BVI, CP, SCI**
1996	Atlanta, USA	103	18	16	25	41	3	3259	17 + 2 Demo	ALA, BVI, CP, ID, SCI

>continued

50 Introduction to Adaptive Sport and Recreation

TABLE 4.2 >continued

Year	Location	No. of countries	Americas	Africa	Asia	Europe	Oceania	No. of athletes	No. of sports	Impairment groups included
1998	**Nagano, Japan**	**31**	**2**	**1**	**4**	**22**	**2**	**561**	**5**	**ALA, BVI, CP, ID, SCI**
2000	Sydney, Australia	122*	20	20	33	41	7	3882	19	ALA, BVI, CP, ID, SCI
2002	**Salt Lake City, USA**	**36**	**3**	**1**	**5**	**25**	**2**	**416**	**4**	**ALA, BVI, CP, SCI**
2004	Athens, Greece	135	24	28	36	42	5	3808	19	ALA, BVI, CP, SCI
2006	**Torino, Italy**	**38**	**4**	**1**	**6**	**25**	**2**	**474**	**5**	**ALA, BVI, CP, SCI**
2008	Beijing, P.R. China	146	24	30	40	45	7	4011	20	ALA, BVI, CP, SCI
2010	**Vancouver, Canada**	**44**	**5**	**1**	**6**	**30**	**2**	**502**	**5**	**ALA, BVI, CP, SCI**
2012	London, UK	164	28	39	42	47	8	4237	20	ALA, BVI, CP, ID, SCI
2014	**Sochi, Russia**	**45**	**6**	**0**	**7**	**30**	**2**	**538**	**6**	**ALA, BVI, CP, ID, SCI**
2016	Rio de Janeiro, Brazil	157	27	43	39	44	6	4315	22	ALA, BVI, CP, ID, SCI
2018	**Pyeongchang, South Korea**	**48**	**6**	**0**	**9**	**31**	**2**	**534**	**6**	**ALA, BVI, CP, ID, SCI**
2021**	Tokyo, Japan	162	30	44	38	45	4	4393	22	ALA, BVI, CP, ID, SCI
2022	**Beijing, P.R. China**	**46**	**5**	**0**	**8**	**31**	**2**	**564**	**6**	**ALA, BVI, CP, ID, SCI**

*Includes a group titled independent or refugee Paralympic athletes.

**Delayed one year by COVID-19 pandemic

Bold = Winter Paralympic Games. Demo = Demonstration Sport.

A = Amputee, ALA = Amputee and Les Autres, BVI= Blind and Visually Impaired, CP = Cerebral Palsied, ID = Intellectually Disabled, SCI = Spinal Cord Injury

Adapted and updated from Brittain (2016)

Development of the Paralympic Games

As the Paralympic Games grew, two key developments can be identified: (1) the addition of sport for other impairment groups besides spinal cord injuries and (2) expanding to winter games.

Sport for Additional Impairment Groups

To give a fuller picture of how the Paralympic Games developed, it is important to understand how sport for impairment groups other than spinal cord injuries developed (e.g., blind and visually impaired, amputees). This began in earnest in 1961 when the International Working Group on Sports for the Disabled was established under the direction of the World Veterans Federation whose headquarters was in Paris. However, according to Guttmann (1976), the organization was beset with language issues and differing opinions and was eventually dissolved in 1964. It was replaced in 1964 with the International Sports Organization for the Disabled (ISOD; Scruton, 1998), which remained under the patronage of the World Veterans Federation until 1967 before becoming an independent organization based at Stoke Mandeville. Also in 1967, the British Limbless Ex-Servicemen's Association (BLESMA) organized the first-ever international sports competition for amputees at Stoke Mandeville. Guttmann, who had been knighted by the Queen in 1966 for services to disabled people, became president of both ISMGF and ISOD, and this dual role played an important part in bringing the impairment groups together in one Games (Goodman, 1986).

At its inception, ISOD represented several impairment groups, but by 1981, people who were blind and living with cerebral palsy had broken away to form their own international federations. In 2004, ISOD, then representing amputees and les autres, merged with the International Stoke Mandeville Wheelchair Sports Federation (ISMWSF) to form the International Wheelchair and Amputee Sports Federation (IWAS; Brittain, 2016). In early 2023, IWAS merged with the Cerebral Palsy International Sports and Recreation Association (CP-ISRA) to form a single body called World Abilitysport representing all physically impaired athletes who compete at the Paralympic Games. As stated previously, initially ISOD represented several disability groups and together with ISMGF co-operated in the organization of the Summer Paralympic Games in Toronto 1976 and Arnhem 1980. They also initiated the first-ever Winter Paralympic Games in Örnsköldsvik, Sweden, in 1976, which was just for amputee athletes and those who were blind or visually impaired (IPC, 2006).

Addition of the Winter Paralympic Games

The Winter Paralympic Games came about as a result of discussions held at the annual general meeting of ISOD in 1974. The initial idea came from the Swedish delegation, a country with a strong winter sports tradition. In around 18 months, the Games went from an idea to a reality taking place in Örnsköldsvik in Sweden (IPC, 2006). They were quite a small Games, catering only for amputations or visual impairments, and had under 200 competitors (Brittain, 2014). But they were hailed as a great success nonetheless. The first six incarnations of the Games all took place in Europe, where winter sports were highly developed and winter sports for athletes with disabilities first began in the 1950s (IPC, 2006). Athletes with spinal injuries joined the second Games in Geilo, Norway, and they were quickly joined by athletes with cerebral palsy and les autres athletes in Innsbruck, Austria, four years later. The Winter Games did not occur at the Olympic host city venues until their fifth incarnation in Tignes-Albertville in 1992, although demonstration events for disability skiing were held at the Sarajevo Winter Olympic Games as early as 1984 (Brittain, 2014). A complete chronology of the summer and winter Paralympic Games from 1960 to 2022, including a breakdown of national participation by continental association, can be found in table 4.2.

Impact of the Paralympic Games Linking to the Olympic Movement

Guttmann made concerted efforts from the beginning to link the Games at Stoke Mandeville with the Olympic Games, probably to motivate his patients. This began with an archery competition at the first Stoke Mandeville Games in 1948, which was held on July 29, the same day as the opening ceremony of the 14th Olympic Games at Wembley some 30 miles south of Stoke Mandeville (Bailey, 2008). At the closing ceremony of the second Games in 1949, which saw the addition of netball (later wheelchair basketball) and had 37 competitors, Guttmann made what might appear like an incredible claim. He stated that he hoped that one day the Stoke Mandeville Games would become recognized as the paraplegic's equivalent of the Olympic Games (Brittain, 2014). Guttmann consistently made this comparison, and his persistence paid off in 1960 when the International Stoke Mandeville Games first moved away from Stoke Mandeville and were held in the Olympic host city of Rome a few weeks after the Olympic closing ceremony (Brittain, 2016).

Guttmann's linkage of the Games at Stoke Mandeville with the Olympic Games was not without controversy with the International Olympic Committee (IOC). They threatened to sue the organizers for using Olympic terminology during the 1970s and early 1980s when new impairment groups were added to the Games, and they started calling the Games things like "Olympics for the Disabled" (Brittain, 2008). Following Guttmann's death in 1980 and many meetings between the IOC and the Games organizers, it was agreed that they would be held in the Olympic host city a couple of weeks after the Olympic closing ceremony from the 1988 Seoul Games onward—a pattern that has continued ever since. Being hosted by the Olympic host city affected the number of participating nations at the Paralympic Games, as Figure 4.1 shows.

The ties between the Olympic and Paralympic movements have grown closer since then with a first memorandum of understanding and cooperation agreement being signed at the Sydney Games in 2000 (Legg et al., 2015) and the current agreement running until 2032 (Brittain, 2018).

How the Term *Paralympic* Has Changed Over Time

Guttmann constantly compared the Stoke Mandeville Games and the Olympic Games. The early Stoke Mandeville Games were primarily for paraplegics (quadriplegics were added later), and as early as 1951, they were being called the Paraplegic Olympics (Merchant, 1954). This was shortened to para-Olympics (Bell, 1954) or Paralympics (Brittain, 2016). This title was used more in newspapers rather than directly as a title for the Stoke Mandeville Games themselves up until 1960, when the Stoke Mandeville Games started moving away from Stoke Mandeville every four years, following the Olympic cycle. The media only started using it for Stoke Mandeville Games held in the Olympic year. However, in 1976, when other impairment groups started competing in these Games, the term *Paralympic*, in the Paraplegic Olympics context, was no longer applicable. Today, the term *Paralympic* derives from the Greek preposition *para* meaning "next to," giving a meaning of parallel or next to the Olympic Games. The IOC officially recognized it in 1988 when the Games finally returned to being hosted by the same host city as the Olympic Games, as they have been ever since (Brittain, 2016).

Impairment Groups That Participate in the Paralympic Games

The participants at the current Summer and Winter Paralympic Games are drawn from five **participating impairment groups**, outlined as follows.

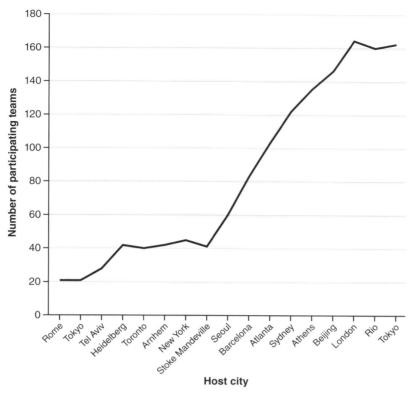

FIGURE 4.1 Nations participating in the Summer Paralympic Games, 1960-2020.
Data from Brittain (2016).

- *Amputees and les autres athletes.* The classification system for athletes with amputations includes those athletes with acquired or congenital amputations. *Les autres*, literally meaning "the others," describes athletes with a range of conditions that result in locomotive disorders, such as dwarfism, that do not fit into the traditional classification systems of the established impairment groups such as amputees, medullar lesions, and cerebral palsy (BBC, 2000). Examples include muscular dystrophy, multiple sclerosis, arthrogryposis, Friedrich's ataxia, and arthritis. Amputee athletes first competed in the Summer and Winter Paralympic Games in 1976, and les autres athletes were added to both in 1984.
- *Athletes with spinal cord injuries.* Athletes with spinal cord injuries include athletes having a spinal cord lesion, spina bifida, or polio. Athletes with spinal cord injuries can also be split into two broad categories of paraplegia, which involves a neurologic affliction of both legs, and quadriplegia or tetraplegia, which involves a neurologic affliction of all four extremities (Auxter et al., 1993). Athletes with spinal cord injuries have competed at Summer Paralympic Games since 1960 and the Winter Paralympic Games since 1980.
- *Blind and visually impaired athletes.* This group of athletes ranges from those who are totally blind to those who can recognize objects or contours between 2 and 6 meters away that a person with typical vision can see at 60 meters (i.e., 2/60 to 6/60 vision) or a field of vision between 5 and 20 degrees. Blind and visually impaired athletes first competed in the Summer and Winter Paralympic Games in 1976.

- *Cerebral palsied athletes.* Cerebral palsy is a condition in which damage inflicted on the brain has led to motor function impairment (Auxter et al., 1993). There are three types of cerebral palsy (Cerebralpalsy.org.uk, 2022). Spastic is characterized by tense muscles that are contracted and resistant to movement, athetoid is characterized by involuntary movements of the affected body parts, and ataxia is characterized by a disturbance or lack of balance and coordination. Athletes with cerebral palsy first competed in the Summer and Winter Paralympic Games in 1980.

- *Intellectually disabled athletes.* The Paralympic movement identifies intellectual impairment as "a disability characterized by significant limitation both in intellectual functioning and in adaptive behavior as expressed in conceptual, social, and practical adaptive skills. This disability originates before the age of 18" (IPC, 2022a, para. 10). The diagnostics of intellectual functioning and adaptive behavior must be made using internationally accepted and professionally administered measures as recognized by Virtus, the brand name of the international sport federation for athletes with an intellectual impairment. Athletes with intellectual disabilities first took part in their own separate Paralympic Games in Madrid in 1992 and then competed alongside the other impairment groups in 1996. Following a classification scandal at the Sydney 2000 Games, they were banned from the Paralympics until London 2012 while a new, more robust classification system was designed (Brittain, 2016; see also chapter 8).

Ensuring Fair Competition at the Paralympic Games

Athlete classification is the system used to ensure fair competition. It is one of the most contentious issues in the Paralympic Games (and disability sport more generally) and often one of the most confusing issues for spectators. It is also one of the most difficult issues to find a fair and workable solution that satisfies the demands of all concerned. Each individual's impairment will influence their functional ability to participate in sports in differing ways and to differing levels, but in most cases, it will lead to a competitive disadvantage if they were to compete against athletes without disabilities or even those with different or lesser degrees of impairments (Connick et al., 2018). Therefore, to ensure that success is determined by "skill, fitness, power, endurance, tactical ability and mental focus" (BOCOG, 2008, p. 1), as it is in nondisabled sport, it is necessary to put criteria or classifications in place for each athlete. The classification system is a constantly evolving process as more is learned about the impact of various impairments upon sporting performance. In addition, given that impairments may degenerate over time for some people, classification may change throughout an athlete's career. In general, classification decides two main issues:

1. Which impairment groups can compete in a particular sport (i.e., in blind football, only people with a visual impairment can compete, but swimming is open to all impairment groups)?
2. Which individual athletes, with which impairments and at what levels of impairment, may compete against each other in a particular medal event?

Those involved in the classification and organization of the Paralympic Games need to provide categories for athletes that are both entertaining for spectators and fair for the athletes involved. This requires "striking a very difficult balance between categories that are sufficiently broad to provide compelling competition yet sufficiently well defined so that people with relevantly similar skills are paired against each other" (Pickering Francis, 2005, p. 129).

> Classification is the key to fair competition but is often difficult for spectators to understand because they may not realize the impacts of various impairments on performance.

Current Governance Structure for the Paralympic Movement

The International Paralympic Committee (IPC) was founded in September 1989 and took over responsibility for organizing the Paralympic Games from the 1994 Winter Games in Lillehammer, Norway (Bailey, 2008). Before that, the International Stoke Mandeville Games Federation organized the games, as did the International Coordinating Committee of World Sports Organizations for the Disabled from 1982 to 1994 (Brittain, 2014). The mission statement of the IPC states that its role is to lead the Paralympic movement, oversee the delivery of the Paralympic Games, and support members to enable para-athletes to achieve sporting excellence (IPC, 2019). Each country in membership of IPC has its own **National Paralympic Committee (NPC)** that is responsible for training, selecting, and sending a team to the Paralympic Games. As of January 2022, there were 184 NPCs spread across five continental associations who were members of IPC, which compares with 206 National Olympic Committees (NOCs) worldwide (see table 4.3).

The IPC headquarters is based in Bonn, Germany, and is structured along similar lines to the International Olympic Committee with a president and 10 elected members of a governing board who discuss and recommend new policies that are put to the members to vote on at the General Assembly. They are supported by paid staff who oversee the day-to-day running of IPC and the preparation of future Paralympic Games.

Sports on the Winter and Summer Paralympic Games Programs

As of 2022, there were six sports on the winter Paralympic program and 22 sports on the summer Paralympic program. The sports, the number of medal events in each sport, and the number of NPCs and athletes competing in each sport at the Pyeongchang winter and Tokyo Summer Paralympic Games can be seen in tables 4.4 and 4.5.

What these tables also highlight, with the possible exceptions of alpine and cross-country skiing at the Winter Games and athletics (track and field) at the Summer Games, is the relatively low number of NPCs represented in most of the sports compared to the total number of NPCs present at the Games. With some sports, this is easily explained by the fact that only a small number of NPCs can qualify for a particular sport (e.g., eight teams in football five-a-side for blind and visually impaired athletes where continental qualifying competitions may have been held to decide who will compete at the Games). Even with individual sports, there will be a cap on the number of athletes who can qualify for a particular sport

TABLE 4.3 **National Paralympic and Olympic Committees by Continental Association (January 2022)**

	Africa	Americas	Asia	Europe	Oceania	Total
NPCs	51	32	44	48	9	184
NOCs	54	41	44	50	17	206

56 Introduction to Adaptive Sport and Recreation

TABLE 4.4 Sports, Events, NPCs, and Athletes at the Pyeongchang 2018 Winter Paralympic Games

Sports	Events	NPCs (Out of 49)	Athletes	
			Male	Female
Alpine skiing*	30	33	101	40
Biathlon	18	16	55	40
Cross-country skiing*	20	31	98	57
Para ice hockey	1	8	133	1
Snowboarding	10	24	56	13
Wheelchair curling	1	12	40	20

*On the program at first Winter Paralympic Games (1976)

Data from IPC (2022b).

TABLE 4.5 Sports, Events, NPCs, and Athletes at the Tokyo 2020 Summer Paralympic Games

Sports	Events	NPCs (Out of 162)	Athletes	
			Male	Female
Archery*	9	42	79	60
Athletics*	167	155	653	489
Badminton	14	28	46	44
Boccia	7	25	73	41
Canoe	9	29	51	40
Cycling	51	50	150	80
Equestrian	11	27	22	55
Football five-a-side	1	8	62	0
Goalball	2	15	60	58
Judo	13	41	80	56
Powerlifting	20	54	90	88
Rowing	4	25	48	48
Shooting	13	44	100	54
Swimming*	146	74	341	263
Taekwondo	6	37	36	34
Triathlon	8	19	40	40
Table tennis*	31	55	172	105
Volleyball	2	12	95	92
Wheelchair basketball*	2	14	144	118
Wheelchair fencing*	16	20	48	48
Wheelchair rugby	1	8	88	4
Wheelchair tennis	6	31	72	32

*On the program for the first Summer Paralympic Games (1960)

Data from IPC (2022c).

(e.g., triathlon, in which only 40 male and 40 female athletes could compete in Tokyo), and so qualifying tournaments are held before the Games.

However, as Brittain (2019) has highlighted, developed nations have a distinct advantage when it comes to participating at the Paralympic Games (as they do with the Olympic Games). Brittain showed that the more developed a nation in terms of the Inequality-Adjusted Human Development Index, the larger the team it can afford to train and take to the Games and the more medals it is likely to win. More developed nations can also afford to build and maintain the necessary training facilities or send their athletes abroad to train, especially for winter sports where they may not have the necessary climatic or topographical conditions to practice winter sports at home. This then translates into distinct advantages in the ability to both qualify athletes for the Games and increase the possibilities of winning medals. Overall, this highlights the distinct inequalities of opportunity that underpin Paralympic Games participation globally. The impact of this can be seen in tables 4.6 and 4.7 following the same method as Brittain (2019) and grouping the competing nations in the Pyeongchang Winter Paralympic Games (table 4.6) and the Tokyo Summer Paralympic Games (table 4.7) by their Inequality-Adjusted Human Development Index level. In both cases, nations in the very high Inequality-Adjusted Human Development Index level tend to take larger teams and win the largest share of the medals.

> Developed nations generally can take larger teams to the Paralympic Games and therefore have increased opportunities to win medals.

TABLE 4.6 **Pyeongchang 2018 Paralympic Games NPC Team Sizes and Medal Success by Inequality-Adjusted Development Index Level**

| IHDI level | Number of NPCs | Average team size | | | Percentage of medals won* |
		Males	Females	Team	
Very high	22	14.25	3.95	18.18	78.89
High	15	4.73	1.27	6.00	20.42
Medium	10	3.10	1.00	4.10	0.69
Low	1	2.00	0	2.00	0
Overall	48**	8.69	2.42	11.11	100.00

*Gold = 3 pts, Silver = 2 pts, Bronze = 1 pt. Does not include medals won by Neutral Paralympic Athletes.

**Does not include Neutral Paralympic Athletes.

TABLE 4.7 **Tokyo 2020 Paralympic Games NPC Team Sizes and Medal Success by Inequality-Adjusted Development Index Level**

| IHDI level | Number of NPCs | Average team size | | | Percentage of medals won* |
		Males	Females	Team	
Very high	41	26.85	20.32	47.17	42.36
High	29	20.83	14.21	35.04	25.05
Medium	43	15.63	10.95	26.58	29.00
Low	48	3.44	2.69	6.13	3.59
Overall	161**	15.79	11.46	27.25	100.00

*Gold = 3 pts, Silver = 2 pts, Bronze = 1 pt. **Does not include Refugee Paralympic Team.

Aims of the Paralympic Games Beyond Sport

Guttmann (1976) highlighted three main areas in which participation in sport could benefit disabled people:

1. Improving the health of disabled people to improve their day-to-day living

2. To use sport to help develop an active mind, self-confidence, self-dignity, self-discipline, competitive spirit, and camaraderie, all of which are essential in helping to overcome the all-consuming depression that can occur with sudden traumatic disability

3. To create a better understanding between disabled people and their nondisabled peers, which then aids in their social reintegration through the medium of sport

Indeed, the message underneath the Stoke Mandeville Games flag that flew in the 1950s included the line "No greater contribution can be made to society by the paralyzed than to help, through the medium of sport, to further friendship and understanding amongst nations" (Brittain, 2014, p. 15).

During the last decade or so, a large body of work has examined the idea that major sports events such as the Olympic Games or the FIFA World Cup can produce "legacies" for the host city and country well beyond the event itself. However, Misener and colleagues (2013) claim that "few studies have evaluated the comparative outcomes, legacies, and event leverage that the Paralympic Games have generated" (p. 1). This is even though, in many ways, the Paralympic Games, and their forerunner, the Stoke Mandeville Games, were founded on the idea of legacy as a process designed to improve the lives of disabled people. Guttmann (1976; pp. 12-13) highlighted three main areas in which he felt participation in sport could benefit disabled people and that underpin many of the legacy claims made by the International Paralympic Committee today. Here, they are highlighted in slightly more detail:

1. *Sport as a curative factor.* According to Guttmann, sport represents the most natural form of remedial exercise. It can be used to successfully complement other forms of remedial exercise and can be invaluable in restoring the overall fitness, including strength, speed, coordination, and endurance of someone receiving a disabling injury. Indeed, Groff and colleagues (2009) claim that "several studies have suggested that participation in sport may impact elements of quality of life such as one's overall enjoyment with life, sense of well-being, and ability to complete daily life activities. Researchers have concluded that athletes with disabilities exhibit higher levels of positive mood, increased wheelchair mobility skills, lower levels of tension and depression, and have better perceived health and well-being" (p. 319).

2. *The recreational and psychological value of sport.* Guttmann (1976) claims that the big advantage of sport for disabled people over other remedial exercises lies within its recreational value in that it restores "that passion for playful activity and the desire to experience joy and pleasure in life, so deeply inherent in any human being" (p. 12). Guttmann also points out that much of the restorative power of sport is lost if the person with a disability does not enjoy their participation in it. As long as enjoyment is derived from the activity, then sport can help develop an active mind, self-confidence, self-dignity, self-discipline, competitive spirit, and camaraderie, all of which are essential in helping to overcome the bouts of depression that can occur with sudden traumatic disability (Brittain et al., 2022).

3. *Sport as a means of social reintegration.* There are certain sports where disabled people can compete alongside their nondisabled peers (e.g., archery, bowls, and table tennis), as Neroli Fairhall of New Zealand proved when

she competed from a wheelchair in archery at the 1984 Olympic Games in Los Angeles (Brittain, 2016). Guttmann (1976) claims this was especially true at a recreational level, whereby disabled people were given the opportunity to integrate into their local community by competing on an equal footing against nondisabled athletes. Guttmann believed this creates a better understanding between disabled people and their nondisabled peers and aids in their social reintegration through the medium of sport.

These three ideas still form the underpinnings of the "ultimate aspiration" of the IPC stated in their strategic plan (2019-2022) to "make for an inclusive world through Para sport" (IPC, 2019, p. 6). This overarching vision is further reinforced in the IPC's Strategic Priority 3, which it says aims to "drive a cultural shift through Para sport for a truly inclusive society" (IPC, 2019, p. 14). This is despite there being relatively little in the way of hard evidence or scientific studies to back these claims (Misener et al., 2013).

Even former Paralympians and Paralympic medalists who have gone on to become academics have questioned these claims. They include Dr. Stuart Braye and Dr. David Howe (athletics) and Dr. Danielle Peers (wheelchair basketball). Peers (2012) is quite scathing of those involved in the running and promotion of the Paralympic movement, painting them as self-serving and claiming that the IPC "continually reproduces the figure of the tragic disabled in order to reproduce itself" (p. 303). She claims that historically the IPC and its forebears have used the image of the tragic disabled to justify its aims and existence and that IPC continues this practice. Purdue and Howe (2012) argue that the IPC is endeavoring to situate the Paralympic Games as an elite sports competition operating within a self-contained social vacuum in which social perceptions about the impaired body are nullified by the assertion that it is the athletes' sport performances, not their individual impairments, that should be the focus. However, this is problematic because the athletes must perform for two distinct audiences: a nondisabled audience that is expected to only focus on the sporting performance and a disabled audience that is "encouraged to identify with the impairment the athlete has, whilst also appreciating their performance" (Purdue & Howe, 2012, p. 194). For London 2012, Braye and colleagues (2013) concluded that "the IPC's positive rhetoric on improving equality can also be regarded as having a limited effect on the negative daily reality faced by disabled people living in the UK today" (p. 3).

The media coverage of the Paralympic Games provides a vital platform from which to start a discussion about the issues disabled people face in a wider society. Those involved in the Paralympic movement are trying to do this by using Paralympic history and memorabilia as a vehicle from which to take this discussion to a wider audience.

> The media coverage of the Paralympic Games provides a vital platform from which to start a discussion about the issues disabled people face in a wider society.

Paralympic History and Memorabilia Used to Promote Paralympic Legacy

Over the last decade or so, particularly among countries in which Paralympic sport is now well developed and successful, there has been an increase in collecting and using the country's participation in the Paralympic Games to further highlight awareness of the Games and movement themselves. Three key examples of these are the following:

1. *Australian Paralympic History Project (www.paralympic.org.au/about-us/history-project/).* Australia was probably the first nation to make a serious attempt to collate a complete national Paralympic history in 2010 that

culminated in, among other things, the current website, Paralympic Stories, and a forthcoming book, *A History of the Paralympic Movement in Australia*, written by University of Queensland professors Murray Phillips and Gary Osmond. The program "has been established to capture, manage and preserve the history of the Paralympic movement in Australia in a way that is relevant, accessible and places the Paralympic movement within its broader social context" (Paralympics Australia, 2022, para. 3). Through the program, "Paralympics Australia also seeks to accredit universities which it can work with to promote research into, and teaching about, Paralympic sport" (Paralympics Australia, 2022, para. 25).

2. *National Paralympic Heritage Trust (www.paralympicheritage.org.uk/).* Based at Stoke Mandeville Stadium, the spiritual home of the Paralympic movement, the National Paralympic Heritage Trust (NPHT) was established in July 2015 to protect and share British Paralympic Heritage with the aim "to enlighten and inspire future generations by celebrating, cherishing, and bringing the Paralympic heritage and its stories of human endeavour to life" (NPHT, 2022, para 2). It has established a small museum inside the Stoke Mandeville sports facilities, supports traveling exhibitions that tour the United Kingdom, and is actively gathering memorabilia and information about British participation in the Paralympic Games and oral histories from British Paralympians.

3. *United States Olympic and Paralympic Museum (https://usopm.org/).* The museum was established in 2020 and comprises a 60,000-square-foot facility in Colorado Springs dedicated to America's greatest Olympians and Paralympians and their stories. Its mission is to "honor the Olympic and Paralympic ideals; document and share the history of the United States' Olympic and Paralympic participation; and celebrate the achievements of U.S. Olympic and Paralympic competitors" (USOPM, 2022, para. 2). It was voted America's Best New Attraction in 2020 by *USA Today's* 10 Best Readers' Choice Awards.

The media has also taken an interest in Paralympic history and Paralympic athletes with 2020 release of a Netflix documentary titled *Rising Phoenix*. It was made with the International Paralympic Committee. It tells the stories of nine Paralympic athletes and their journeys in competition and has some historical aspects of how the Paralympic Games came about and why they exist. It was supposed to be released in time for the 2020 Tokyo Paralympic Games. However, the worldwide COVID-19 pandemic resulted in the Tokyo Games being postponed by a year.

Summary

The Paralympic Games were the brainchild of a German-Jewish neurosurgeon who escaped Nazi Germany in 1939 and introduced sport to the rehabilitation process of spinally injured civilians and military personnel at Stoke Mandeville Hospital. This was not only to improve their physical and psychological well-being but also demonstrates to nondisabled society that disabled people can still be productive members of society at a time when most people assigned them to the scrapheap of society. Through the hard work of Dr. Ludwig Guttmann and his team at Stoke Mandeville, what started out as a small demonstration event to mark the donation of an accessible bus grew in less than a decade to become an international event attracting teams annually from around the world. Guttmann's constant linking of the Stoke Mandeville Games with the Olympic Games led to the first Paralympic Games in Rome in 1960. It is now one of the world's largest multisport events, after the Olympic Games. It is strongly linked to the Olympic

Games because it is held a couple of weeks after each Summer and Winter Olympic Games in the same host city and using the same venues.

Just as the International Olympic Committee claims that the Olympic Games have social impact beyond the Games themselves, the International Paralympic Committee claims that Paralympic Games affect the lives of disabled people within the wider society by increasing understanding and changing attitudes toward disabled people in a positive manner. In several nations such as Australia, Great Britain, and the United States, they have started trying to use the history of the Paralympic Games and memorabilia connected with it to assist with this process of increasing awareness and understanding.

CRITICAL THINKING EXERCISES

1. What are some of the advantages and disadvantages of the close linkage between the Olympic and Paralympic movements?
2. How can classification be made more easily understandable to increase spectator enjoyment of Paralympic and disability sport?
3. How can less-developed nations be assisted to increase their opportunities to be competitive at a Paralympic Games?
4. In what ways can Paralympic history and memorabilia be used to raise awareness of disability issues within the wider society?

CHAPTER 5

Legal Aspects of Disability Sport and Recreation

Anita Moorman, JD

LEARNING OBJECTIVES

After reading this chapter, you will be able to do the following:

- Understand the history of disability rights advocacy and the creation of the first sporting events for people with disabilities.
- Explain the importance and scope of the United Nations Convention on the Rights of Persons with Disabilities (CRPD).
- Understand the interconnectedness of the U.S. federal laws providing protections for people with disabilities across a broad spectrum of cultural and life activities.
- Gain a working knowledge of how the Americans with Disabilities Act of 1990 (ADA) affects the operation of sport and recreation programs, and venues.
- Create strategies for compliance with federal nondiscrimination laws and for implementing inclusive risk management practices to meet the needs of participants or customers with disabilities.

Sport and recreation opportunities for people with disabilities have expanded significantly during the past 50 years due in large part to dedicated activism and advocacy for disability rights resulting in legal protections for people with disabilities. This chapter will first explore the history of the disability rights movement. It will then examine both the international and U.S. legal landscape of disability rights, including key international and U.S. legal and policy efforts recognizing fundamental rights of people with disabilities. Next, we consider how the legal protections in the United States have affected the participation rights of athletes with disabilities in a variety of contexts, including educational programs, recreation programs, competitive sport programs, and Olympic and Paralympic sports programs. The chapter concludes by investigating the impact of disability laws on sports venues such as stadiums and arenas.

Understanding the history of the disability rights movement, the international declarations related to disability rights and education, and U.S. laws and regulations applicable to creating and protecting these important rights is vital for decision makers and managers across the sport industry, physical education, and recreational environments.

History of the Disability Rights Movement

The disability rights movement tracks activism related to disability rights back to the 1800s. By the 1930s and 1940s, numerous organizations and initiatives were established to promote equality in employment, health care, education, and access to public services and buildings for people with disabilities. Sport and physical activity played an important role in the movement because it was seen as a mechanism to improve vitality and productivity of the community, children, and those with injuries or other impairments. Thus, developing physical education curriculum, fields of physiotherapy, movement-based leisure, and competitive sport opportunities were closely aligned with the expanding disability rights movement.

The movement gained significant momentum after the end of World War II, prompting international organizations such as the United Nations to advocate for the recognition and expansion of fundamental rights for people with disabilities. Several key international declarations recognized basic human rights for persons with disabilities. Physical education and physical activity were identified as essential components of the educational experience for children and students with disabilities.

Some of the first national and international sports competitions for people with disabilities emerged in the 1940s and 1950s. The modern Paralympic movement began in 1948 at the Stoke Mandeville Games to coincide with the 1948 London Olympic Games. These Games resulted in the founding of an International Stoke Mandeville Games Committee (ISMGC), which was the precursor to the first Paralympic Games in 1960 in Rome featuring eight parasports for athletes with spinal cord injuries. The ISMGC eventually became the International Paralympic Committee (IPC; see chapter 4 for more in-depth information about the Paralympic Games). The 1960s also introduced organized sport competitions for people with intellectual disabilities through the advocacy of Eunice Kennedy Shriver establishing what is now Special Olympics providing participative and competitive sport opportunities for persons with intellectual disabilities (see more on the Special Olympics in chapter 8).

In U.S. federal law, the term *disability* first appeared in 1790 to define persons who would receive compensation for injuries sustained in war because they had an incapacity that precluded manual labor (Colker, 2000). Beginning in the late 1950s and early 1960s, attitudes about people with disabilities began to evolve from paternalism, where the government's role was to provide funding to rehabilitate or care for people with disabilities, to inclusion, where the government's role was to eliminate barriers that prevented people with disabilities from seeking full and equal access to society (Weber, 2000). By the late 1970s in the United States, broad and sweeping federal legislation was enacted that began to alter the landscape in employment and education for people with disabilities (Section 504 of the Rehabilitation Act of 1973; Individuals with Disabilities Education Act, 1975). Then, in 1990, the United States enacted its most sweeping legislation known as the Americans with Disabilities Act of 1990 (ADA). A central component of U.S. federal legislation focused on recognizing the fundamental rights of people with disabilities and prohibiting discrimination based on disability across lived environments such as education, employment, and access to public and private services and facilities.

International Legal and Policy Efforts on Disability Rights

Following years of policy efforts to advance the rights of persons with disabilities in society, a benchmark moment occurred in 2006 with the adoption of the United Nations Convention on the Rights of Persons with Disabilities (CRPD). It established a framework for national policymaking and legislation for building an inclusive society and fostering disability-inclusive environments. Most significantly for disability sport and recreation, the CRPD recognized the essential nature of physical activity and sport to human development and social inclusion.

Article 30 of the CRPD is titled *Participation in Culture Life, Recreation, Leisure, and Sport.* Article 30 is the first international treaty specifically recognizing the importance of sport and physical activity as a fundamental human right for people with disabilities to experience full inclusion in society. Section 1 of Article 30 says: "States Parties recognize the right of persons with disabilities to take part on an equal basis with others in cultural life" (CRPD, 2008b, p. 22). It further emphasizes the importance of providing sport and physical activities across a broad spectrum of life, including activities at all skill levels, the opportunity to have disability-specific activities, access to venues, and access to activities in school systems, recreation, and tourism spaces. For example, Section 5 says:

> With a view to enabling persons with disabilities to participate on an equal basis with others in recreational, leisure and sporting activities, States Parties shall take appropriate measures:
>
> a. To encourage and promote the participation, to the fullest extent possible, of persons with disabilities in *mainstream sporting activities at all levels*
>
> b. To ensure that persons with disabilities have an opportunity to organize, develop, and participate in disability-*specific sporting and recreational activities* and, to this end, encourage the provision, on an equal basis with others, of appropriate instruction, training, and resources

> c. To ensure that persons with disabilities have access to sporting, recreational and tourism *venues*
>
> d. To ensure that children with disabilities have equal access with other children to participation in play, recreation, and leisure and sporting activities, including those activities in the *school system*
>
> e. To ensure that persons with disabilities have access to services from those involved in the organization of *recreational, tourism, leisure*, and sporting activities (CRPD, 2008b, p. 23; emphasis added)

> **Article 30 of the CRPD is the first international treaty expressly recognizing sport and physical activity as a fundamental human right for people with disabilities.**

For the nations that have ratified the CRPD, it represents binding international law. Nations who become signatories and then ratify the CRPD are legally bound to respect the standards in the Convention and to implement those standards into their national legal system. Before the adoption of the CRPD, only about 40 nations had some form of disability rights protections included in their legal systems. Now with 164 signatories and 185 ratifying countries (United Nations, 2022), nations continue to implement legal protections for persons with disabilities (see Stein & Lord, 2008). The United States became a signatory to the CRPD on July 30, 2009 but has yet to ratify it in Congress (United Nations, 2022b). Canada is one of the 185 ratifying countries, becoming a signatory in 2007 and ratifying in 2010 (United Nations, 2022b).

The CRPD represents an international standard that nations should endeavor to respect and provides lawmakers and advocates a foundation for implementing legal protections at the national level for persons

Accessibility Laws in Canada

Robin Hardin and Joshua Pate

The Canadian Human Rights Commission's goal is to ensure that all Canadian residents are treated equally and fairly. The Commission provides oversight of the Canadian Human Rights Act of 1977, which protects people in Canada from discrimination based on gender and ethnicity as well as disability. This is applicable to all 10 Canadian provinces as well as Canada's three territories.

While the Canadian Human Rights Act protects from discrimination, the Accessible Canada Act (ACA) was adopted in 2019 with a goal to create a Canada without barriers by 2040. The guidelines set forth in this act are applicable to federally funded programs and organizations, similar to the way Title II of the Americans with Disabilities Act of 1990 (ADA) in the United States prohibits discrimination within public entities. The Canadian Human Rights Commission is also charged with overseeing the implementation of ACA standards. ACA is applicable only to programs and organizations that receive federal funding, such as Air Canada, Canadian Armed Forces, and Canada Post.

Programs, organizations, and businesses that do not receive federal funding are governed by standards adopted by each province and territory. Private and provincial funding organizations and programs in Ontario are guided by the standards set forth in the Accessibility for Ontarians Disability Act (AODA). This act was adopted in 2005 with the "purpose to develop, implement, and enforce standards for accessibility related to goods, services, facilities, employment, accommodation and buildings" (Accessibility for Ontarians Disability Act, 2023, para. 1).

A watershed moment for this act was the Pan American Games and Parapan American Games hosted by Toronto in 2015. This was an opportunity for the province to demonstrate its commitment to accessibility and serving people with disabilities. The Organizing Committee and its stakeholders who were charged with the strategy and development of infrastructure for the Games were purposeful in the decision-making process of adhering to AODA policies. These polices were not only applicable for accommodating para-athletes but also for staff members, volunteers, and spectators. For example, all shower facilities were step-free to accommodate para-athletes with mobility impairments. Public spaces (i.e., cafés, restaurants, competition venues) were constructed with accessible doors, curb cuts, and aids for people with visual impairments. Accommodations were present throughout the athletes' village, competition venues, training areas, and commercial spaces to adhere to the standards of AODA.

The ACA and AODA are similar Canadian laws created to enable full and equal participation for anyone with a disability without barriers or restrictions. There is no national standard for accessibility similar to the ADA, so it is important to be aware of the specific standards for each province or territory in Canada. The standards throughout Canada are similar in nature, but an awareness of the subtleties is important as well as the level of adherence and enforcement.

Accessibility for Ontarians with Disabilities Act (2023). *Guide to the act*. https://aoda.ca/guide-to-the-act/

---

with disabilities (CRPD, 2008a). Even for nations that are not signatories or that have not ratified the CRPD, it is still highly influential in developing policies and laws related to disability sport and persons with disabilities more broadly (Cooper & Whittle, 1998). For example, even though the United States has yet to ratify the CRPD, the United States has enacted significant laws and policies to protect the rights of persons with disabilities.

United States Legal Framework for Disability Rights

The United States has a complex and overlapping legal framework for recognizing the rights of people with disabilities and preventing discrimination based on disability. U.S. laws have primarily framed disability protections from the dual perspective of *ensuring rights* and *addressing inequality or discrimination*. The United States has three primary federal statutes focused on disability rights and disability discrimination:

- Individuals with Disabilities Education Act (IDEA; public schools, K-12)
- Section 504 of the Rehabilitation Act of 1973 (Section 504; recipients of federal funds)
- Americans with Disabilities Act of 1990 (ADA; employers, public services, public accommodations)

Both IDEA and Section 504 were enacted in the 1970s. IDEA applied to state and local education agencies (public schools), and its focus was to establish special education programs for K-12 students with disabilities. Section 504 sought to eliminate discrimination in any programs or services offered by public or private entities who received federal financial assistance. Section 504 set the stage for the ADA, which broadly prohibits discrimination based on disability in employment (Title I), in public services (Title II), by private entities providing public accommodations (Title III), and in telecommunications (Title IV). ADA also prohibits retaliation against people who have disabilities or those who aid people with disabilities in asserting their rights under the ADA (Title V).

Individuals with Disabilities Education Act

In 1975, Congress enacted specific legislation to guarantee that children with disabilities could receive an education. Previously, the courts had already introduced the principle that children with disabilities had a civil right to receive an education (*Pennsylvania Ass'n for Retarded Children v. Commonwealth of Pennsylvania* (1972); *Mills v. Board of Education of District of Columbia* (1972)). Congress enacted the Education of All Handicapped Children Act in 1975 (now renamed as the Individuals with Disabilities Education Act; IDEA) to ensure that children with disabilities (1) received an education that met their unique needs and prepared them for further education, and (2) protected the rights of children with disabilities and their parents to be involved in determining how to meet those needs (Colker, 2000).

IDEA mandates that each child with disabilities have an **individualized education program (IEP)** so that the child can receive a **free appropriate public education** (FAPE). IDEA covers children from age 3 through 21. The act also provides federal funding for educating children with disabilities and is enforced and administered by the Department of Education (DOE). The DOE has issued regulations to guide implementation of IDEA, which expressly includes "instruction in physical education" in the educational instruction required as needed to ensure the unique needs of a child with a disability are being met (Wright & Wright, 2007, 2021). When IDEA was amended in 2004, it included a requirement that students with disabilities have access to physical education, which includes developing physical and motor skills. Adapted physical education and sport participation opportunities are often included in a student's IEP.

Block (1996) observed that U.S. legislation provides a framework for policy and decision making supported by extensive rules and regulations to assist with implementation of the legislation, but it also has a long history of court decisions resolving disputes and disagreements as school administrators, teachers, parents, and students attempted to implement the legislative mandate. These court cases, both in the context of physical education and disability sport, have played a critical role in defining the duties and responsibilities of schools to comply with IDEA.

The key operational features that have been shaped through both regulations and court decisions often related to (1) how FAPE is defined, (2) the reasonableness of the IEP, and (3) the application of the least restrictive environment standard.

Defining Free Appropriate Public Education

Under IDEA, FAPE includes both special education and related services. Special education can be any "specially designed instruction to meet the unique needs of a child with a disability." This would include adapted physical education. Related services are the support services "required to assist a child to benefit from that instruction" (§ 1401(9)). IDEA defines physical education as the development of the following:

- Physical and motor skills
- Fundamental motor skills and patterns
- Skills in aquatics, dance, and individual and group games and sports (including intramural and lifetime sports)

Physical education must be made available equally to children with and without disabilities. If physical education is provided as part of the general education curriculum for children without disabilities, it must also be available to children with disabilities.

> Special education includes instruction in physical education, and adapted physical education is specially designed instruction, not a related service.

Reasonableness of the IEP

The reasonableness of the IEP and determining whether a school has met IDEA obligations has largely been defined and clarified through litigation. The standard was established in the seminal case decided by the U.S. Supreme Court in *Board of Education*

v. Rowley (1982; hereafter *"Rowley"*) where the Court held:

> [T]he requirement that a State provide specialized educational services to handicapped children *generates no additional requirement that the services so provided be sufficient to maximize each child's potential commensurate with the opportunity provided other children* . . . . . The educational opportunities provided by our public school systems undoubtedly differ from student to student, depending upon a myriad of factors that might affect a particular student's ability to assimilate information presented in the classroom [emphasis added]. 458 U.S. at 198-99

The *Rowley* decision has been applied to provide that an IEP is reasonable so long as it provides a student *some or minimal educational benefit.* Thus, if a student is generally progressing from grade to grade, the state has met its burden under IDEA. This has been referred to as the *de minimis standard,* which only requires a minimal educational benefit. *Rowley* has generally been understood to impose no burden on the school to provide an ideal educational program or to maximize the student's educational potential.

Least Restrictive Environment

The basic idea of the **least restrictive environment** is straightforward: ensure that students with disabilities who receive special education instruction are included in the general education classroom as often as possible ("maximum extent appropriate," 20 U.S.C. 1412(a)(5)). The physical education regulations stipulate that each child with a disability must be afforded the opportunity to participate in the general physical education program unless the child is enrolled full time in a separate facility or the child needs specially designed physical education as prescribed in the IEP (34 CFR § 300.108(b)). Since federal law mandates physical education be included with the special education services provided to children

CHAPTER 5 ▮ Legal Aspects of Disability Sport and Recreation

with disabilities, physical education teachers should be actively involved in and understand the IEP development process.

For a more in-depth discussion of the laws and regulations related to implementing IDEA, several excellent resources are available for a detailed analysis of special education law in the United States and resources for adapted physical education standards (NCPEID, 2021, 2022; SHAPE America, 2018; Wright & Wright, 2021).

Section 504 and the Americans With Disabilities Act

Section 504 and the ADA work together along with IDEA to protect children and adults with disabilities from exclusion and unequal treatment in schools, jobs, and the community. IDEA is applicable only in the school setting. However, Section 504 and the ADA are both broad civil rights statutes designed to promote equal access to and participation in public and private programs and services for people with disabilities.

The ADA is modeled after Section 504 and is even broader in scope. Section 504 casts its mandate over federal agencies and any institutions receiving federal financial assistance; the ADA extends that mandate even more broadly to include all private employers, state and local governments, and privately owned businesses. Many organizations can be subject to both Section 504 and the ADA, and public schools can even be subject to IDEA, Section 504, and the ADA simultaneously. Providers of sport, recreation, or exercise programs and activities need to understand the legal requirements of 504 and the ADA.

The regulatory framework for Section 504 and ADA have many enforcement similarities. Table 5.1 compares the statutory language between Section 504 and Titles II and III of the ADA. The key operational features Section 504 and the ADA share include the following:

- Definition of disability
- Requirement that to be covered, a person must be **"otherwise qualified"** to access the programs, services, or opportunities at stake

TABLE 5.1 **Comparison of the Statutory Language for Section 504 and the ADA**

Statute	Key operational language	Scope of coverage
Section 504	No otherwise qualified individual with a disability . . . shall solely by reason of her or his disability be excluded from the participation in, be denied the benefits of, or be subjected to discrimination under any *program or activity receiving Federal financial assistance* [emphasis added].	Any recipient of federal financial assistance
ADA, Title II	No qualified individual with a disability shall, on the basis of disability, be excluded from participation in or be denied the benefits of the *services, programs, or activities of a public entity*, or be subjected to discrimination by any public entity [emphasis added].	Public entities: state and local governments
ADA, Title III	No individual shall be discriminated against on the basis of disability in the full and equal enjoyment of the *goods, services, facilities, privileges, advantages, or accommodations of any place of public accommodation by any private entity* who owns, leases (or leases to), or operates a place of public accommodation [emphasis added].	Private entities owning or operating public accommodations

- Requirement to make **reasonable modifications** to policies, practices, or procedures when modifications are necessary, unless modifications would operate as **fundamental alteration** or impose an undue burden
- Prohibition of separate but equal concept of service delivery, instead requiring services or programs be offered in the most **integrated setting** appropriate to the needs of the individual
- That all the aforementioned factors be determined using an **individualized inquiry** approach

Definition of Disability

Section 504 and ADA both define a disability as a substantial impairment that affects one or more major life activities, such as learning, breathing, or walking. In 2016, Section 504 was amended to reinforce the broad scope of coverage provided under Section 504 and the ADA and to reinforce a broad construction of the term *disability* to favor expansive coverage to the maximum extent permitted under the law. Section 1251.100(b) states: "The primary object of attention in cases brought under this part should be whether entities have complied with their obligations and whether discrimination has occurred, not whether the individual meets the definition of disability. The question of whether an individual meets the definition of disability under this part should not demand extensive analysis."

Under Section 504 and ADA, the existence of a disability triggers coverage and the coverage extends across the lifespan. This contrasts with IDEA, where special education or related services must be provided only while the student is in the public school system (coverage from age 3 through age 21).

Otherwise Qualified

To be covered by Section 504 and ADA, a person must "be an otherwise qualified individual with a disability," meaning the individual must be qualified to participate in the program or activity. **Otherwise qualified** is defined as "satisfying all the essential skill, ability, physical and eligibility requirements for participation, either in spite of the disability or with reasonable accommodations for the disability." For example, a student with attention deficit hyperactivity disorder (ADHD) may try out for a basketball team but lacks the dribbling, shooting, and passing skills needed to make the team if the team is a competitive team with limited participation slots. A coach would not be required to permit the student to play on the team because the student is not "otherwise qualified." There can be a critical distinction between community or recreation sports teams and elite or competitive sports teams in this area. Community, intramural, and recreational sports teams may not have a minimum skills threshold to participate, and therefore most participants would be "otherwise qualified" to participate.

Reasonable Modifications

If a person is otherwise qualified, the next question becomes whether that individual can participate in the sports or recreation program with or without modifications of the program or activity. Section 504 and ADA require a provider to make reasonable modifications that will allow one to participate. However, Section 504 and ADA do not require modifications that would be *unduly burdensome* or would *fundamentally alter* the programs or services the schools provide.

Several organizations provide strategies for making modifications to sport and recreation programs. These modifications can influence coaching styles, competition rules, the playing surface or venue, or sports equipment. As noted in chapter 2, the Office of Civil Rights issued a Dear Colleague Letter in 2013 providing numerous common-sense modifications for athletics competitions including allowing for two bounces in tennis or racquetball, visual cues for a hearing-impaired track and field athlete, alteration of the two-hand touch rule in swimming for a one-handed swimmer, and providing assistance with glucose testing or

Reasonable Modification in Practice

Kempf v. Michigan High School Athletic Association (MHSAA; 2015) illustrates the importance of using best practice for resolving disputes surrounding reasonable modification requests. A hearing-impaired high school wrestler, Kempf, used an external cochlear device but due to safety reasons was unable to wear the device during wrestling matches. He was permitted to use an American Sign Language interpreter to interpret his coach's instructions during matches. During unsanctioned matches, the interpreter was permitted to move freely around the perimeter of the mat so Kempf could always see him. However, during sanctioned matches, the MHSAA restricted the interpreter to a designated area near the coach. After a year of unsuccessful negotiations with the MHSAA to allow his interpreter greater access around the perimeter of the mat, Kempf sued in federal district court. The MHSAA ultimately entered a consent decree that permitted the interpreter 360-degree access around the mat (Green, 2020). The interpreter was required to stay at least six feet away from the active wrestling circle to avoid any contact or interference with the wrestlers, scorers, coaches, and referee. In this situation, it was clear that the requested accommodation would not fundamentally alter the activity or impose an undue burden on the governing body or program operator. In such instances, acknowledging the reasonableness of the request and providing enthusiastic support for providing the participation opportunity is a much better ADA compliance strategy, avoids costly litigation, and will align and support organization's goals to be inclusive.

insulin administration for a diabetic athlete (U.S. Department of Education, 2013).

The reasonable modification principle also places the *burden of proof* on the public accommodation to prove that a modification is not reasonable and is instead an undue hardship or **fundamental alteration.** A landmark case in the United States examined the "fundamental alteration" language in the ADA in the context of whether requested modifications to the "walking rule" of the PGA Tour for an elite professional golfer was a reasonable modification of the rules of competition (*PGA Tour v. Martin,* 2001). The case involved professional golfer Casey Martin who requested to use a golf cart during the PGA Tour competition due to his mobility disability.

The Supreme Court held that Martin's requested modification was not a fundamental alteration of the PGA Tour and therefore was a reasonable modification under the ADA. The Supreme Court developed a two-step analysis to determine whether a modification of a substantive rule of competition would result in a fundamental alteration of the competition. First, the requested modification must not fundamentally alter the *essence of the sport*. Second, the requested modification must not give the athlete with a disability a *competitive advantage*. In its analysis, the Court held that walking was not a fundamental part of the sport of golf—golf tests one's shot-making skills, not walking skills; thus, walking was not the "essence of the sport" of golf. The Court next held that given Martin's individual circumstances, affording him the use of a cart would not give him a competitive advantage.

> To deny a requested modification based on the fundamental alteration defense, the program operator must prove that the requested modification would (1) alter the essence of the sport or activity or (2) would give the athlete with a disability a competitive advantage.

Most Integrated Setting

ADA regulations require entities to administer "services, programs, and activities in the most integrated setting appropriate" (§ 35.108(a)(1)(iii)). Integrated settings provide individuals with disabilities opportunities to live, work, and receive services in the greater community, just like those without disabilities. The primary goal of the ADA is equal participation in mainstream American society. The main principles of **mainstreaming** include:

a. Individuals with disabilities must be integrated to the maximum extent appropriate.

b. Separate programs are permitted where necessary to ensure equal opportunity. A separate program must be appropriate to the particular individual.

c. Individuals with disabilities cannot be excluded from the regular program or required to accept special services or benefits. (United States Department of Justice, n.d.a,§ 3.4000-3.4200)

The ADA's technical assistance manuals provide several illustrations of integrated settings and separate programs that would satisfy the ADA's integration mandate (see table 5.2).

Individualized Inquiry

The Supreme Court in *Martin* held that when evaluating accommodation requests under Title III of the ADA, the provider must conduct an individualized inquiry. This is a fact-specific inquiry relative to the stated purpose of a rule and a person's individual disability and circumstances. For example, in *PGA Tour v. Martin*, instead of evaluating

TABLE 5.2   **Illustrations of Integrated Settings and Separate Programs**

Venue or event	ADA TAM illustration	Operational issue
Museum	Museums generally do not allow visitors to touch exhibits because handling can cause damage to the objects. A museum may offer a special tour for individuals with vision impairments during which they are permitted to touch and handle specific objects on a limited basis. (It cannot, however, exclude a blind person from the standard museum tour.)	Separate program offering
Private athletic facility	A private athletic facility may sponsor a separate basketball league for people who use wheelchairs.	Separate program offering
Basketball league	Even if separate program is available, participation in regular program should be permitted unless some other limitation applies. For example, an individual who uses a wheelchair may be excluded from playing in a basketball league if the recreation center can demonstrate that the exclusion is necessary for safe operation.	Integration into existing program
Museum	If person with a disability prefers the standard museum tour, where touching is not permitted, a public accommodation cannot exclude the person. The public accommodation cannot exclude based on assumptions about their ability to appreciate or benefit from the standard tour experience.	Integration into existing program

Adapted from Title III Technical Assistance Manual (with 1994 supplement). Available: https://www.corada.com/documents/title-iii-technical-assistance-manual/III-3-4000-Separate-benefit-integrated-setting.

Martin's individual circumstances, the PGA Tour argued that rules it deemed essential, such as a substantive competition rule (the walking rule), could not be waived without fundamentally altering the nature of the competition; therefore, an individual inquiry was unnecessary. In essence, the PGA Tour's argument was that once a rule is designated as a substantive rule by the provider, any modification would result in a fundamental alteration. However, § 12182 of the ADA provides that "reasonable modification in policies, practices, or procedures" *must be made*. The statute does not say that only policies, practices, or procedures that are not substantive are subject to modification. The court in *Martin* reinforced the importance of the individualized inquiry to evaluate modification requests. Thus, a provider cannot unilaterally declare a requested modification as unreasonable or a fundamental alteration without first conducting an individualized inquiry of the requested modification.

> **The individual inquiry is a required and vital part of the disability discrimination paradigm.**

Impact of Disability Rights Laws on Athletic Participation

In the context of sport and recreation, the ADA mandate does not stop at the physical structure or physical access to a sport space or venue, nor is it limited only to spectators at stadiums and arenas. Instead, eligibility policies, competition rules, and other operating practices that determine who is permitted to participate in the services offered at sport and recreation venues are also subject to the mandates contained in Section 504 and the ADA. Thus, any person with a disability, whether a casual participant in a community recreation program or a professional athlete participating in an elite sports competition, must be afforded an equal opportunity to access those programs and services.

The ADA expressly provides "a public accommodation shall make reasonable modifications in *policies, practices, or procedures* when the modifications are necessary to afford *goods, services, facilities, privileges, advantages, or accommodations* to individuals with disabilities" (28 CFR, Part 36 § 36.302, 2018; emphasis added).

The following are examples involving competition rules, eligibility rules, and operating practices to illustrate how policies, practices, or procedures may deny access to sport or recreation participation opportunities to people with disabilities.

Competition Rules

The *Martin* case previously discussed involved a competition rule, the PGA Tour's "walking rule," and reaffirmed that even sports competition rules must be subject to modification to meet the broad mandate of the ADA. The *Martin* case also addressed the issue of fundamental alteration and whether modifying a competition rule would provide the individual with a disability with a competitive advantage. This question of accommodation versus advantage can often occur in the elite sport realm, where presumably even the slightest competitive advantage could serve to alter the nature of the competition.

In the international sports context, this issue arose when South African sprinter Oscar Pistorius sought to compete in events sanctioned by International Association of Athletics Federations (IAAF) alongside able-bodied athletes. Pistorius is a double amputee and decorated Paralympic athlete. He used prosthetic legs, known as the Flex-Foot Cheetah, to compete. The IAAF banned him from competing during the 2008 Olympics on the basis that his prosthetic device was an illegal technical device prohibited by IAAF rules of competition and gave him a competitive advantage. Following a complicated and lengthy dispute resolution process before the Court of Arbitration for Sport (CAS), CAS determined that the scientific evidence did not prove that the prosthesis gave Pistorius a metabolic or biomechanical advantage; therefore, he should be permitted to compete on an equal basis with nondisabled athletes (*Pistorius v. IAAF*, 2008).

Interestingly, CAS did not rely on the CRPD in its analysis; of course, the ADA was inapplicable since this dispute was between a South African athlete and an international sports federation. But CAS did evaluate Pistorius and IAAF claims using several principles similar to those seen in ADA cases in the United States—namely, the notions of equal access, individual inquiry, and placing the burden to prove competitive advantage on the provider, which was IAAF (see Weston, 2017).

In fact, after this CAS decision, IAAF (now World Athletics) amended their rules to shift the burden of proof to the athlete to prove they do not have a competitive advantage. Thus, when a similar issue came up in 2017 involving another dual amputee sprinter, Blake Leeper, his racing times were annulled because he had not met his burden of proof that his prosthetics did not give him a competitive advantage, specifically extra height and a running speed advantage. Leeper appealed to CAS, and after another lengthy dispute resolution process, CAS determined that the prosthetics Leeper used were more likely than not giving him an overall competitive advantage (Court of Arbitration for Sport, 2021; Wittmer, 2021). However, CAS also declared that the World Athletic rule shifting the burden of proof upon the athlete was unlawful and invalid. So, while Leeper lost his appeal, the burden of proof related to competitive advantage in international elite sport cases would appear to remain on the sports federation instead of the athlete, consistent with the burden of proof framework used in ADA cases in the United States.

Eligibility Rules

Claims brought under Section 504 and ADA often involve athletic eligibility requirements that high school or collegiate athletic associations impose. Typically, the requirements most often challenged include (1) age

requirements preventing athletes from participating who turn 19 before the beginning of the school year, (2) maximum semester or year rules prohibiting athletes from participating beyond eight semesters or four years in high school, and (3) minimum academic requirements excluding certain classes from GPA or other qualifying academic credits. Athletes denied the opportunity to participate would request that the eligibility requirements be modified or waived, triggering the reasonable modification provisions of Section 504 and ADA.

In *Dennin v. Connecticut Interscholastic Athletic Conference* (1996), Dennin was a 19-year-old with Down syndrome who was a member of the swim team. He had been held back a year in middle school due to his educational needs with the result that he was 19 during his senior year in high school. He was thus denied eligibility for his senior year under the Connecticut Interscholastic Athletic Conference (CIAC) age-limit rule. His request for a waiver of the rule was denied, but because his participation on the team was written into his IEP, the CIAC said they would allow him to continue to participate as a nonscoring exhibition swimmer on his relay team. This meant that his relay team could not earn any points for the overall team. Dennin sued under Section 504 and the ADA. The court found in favor of Dennin, holding that it would be a reasonable accommodation for the CIAC to grant a waiver in his case. According to the court, allowing Dennin to participate only as an exhibition swimmer would be to treat him differently on the basis of his disability, thus potentially damaging his self-esteem and his willingness to attempt to function in the larger community.

With regard to age eligibility rules, the courts have reached inconsistent outcomes. In *Dennin*, the CIAC argued that their age-limit rule was a neutral rule neutrally applied, and the court found that this argument ignored the reality that the sole reason he was past the designated age requirement was due to his disability. Other courts have disagreed with the *Dennin* rationale. These courts have held that age-limit rules are neutral rules and instead concluded the students were excluded simply based on their age because they became too old during their senior year (see *Sandison v. Michigan High School Athletic Association,* 1995).

In *Dennin* and *Sandison,* both high school athletic associations defined eligibility based on age. However, the Florida High School Athletic Association (FHSAA) limits the athletic eligibility of high school students based on criteria setting maximum years of eligibility at four years. Thomas Pritchard requested a waiver and a fifth year of eligibility. Pritchard had participated in high school athletics for two years in Virginia before transferring to Florida, at which time he was recommended to and did repeat 10th grade. Thus, during his senior year, he was deemed ineligible because by then he had participated for four consecutive years in high school. The FHSAA denied his requested waiver and fifth year of eligibility. The Florida federal district court denied Pritchard's request for an injunction and dismissed his Section 504 and ADA claims. The court held that since Pritchard had participated for four years, he was not "otherwise qualified" to participate. The court found that the student was prevented from participating because he has completed four consecutive years and not because of his disability (see *Pritchard v. FHSAA,* 2019).

Eligibility rules may be some of the more challenging circumstances to evaluate based on the intersection of the "otherwise qualified" standard and the "reasonable modification" standard; however, the best practice for inclusion is to refer to the question: Is the modification request reasonable given the individual circumstances of the athlete or participant?

> The best practice for inclusion is to refer to the question: Is the modification request reasonable given the individual circumstances of the athlete or participant?

Operating Practices and Auxiliary Aids and Services

The *Kempf* case is a good example of an event operations practice that was required to be modified to permit Kempf to benefit from his interpreter during the wrestling match. The Department of Justice also maintains a useful database of settlement agreements under Section 504 and ADA that it negotiates upon the filing of a discrimination complaint. These agreements cover a range of topics involving the operation of summer camps, sports clubs, and recreational programs. It also covers the operator's responsibility to not exclude participants who may have severe food allergies, diabetes, or other disabilities from their programs and to provide necessary auxiliary aids for participants.

One settlement agreement reached with the Indianapolis Department of Parks and Recreation covered 13 different golf courses operated by the city. The agreement required the city golf course to purchase and provide two different models of adapted individual golf mobility aid devices and locate those devices at two different courses (U.S. Department of Justice, 2002). Another settlement agreement was reached when the parents of a deaf child filed a complaint against a Colorado youth soccer club who had ceased providing sign language interpretation services for their eight-year-old son for practices and games and failed to offer any other auxiliary aids for communication. The soccer club was required to furnish appropriate auxiliary aids and services free of charge to ensure effective communication with individuals with disabilities, but the club did have some flexibility to determine the type of auxiliary aid provided so long as it provided effective communication (Karlik, 2020; U.S. Department of Justice, 2020).

These settlement agreements are useful tools for sport and recreation managers operating sport camps, recreational programs, and after-school programs to better understand the disputes that may arise when responding to an accommodation request from a participant with a disability.

Impact of Disability Rights Laws on Sports Venues

The ADA has had a profound impact on accessibility of sport venues in the United States. It requires stadiums, arenas, and other sport venues to be accessible to people with disabilities so that they, their families, and their friends can enjoy equal access to entertainment, recreation, and leisure.

Title III says: "[n]o individual shall be discriminated against on the basis of disability in the full and equal enjoyment of the goods, services, facilities, privileges, advantages, or accommodations of any *place of public accommodation* by any person who owns, leases (or leases to), or operates a place of public accommodation" (42 U.S.C. § 12182; emphasis added).

Places of public accommodation include several specific sport facilities, such as gymnasiums, health clubs, bowling alleys, golf courses, and stadiums (see figure 5.1). More importantly, the general categories of places deemed places of public accommodation under ADA encompass virtually all sport facilities. Parks, fitness clubs, sports museums, arenas, stadiums, yoga clubs, recreation centers, a community road race, a marathon, a pickleball tournament, and so on are all places of public accommodation. In addition, within a single facility, separate elements or areas are also places of public accommodation, such as restaurants, museums, galleries, day care centers, bars, concessions areas, convention meeting halls, and auditoriums; these are also subject to the ADA. Essentially, any facility, event, or activity that is a place of exhibition, entertainment, exercise, or recreation is covered by the ADA. For venue and event managers, understanding ADA requirements is essential to effectively operating the venues and events. Figure 5.1 highlights the definition of public accommodation.

ADA Regulations and Guidance for Sports Venues

As part of ADA implementation, the U.S. Department of Justice (USDOJ) released regulations and standards to guide businesses,

---

A public accommodation is defined as the following private entities if the operations of such entities affect commerce:

a. An inn, hotel, motel, or other place of lodging, except for an establishment located within a building that contains not more than five rooms for rent or hire and that is occupied by the proprietor of such establishment as the residence of such proprietor

b. A restaurant, bar, or other establishment serving food or drink

c. A motion picture house, theater, concert hall, stadium, or other *place of exhibition or entertainment*

d. An auditorium, convention center, lecture hall, or other *place of public gathering*

e. A bakery, grocery store, clothing store, hardware store, shopping center, or other sales or rental establishment

f. A *park*, zoo, amusement park, or other *place of recreation*

g. A nursery; elementary, secondary, undergraduate, or postgraduate private school; or other place of education

h. A *gymnasium, health spa, bowling alley, golf course, or other place of exercise or recreation* (42 U.S.C. § 12181(7)(2013)).

FIGURE 5.1 Definition of a "public accommodation" under the ADA (emphases on places covering sport and recreation).

42 U.S.C. § 12181(7)(2013)

service providers, employers, and governmental entities in complying with Title III of the statute (42 U.S.C. § 12134(a) & 12186(b)). Congress required that these regulations be consistent with the minimum guidelines issued by the Architectural and Transportation Barriers Compliance Board, now known as the United States Access Board ("Access Board"). The Access Board is an independent federal agency charged with issuing guidelines to ensure that public accommodations are accessible to individuals with disabilities. The Access Board published its first proposed Guide to ADA Accessibility Standards (ADA Guides) in July 1991 for designers and operators to ensure that a sport facility is accessible and compliant with ADA requirements (U.S. Access Board, 2003). In addition, the Access Board has published ADA accessibility guidelines for several specific recreation facilities, such as golf facilities, boating facilities, fishing piers, and swimming pools. The USDOJ publishes technical assistance manuals (TAMs) to guide entities through the more technical elements of complying with the regulations (U.S. Department of Justice, 1993, 1994). USDOJ also publishes more informal guidelines regarding its interpretations of the ADA, the ADA Guides, and its own regulations. For example, the U.S. Access Board provides guidance for sports facilities, which includes exercise facilities, locker rooms, swimming pools, and golf courses (U.S. Access Board, 2003).

In 2004, the Access Board comprehensively updated the 1991 guides, which the USDOJ adopted on September 15, 2010. Under the 2010 ADA guide, any stadiums or arenas constructed after March 2012 must comply with the 2010 standards. An initial question often arises as to whether a sport facility has to comply with 1991 or 2010 ADA standards. Generally, 1991 standards apply to venues built before September 2010 (28 C.F.R. § 36.406(a)(1)), while 2010 standards apply to construction after March 2012 (28 C.F.R. § 36.406(a)(3)).

Responsibility of Owners and Operators of Sports Venues

An issue frequently raised in ADA cases relates to who has the responsibility for compliance with the ADA. The congressional mandate of the ADA is broad, not only as to the places considered a public accommodation but also the scope of persons responsible for ADA compliance. Any owner, operator, lessor, or lessee has a responsibility to ensure ADA compliance and can be sued under Title III for noncompliance. For example, in *Clark v. Simms* (2009), patrons of a hunting store sued the owners of the building as opposed to the operators of the business, alleging that architectural barriers prevented them from accessing the premises. The building lacked accessible parking spaces and an accessible route to the store. The owners had leased the store to the hunting store operators, the Hunt 'N' Shack. The court held that the plain terms of the ADA apply to those who own, lease, or lease to others a place of public accommodation. In no way does the language of the statute suggest that a person must both own and operate a place of public accommodation to be held liable. As the owners and the lessors of the property on which the Hunt 'N' Shack is located, the Simms could be held liable under the ADA. Furthermore, the owners may not assign their responsibilities for compliance with the ADA to the tenants who operate the Hunt 'N' Shack because "a landlord has an independent obligation to comply with the ADA that may not be eliminated by contract" (*Clark v. Simms*, 2009, p. 6).

> Any owner, operator, lessor, or lessee has a responsibility to ensure ADA compliance and can be sued under Title III for noncompliance.

For a professional sport venue, ownership structures can be quite complex. Often, the state or city has some ownership interests in the venue, the professional sports team may be the sole or primary tenant, and a third-party management company may be responsible for day-to-day venue operations and management. These complex contractual relationships may leave one party attempting to either shift or delegate their ADA compliance responsibilities to another party. However, as we saw in the *Clark* case, ADA applies to all owners, operators, lessors, or lessees, regardless of how large the facility is or how complex the contractual relationships are between the parties. For example, in *Bailey v. Board of Commissioners* (2019), a New Orleans Saints season ticket holder who uses a wheelchair for mobility filed a complaint naming as defendants SMG as the *operator* of the Superdome, the Board of Commissioners of the Louisiana Stadium and Exposition District (the "Board") as the *owner* of the Superdome, and Kyle France ("France") in his official capacity as chairman of the board (collectively, "Defendants").

Bailey had been a Saints season ticket holder for more than 30 years and alleged that before 2011, his seat was located on a wheelchair-accessible raised platform in the 100-level section of the Superdome. According to Bailey, as a result of extensive renovations in 2011, the wheelchair-accessible seating at the Superdome was moved to other positions where the views were obstructed by barriers and other patrons or players standing during the game and that the seating is not fully accessible by wheelchair in violation of the ADA and Section 504.

SMG argued that it cannot be held liable as an operator of a place of public accommodation because it is not in charge of ticketing or programming for Saints games. The district court disagreed. The court said that the relevant question is whether the defendant controls the modification of the public accommodation such that the defendant could cause the accommodation to comply with the ADA. The Stadium Agreement states that SMG "shall provide all services to manage and operate the Superdome in a first-class, businesslike, and efficient manner substantially consistent with the operation and management of other NFL stadiums." Further, SMG was obligated to "maintain the physical structure of the Superdome and all features, fixtures, equipment, and improvements therein, including but not limited to . . . spectator and other seating" (*Bailey v. Board of Commissioners*, 2019). Although SMG did not have control over ticketing for Saints games, SMG was obligated to maintain the physical structure of the Superdome, including spectator and other seating. SMG could be held liable as an operator of the Superdome because SMG controls modification of the Superdome and could cause the Superdome to comply with the ADA.

These cases illustrate not only the scope of the ADA but also the relationships among owners, lessees and lessors, and operators of places of public accommodation. The *Clark* case reminds us that the ADA is applicable to many places related to the sport industry, such as a retail sporting goods store, not just stadiums and arenas. *Bailey* reinforces that owners and operators with any control or management of the functioning of the facility fall under the broad umbrella of ADA compliance framework.

Equal Access to All and Amenities

The ADA requires that that people with disabilities be able to access a sports facility and the various amenities and services offered within it. When examining whether all services and amenities are accessible, the guest's overall enjoyment and ability to access the benefits and services offered to all patrons must be considered. To ensure that a venue's amenities and services are accessible, it is helpful to think about how a guest experiences the venue by asking the following questions.

- Do guests with disabilities have equal access to the venue? This includes accessible sidewalks, parking, pathways or doorways, restrooms and concession areas with accessible features, signage readable to visually impaired people, website accessibility for the visually impaired, and ticket sales policies for accessible seating and accessible shuttles.

- Do guests with disabilities have an equal opportunity to enjoy the services and amenities at the venue? This includes unobstructed sightlines blocked by railings or standing spectators, closed captioning for the hearing impaired, seating areas designated for a guest with sensory disability, ticket sales policies related to companion seating and resale, and access to services and amenities provided in concession areas and suites.
- Are their operational barriers to access and enjoyment? This includes website accessibility for the visually impaired, ticket sales policies, ADA policies, and staff training.

In addition to considering physical access for guests with mobility disabilities, it is important to consider how guests with sensory, auditory, or other invisible disabilities may experience the venue.

Ticketing Policies

The 2010 ADA standards established ticketing requirements governing accessibility for persons with disabilities. In the past, some public and private venues, ticket sellers, and distributors have not provided the same opportunity to purchase tickets for wheelchair-accessible seats and nonaccessible seats (U.S. Department of Justice, 2010). Up until 2010, direct ticket purchase options available to the public were not available to those with disabilities because transactions could not be completed. Patrons seeking accessible seating had to comply with a myriad of different ticket request policies and practices, resulting in either not being able to successfully purchase tickets or having to endure a particularly burdensome process.

Beginning on March 15, 2011, venues that sell tickets for assigned seats must implement policies to comply with the 2010 ADA ticketing requirements. The requirements shown in table 5.3 affect a variety of different policies and practices for sports

and recreation venues. A critical and often overlooked component of ensuring successful ADA compliance is comprehensive and ongoing ticket sales staff training. Venue and event managers must proactively consider the needs of customers with disabilities as a central feature of customer service and sales training. This will not only minimize the likelihood of ADA complaints but also attract a loyal customer base to the venue.

Service Animals

The ADA permits people with disabilities to bring their service animals into a sports facility in whatever areas customers are generally allowed. The ADA defines a service animal as any guide dog, signal dog, or other animal individually trained to provide assistance to an individual with a disability. Beginning in 2010, the only recognized service animal other than a dog is a miniature horse.

The ADA does not require licensure or certification to meet the definition of a service animal, and there is no national registry for service animals. The USDOJ specifically warns that "there are individuals and organizations that sell service animal certification or registration documents online. These documents do not convey any rights under the ADA, and the DOJ does not recognize them as proof that the dog is a service animal" (U.S. Department of Justice, 2015, p. 4). In situations where it is not obvious that the dog is a service animal, staff may ask only two specific questions: (1) Is the service animal required because of a disability? and (2) What work or task has the animal been trained to perform? Staff are not allowed to request any documentation for the animal, require that the animal demonstrate its task or inquire about the nature of the person's disability.

> Two questions staff may ask concerning service animals: (1) Is the animal required because of a disability? and (2) What work or task has the animal been trained to perform?

80 Introduction to Adaptive Sport and Recreation

TABLE 5.3 **ADA Ticketing Requirements, 2010 ADA Standards**

Practices impacted	Requirements
Ticket sales	Venues are required to sell tickets for accessible seats in the same manner and under the same conditions as all other ticket sales. Tickets for accessible seats must be sold during the same hours; through the same methods of purchase (by telephone, on-site, through a website, or through third-party vendors); and during the same stages of sales (presales, promotions, general sales, wait lists, or lotteries) as nonaccessible seats.
Ticket prices	Venues cannot charge higher prices for accessible seats than for nonaccessible seats in the same seating section. Venues must offer accessible seats in all price categories available to the public.
Identification and release of accessible seating	The information provided about accessible seats should be the same as nonaccessible seats, using the same text and visual representations. Generally, tickets for accessible seats may not be sold to members of the public. However, in three specific circumstances—typically involving sold-out sections, sold-out price categories, or sold-out events—unsold accessible seats may be released and sold to members of the public, but venues are not required to release unsold accessible seats.
Multiticket purchase and group sales	People purchasing a ticket for an accessible seat may purchase up to three additional seats for their companions in the same row, and these seats must be contiguous with the accessible seat. If a group includes one or more individuals who need accessible seating, the entire group should be seated together in an area that includes accessible seating.
Transfers and secondary markets	If venues permit patrons to give or sell their tickets to others, the same right must be extended to patrons with disabilities who hold tickets for accessible seats.
Fraud prevention	Venues cannot require proof of disability as a condition for purchasing tickets for accessible seats. Venues may ask purchasers to state that they require, or are purchasing tickets for someone who requires, the features of an accessible seat.

Adapted from U.S. Department of Justice (2010).

Service animals perform functions and tasks that the individual with a disability cannot perform for themselves. The task the dog performs must be directly related to the person's disability. Guide dogs are a common example of service animal used by those who are visually impaired. This is the type of service animal that is most familiar, but there are service animals that assist persons with other kinds of disabilities in their day-to-day activities as well. Some examples include alerting persons with hearing impairments to sounds, pulling wheelchairs or carrying and picking up things for persons with mobility impairments, assisting persons with mobility impairments with balance, or alerting a diabetic to a sudden change in blood sugar. A service animal is not a pet, and the ADA definition of a service animal excludes emotional support animals. This can raise questions if a patron indicates that their service animal helps them with their anxiety. The ADA makes a distinction between psychiatric service animals who are trained to sense an anxiety attack and take specific action to avoid the attack and emotional support animals whose mere presence provides comfort to a person who experiences anxiety.

The service animal must be permitted to accompany the individual with a disability to all areas of the facility where customers are normally allowed to go. A venue operator may also exclude a service animal from the facility when that animal's behavior poses a direct threat to the health or safety of others. For example, any service animal that displays vicious behavior toward other guests or customers may be excluded. Although a public accommodation may exclude any service animal that is out of control, it should give the individual with a disability who uses the service animal the option of continuing to enjoy its goods and services without having the service animal on the premises. Staff must also avoid making assumptions about how a particular animal is likely to behave based on past experiences with other animals. A guest may have a Doberman as a service animal, and it cannot be assumed that their service animal will be aggressive based on general knowledge about that particular breed of dog or past experiences with an aggressive Doberman. Each situation must be considered individually (individual inquiry paradigm). Staff should be trained properly on how to manage situations when customers seek entry with a service animal.

Website Accessibility

For many sports and recreation entities today, the website is the front door to the facility. Websites are likely to be the first interaction that guests will have with a venue or event. Many services have moved online, and people rely on web-based information to access goods and services. An inaccessible website can exclude people with disabilities to the same extent that steps at a doorway can deny them entry. USDOJ's guidance for web accessibility lists several examples of barriers, including poor color contrast, using color alone to communicate information, lack of text alternative (alt text) on images, no captions on videos, lack of screen readers for online forms, and mouse-only navigation, to name a few.

This is also one of the fastest-growing areas of ADA litigation (Kramer, 2015), and sport venue and event operators must be proactive in designing (redesigning) websites to ensure accessibility. The USDOJ has made web accessibility a priority and will more aggressively pursue these claims. For example, the Golden State Warriors had a class action suit filed against them alleging their online store violated the ADA because it was not fully accessible to blind and visually impaired consumers (Klein, 2021). The NHL's Anaheim Ducks and Minnesota Wild, the U.S. Tennis Association, and DraftKings have all faced ADA web accessibility lawsuits (Hayes, 2022; Jewett, 2022).

A few best practices to avoid lawsuits and fulfill obligations to patrons with disabilities are shown in the following list:

1. Regularly audit websites related to color contrast in text, text cues, alt text, video captions, online forms, text size and zoom capability, headings, and keyboard and mouse navigation.
2. Provide a reporting mechanism so users can report accessibility problems, and keep a log of the reports.
3. Post an accessibility statement prominently on the website identifying available resources and provide a contact person.
4. Integrate ADA web accessibility in staff training as an integral part of customer service, not just compliance.

Of course, it is important from a sales perspective that websites be attractive and that customers interact positively with them, but it is also critical under the ADA to ensure that guests with disabilities are able to fully access it.

Number and Placement of Wheelchair-Accessible Seating

The ADA requires wheelchair spaces and companion seats in proportion to the total available fixed seating in a venue.

For assembly areas, which would include stadiums, arenas, and grandstands, the minimum number of required wheelchair spaces is specified in 2010 ADA Standards (§ 221.2.1.1) and summarized in table 5.4. Wheelchair spaces must also be provided in luxury boxes, club seating, and suites (§ 221.2.12); team or player seating areas (§ 221.2.1.4); and are dispersed throughout the venue, providing spectators using wheelchairs with a choice of seating locations (§ 221.2.2 and 221.2.3).

The minimum number requirements and the dispersion requirements are separate. The minimum number requirement focuses on the total number of wheelchair-accessible seats available in the facility. The dispersion requirement looks at whether those accessible seats are sufficiently dispersed throughout the facility to afford a person using a wheelchair with equal access to a variety of seating locations. If a facility has sufficient wheelchair-accessible seats, but all the seats are located in the last row in a single section, the seats may not be adequately dispersed to satisfy the ADA wheelchair-accessible seating requirements. At least one companion seat must also be provided for each wheelchair space. The companion seat is a conventional seat that accommodates a friend or companion.

For a facility built before 1992, the 2010 ADA standards may not apply unless the facility is renovated or expands its structures or operations. The ADA distinguishes between *repairs* and *alterations* and requires a different standard of compliance under these circumstances. Simply making repairs to an older sport facility, such as replacing the roof, installing tile in a restroom, or refinishing a gymnasium floor, would not trigger the ADA's minimum accessible seating requirement. However, if the renovation project involves an *alteration* of an existing facility built before 1992, the areas being altered are subject to 2010 ADA standards. With a few exceptions, most professional sports venues in the United States have been altered or completely replaced with new stadiums or arenas and therefore are subject to the 2010 ADA standards. For high school, college, and community facilities, this may be a threshold question to determine first whether the venue to subject to the minimum accessible seating requirements and then whether they are compliant with the applicable rule. Best practice would be to aspire to the 2010 ADA standards, even if the venue was constructed before 1992.

Even for historic professional and collegiate sports venues, undertaking a major renovation will likely trigger ADA compliance with 2010 ADA standards. This was the situation Chicago Cub's famous Wrigley Field faced when it completed its $1 billion makeover only to be subject to a lawsuit alleging the renovations did not comply with 2010 ADA standards (Kozlarz, 2019). The

TABLE 5.4   **2010 ADA Standards for Wheelchair Spaces and Companion Seats**

Number of seats	Minimum number of required wheelchair spaces*
Less than 4	0
4 to 300	1-5 (see 2010 ADA Standards for breakdown)
301 to 500	6
501 to 5,000	6, + 1 for each 150 seats or fraction thereof between 501 and 5,000, e.g., 1,000-seat venue = 10
5,001 and over	36, + 1 for each 200, or fraction thereof more than 5,000, e.g., 10,000 seat venue = 61

*At least one companion seat for each wheelchair space must also be provided

complaint alleged that the stadium did not contain sufficient wheelchair-accessible seats and that the seats provided were not properly distributed through the venue. Wrigley Field had been exempted from 2010 ADA standards, but the scope of its renovation brought it under the new standards requiring substantially equivalent choice in seating locations and viewing angles (Kozlarz, 2019). In conjunction with the lawsuit, the USDOJ also launched an official review, and the Cubs promised to drastically improve the number and dispersion of seats by the 2020 season (Eadens, 2019; Kozlarz, 2019). However, the Cubs continued to face legal challenges and criticism. The team was sued by ticket holders who said the Cubs had eliminated general admission wheelchair seats that had excellent views and replaced them with the Budweiser Patio, group seating. Club areas in the lower grandstands were not accessible, and club areas in the upper deck lacked adequate sightlines over standing spectators. Most wheelchair-accessible seats were relocated to the last row of the newly constructed patio areas (Seidel, 2022). In 2022, the U.S. Attorney's office opened an investigation into the Cubs' ADA compliance.

The University of Michigan also encountered a legal challenge when it began a $226 million renovation of its football stadium (Wolverton, 2007). A group for veterans with disabilities sued, claiming people who used wheelchairs were being denied equal access to the stadium and that the University of Michigan was avoiding compliance with ADA requirements regarding the number and location of wheelchair seating in stadium. The renovation would add luxury suites; 3,200 club seats; and widen seating and aisles in the 107,501-seat stadium. Ultimately, the University of Michigan signed a consent agreement with the USDOJ and the disabled veterans group to resolve the lawsuit. By 2010, the stadium had a total wheelchair seating of 329, including companion seats and seats in multiple locations throughout the stadium (Gershman, 2008).

To avoid these disputes, include perspectives from customers who use wheelchairs for accessibility during the redesign and planning phases of renovations and even solicit a review and input from disability advocacy groups in the local community so that other accommodations are fully considered.

Sightlines

Sightlines for patrons in wheelchairs has been a central question under the USDOJ guides and in lawsuits against sport venues. The 2010 ADA standards include a requirement that people who use wheelchairs are provided with a choice of seating locations and viewing angles that are substantially equivalent to, or better than, those available to all other spectators. The 2010 ADA standards further provide that when spectators are expected to stand during events, spectators seated in wheelchair spaces shall be afforded lines of sight *over the shoulders and between the heads* of seated spectators in the first row in front of wheelchair spaces (USDOJ, 2010, § 802.2). If standing spectators are provided lines of sight over the heads of spectators standing in the first row in front of their seats, spectators seated in wheelchair spaces shall be afforded lines of sight over the heads of standing spectators in the first row in front of wheelchair spaces (USDOJ, 2010, § 802.2.2).

Several federal appellate circuit courts have struggled to interpret what exactly comparable lines of sight entail under the 2010 ADA standards. The Oregon federal district court (*Independent Living Resources v. Oregon Arena Corp.*, 1997) and the Third Circuit (*Caruso v. Blockbuster-Sony Music Entertainment Centre at the Waterfront*, 1999), concluded that USDOJ regulations do not require lines of sight over standing spectators. However, the D.C. Circuit (*Paralyzed Veterans of America v. D.C. Arena L.P.*, 1997), the Minnesota federal district court (*United States v. Ellerbe Becket Inc.*, 1997) held that 100% of accessible seating did not need sightlines over standing spectators; instead, substantial compliance was sufficient.

Sightlines for spectators using wheelchairs should be substantially equivalent to, or better than, those available to all other spectators.
Nobuo Yano/Getty Images Sport

In 2008, Robert Miller, a NASCAR fan who is a quadriplegic and uses a wheelchair, attended three to six events a year at the California Speedway in Fontana. Miller's view of the track and the cars from his viewing area in the grandstand was regularly blocked by fans standing immediately in front of him. Unable to fully enjoy his spectator experience, Miller filed suit, claiming that California Speedway had violated Title III of the ADA. The district court dismissed Miller's case, finding that the USDOJ guidelines requiring lines of sight over standing spectators was perhaps a good recommendation but was not entitled to judicial deference as part of the regulatory scheme for the ADA (*Miller v. California Speedway Corp.*, 2006). The Ninth Circuit reversed the district court and held that it is perfectly reasonable to interpret the term "lines of sight comparable to those for members of the general public" as requiring lines of sight that are comparable in the actual conditions under which a facility operates. If spectators are widely expected to stand during the key moments of an event—from the singing of the national anthem to the fourth quarter—it does not take a fertile legal imagination to understand that relatively immobile patrons will not have a comparable line of sight. The court finally stated that "the regulatory scheme at issue in this case is complex, but our conclusion is simple: The USDOJ's interpretation of its own regulation is reasonable and therefore entitled to substantial deference" (*Miller v. California Speedway Corp*, 2008).

Since *Miller*, the prevailing practice was to provide sightlines that enabled patrons in wheelchair spaces to be able to see over the shoulders and between the heads of spectators standing in the row directly in front of them. Yet another court considered this issue in 2021 in *Landis v. Wash. State Major Baseball Pub. Facilities Dist. Baseball of Seattle* (2021). In *Landis*, the plaintiff challenged inadequate sightlines over standing spectators at T-Mobile Park, home of Major League Baseball's Seattle Mariners. Central to the *Landis* case was the dueling sightline requirements of 1991 ADA standards and 2010 ADA standards. The parties agreed the 1991 ADA standards applied and that it was also appropriate to apply the USDOJ 1996 TAM, *Accessible Stadiums*. The U.S. Department of Justices (n.d.a). guide *Accessible Stadiums* requires that a person using a wheelchair have comparable sightlines over standing spectators only when two requirements are met:

1. A person using a wheelchair must be able to see the playing surface *between the heads and over the shoulders* of the *persons standing in the row immediately in front*.
2. A person using a wheelchair must be able to see the playing surface *over the heads* of the *persons standing two rows in front*.

At the appellate level, this case turned into largely a procedural one, focused on administrative deference to federal agency's interpretations of its own guidelines, similar to the substantial deference used in *Miller*. The appellate court ultimately held the district court's deference to the *Accessible Stadiums* guidance was appropriate because the parties stipulated it. However, the court of appeals does note that the validity of *Accessible Stadiums* may be properly raised in the future. The 2010 ADA standards do not expressly include the second requirement from *Accessible Stadiums*. Instead, it requires that patrons in wheelchair spaces be provided lines of sight comparable to the lines of sight for standing spectators. Thus, *Landis* does insert some uncertainty into what the precise legal standard is for providing comparable lines of sight for spectators in wheelchair spaces and whether the 2010 ADA Standards have

essentially replaced the 1991 ADA standards and the 1996 *Accessible Stadiums* TAM.

Assistive Devices

Patrons with visual or hearing impairments are entitled to assistive devices that will give them equal access to the services and amenities of sports venues. These assistive devices may include listening devices, closed captioning, and braille signage. The DOJ's guidelines for accessible stadiums provide that when audible communications are integral to the use of a stadium, assistive listening systems are required for people who are hearing and visually impaired (U.S. Department of Justice, n.d.). Additional changes as part of the *2010 ADA Standards for Accessible Design* went into effect in 2012. Assisted listening devices amplify and deliver sound to a special receiver worn by the spectator or to their hearing aid, depending on the type of system used. The stadium must provide receivers for the assistive listening system. The number of available receivers must equal 4% of the total number of seats. Further, signs must be provided to notify spectators of the availability of receivers for the assistive listening system. Given that new stadiums are frequently multipurpose facilities that also host concerts, conventions, and other events, venue managers must be aware that the ADA standards require any facility to have a permanently installed assistive listening system.

Closed captioning demonstrates how facilities can further help deaf and hearing-impaired patrons more fully enjoy the services and experiences of attending a sporting event (Peers, 2018). Closed captioning can be made available on video boards and concourse televisions. In 2006, patron Shane Feldman and two other plaintiffs sued Pro Football, Inc. and WFI Stadium Inc, the operators of the Washington Redskins (now Washington Commanders) and FedEx Field. The plaintiffs, who are deaf or hearing impaired, argued that the ADA obligated the team and stadium to provide auxiliary aids such as closed captioning at their football games. Before the 2006 football season, FedEx Field did not caption any announcements made over its public address system. The team or stadium had offered listening devices to fans who requested one; however, Feldman did not benefit from an assistive listening device. In September 2008, the Maryland federal district court ruled that the ADA requires facility operators to provide deaf or hearing-impaired fans equal access to the aural information broadcast over the stadium public address system (*Feldman v. Pro Football, Inc.,* 2008). This information includes music with lyrics, game commentary, advertisements, referee calls, and safety and emergency information.

Related to web accessibility discussed previously is the requirement to ensure that team smartphone apps are screen reader–friendly for guests with visual disabilities. A screen reader allows visually impaired individuals to use apps by reading the subsequent banners and headings to help assist with navigation. An example of this type of case was seen with the San Jose Sharks and their mobile app, San Jose Sharks + SAP Center, which was introduced to improve fan engagement and experiences. However, this mobile app was not screen reader–friendly, and when concerned visually impaired patrons raised the problems, the Sharks did nothing. The suit filed against the Sharks in 2019 called for equal access to the digital fan experience via websites and mobile apps (*Salsiccia v. Sharks Sports & Entertainment LLC,* 2019).* The digital fan experience is becoming increasingly important for sport venues and event operators; therefore, they must ensure that their interactive promotions, websites, and mobile apps meet ADA accessibility guidelines.

Summary

This chapter provided a brief history of the disability rights movement and the importance of that movement to the adoption of international treaties and national laws to recognize and protect the rights of persons with disabilities. For the sport and recreation managers in the 21st century, understanding the legal requirements applicable to programs, policies, operating practices, and venues will enable avoiding disability discrimination claims and ensure that guests and customers with disabilities are able to enjoy and fully participate in your programs and services. This chapter illustrates the importance of being a proactive facility manager to ensure ADA compliance. Many components of a sport event or a sports venue can serve as barriers to people with disabilities. In addition to understanding the legal requirements, considering how your guests experience your events and being responsive to requests made by patrons with disabilities can also avoid many legal claims as well as dissatisfied customers.

CRITICAL THINKING EXERCISES

1. Facts versus assumptions: For this exercise, read each statement and try to determine whether it sounds like an objective fact or a stereotype or assumption. This can be completed alone or with a study partner.

    ◦ A student with a disability is more likely to be injured when playing a contact sport than a student without a disability; therefore, we should not risk allowing them to participate.
    ◦ A student with a hearing disability is not capable of participating in basketball since they cannot hear their coach's instructions during the game.
    ◦ A track and field athlete who uses a wheelchair poses a safety risk to other runners on the track and therefore should not participate alongside runners who are not using wheelchairs.

As you determine whether these statements reflect known facts versus assumptions or stereotypes, also consider whether any modifications to the activities would alter your assessment of the "truth" of the statement.

2. You are the gate and ticket manager for your high school athletics department. A parent arrives at your gate during a football game seeking entry with a small dog. The dog is wearing a halter with "Service Dog" emblazoned on it. Your gate attendant asked whether the dog was a service animal under the ADA and what service the animal was trained to provide. The patron said, "It helps me with my anxiety and keeps me calm." The parent insists that she has registered the dog as a service animal with a national service dog registry and even presents an official decal and membership card validating her registration with the National Service Animal Registry (nsarco.com). Based on the responses, the gate attendant felt that the dog was an emotional support animal, not a service animal, and denied entry for the parent. The parent has sent a letter to the school asserting that denying access to her was a violation of her rights under the ADA.

   ◦ Is the high school football game a place of public accommodation? Why or why not?
   ◦ Does it appear your gate attendant properly denied the fan entry to the stadium based on your understanding of the difference between service animals and emotional support animals? Explain your conclusion and be sure and demonstrate (1) your understanding of how to differentiate service animals and emotional support animals under the ADA and (2) what actions of the gate attendant were or were not appropriate under the ADA.
   ◦ How would you respond to the parent? What steps would you take to ensure that parents understand your access policies for service animals?

3. Select any large multipurpose sports venue for this exercise. Locate that venue's main webpage. Using the criteria discussed in the Website Accessibility section, conduct an accessibility audit for the website to determine if the website would be accessible for patrons with disabilities. In addition to evaluating its accessibility, using a consumer lens to consider whether the website provides sufficient information for patrons with disabilities related to (1) ticket purchases, (2) availability of accessibility services, and (3) the range or types of accessibility services available. Prepare a brief memo of your findings and conclusions.

CHAPTER 6

Media and Disability Sport

Erin Pearson, MA, and Laura Misener, PhD

> **LEARNING OBJECTIVES**
>
> After reading this chapter, you will be able to do the following:
>
> - Discuss the history of disability sport coverage.
> - Identify the dominant frames and narratives the media has used to represent disability sport.
> - Compare and contrast media personnel perspectives versus athlete perspectives of disability sport media coverage.
> - Discuss the challenges and opportunities for future disability sport coverage.

This chapter examines the history and current trends of disability sport media coverage with a specific focus on Paralympic media coverage. It demonstrates how disability sport coverage has evolved from complete invisibility in media coverage to the growth of coverage in and outside the time frame of the Paralympic Games. It discusses the dominant ways the media has represented athletes with disabilities and the different approaches media have used to cover disability sport. The conflicting history of media personnel perspectives versus athlete perspectives of how disability sport should be represented is highlighted. Finally, it describes the challenges and opportunities for future directions of disability sport coverage that is proportionate to able-bodied sports coverage.

Introduction

Interest in disability sport is demonstrated by the growth of disability sport representation in the mainstream media and popular press. The Tokyo 2020 Paralympic Games, for example, had the most comprehensive broadcast and digital coverage to date. Coverage featuring Paralympic sport increased in the number of broadcast hours, live streaming options, and digital shows on social media platforms such as Facebook and X (formerly known as Twitter). NBC reported the highest number of viewers on average in the United States at 1.2 million, nearly doubling the 2016 Paralympic Games average of 640,000 viewers (NBC, 2021). There have also been advances outside of the Paralympic Games broadcasting, such as the release of Netflix's documentary *Rising Phoenix* in 2021, featuring stories of the Paralympic movement and of Paralympic athletes.

The increase in the quantity of coverage across diverse mainstream media platforms is significant for disability sport growth, which has been absent from mainstream sports media coverage. But this increase is not the only metric by which to measure positive trends in disability sports coverage;

the *quality* of coverage must be considered as well. Historically, when the media has represented disability, it has been in negative, stereotypical ways. This is concerning for the lived experience for people with disabilities because the media can affect public attitudes toward disability (Goodley, 2011). The World Health Organization (2011) highlighted how the lived experiences of people with disabilities are often linked to negative attitudes about disability, which can affect how people with disabilities participate in different aspects of everyday life (e.g., employment, education, recreation). It is, therefore, critical that the media represent people with disabilities in nonstereotypical ways.

> It is critical that the media represent people with disabilities in nonstereotypical ways.

Media Representation of Disability

In 2006, the United Nations introduced the *Convention on the Rights of Persons with Disabilities* (CRPD) to guarantee the rights of persons with disabilities in all spheres of life, including sport, and via media representation. The CRPD states that "disability is an evolving concept and that disability results from the interaction between persons with impairments, and attitudinal and environmental barriers that hinders their full and effective participation in society on an equal basis with others" (United Nations, 2006, p. 21). For example, Article 30 recognizes the rights of persons with disabilities in cultural life, recreation, leisure, sport, and tourism. People with disabilities should, therefore, have the right to participate on an equal basis, and this includes having access to a television. Furthermore, Article 8 encourages "all organs of the media to portray persons with disabilities in a manner consistent with the purpose of the present

Convention" (United Nations, 2006, p. 10). Yet, significant barriers to sport participation (e.g., inaccessible facilities, lack of transportation) remain, and stereotypes of disability are prevalent in disability sport media representation.

Although 16% of the world's population identifies as having a disability (WHO, 2023), media coverage of people with disabilities remains scarce, and when they are represented in the media, they are often anchored in disability stereotypes. This issue of representing disability in the media is not unique to disability sports coverage but includes disability coverage in general. Barnes' (1992) early work examined how the media use of imagery and language has negative implications for people with disabilities and impairments. Barnes (1992) emphasized a need for media outlets to use language that empowers people with disabilities rather than language that stereotypes and discriminates against them. In addition, Cumberbatch and Negrine's (1992) work found 10 main ways in which people with disabilities have been represented in television:

1. Disability or handicap as an emblem of evil
2. The disabled as monsters
3. Disability as a loss of one's humanity
4. Disability as total dependency and lack of self-determination
5. The image of the disabled as a maladjusted person
6. Disability with compensation or substitute gift
7. Disability leading to courageousness or achievement
8. Disability and sexuality: as sexual menace, deviancy, and danger stemming from loss of control
9. Disability as an object of fun or pity
10. The disabled as an object of charity

Cumberbatch and Negrine's (1992) findings demonstrated that people with disabilities had rarely been represented in a positive manner. These portrayals of people with disabilities on television continue to reinforce negative stereotypes of disability and reflect the dominant way society has historically understood disability—that is, through the medical model. According to the medical model, disability is understood as "any lack of ability resulting from impairment to perform an activity within the range considered normal for a person" (Smith & Bundon, 2018, p. 16). Therefore, within this model, disability is understood as a medical condition that needs to be "fixed" for a person to be considered "normal." The medical model fails to consider other factors for disability, such as social, political, or environmental factors that may contribute to disablement. This medicalized understanding of defining disability extends to the ways the Paralympic Games were first formalized and consequently how athletes with disabilities have been represented in coverage.

Media Representation of Disability Sport and the Paralympic Games

The Paralympic Games were formed by able-bodied medical professionals and sport administrators, which has influenced the way Paralympic sport continues to be covered by the media. As mentioned in chapter 4, the origins of disability sport are intimately tied to the medical profession because Dr. Ludwig Guttmann, a German neurologist at Stoke Mandeville Hospital in England, embraced sport as part of rehabilitative practice for ex-military personnel with spinal cord injuries (Legg & Steadward, 2011; Wedgwood, 2014). Guttmann understood disability through the lens of the medical model and used sport as a tool to rehabilitate or even complement an individual's physical impairment so they could successfully integrate back into society (Wedgwood, 2014). Guttmann viewed engagement in the Stoke Mandeville Games as participation rather than sporting competition (Legg & Steadward, 2011). Participants in the Stoke Mandeville Games were referred to as patients

rather than as athletes or competitors in his sporting event (Legg & Steadward, 2011).

> **The origins of disability sport are intimately tied to the medical profession.**

The ninth edition of that sporting event was held in 1960 in Rome and is considered to be the first official Paralympic Games (Legg & Steadward, 2011). The first "modern" Paralympic Games occurred in 1988 in Seoul and was hosted in the same venue and year as the Olympic Games (Howe, 2008a). This was the first time the Olympic and Paralympic Games were hosted in the same location since 1964. The 1988 Seoul Paralympic Games signified an increase in professionalism of disability sport and marked the beginning of a shift away from medicalized discourses of disability sport (Howe, 2008a). Athletes competing at the Paralympic Games began to be seen as athletes competing in elite sporting competitions rather than patients participating in rehabilitative exercise (Howe, 2008a).

The 2000 Paralympic Games in Sydney marked the first occurrence where both the Olympic and Paralympic Games were marketed together as one entity (Howe, 2008a). The partnership formed between the International Paralympic Committee and International Olympic Committee helped shift the Paralympic movement into its current form as an elite mega-sporting competition (Howe, 2008a). The Sydney Paralympic Games broke ticket sales records and was covered by 2,300 accredited members of the media (Howe, 2008a; Legg & Steadward, 2011). The success of the Sydney Paralympic Games led other news organizations to make efforts to view Paralympic sport more seriously (Goggin & Hutchins, 2017). The success of the 2000 Sydney Paralympic Games also sparked an uptick in the number of researchers interested in examining media representations of the Paralympic Games and of Paralympic athletes (Rees et al., 2019).

The 2000 Sydney Paralympic Games marked an increase in researchers who began to focus their attention on examining how the media represents athletes with disabilities and disability sport during the Paralympic Games. Goggin and Newell's (2000) investigation of media representation of the 2000 Sydney Paralympic Games was one of the first studies to specifically address media representation of Paralympic athletes with only one study before 2000 cited in their research. Since the turn of the century, researchers have explored how athletes with disabilities have been represented (Beacom et al., 2016; Rees et al., 2019). The following section is a brief overview of the main ways athletes with disabilities have been represented in Paralympic coverage and trends toward positive representations. Figure 6.1 outlines the four frames of representation that will be discussed.

Stereotypical Frame

Researchers have consistently found that stereotypical representations of disability, rooted in medical understandings of disability, have been the dominant way Paralympic athletes have been represented in coverage (Howe, 2011; Maika & Danylchuk, 2016; Peers, 2012; Silva & Howe, 2012; Tynedal & Wolbring, 2013). This **stereotypical frame** represents Paralympic athletes' involvement in the Paralympic Games as participatory as opposed to representing them as high-performing, elite athletes commonly seen in able-bodied sport such as the Olympic Games (Pearson & Misener, 2019). Limited focus is placed on athletic results or capabilities, and instead the focus is primarily on celebrating athletes for their ability to overcome their disability to participate in the Games, often celebrating them as superhuman or heroic for doing so or by justifying their success by making comparisons to able-bodied counterparts. The most common stereotypical representations scholars found are (1) supercrip, (2) overcoming, (3) cyborg, (4) passive victim, and (5) comparison narratives:

1. *Supercrip.* The supercrip narrative is the most common stereotype for Paralympic athletes. The **supercrip narrative**, also called the *superhuman narrative*, frames a Paralympic athlete as a hero, or like a superhuman, for being able to "overcome" their disability to achieve success (Silva & Howe, 2012). Marketing campaigns for the Paralympic Games have commonly used the supercrip narrative to sell the Games to a larger audience. Examples of marketing campaigns focusing on the supercrip narrative include the Superatleta campaign

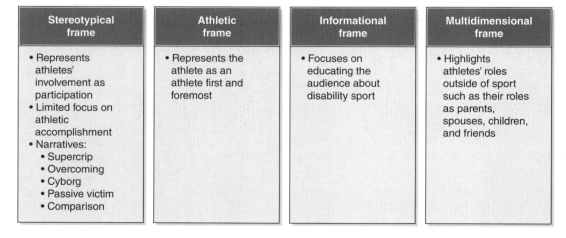

FIGURE 6.1 Four frames used to represent athletes with disabilities in the media.

at the 2008 Olympics in Beijing, the United Kingdom's Meet the Superhumans campaign in 2012 and We're the Superhumans in 2016, and Canada's #ParaTough Campaign in 2016 (Pearson & Misener, 2022). The problem with using the supercrip narrative in media and marketing campaigns for the Paralympic Games is that it reinforces ableism by downplaying the bodily experience of disability for Paralympic athletes. This can distance and misrepresent the everyday lived experiences of people with disabilities from those who do not have the resources, capacity, or desire to achieve "superhuman" status (Cherney & Lindemann, 2019; Silva & Howe, 2012).

2. *Overcoming.* Often categorized with the supercrip narrative, the **overcoming narrative** reflects the idea that an athlete must overcome their disability (through individual and internal motivation) to achieve success (Pearson & Misener, 2019). The difference between the overcoming narrative and the supercrip narrative is that it does not formally give "superhuman" status or use that specific "super" or "hero" language in marketing and coverage. In particular, the overcoming narrative emphasizes feelings of pity, with the audience presenting the Paralympic Games as a form of therapeutic technique rather than an elite sporting competition. For example, the official song of the 2000 Sydney Paralympic Games was "Being Here." The song was written to evoke sympathy with the audience by promoting the idea that just simply "being here" to "participate" in the Paralympic Games was enough of an accomplishment (Darcy, 2003). The overcoming narrative thus disempowers Paralympic athletes by not recognizing their athletic prowess, dedication, and strength for training and competing in the Paralympic Games. Like the supercrip narrative, it misrepresents the lived experience of people with disabilities by further marginalizing those who are unable to fulfill these preconceived roles about ability or overcoming impairment.

3. *Cyborg.* A **cyborg** is a hybrid body made of organism and machine (Haraway, 1991; Hartnett, 2000). The cyborg narrative is commonly used in media representation and marketing of the Paralympic Games when featuring athletes with movement-enhancing technology, such as prosthetics, wheelchairs, and other mobility devices (Howe, 2017). The **cyborg narrative** focuses on a Paralympic athlete's prosthetics or mobility devices as the central story rather than focusing on their athletic ability or achievements (Howe, 2011). Cyborg bodies have been the most celebrated by the public and featured in the media representation of disability sport (Howe, 2017). One example is the popularity (and fall) of South African Oscar Pistorius, who was marketed as "Blade Runner" and "the fastest man on no legs" (Howe, 2011; Swartz & Watermyer, 2008). This narrative is problematic because it creates a hierarchy of disability within coverage: those with visible disabilities are celebrated and featured more in coverage than those with invisible or greater impairments.

4. *Passive victim.* The **passive victim narrative** is intrinsically linked with medical understandings of disability and uses language such as "tragedy," "suffering," and "afflicted by" to describe a Paralympic athlete's disability in coverage (Howe, 2008b; Maika & Danylchuk, 2016). The passive victim narrative is also demonstrated in visual images of the Paralympic Games such as showing Paralympic athletes in passive positions rather than in active positions (Peers, 2012). An example of passive position may show an athlete

sitting on the sidelines of their sport competition rather than showing an action shot of the athlete competing within their sport. The passive victim narrative is problematic because it reinforces medical understandings of disability by reinforcing Paralympic athletes' participation at the Paralympic Games as therapeutic rather than participating in an elite sporting competition.

5. *Comparison.* Finally, the **comparison narrative** focuses on stories that compare Paralympic athletes to able-bodied athletes, often with Olympic athletes who competed in a similar event, to justify or explain their athletic success (Pearson & Misener, 2019). For example, Paralympic athletes might be marketed or celebrated as "Olympians 2.0." This appears to be a way for the media to justify the success of a Paralympic athlete and explain their success to an able-bodied audience as opposed to celebrating a Paralympic athlete's athletic abilities in their own rights.

Athletic Frame

Scholars have begun to see a positive shift away from stereotypical representations being used within disability sport coverage to primarily focusing on athletic achievement (Maika & Danylchuk, 2016; Pearson & Misener, 2019; Pullen et al., 2018). The **athletic frame**, also called athlete-first representation, focuses on representing an athlete as an athlete first. For example, the media may describe the sport events as competitions, highlighting an athlete's training and dedication to athletic excellence, or report on athletic accomplishments and results in coverage (Maika & Danylchuk, 2016; Pearson & Misener, 2019). This is the primary way able-bodied athletes and able-bodied sport has been and continues to be represented within sports coverage and marketing campaigns.

> Scholars have begun to see a positive shift away from stereotypical representations being used within disability sport coverage to primarily focusing on athletic achievement.

Informational Frame

The stereotypical and athletic frames are the two most common ways athletes with disabilities have been represented in disability sport coverage. The informational frame is an additional trend being included within Paralympic media coverage. The **informational frame** refers to the coverage of the Paralympic Games and of Paralympic athletes that focuses on educating the audience about parasport and the Paralympic movement (Pearson & Misener, 2019). The informational frame also includes articles Paralympic athletes write as a mechanism for them to share their stories via a media company's platform. For example, this may include educating the audience on the classification process in parasport, the rules of certain parasport events, or "Player's Own Voice" pieces. Howe and Silva (2012) argued that "media coverage must play a crucial educative role in increasing public knowledge on the specificities of the Paralympics, namely, classification, new sports, records, and performances to develop informed and educated audience" (p. 191). To build a fan base for disability sport, the audience must understand the rules and regulations of adaptive sport.

Multidimensional Frame

Finally, the **multidimensional frame** is emerging as an alternative feature in disability media coverage focusing on highlighting a Paralympic athlete's nonathletic roles. For example, stories using the multidimensional frame discuss their roles as parents, spouses, children, and friends to connect with the audience. Quinn and Yoshida (2016) first introduced this frame. It is important because it can help create role models for other people with similar impairments and represent Paralympic athletes as having full lives outside of sport. These backstories are often included in able-bodied sports coverage and have been absent from disability sports coverage.

Intersections of Ableism and Gender in Coverage

In addition to the main frames used to represent disability, scholars have found that ableist and gendered stereotypes are commonly reinforced in coverage via the language, visual images, and location of content media used to represent Paralympic athletes (Pearson & Misener, 2019; Pullen et al., 2018; Rees et al., 2018). Researchers have found that a hierarchy exists in disability representation in sports coverage based on an athlete's impairment, sport, and gender (Haller, 2000; Pearson & Misener, 2019; Quinn & Yoshida, 2016). DePauw (1997) explained this hierarchy in the example that male-identifying wheelchair athletes typically receive more coverage than other athletes due to society's ableist and gendered understandings that sport is a masculine and physical. The disability sports with the most coverage tend to be those that are also popular in able-bodied sport, such as basketball and rugby. Thus, on a spectrum of impairment, Paralympic athletes that are "more" able, are male, and compete in common able-bodied sports (e.g., wheelchair basketball) have historically received more coverage (Rees et al., 2019). This singular type of representation is problematic because it does not reflect the diversity of the Paralympic sport community (Quinn & Yoshida, 2016). For example, it fails to represent women, athletes who compete in nonmainstream sports, and athletes who are "less" able, marginalizing them from coverage.

Ableist and gendered stereotypes are also further reinforced through using stereotypical frames. Athletes who use technologies are often featured more than athletes without technologies by using the cyborg narrative (Howe, 2011). Pearson and Misener (2019) found that the media favored visual images of athletes who used technologies (e.g., wheelchairs or prosthetics) and whose impairment was almost invisible from visual representation (e.g., athletes who are "more" able). Ableism is thereby also commonly reinforced in Paralympic media coverage when the media uses images that do not feature or include an athlete's impairment (Bruce, 2014; Crow, 2014; Pearson & Misener, 2019; Schell & Rodriguez, 2001). In addition to the cyborg narrative, scholars found that the passive victim narrative was also commonly reinforced in visual images by the media primarily featuring athletes in passive positions (Pearson & Misener, 2019). Passive positions are used more often for women athletes, and action shots are more often used for male athletes in coverage (Brookes, 2019). Pearson and Misener (2019) found that this is beginning to change because both men and women athletes received an equal amount of coverage and framing across passive versus action images more recently. However, the coverage quality was not equal in terms of men receiving more multidimensional views of the self and language describing their athleticism first and foremost (Pearson & Misener, 2019).

Female Paralympic athletes face **double discrimination** (also known as *double jeopardy* or *double whammy*) within disability sport and coverage. This double discrimination can be explained as the discrimination women with disabilities face based on ableist and gendered stereotypes in society. Some women athletes with disabilities called their experience a "double whammy" when discussing the complexities they have faced as being a woman and having a disability in sport (Blinde & McCalister, 1999). This historically has resulted in female Paralympic athletes receiving less coverage than their male counterparts because they do not fit the hegemonic understandings of a sporting body on the aspects of masculinity and physicality (DePauw, 1997). When female Paralympic athletes have been included, scholars have found that they are often represented in a

Female Paralympic athletes face discrimination based on both ableist and gendered stereotypes.
Yang Zhisen/Xinhua via Getty Images

unidimensional view of the self and asexualized (Hardin & Hardin, 2005; Pearson & Misener, 2019; Quinn & Yoshida, 2016). This is beginning to change with more women Paralympic athletes becoming sexualized like women able-bodied athletes in representation. *ESPN The Magazine*'s Body Issue has presented overly gendered and sexualized images of women Paralympic athletes (Weaving & Samson, 2018) and highlighted this portrayal in recent coverage of the Paralympic Games (Pearson & Misener, 2019, 2022). This finding reflects a positive shift from the full exclusion of women Paralympic athletes from media coverage. However, this shift ultimately demonstrates that female Paralympic athletes are also now subjected to the same problems as their able-bodied counterparts because gender is viewed as incongruent with dominant understandings of the ideal sporting body (DePauw, 1997).

Competing Perspectives of Disability Sports Coverage

With an understanding of how athletes with disabilities have traditionally been represented in media coverage, it is important to consider (1) why the media has represented athletes with disabilities in these ways, and (2) what athletes think of such representations.

Media Personnel Perspectives of Coverage

The tendency to represent athletes with disabilities in stereotypical ways is based on the media's effort to provide an audience with palatable, ableist understandings of disability sport (Purdue & Howe, 2012). Using stereotypical representations in coverage may reflect the media's struggle to understand disability in nonmedicalized terms when covering Paralympic sport (Howe, 2008b; Purdue & Howe, 2012). People with disabilities have historically been largely underrepresented within media organizations (Brittain, 2004; Haralambos & Holborn, 2000). Because able-bodied people hold key positions within media organizations and institutions, representations of people with disabilities are defined by those with no or minimal experience of disability or disability sport (Brittain, 2004; Haralambos & Holborn, 2000). Researchers have found that, historically, media personnel covering the Paralympic Games have little or no experience with disability or knowledge of disability sport (Howe 2008b; Misener, 2013). Media personnel have also been shown to provide a lower status to reporting on disability sport, compared to able-bodied sports, by framing it as lesser, unimportant, and not "true" sports competition (Golden, 2003; Thomas & Smith, 2009).

> **People with disabilities have historically been largely underrepresented within media organizations.**

Researchers are seeing notable shifts by media toward representing athletes with disability and disability sport in nonstereotypical ways (e.g., Maika & Danylchuk, 2016; Pearson & Misener, 2019; Pullen et al., 2018). This shift began after the success of the 2000 Sydney Paralympic Games when media personnel started to address the "deeply embedded journalistic practices and perceptions, such as news values, the role of the journalist, approach to sources, and audience appeal and interest" of covering Paralympic sport (Goggin & Hutchins, 2017, p. 226). Researchers found that media personnel began trying to report on the Paralympic Games in an enlightened manner by featuring disability sport as elite sporting competition (Golden, 2003). The shift

toward seeing fewer stereotypical narratives in media representation of the Paralympic Games, however, did not result in tangible changes until the 2012 Paralympic Games. Scholars at this time began seeing a shift toward athlete-first coverage as the primary way to represent Paralympic athletes in their examinations of Paralympic media coverage for the 2012 and 2016 Paralympic Games (Maika & Danylchuk, 2016; Pearson & Misener, 2019). This was also when media companies such as Channel 4 (C4) in the United Kingdom and the Canadian Broadcasting Company (CBC) in Canada (i.e., the official broadcasters for the Paralympic Games) publicly recognized and began to work toward improving Paralympic media coverage on their platforms (Beacom et al., 2016; CBC Media Centre, 2017; Pullen et al., 2018). Both networks provided greater quantity of coverage (e.g., increased broadcast hours, broadcasting across diverse mediums) and quality of coverage (e.g., athlete-first representation; Beacom et al., 2016; CBC Media Centre, 2017; Pullen et al., 2018).

Despite these positive shifts toward increasing the quantity and quality of coverage, research demonstrates that stereotypical narratives remain common in coverage. The tension media companies demonstrate by declaring a dedication to providing empowering coverage yet portraying Paralympic athletes in stereotypical ways can be understood as the Paralympic Paradox. The term **Paralympic Paradox** was coined by scholars Purdue and Howe (2012) to explain this tension that exists when covering disability sport. When athletes with disabilities are represented in a way that highlights their athleticism and not their disability, it may be seen as empowering for people with and without disabilities watching the Paralympic Games. Yet, athletes with disabilities are often desired to be represented as role models within the disability community by foregrounding their disability in representation. Paralympic stakeholders expressed this tension and the complexities of navigating the Paralympic Paradox when covering the Paralympic Games (Purdue & Howe, 2012).

Some stakeholders thought that media should only report on sport and not on an athlete's disability. Other stakeholders, however, believed the focus should include both the sport and disability in Paralympic media coverage (Purdue & Howe, 2012).

Athlete Perspectives of Coverage

Such a paradox presents the question: What do athletes with disabilities think of the stereotypical representations in coverage and the tensions of navigating athlete-first coverage? More importantly, how do athletes with disabilities want to be represented in media coverage? The following section provides an overview of athletes' perspectives on both the quantity of coverage and the quality of disability sports coverage.

Quantity of Coverage

The quantity of disability sports coverage has been a consistent topic of discussion with athletes. Brittain (2004) found that Paralympic athletes who competed at the 2000 Sydney Paralympic Games were unhappy with the lack of the media coverage. This trend has continued, with athletes continuing to report disappointment in the lack of coverage that exists compared to coverage of able-bodied sport. Although positive increases have been made with the increase in coverage compared to coverage provided for the 2000 Sydney Paralympic Games, a gap remains in terms of the quantity compared to the Olympic Games. For example, for the 2020 Tokyo Summer Olympic and Paralympic Games, CBC (the official broadcaster for the Olympic and Paralympic Games in Canada) provided 3,775 hours of broadcast coverage for the Olympic Games (CBC Sports, 2021). In comparison, CBC provided 120 hours of television coverage and more than 1,000 additional hours of live streaming coverage via its multiple platforms for the Paralympic Games (CBC Media Centre, 2021). Pearson and Misener (2022) examined Canadian Paralympic athletes' perspectives of Paralympic media coverage. Paralympic athletes discussed seeing the positive changes in the increase of coverage over time, but they hoped to see increases in coverage proportionate to able-bodied sports. For example, the athletes discussed hoping to see increases in the quantity of coverage across diverse platforms such as live streams (e.g., what CBC is providing), social media platforms (e.g., TikTok, Instagram, X, Facebook, and YouTube), and seeing representation outside the media time frame of when the Games take place (Pearson & Misener, 2022). Coverage outside the Paralympic Games has increased but still largely remains minimal or absent in comparison to able-bodied sports coverage.

Why is increasing the quantity of disability sports coverage important? Brittain (2004) found that Paralympic athletes "felt that greater coverage in the media would both change perceptions of their abilities as sportspeople as well as encourage more people with disabilities to take up sport" (p. 445). Pearson and Misener (2022) also found that some athletes felt that proportionate representation would provide them with the same level of "normalcy" or opportunities that are afforded to able-bodied athletes. However, no amount of increase in the quantity of disability sports coverage will have such positive effects without changes in the quality of coverage away from stereotypical representations of disability (Brittain, 2004; Pearson & Misener, 2022).

Quality of Coverage

Researchers have found that athletes with disabilities have rejected stereotypical representations in disability sports media coverage (e.g., Brooke & Khoo, 2021; Hargreaves & Hardin, 2009; Pearson & Misener, 2022). In addition, Howe (2008b, 2011) and Peers (2009, 2012) are both scholars and Paralympic athletes and have argued against the use of stereotypical discourses within disability sports coverage. They suggest that stereotypical representations provide a singular perspective of disability experiences, resulting in the loss of an opportunity for media to "acknowledge the pervasiveness of difference" that exists in the disability sports community (Silva & Howe, 2012, p. 191). Furthermore, Peers (2012) called on members of the disability sport community to stop using and accepting stereotypical representations of disability in coverage. The scholar called on members to begin participating "in de-composing the stories, cultures and industries that disable" (Peers, 2012, p. 186).

Athletes with disabilities have grown tired of the most common stereotypical representation, the supercrip narrative. For example, Hargreaves and Hardin (2009) investigated women wheelchair basketball players in the United States and the perceptions of disability sport media coverage and found the athletes were frustrated with the "inspiration" and "supercrip" terms used in coverage. The athletes discussed how they felt the supercrip narrative was not used to demonstrate their accomplishments but to tell an inspirational story to an able-bodied audience (Hargreaves & Hardin, 2009). Brookes and Khoo (2021) found support from Malaysian and Singaporean Paralympic athletes for using alternative representations such as the multidimensional frame and avoiding the supercrip representations. The scholars explained that Paralympic athletes felt:

> For the movement to become more sustainable, stories about how these PWD [people with disabilities] embrace their difficulties and "aspire to lead fulfilling and meaningful lives," without moving into extremities about heroics or being burdens, should be more commonplace in the media. (Brookes & Khoo, 2021, p. 7)

However, as Marques et al. (2014) found that in their exploration of Brazilian Paralympic athletes' perceptions of Brazilian Paralympic media coverage, there sometimes is a lack of consensus for how to appropriately represent Paralympic athletes and disability sport. Pearson and Misener's (2022) examination of Canadian Paralympic athletes found some athletes did not mind campaigns such as Channel 4's Meet the Superhumans, which used the supercrip narrative in its marketing. Upon further discussion, some athletes discussed liking the advertisement because they felt it demonstrated athleticism (Pearson & Misener, 2022). All athletes discussed wanting to be represented as athletes first and not for being inspirational or for "overcoming" their disability (Pearson & Misener, 2022). One Paralympic athlete demonstrated their frustration with coverage by explaining that:

> I have no problem talking a little bit about how I got started in the sport or whatever. I just don't want that to be the primary focus of the article. I don't want it to be focused on my disability. I want it to be focused on my ability. (Pearson & Misener, 2022, p. 14)

Athletes with disabilities do not want to be, and should not be, represented using stereotypical frames within disability sports coverage.

This tension between how to represent athletes with disabilities via the athletic narrative has become an important issue for Paralympic media coverage. It is important to note that using the athletic narrative to represent Paralympic athletes does not mean ignoring, or not discussing, an athlete's disability. Often, to achieve this athlete-first representation, the media has eliminated or ignored discussing any disability. Paralympic athletes have expressed how including their impairment is a part of what makes their story unique and is an important part of their identity (Pearson & Misener, 2022). Some athletes even felt that coverage that only focused on athletic achievements was less enjoyable than coverage that included their athletic achievements and backstory (e.g., inclusion of disability; Pearson & Misener, 2022). DePauw's (1997) construction of sporting bodies highlighted how sport remains a masculinized, heterosexual, and able-bodied space. The athletic frame in representation (that includes disability) has the power to disrupt dominant understanding of sporting bodies and practices (DePauw, 1997; Pearson & Misener, 2022). Paralympic athletes can be represented as elite, high-performance athletes with a unique history. It does not have to be, and should not be, represented as one without the other in coverage and campaigns. A high-performance elite athlete is synonymous with disability.

> The athletic frame does not erase an athlete's disability from coverage but includes it.

The Future of Disability Sports Coverage

The goal for future disability sports coverage is to become proportionate to able-bodied sports coverage in terms of quantity and quality. It is promising to see the growth in terms of the quantity of coverage of the Paralympic Games and the quality of coverage moving toward athletics-first representation. But there is still progress to be made before achieving proportionate media representation for disability sport. The literature, however, provides different suggestions and opportunities to support media personnel with achieving proportionate representation for disability sport in the future.

The quality of coverage needs to improve by removing the stereotypical representations of disability sports from coverage. Until stereotypical representations are no longer used within disability sports coverage, there can never be proportionate representation, representation that has the power to generate positive impacts from representation. This may include influencing public attitudes toward people with disabilities, inspiring people with disabilities to participate in sport, and creating more opportunities for people with disabilities in sport and other aspects of public life (e.g., education, transportation, employment). Media personnel are, therefore, encouraged to focus on

athlete-first representation and ensure the inclusion of disability within that athletic representation.

A way to help support this focus on athlete-first representation can be by ensuring that media personnel responsible for covering disability sport are educated and trained on disability and disability sport. Media personnel should understand the history of stereotypical representations, the Paralympic movement, and the rules of disability sport events they are covering. This may seem like basic standards for good journalistic practice, but unfortunately research has shown a history of media personnel not having prior knowledge, education, or training when covering the Paralympic Games (Howe, 2008b; Misener, 2013). As Pearson and Misener (2022) found in their study, Paralympic athletes explained how a journalist's prior knowledge, education, or training affected their media experience. It affected their interactions with some athletes to where the athletes felt pressure to educate the journalist on their sport or disability and sometimes tried to get the journalist interested in disability sport during their conversation (Pearson & Misener, 2022). This, in turn, affected the coverage of themselves and their sport as they explained how journalists with less knowledge, education, or training would then report on them in stereotypical ways (e.g., using supercrip narrative or even gendered language; Pearson & Misener, 2022). It is, therefore, critical that media organizations and education institutions provide training to journalists on disability.

> The goal for future disability sports coverage is to become proportionate to able-bodied sports coverage in terms of quantity and quality.

Another important way to create positive change and relieve some of the burden Paralympic athletes express (e.g., feeling obligated to train and educate journalists

Channel 4's Disabled Presenting Team for the 2022 Winter Paralympics

For the 2022 Winter Paralympics, Channel 4, the official broadcaster for the Games in the United Kingdom, announced the first-ever 100% disabled presenting team. The team was on the ground in China during the Games and represented a global first for a broadcasting company to ever have an entire disabled presenting and punditry team for an international sporting event. The schedule included more than 80 hours of coverage on Channel 4 and streaming options on their YouTube platform. The format for the broadcast included Broadcast Sports award-winning presenter Ade Adepitan providing daily highlight shows with triathlete Lauren Steadman and rugby player Ed Jackson having a breakfast show. On-screen reporting was done by retired swimmer Ellie Robinson, racing car driver Billy Monger, and sit-skier Sean Rose. Finally, Tokyo 2020 presenter Arthur William led the overnight sports coverage.

Channel 4 has been a supporter of the Paralympic Games since 2012, being the first broadcaster to showcase more hours of Paralympic sport than any other broadcaster in history. Off-screen, Channel 4 has been committed to progressing the careers of disabled people. One example is its "Engage & Enable" disability strategy. It was launched in 2021 and included the "RISEits" new mentorship scheme for mid- to senior-disabled production talent in television. Channel 4 also created shareable best practice guidelines for those working in media organizations to hire and progress disabled production talent in their organizations. These guidelines also included expectations for the production companies when featuring disabled people on-screen. More broadcasters around the world will hopefully continue to follow Channel 4's example for making strides toward improving disability sports coverage on- and off-screen.

while on-site for competition) for future coverage is to hire people with disabilities on staff in media organizations. Having people with disabilities on staff, and in positions of authority within media institutions, helps create and facilitate change for the disability community through coverage. This is becoming more common practice with CBC, for example, not only including "Player's Own Voice" pieces but hiring past Paralympic athletes on staff in the newsroom during the Games as well. For the 2022 Winter Paralympic Games in Beijing, Channel 4 made history with having the first 100% disabled team for the Paralympic Games (Channel 4, 2022). The broadcasting company has made public strides toward improving disability sports coverage on- and off-screen through its organization and will hopefully set an example for other broadcasting companies to follow suit.

Achieving proportionate coverage involves more than only stopping the use of stereotypical representations in disability sports coverage. For proportionate representation to be achieved, the quality of content needs to go beyond the time of Paralympic Games and include content beyond what is called the cycle of reintroduction. The **cycle of reintroduction** is a term (coined by a Paralympic athlete in Pearson & Misener's [2022] study) explaining the process of Paralympic athletes having to reintroduce themselves to media personnel and the public every four years the Paralympic Games takes place. Importantly, it highlights the lack of in-depth or critical coverage that exists for Paralympic Games. For example, the athlete explained how every Paralympic Games, they must reintroduce themselves to the public because there is little disability sports coverage outside of the Games, and that is the primary style journalists choose to follow during each Games cycle (Pearson & Misener, 2022). To build a fan base for disability sport, coverage needs to occur outside of the Games and go beyond the reintroduction cycle format. Breaking this cycle would mean the media provides coverage common in able-bodied sports coverage such as critiques of athletes in disability sports.

> **What other unique opportunities or challenges do you predict for covering disability sports in the future?**

It is great to see advances in the number television hours and the use of streaming platforms for broadcasting the Paralympic Games. But media should go beyond standard platforms to consider other mediums such as social media and engagement techniques as seen commonly in able-bodied sports. Pullen et al.'s (2022) study found that in the United Kingdom, there is enough evidence of a parasport media market beyond the Paralympic Games. Broadcasters and media personnel have "yet to fully realize both the commercial and cultural potential of parasport beyond the dictates of the mega-event marketplace" (Pullen et al., 2022, p. 384). But these changes could generate positive impacts for people with disabilities in sport on- and off-screen.

Summary

This chapter examined the dominant ways disability sport and athletes with disabilities have been represented in disability sports coverage to date. The Paralympic Games were developed by able-bodied people, and this has shaped how the Games were designed, marketed by media, and understood by the broader audience. The stereotypical frame has been the most common way disability sport has been represented, using the supercrip, overcoming, cyborg, passive victim, and comparison narratives. The athletic frame is becoming the primary way to represent athletes and has been advocated for by scholars and athletes with disabilities as their desired mode of representation. Importantly, the athletic frame does not erase disability from representation. Athletes must be featured as high-performance elite athletes with disabilities. Next, media personnel's and athletes' perspectives were discussed highlighting why and how disability sport media has and should be represented. Finally, several opportunities were discussed in relation to the challenges that exist for achieving proportionate representation to able-bodied sports coverage in the future.

CRITICAL THINKING EXERCISES

1. What are the differences between the stereotypical frame and the athletic frame? Why is the athletic frame the preferred frame of representation by athletes?

2. Many stakeholders and scholars have argued that Paralympic media representation can change public attitudes about disability. Do you believe media coverage of disability sport can change public attitudes about disability? Why or why not?

3. What are some ways you think media could market athletes with disabilities using the athletic frame?

4. Why is it important that media personnel be trained and educated about disability before reporting on disability sport? Who do you think should be responsible for this training?

CHAPTER 7

Elite Adaptive Sport

Jeff Ward, PhD, and Mary Hums, PhD

LEARNING OBJECTIVES

After reading this chapter, you will be able to do the following:

- Identify major disability sport organizations and explain their differences.
- Define terms related to major disability sport events.
- Make the connection from disability sport to larger society.
- Understand current issues facing disability sport managers.
- Explain classification of disabilities.

This chapter provides an overview of major international games for athletes with disabilities. In these events, thousands of elite athletes compete in front of millions of viewers each year. More viewers translate to more recognition for athletes with disabilities, which in turn creates more interest in disability sport. However, disability sport represents so much more than a collection of yearly sporting events. Each separate event can be the impetus for social change that extends far beyond a stadium or, most times, a television, computer screen, or mobile device. Each event helps shift attitudes and assumptions about what people with disabilities can accomplish.

Throughout disability sport history, the organizations striving for mainstream acceptance have been willing to showcase athletes with disabilities and their sports as a force for all that is good while working to change people's perceptions of disability. Even with the increased success of each edition of the Paralympic Games and other international games, much work still needs to be done to heighten awareness of and interest in disability sport (Nielson Sports, 2016). Disability sport should be considered a social movement as much as it is a sport. The work of increasing awareness and interest in disability sport begins with each potential future sport manager.

Major Games Featuring Disability Sport

Just like events for able-bodied athletes, there are a wide variety of competitions for elite athletes with disabilities. The following sections address several these, including the Paralympic Games, Commonwealth Games, Parapan American Games, Asian Para Games, Warrior Games, Invictus Games, and Cybathlon. Table 7.1 presents an overview of when these games take place.

TABLE 7.1 Major Games Schedule Overview

Games	Schedule	Most recent location
Summer Paralympic Games	4-year cycle	Paris 2024
Winter Paralympic Games	4-year cycle	Beijing 2022
Commonwealth Games	4-year cycle	Birmingham 2022
Parapan American Games	4-year cycle	Santiago 2023
Asian Para Games	4-year cycle	Hangzhou 2023
African Para Games	First held in 2023	Accra 2023
Warrior Games	Annual event	Orlando 2024
Invictus Games	2-year cycle	Düsseldorf 2023
Cybathlon	4-year cycle	Zürich 2023

Paralympic Games

The first competition for wheelchair athletes, the Stoke Mandeville Games, was organized at Stoke Mandeville Hospital in 1948 in London (IPC, n.d.g). The original games involved 16 injured military members who took part in archery (Paris2024, 2021). The first International Stoke Mandeville Games took place in 1952, and from then on, the Games occurred every year. In 1960, the 9th International Stoke Mandeville Games were held in Rome (where the Summer Olympic Games were also taking place) and were considered the first Paralympic Games (IPC, n.d.a). However, the term *Paralympic Games* was not officially used until the International Olympic Committee (IOC) approved it in 1984 (Paris2024, 2021). The word *Paralympic* derives from the Greek preposition "para," meaning beside or alongside, and the word *Olympic*. The intended meaning is that the Paralympic Games are parallel to the Olympic Games, demonstrating how the two movements exist side by side (IOC, 2021). Not until the 1988 Summer Games, in Seoul, South Korea, and the 1992 Winter Games in Albertville, France, would the Paralympic Games take place in the same cities and venues as the Olympic Games (International Paralympic Committee, n.d.).

Paralympic Games Vision, Mission, and Values

- Vision: Make for an inclusive world through parasport.
- Mission: To lead the Paralympic movement, oversee the delivery of the Paralympic Games, and support members to enable para-athletes to achieve sporting excellence.
- Values: Courage, determination, inspiration, and equality.

On September 22, 1989, the International Paralympic Committee was founded as an international nonprofit organization in Düsseldorf, Germany. This organization acts as the global governing body of the **Paralympic movement**. The International Paralympic Committee headquarters have been in Bonn, Germany, since 1999 (IPC, n.d.a). It is governed by the General Assembly, which meets every two years and is comprised of representatives from international sports federations, National Paralympic Committees, International Organizations of Sports for the Disabled, and Regional Organizations (IPC, n.d.a). The membership and commitment of these organizations are outlined in the International Paralympic Committee (IPC) Handbook, the

CHERI BLAUWET, MD

Athlete. Advocate. Physician. Role model. Most people would be happy to have one of these descriptors associated with their names. In the world of Paralympic sport and promoting the inclusion of people with disabilities in society, Dr. Cheri Blauwet is all these things.

Dr. Blauwet was injured in a farm equipment accident at a young age while growing up in rural Iowa and has used a wheelchair to move through life at top speed ever since. Her disability never stopped her or her family from supporting her in her life's dreams. She became active in sport at a young age and even today retains her commitment to encouraging young people with disabilities to achieve all they can be in sport and life.

Before enrolling at Stanford for medical school, Dr. Blauwet attended the University of Arizona for her undergraduate degree. Along the way, she became an accomplished athlete, specifically in the sport of wheelchair racing. Over the course of three Paralympic Games, she amassed seven medals. In addition, she won several major international marathons, including Boston, New York, and Los Angeles.

Cheri Blauwet

Retired from competition now, Dr. Blauwet has taken her commitment to promote sport and physical activity for people with disabilities into her professional life. She pursues a sports medicine practice at Spaulding Rehabilitation and the Brigham and Women's Hospital in Boston. In addition, she has an appointment as an associate professor in physical medicine and rehabilitation at Harvard Medical School. She is an active voice on behalf of physicians with disabilities and works to promote the greater inclusion of people with disabilities in the medical profession. A frequent guest on podcasts and media interviews, Dr. Blauwet uses her platform to be a voice for including people with disabilities not just in sports but across society as a whole.

Dr. Blauwet continues her active involvement in the Paralympic movement as a U.S. Olympic & Paralympic Committee Board of Directors member. She also serves on the IPC Medical Commission. In addition, she is a member of the International Olympic Committee Medical and Scientific Expert Group. Her legacy will live on in the many people whose lives she has touched up to now and those she will interact with in the future.

Paralympic movement's ultimate reference document and framework (IPC, n.d.c). A 14-member Governing Board sets organizational policy and ensures the directions of the General Assembly are being implemented (IPC, n.d.b).

The IPC acts as the international federation for 10 disability sports (although this is evolving). Their primary responsibilities are supporting more than 200 members in developing disability sport and advocating social inclusion (IPC, n.d.a). This ensures the successful delivery and organization of the Paralympic Games.

The athletes who participate in the Paralympic Games live with spinal injuries, are amputees, may have vision impairments, have cerebral palsy, and have intellectual disabilities (IPC, n.d.e). As of 2022, the IPC sanctions 28 total Paralympic sports: 22 summer sports and six winter sports (IPC, n.d.f). Because of the unique combination of ever-improving athletic performance and increasing global awareness, the Paralympic Games are firmly established as the world's primary sports event for driving social inclusion. Moreover, the event boasts an excellent record for transforming attitudes, cities, countries, and the lives of millions of people worldwide (IPC, n.d.d).

See chapter 4 for more in-depth information about the Paralympic Games.

National Olympic and Paralympic Committee Cooperative Efforts

In most countries, National Paralympic Committees and National Olympic Committees are two separate and independent organizations. A handful of countries, however, have combined organizations for both. Some of these countries include the Netherlands, the United States, and, most recently, Saudi Arabia.

The Nederlands Olympisch Comité*Nederlandse Sport Federatie (NOC*NSF) is the overarching organization for sports in the Netherlands. As the "country's Olympic and Paralympic Committee, it develops, promotes, and protects the Olympic and Paralympic movement in the Netherlands. NOC*NSF is responsible for the participation of Dutch athletes in the Olympic and Paralympic Games" (NOC*NSF, 2020, para. 1).

In a move celebrating Paralympic athletes, in 2019, the United States Olympic Committee (USOC) announced an official name change to the United States Olympic and Paralympic Committee (USOPC). According to USOPC CEO Sarah Hirshland, "The decision to change the organization's name represents a continuation of our longstanding commitment to creating an inclusive environment for Team USA . . . . Paralympic athletes are integral to the makeup of Team USA and our mission to inspire current and future generations of Americans. The new name represents a renewed commitment to that mission and the ideals that we seek to advance, both here at home and throughout the worldwide Olympic and Paralympic movements" (Pimer, 2019, para. 5).

Saudi Arabia decided to merge its Saudi Arabia Olympic and Paralympic Committees in late 2021. "This integration is aimed at the development of the sports sector, the consolidation of the efforts and services provided to all categories of athletes, compliance with clear and unified plans, the provision of a link between athletes of all categories, the strengthening of the Saudi presence at various international platforms and encouraging the practice of sport among society," said Prince Abdulaziz Bin Turki Al-Faisal, President of the Saudi Olympic Committee (Nelsen, 2021, para. 5).

These countries have publicly recognized the importance of Paralympic sport by setting up governance structures that embrace the Paralympic experience. As the Paralympic movement evolves, perhaps more countries will follow suit.

Commonwealth Games

The Commonwealth Games Federation (CGF) manages the direction and control of the Commonwealth Games and Commonwealth Youth Games while working to deliver the vision of the Commonwealth Sports Movement (CGF, 2020c). The CGF organization is headquartered in the United Kingdom, but operates across 72 member nations and territories, all of which were colonized (with the exceptions of Rwanda and Mozambique; BBC Reality Check Team, 2021) or established by the British Empire.

Commonwealth Sport

- Mission: To be an athlete-centered, sport-focused Commonwealth Sports Movement, with integrity, global impact and embraced by communities that accomplish the following: (1) delivering inspirational and innovative Games built on friendships and proud heritage and supported by a dynamic Commonwealth Sports Cities Network, (2) to nurture and develop one of the best governed and well-managed sports movements in the world, (3) to attract and build on public, private, and social partnerships that widely benefit Commonwealth athletes, sports, and communities, and (4) champion, through our brand, Commonwealth athlete, citizen, and community engagement in everything that they do (CGF, 2020c).

- Vision: The Commonwealth Games aims to build peaceful, sustainable, and prosperous communities through sport.
- Values:
  - Humanity: To embrace all Commonwealth athletes, citizens, communities, and nations.
  - Equality: To promote fairness, nondiscrimination, and inclusion in all they do.
  - Destiny: Through impactful, high-performance sport, help Commonwealth athletes, citizens, and communities realize their aspirations and ambitions.

The concept of a united Commonwealth sporting event bringing together the members of the British Empire was first proposed in 1891 (Team Scotland, 2021). In 1930, the first Commonwealth Games, then known as the British Empire Games, were held in Hamilton, Ontario, Canada. Because of their success, they were transitioned into a regularly occurring event. Since 1930, they have taken place every four years except for 1942 and 1946, when they were disrupted because of World War II. After undergoing a series of name changes, the event is now known simply as the Commonwealth Games and has been since 1978 (Wood, 2010).

Events for athletes with a disability were first included at the Commonwealth Games as exhibition sports at the 1994 Commonwealth Games. Unlike most major sporting events, the disability sport program at the Commonwealth Games is fully integrated. For example, a medal won by a para-athlete contributes to a nation's overall medal tally, just as a non-para-athlete's does, and regular ticketing practices apply to both disability and non-disability sport events. The 2002 Commonwealth Games marked the first time para-athletes were fully integrated into their national teams (CGF, 2020b). This made the competition the first fully inclusive international multisport games. Elite male and female para-athletes representing 20 nations compete in 10 events across five different disability sports—athletics, lawn bowls, swimming, table tennis, and weightlifting (CGF, 2020b).

The CGF has positioned itself in the sports landscape not just by the success of its event and athletes but by the stand its leadership has taken to promote the inclusion of people with disabilities in sport. Under the leadership of former CEO David Grevemberg, the CGF became a leader in the sport and human rights ecosystem.

For more than a decade, Grevemberg worked with the Commonwealth sport movement. He served as both the chief executive officer of the Glasgow 2014 Commonwealth Games and, most recently, for the CGF itself. As seen from the sidebar, his story illustrates the influence a sport executive can have in shaping a sport organization's commitment to inclusion and social justice. His work was on a global level, but sport managers can make a difference at any level.

Parapan American Games

Similar to the Commonwealth Games, major regional games are open to a defined group of nations, countries, and territories. The Pan American Games are a multisport competition with representatives from North America, South America, Central America, and the Caribbean. The Pan American Games are globally the third-largest multisport games, surpassed only by the Summer Olympic Games and the Asian Games. The Pan American Games include all the sports and events featured on the Summer Olympic program and additional sports that the IOC recognizes (COC, 2022). The Pan American Games are held every four years in the year prior to the Olympic Summer Games. The games have been held in cities throughout North, Central, and South America. Canada and Mexico are the only countries to host the Games three times (FÉI, 2021). The Pan American Games are governed by the Pan American Sports Organization, headquartered in Mexico. Members include 41 countries and roughly 6,000 athletes and 4,000 officials (COC, 2022).

DAVID GREVEMBERG

David Grevemberg's connection to the disability sport movement runs deep, dating back to the Manchester 2002 Commonwealth Games while he worked as the sports director for the IPC (CGF, 2020a). Speaking about his experiences, he said he "discovered that sport in the Commonwealth was distinctly positioned not only to celebrate and commemorate individual and collective perseverance and achievement in all its forms but as a platform for reckoning with our common humanity, as a vehicle for strengthening our pursuit for greater equality and as a call to action for unleashing our common destiny in creating a more peaceful, sustainable and prosperous world" (CGF, 2020a).

Two accomplishments that speak to his humanitarian efforts are his role in planning the 2014 Glasgow Games and his involvement in the 2018 Gold Coast Games. Glasgow 2014 embraced respecting, protecting, and promoting human rights, aligning its planning and delivery with the United Nations Guiding Principles on Business and Human Rights. The Organizing Committee published its approach and results in reports. This was the first global sporting event to do so in history. This was applauded by sports and human rights entities worldwide and has continued to be used as the standard for all future games (CGF, 2020a).

After spearheading efforts to integrate human rights principles and standards, Grevemberg left the CGF in early 2021 to become the chief innovation and partnerships officer for the Center for Sport and Human Rights (CSHR). His role there focuses primarily on engaging with the sport sector and developing new partnerships. He also oversees projects that drive positive change in sport, including education and training programs and leading and developing significant new initiatives (Mackay, 2021).

Parapan American Games Values

- Courage: The ability of athletes to persevere with strength and claw.

- Determination: The perseverance of athletes to achieve their goals and earn a gold medal.

- Equality: The value of equality is decisive to parallel the Pan American and Parapan American Games. Both Para and Pan American athletes should be treated in the same way in their respective sports.

- Inspiration: Para-athletes inspire effort, perseverance, and discipline. The inspiration of each athlete ensures that an athlete or team competes in the same conditions as other athletes.

(Lima2019, 2019)

Athletes who compete in the Parapan American Games have impairments that fall into three categories: physical, visual, and intellectual (Lima2019, 2019). Athletes with physical impairments can be further divided into the following eligible impairment types: impaired muscle power, impaired passive range of movement, loss of limb or limb deficiency, leg-length difference, short stature, hypertonia, ataxia, and athetosis (World Para Athletics, n.d.).

In November 1999, the first Parapan American Games were held in Mexico City. One thousand athletes from 18 countries competed across four sports: athletics, swimming, table tennis, and wheelchair basketball. The gold medal winners at Mexico 1999 secured a place at the Sydney 2000 Paralympic Games. Since then, the Parapan American Games have taken place every four years (IPC, n.d.d). The second edition of the Parapan American Games was held in 2003, with 1,500 athletes from 28 countries competing across nine sports: athletics, boccia, cycling, equestrian, swimming, table tennis, wheelchair basketball, wheelchair fencing, and wheelchair tennis. However, in 2007, the Games took place in the same city as the Pan American Games. The Parapan American Games have since followed the Olympic and Paralympic model, with the Parapan American Games taking place shortly after the conclusion of the Pan American Games (IPC, n.d.d). The 7th Parapan American Games took place in November 2023, in Santiago, Chile, marking the first time the South American country hosted the event (IPC, n.d.d).

Asian Para Games

The Asian Games are the oldest and most prestigious event on the Olympic Council of Asia (OCA) calendar, dating back to the inaugural edition in 1951. Like the Olympic Games, they are held every four years. The Games follow the sports program of the Olympic Games, with athletics and swimming as core sports, and feature disciplines that reflect the diverse sporting culture of the continent (Dunsar Media Company Limited, n.d.).

> ### Asian Paralympic Committee Vision and Mission
>
> - Vision: Make for an inclusive Asia through parasport.
> - Mission: To lead the Paralympic movement in Asia, deliver successful and sustainable Asian Para Games, and support the NPCs to enable Para-athletes to achieve sporting excellence from grassroots to elite level.
>
> (APC, 2021d)

The first edition of the Asian Games was held in New Delhi in March 1951. A total of 489 athletes from 11 National Olympic Committees competed in 12 sports. The torch relay, now a well-established tradition in the buildup to the Olympic, Paralympic, and Commonwealth Games, was introduced as a new tradition of the Asian Games for Tokyo in 1958 (Dunsar Media Company Limited, n.d.) when the sacred flame was ignited at the opening ceremony by triple jumper Mikio Oda, who had become Japan's first Olympic champion three decades earlier when he won the gold medal at Amsterdam in 1928.

When it comes to disability sport and para-athletes, the Far East and South Pacific Games for the Disabled (FESPIC) existed before the Asian Para Games and included athletes from the Asia-Pacific region. The FESPIC Games were first held in 1975 in Japan with 18 participating nations. The FESPIC Games were multisport games. They were the precursor to the Asian Para Games, and two of its competitions were held parallel to the Asian Games in 1998 and 2002 (Disability Sport, 2014).

The Asian Para Games dissolved the FESPIC Games and the FESPIC Federation, the Games' governing body. They merged with the Asian Paralympic Council, which was renamed the Asian Paralympic Committee at the closing of the final FESPIC edition held in November 2006 in Malaysia. The first Asian multisport event for athletes with a disability, the inaugural Asian Para Games, took place in China in 2010 (Mackay, 2010).

The Asian Para Games, also known as Para Asiad, is a multisport event regulated by the Asian Paralympic Committee and is held every four years following the Asian Games. However, the exclusion of the Asian Para Games from the Asian Games host city contract meant that both events run independently. The IPC recognized the Games, the second-largest multisport event after the Paralympic Games. Three nations have hosted the Asian Para Games in its history, and 44 nations have participated (APC, 2021).

The Asian Para Games officially began on October 30, 2002, when the Asian Paralympic Council was established. Initially, the regions included East Asia, South Asia, and Southeast Asia (APC, 2021b). In 2004, aligning with the structure the International Olympic Committee followed, the International Paralympic Committee decided that the Central Asia and West Asia subregions would also be included. In 2006, the Asian Paralympic Council became the Asian Paralympic Committee (APC), with a president directly elected by the APC General Assembly (APC, 2021c). The Asian Paralympic Committee comprises 44 member nations that are

Athletes compete in men's badminton singles in the 4th Asian Para Games.
Wu Zhizun/Xinhua via Getty Images

divided up into five subregions: East Asia, Central Asia, West Asia, South Asia, and Southeast Asia (APC, 2021b).

Four years later, in 2010, the first Asian Para Games took place in Guangzhou, China. The 2014 Asian Para Games took place in Incheon, South Korea. The 2018 Games were held in Jakarta, Indonesia (APC, 2021c). The 2022 Games were held in Hangzhou, Zhe-jiang, China, with an estimated 3,000 athletes participating in 22 sports (International Wheelchair Basketball Federation, n.d.).

The new vision and mission statements of the Asian Para Games were developed in July 2019. They were launched officially in December 2019 with the Asian Paralympic Committee's new strategic plan. The strategic plan identifies three new core values for the Asian Paralympic Committee: solidarity, diversity, and sustainability. These values were designed to meet the region's specific needs while complementing the Paralympic values (APC, 2021a). The core values are the following:

- Courage. Para-athletes, through their performances, showcase to the world what can be achieved when testing the body to its absolute limits.
- Inspiration. As role models, Para-athletes maximize their abilities, empowering and exciting others to be active and take part in sport.
- Determination. Para-athletes have a unique strength of character that combines mental toughness, physical ability, and outstanding agility to produce sporting performances that regularly redefine the boundaries of possibility.
- Equality. Through sport, para-athletes celebrate diversity and show that difference is a strength. As pioneers for inclusion, they challenge stereotypes, transform attitudes, and break down

social barriers and discrimination toward persons with disabilities. While adhering to IPC values, APC has developed the following values specific to the region's needs.

- ° Diversity. They celebrate and champion the many unique cultures that make their region diverse.
- ° Solidarity. They recognize that diversity becomes a considerable strength through unity of purpose and supporting one another, no matter how big or small.
- ° Sustainability. They ensure that everything they do can be maintained, replicated, and built upon so that the Paralympic movement continues to grow and develop in their region.

The Asian Paralympic Committee has further outlined these strategic priorities:

- Enhancing the positive impact of the Paralympic movement in Asia
- Improving the standard of the Asian Para Games and leaving a legacy
- Driving a cultural shift through parasport for an inclusive Asia
- Strengthening both the Asian Paralympic Committee and Asian Para Games brands
- Developing excellence in their organization's operations and governance

The reasons for the shift in strategy were many, but the main reasons were greater gender parity across the region and more athletes from Asia competing in the Paralympic Games. They also wanted more recognition for the role of the Paralympic movement and its social impact and inclusion in Asia, and to develop close relationships with key strategic partners and stakeholders to activate audiences in and around the Games. Finally, they wanted to increase the volume of media exposure and number of social media followers (APC, 2021a).

With the Summer and Winter Paralympic Games in 2021 and 2022 and the Hangzhou 2022 Asian Para Games all taking place in the Asian region, these new values and strategic plans provide an opportunity to achieve each objective (APC, 2021a).

Warrior Games

The U.S. Department of Defense (DoD) organized the Warrior Games in 2010 as an annual event that champions the resiliency and dedication of wounded, injured, or otherwise impaired active duty and veteran U.S. service members. The Games also allow service members from international allied nations to take part (DOD, n.d.).

Elite athletes compete in adaptive sporting events, including wheelchair basketball, cycling, indoor rowing, and wheelchair rugby. The Warrior Games enhance the recovery and rehabilitation of wounded service members by exposing them to the transformative power of adaptive sports. Participation in the Warrior Games represents the culmination of a service member's involvement in an adaptive sports program. In addition, it shows the unbreakable determination and perseverance of wounded service members through competitive sports (DOD, n.d.).

Initial talks to establish the event were held in 2009 during a meeting at the Pentagon with the USO. Later the then-named United States Olympic Committee became involved. The first event was in 2010 at the U.S. Olympic and Paralympic Training Center in Colorado Springs, Colorado, where the event was held through 2014 (Wounded Warrior Regiment, 2010).

The DoD organized the 2015 Warrior Games. They were held at Marine Corps Base Quantico in Virginia. At that event, 250 athletes representing the United States and the British armed forces took part and competed in eight adaptive sports (USMC, 2015).

In 2016, the Warrior Games took place at the United States Military Academy in West Point, New York, with 250 athletes participating (DVIDS, 2016). The 2017 Games were the first time the event took place away from a military installation. The competitions were at the United Center, Soldier Field, and

Athletes compete in handcycling at the 2012 Warrior Games.
Craig F. Walker/The Denver Post via Getty Images

other venues in Chicago, Illinois, where 265 athletes took part, including a team of elite athletes from Australia (Wounded Warrior Regiment, 2017). The 2018 edition of the Warrior Games took place at the U.S. Air Force Academy, with 300 athletes competing across 11 sporting events (DoD, 2018).

The 2019 event was in Tampa, Florida. The competitions were held in public venues for the second time since the Games began. More than 300 wounded and impaired service members and veterans competed. Three new allied nations took part in the Games: Canada, Denmark, and the Netherlands. Two more competitions were added, bringing the total to 13 adaptive sports: archery, cycling, indoor rowing, powerlifting, shooting, sitting volleyball, swimming, track, field, wheelchair basketball, wheelchair tennis, wheelchair rugby, and golf (Military Times, 2019). The 2020 Games were initially scheduled to occur in San Antonio, Texas. They would have marked the 10th anniversary of the annual competition. However, the Games were ultimately canceled because of the COVID-19 pandemic (Altman, 2020). In 2021, the Games had to be canceled for the second year in a row. They were scheduled to take place at the ESPN Wide World of Sports Complex at Walt Disney World Resort in Florida. The 2022 Warrior Games were held in San Antonio, with the 2023 competition at the Pro Football Hall of Fame in Canton, Ohio (Ruiz, 2021). The Games returned to the ESPN Wide World of Sports Complex at Walt Disney World Resort in Florida in 2024.

Invictus Games

The word *Invictus* is a Latin adjective for "unconquered, unsubdued, and invincible." The term was specifically chosen because it embodies and awakens the fighting spirit of the service members who were injured while executing their duties. The Games show how tenacious and resilient these warriors truly can be. However, the Games are more than just sports, and they have captured the hearts and minds of millions of people worldwide. They also challenge preconceived thinking on wounded veterans while challenging those same service members to live their best lives (IGF, 2019b).

Invictus Games Mission and Vision

- Mission
  - The mission is to provide new opportunities for active service members and veterans who paid a high price for their dedication to their country and its people. Their primary objective is to build a community that brings together people with similar experiences and supports them. They accomplish this through social support structures that help them overcome the consequences of their war wounds, injuries, and illnesses.
  - It will offer full support for physically impaired service members and veterans on their road to recovery, psychological rehabilitation, social integration, and self-development by helping them form a positive outlook and motivating them to participate in sports.
  - It will promote the development and popularization of sports as an effective agency for rehabilitation for wounded soldiers and to encourage society to create the conditions necessary for this.
- Values
  - Support: They believe that the support of fellow service members, family, and friends is the foundation for a successful recovery from wounds and injuries.
  - Expanded capabilities: They believe that wounded soldiers should have proper opportunities for their rehabilitation. In doing so, service members can return to living a full life regardless of the level or type of wound, injury, or illness.
  - Dedication: They support the participants in their desire to reach new goals in their rehabilitation through sport.
  - Respect: They respect the participants' experience and want to create a community based on mutual understanding and respect for the lived experiences of each participant.
  - Courage: They are inspired by the unconquered spirit of their participants and motivate them to go outside their comfort zone and look at their future bravely.

Most people have never faced the horrors or consequences of being in a military war zone. Further, even more will never know or fully appreciate the sacrifices these men and women made so that citizens can have the best lives possible (IGF, 2016b). Thousands of service members globally have experienced life-changing injuries, visible or otherwise, while serving their countries. The challenge for them is how they will successfully and sustainably reintegrate back into nonmilitary society with the motivation and perseverance not to be defined by their impairments (IGF, 2016a).

The Invictus Games were born after Prince Harry, the Duke of Sussex, witnessed the transformative power sports can have on veterans. He was present as the British team competed at the 2013 Warrior Games held in Colorado (BBC News, 2013; IGF, 2016b) and was overcome by the impact those Games had on the service members living with various injuries and impairments physically, psychologically, and socially. He was so inspired that he wanted to help the wounded service members with their challenges and raise awareness worldwide. Because of the Games and what he surely saw firsthand in combat, Prince Harry desired to bring a similar concept of an international sporting event to the United Kingdom (The Royal Household, n.d.).

With the financial backing of several parties and the unwavering support of the 2012 London Organizing Committee of the Olympic and Paralympic Games and the Ministry of Defence, the event was planned over 10 months. In 2014, London hosted the inaugural Invictus Games. More than

400 competitors from 13 nations were present, all of whom fought alongside the United Kingdom in recent military campaigns (IGF, 2019a). The Invictus Games Foundation was established and is the governing body that selects future host cities. The foundation exists to ensure that the Invictus Games continue to adhere to the high standards set at the original Games. It handles sport and competition management, rules and categorizations, and overall branding. The foundation has made possible the transition from a one-time sporting event to a global movement that positively influences all levels of society, not just service members (IGF, 2016a).

In an effort to bring Invictus Games to the United States and build on the success of the 2014 Invictus Games held in London, Military Adaptive Sports Inc. (MASI) was created. The second Invictus Games took place in May 2016 in Orlando, Florida. These Games were built on the premise of the London Games and featured more than 500 competitors across 15 nations (Invictus Games Orlando 2016; MASI, 2016). Toronto, Canada, hosted the third Games in September 2017. Unlike previous Games, which were hosted at a single site, multiple venues around the Toronto metro area hosted the 12 sporting events in addition to the opening and closing ceremonies (Invictus Games Toronto, 2017).

In 2017, before the Toronto Games, the Invictus Games Foundation received a research grant from the Forces in Mind Trust (IGF, 2016a). It wanted to investigate the long-term impact competing in the Invictus Games has on competitors, their families, and friends. Researchers wanted to assess whether the competitors' well-being improved significantly compared to noncompetitors and wanted to measure the duration of any variances (Forces in Mind Trust, 2020c). The researchers leading this comprehensive study sought to identify the best practices to support the long-term well-being of active-duty service members and veterans who were wounded, injured, or otherwise impaired. The longitudinal study was scheduled to take place during a four-year span (2017-2020; IGF, 2018). In 2020, additional funding was made available to extend the study to cover athletes taking part in the 2020 edition Invictus Games scheduled to take place in the Hague. Unfortunately, because of the worldwide pandemic, full results from this study have been delayed (Forces in Mind Trust, 2020a).

Preliminary findings indicated that sport participation has a significant short- and long-term positive impact on the rehabilitation of wounded, injured, and impaired military personnel and veterans. Additional analysis pointed toward competitors experiencing greater post-traumatic recovery, in addition to better psychosocial and physical health, than those who did not take part in competitive sports (IGF, 2020a, 2020b). This suggests that participation in competitive sports may provide distinct benefits in the recovery of impaired service members.

> Sport participation has a significant short- and long-term positive impact on the rehabilitation of wounded, injured, and impaired military personnel and veterans.

In 2018, Australia became the fourth country to host the Invictus Games. The Games were held in Sydney and featured athletes from 18 nations competing in 11 adaptive sports (IGF, 2021a). The 5th Invictus Games were scheduled to take place in 2020 in the Hague, the Netherlands but were postponed until 2021 because of the COVID-19 pandemic (IGF, 2020b). However, the Games had to be rescheduled a second time to April 2022 due to ongoing concerns related to the pandemic. The 2023 Invictus Games were held in Düsseldorf, Germany in September (IGF, 2021b).

Cybathlon

Sometimes competitive sporting events can take on a unique look. An example of this is the Cybathlon, a nonprofit project of the

An athlete competes in the leg prosthesis race in the 2016 Cybathlon.
MICHAEL BUHOLZER/AFP via Getty Images

Swiss Federal Institute of Technology in Zurich (ETH Zürich), a private research university. The impetus behind Cybathlon is international competitions and events. Cybathlon challenges teams worldwide to develop assistive technologies suitable for everyday use with and for people with disabilities. The primary goal is to complete various daily tasks using the latest assistive technologies. Examples include physically impaired participants balancing on rocks with a prosthetic leg, tying shoelaces with a robotic arm prosthesis, or overcoming uneven terrain with an exoskeleton (ETH Zürich, 2021b). Cybathlon was organized for these reasons:

- To give people with severe motor deficits—too severe for the Paralympic Games, where most assistive technologies are not allowed—a chance to compete

- To promote the development and application of the most advanced assistive and wearable technologies, eventually leading to innovative solutions because of the technological competition. (NCCR Robotics, 2021)

Robert Riener, head of ETH Zürich, started the Cybathlon in 2013. Through Cybathlon, ETH Zürich showcases what research and development signify for a global society. Since the project was formed, more than 100 teams from more than 30 countries have taken part in Cybathlon competitions (ETH Zürich, 2021d). The development teams brought to the forefront the barriers that people with physical disabilities face and live with daily (ETH Zürich, 2021d). Further, the event shows how modern technology can help people with disabilities overcome those obstacles. Cybathlon connects society, research and development, and people with disabilities through an emotional, positive, and unique global platform (ETH Zürich, 2021d).

To drive assistive technology development forward, Cybathlon constantly analyzes what already exists and, from there, creates new, forward-looking event formats and projects. They truly embody their brand as "a world without barriers." In Cybathlon competitions, teams from around the world compete with and against each other in eight different disciplines:

- Arms prothesis race (ARM)
- Assistance robot race (ROB)
- Vision assistance race (VIS)
- Brain-computer interface race (BIS)
- Exoskeleton race (EXO)
- Functional electrical stimulation bike race (FES)
- Leg prosthesis race (LEG)
- Wheelchair race (WHL)

Teams are comprised of a technology developer and a participant with a disability, referred to as a pilot. The tasks in the respective disciplines represent everyday activities (ETH Zürich, 2021c).

Pilots must be at least 18 years old and meet the discipline-specific eligibility criteria to be included in the competition. In addition, the assistive devices must always be safe for the users and their surroundings. Between five and 13 teams compete in each discipline (ETH Zürich, 2021b).

ETH Zürich organized the first Cybathlon. It took place in Kloten, Switzerland, in October 2016. This was the first-ever international sports competition to use assisted technologies. Sixty-six pilots from 25 nations competed in front of approximately 4,600 spectators. The event's structure resulted from multiple exchanges with people who use assistive technologies because of disability, disability organizations, hospitals, industry, and political organizations. The objective was to facilitate, strengthen, and deepen the inclusion of people with disabilities within broader society (ETH Zürich, 2021a).

The 2020 Cybathlon took place in November. Because of the ongoing COVID-19 pandemic, teams could not travel to Zürich in person. This resulted in a "global edition" that took place remotely. Teams set up the infrastructure for the competition at their own facilities, Cybathlon officials monitored competitions, making any necessary rulings via video. In total, 51 teams from 20 countries competed against each other. Teams competed in different time zones and locations in an international sporting event for the first time. Each pilot had three hours to make three attempts at an obstacle course, with their best attempt counting toward their result. To heighten anticipation and create a "live" feeling, race results and winners were not revealed to anyone before the Cybathlon organizers streamed the races in two live events (ETH Zürich, 2021e).

The third edition of the Cybathlon took place in October 2024 in Kloten, Switzerland and "worldwide" (ETH Zürich, 2021f). At least 160 international teams from the worlds of academia and industry competed in the event. Two more disciplines were added to the original six: a race with innovative visual assistance technologies for people with severe visual impairment and a race with assistance robots for people with severe impairment of the upper and lower extremities (ETH Zürich, 2021f). Roland Sigrist, head of Cybathlon, said that these competitions incorporate unpredictability and a wide spectrum of tasks (ETH Zürich, 2021f). An example of this includes the wheelchair pilots not knowing the order they will encounter steps of differing heights. This means that they must react to the situation in the moment. As a result, international teams have to develop even more robust, functional, and dynamic assistive technologies for people with disabilities. The purpose of adding variability to the competition tasks is to better account for everyday situations where the exact circumstances are not always known or constant ahead of and over time. This variability also attempts to replicate able-bodied sports, such as baseball, football, and basketball (ETH Zürich, 2021f).

Current Issues in Disability Sport Competition

The disability sport world is in a constant state of change. New complexities arise as this vibrant industry segment continues to grow. Athletes with high support needs, classification, new technologies, and expanding worldwide opportunities are just a few of the issues facing sport managers who work in the world of athletes with disabilities.

Athletes with High Support Needs

The IPC's primary vision is to foster a more inclusive world through parasport. They accomplish this by promoting the Paralympic movement at all levels, including encouraging **athletes with high support needs (AHSN)** to participate (Herbison & Latimer-Cheung, 2021). AHSN are those who compete within eligible sport classes in Paralympic sports and who require additional support at competitions (IPC, 2016). AHSN can have a variety of physical, visual, and intellectual impairments that require additional support and may involve directly assisting an athlete during competition. For example, an athlete with limited hand function may need help loading a pistol in a shooting event. In addition, an athlete may often have a more significant physical impairment (such as cerebral palsy or muscular dystrophy) and use a power chair (Herbison & Latimer-Cheung, 2021).

Despite the rapid growth of the Paralympic movement, AHSN have remained underrepresented. AHSN have historically faced distinct barriers in sport participation and underrepresentation at elite levels of Paralympic sport competition (Slocum et al., 2018). In June 2014, the IPC Governing Board acknowledged that a greater emphasis was needed for these athletes. This prompted the Board to create an AHSN working group. Since then, the working group has been tasked with developing its best structure. The committee has tried to better represent AHSN within the IPC governance structure by focusing on three primary areas: accessibility, visibility, and education (IPC, 2016).

> **Despite the rapid growth of the Paralympic movement, AHSN have remained underrepresented.**

Still, research suggests that AHSN receive far less media coverage than their counterparts because their performances are not considered aesthetically pleasing (Purdue & Howe, 2013). These perceptions also influence the audience to not rate these performances as elite. Unconsciously reinforcing this image of disability sport performances reinforces a lack of inclusion. It also affects the amount of exposure that certain disability sports get, consequently limiting access to financial resources (Desaulniers, 2021).

Classification

According to the IPC, **classification** addresses three fundamental questions:

- Does the athlete have an eligible impairment for this sport?
- Does the athlete's eligible impairment meet the minimum impairment criteria of the sport?
- Which sport class should the athlete be allocated in (based on the extent to which the athlete can execute the specific tasks and activities fundamental to the sport) (IPC, n.d.e)?

While these questions appear straightforward, the answers are not as simple as they may seem.

Classification forms an essential platform for ensuring fairness within disability sport, but it has inspired ongoing debates. There are allegations of athletes purposefully performing less than optimally to be classified in a division that would allow them to be more likely to win a medal (Sanchez, 2020). This has been seen in swimming, for example. In several cases, athletes have been reclassified—or perhaps misclassified, in the athlete's opinion—into categories that they feel are not appropriate for them. Some athletes have been completely ruled out of Paralympic sport altogether as a result (Allan, 2019). For example, Anne Wafula Strike is a Paralympic wheelchair racer who "lost five years of her career after she was reclassified into a more able-bodied category mid competition" (Taylor, 2017, para. 13). According to Wade (2021), the classification system is complex and while athletes agree with the need for classification, they may also disagree with the rationale behind the system. Wheelchair racer Rob Smith (2022) had this to say: "I am concerned about the lack of possibility for selection for those who have had the classification boundaries moved above them to let more able athletes in and other sports where lack of disability is what coaches are looking for rather than talent, ability and determination" (para. 7).

The classification system is far from perfect. Classifiers are human, and evaluating athletes requires using subjective measures. The IPC is constantly working to improve the system, but it is a never-ending process. Evolving technologies may also play a role in classifying athletes using prosthetic devices and wheelchairs and how that affects their performance. The IPC issued Explanatory Guide to Paralympic Classification for both Summer and Winter sports in 2020 to keep athletes and coaches up to date on changes. A tenet of any sport is fairness, and through the classification system, the IPC works to try to make that happen in disability sport.

> A tenet of any sport is fairness, and through the classification system, the IPC works to try to make that happen in disability sport.

New Technologies

With Cybathlon creating the blueprint for how advancing technologies can be used in major games, virtual reality (VR) is an additional avenue being explored. Major sports teams have employed this technology as part of their practice routines. Therefore, it is not beyond the realm of possibility for athletes with disabilities to take part in games and competitions remotely or to have a separate event or classification for VR athletes.

In addition, these technologies could allow able-bodied people worldwide to see, feel, and experience what training and competition are like for elite athletes with disabilities in various sports. VR use could expand knowledge and interest in parasport exponentially, allowing fans worldwide to follow their favorite athletes as they prepare between events. This keeps parasports in the forefront instead of the background between major games.

The VR experience typically involves three areas:

- Hyper-immersive or emotion-based designs (which can involve scents, sights, or sounds)
- Live-action-style POV (first-person point-of-view) events (e.g., experience how to train for an event)
- Games and gamified experiences (Interaction Design Foundation, n.d.)

Imagine what it would be like to virtually experience playing wheelchair rugby or wheelchair tennis from the safety and comfort of your own home, while realistically exploring and immersing oneself in any facet of the disability sport ecosystem—even interacting and training with the athletes themselves. Future potential sport managers could go behind the scenes to find out what it is like, virtually, to put on a major disability sport competition.

Like those technologies, esports is increasing in popularity. Esports competitions are usually presented in organized, multiplayer video game competitions between professional players individually or as teams (IGEA, 2021). Leveraging these athletic competitions could be another way for athletes who are limited in their physical ability or have other health conditions to take part in major games and competitions. Major multisport events like the Asian Games already include esports on their program. The IOC hired its first head of virtual sport "to help the IOC pursue recommendation nine of Olympic Agenda 2020+5, which covers promoting the development of virtual sport and using its increasing popularity to assist with the growth of the Olympic Movement" (Burke, 2022, para. 2). This represents increased acceptance of esports by the greater sports community.

Expanding Opportunities Worldwide

A concept mentioned with Cybathlon was the incorporation of a truly "global" competition. With Cybathlon setting a precedent, especially during the COVID-19 pandemic, it is possible that major high-level games can be adapted and played remotely, especially if the concept of esports and VR are incorporated. Indeed, the pandemic and its viral variants forced competitions, not just Cybathlon, to overcome and adapt, as parasport continually must do. So, the question becomes whether the trend of athletes taking part in games remotely will continue, or whether major games eventually resume having all competition on-site in the host country.

Major games must continually explore all expansion opportunities and possible host countries to stay relevant and truly global. Recognizing that operating framework, IPC President Andrew Parsons gave total IPC commitment to the Republic of Ghana, a country in West Africa, to host the first-ever African Para Games in 2023. It is expected that around 50 countries will compete in the 2023 Games (Dowdeswell, 2022).

Expanding globally does not always refer to a physical place or location. The term *expansion* could also refer to **inclusion** because "inclusion refers to how diversity is leveraged to create a fair, equitable, healthy, and high-performing organization or community where all individuals are respected, feel engaged and motivated, and their contributions toward meeting organizational and societal goals are valued" (O'Mara & Richter, 2014, p. 2). Exemplifying that definition, Majid Rashed, president of the APC, fully committed to ensuring that the Hangzhou 2022 Games boosted inclusion. The hope was that the 2022 Games would be an opportunity to build a more inclusive Asia by developing the Paralympic movement in the region. The APC hoped to accomplish this by examining and making substantial improvements in the areas of arrival and departure from Hangzhou, transportation, catering, accommodation, doping control, competition, training, medical services, ticketing, athletes' village, and ceremonies (Pavitt, 2021).

Summary

This chapter introduces major sports events that feature athletes with disabilities. Some are disability-specific, such as the Paralympic Games, while others, such as the Commonwealth Games, incorporate disability sport as part of the overall event program. The most prominent and modern events differ in their missions, visions, and values; who competes; and the sports included within the specific programs. Understanding current issues indicates how the Paralympic movement continues to evolve to stay current with worldwide demand for its athletes and events. Elite adaptive sport is not static but continues to change, and sport managers must be aware of how to respond to the challenges.

CRITICAL THINKING EXERCISES

1. Let's think beyond the book. The Paralympic Games will be coming to Los Angeles in 2028, and the event will need volunteers and staff. Volunteer work areas are international relations, competition operations, press operations and broadcasting, venue operations, marketing, human resources, technology, cultural programs, logistics, security, sports information, language services, customer relations, transportation, and social media. Volunteer work locations are transportation hubs, the Athlete Village, the broadcast center, competition sites, practice sites, and general venue areas. Of the work areas listed, which one would you most like to work with? Why? Of the work locations listed, where would you most likely want to work? Why?

2. Go to the IPC website and look at a list of sports typically on the Paralympic program.

   - Choose two parasports you would want to watch in person.
   - Explain why you chose these two.
   - Which specific countries or athletes excel at these sports?

3. You have been assigned to cover an upcoming Paralympic Games for NBC. One of your responsibilities will be interviewing some of the athletes. Develop a list of questions you would like to ask when conducting a 15-minute interview.

CHAPTER 8

Sport for Athletes With Intellectual Impairment

Abby Fines, PhD, and Christina Mehrtens, PhD

LEARNING OBJECTIVES

After reading this chapter, you will be able to do the following:

- Discuss the philosophical and structural differences of the Special Olympics and Paralympics.
- Understand intellectual disability and intellectual impairment and explain how they affect sport participation.
- Examine how the historical narratives of each movement influence goals toward inclusion.
- Compare how organizational governance of Special Olympics and the Paralympics (Virtus) affect competition for athletes with intellectual disability and intellectual impairment.

This chapter will clarify pathways for athletes with intellectual disabilities or intellectual impairment to participate in sport. We begin by describing the major differences between the Special Olympics and Paralympics, then contextualize intellectual disabilities and sport participation before looking at each movement more specifically. Sections about the Special Olympics and Paralympics examine the historical narratives of each organization to understand implications of sport management on the inclusion (or exclusion) of athletes with intellectual disabilities in sport.

Special Olympics Versus Paralympics

The Paralympics and Special Olympics are often confused, but they are two separate movements recognized by the International Olympic Committee (IOC). They are similar in that they both focus on sport for athletes with a disability and are managed by international nonprofit organizations. Apart from that, Special Olympics and Paralympics differ in three main areas: (1) the disability categories of their athletes, (2) the criteria and philosophy under which athletes participate, and (3) the structure of their respective organizations (Special Olympics Australia, n.d.).

Athletes

Special Olympics welcomes athletes with intellectual disabilities, cognitive delays, or developmental disabilities that limit functioning in both general learning and adaptive skills. Special Olympics athletes represent all ability levels, which may include individuals with secondary sensory and physical disabilities. Paralympics welcomes athletes from 10 different impairment types that are grouped into three categories: physical, visual, and intellectual impairments. This chapter focuses on the latter, particularly because this group of athletes is rarely associated with the Paralympics. Unlike the Special Olympics, participation in the Paralympic Games requires that athletes meet certain impairment criteria and qualifying standards for eligibility.

Philosophy

Special Olympics believes deeply in the transformative power of sport to promote social inclusion. Excellence is measured by *personal* achievement, the reaching of one's maximum potential. Thus, Special Olympics employs a system of **divisioning**—grouping athletes based on their gender, age, and competitive ability—to ensure all athletes have an equal chance of succeeding. The Paralympics also believes in leading social change through (para)sport, but excellence is measured by *elite* achievement. Athletes must satisfy stringent impairment criteria and qualifying standards determined by the International Paralympic Committee (IPC) and by various disability and sport-specific organizations. For Paralympic athletes with intellectual impairments, **Virtus** is the governing body and a founding member of the IPC.

Structure

Special Olympics is a global movement committed to creating opportunities for people with intellectual disabilities, of all ability levels, to engage in healthy lifestyles through sport while leading social change toward inclusion, acceptance, and dignity for all. The international headquarters is in Washington, D.C., with regional and local programs in more than 170 countries. Special Olympics International governs the 30-plus Olympic-type sports offered to athletes.

The Paralympics work to create an inclusive world through parasport for athletes with physical, visual, and intellectual impairments on a high-performance stage. Located in Bonn, Germany, the IPC is the governing body responsible for supporting its members and managing the Paralympic Games. Membership draws together National Paralympic Committees (e.g., United States Olympic & Paralympic Committee), international sport federations (e.g., World ParaVolley, International Tennis Federation), national sport organizations, and International Sports Organization for the Disabled (ISOD; International Paralympic Committee, n.d.a). Virtus (formerly the International Federation for Athletes with Intellectual Impairments; INAS) is the international governing body for athletes with intellectual impairment; Athletes Without Limits is the national counterpart in the United States. These organizations promote the development of sport for people with an intellectual impairment, which includes eligibility for fair competition.

Contextualizing Intellectual Disability Within Sport

Both disability and sport are a natural part of the human experience. In 2011, the World Health Organization (WHO) and World Bank jointly published the first *World Report on Disability*, estimating that more than 1 billion people experience living with a disability, corresponding to about 15% of the world's population (World Health Organization, 2021). In the United States, Centers for Disease Control and Prevention

Special Olympics athletes celebrate a victory.
Special Olympics Virginia

(CDC) data indicate that the prevalence is greater, suggesting that approximately 61 million (26%) adults are living with a disability. While these numbers are significant, disability is extremely diverse. People living with intellectual disabilities, the most common type of developmental disability, are estimated to account for 1% to 3% of the entire population, about 200 million people globally and 7 million people in the United States (American Psychiatric Association, n.d.; Special Olympics, n.d.l). Although a small fraction compared to the greater disability community, contextualizing intellectual disability (in sport) is also necessary.

> Both disability and sport are a natural part of the human experience.

It is first important to address how intellectual disability should be referenced. Until 2010, the term *intellectual disability* was synonymous with the terms *mental retard*, *mental retardation*, and *retard*. The passing of Rosa's Law (Bill S.2781), signed by former president Barack Obama, replaced these outdated and derogatory terms with **person-first language**—"individual with an intellectual disability" and "intellectual disability"—in all federal health, education, and labor policies (Rosa's Law, Pub.L.No. 111-256, 2010; Special Olympics, n.d.n). This chapter uses person-first (or rights-based) language for these reasons:

- Person-first language is used internationally because of the United Nations Convention on the Rights for Persons with Disabilities and nationally in United States federal law (Rosa's Law, Pub.L.No. 111-256, 2010; United Nations, 2006).

- The Special Olympics disability language guidelines use person-first language (Special Olympics, n.d.o).
- Person-first language allows a more seamless transition in language between *disability* and *impairment* depending on sport context.

Intellectual disabilities is a phrase used when an individual experiences certain limitations in cognitive functioning and skills. These differences in cognitive abilities affect how an individual learns and thrives in areas of social and motor development; however, they should not be confused with other conditions, such as learning disabilities (e.g., dyslexia), attention deficit hyperactivity disorder (ADHD), or mental illness. The American Association of Intellectual and Developmental Disabilities (AAIDD) and the *Diagnostic and Statistical Manual of Mental Disorders, 5th Edition* (DSM-5) specify that an individual has an intellectual disability if they meet three criteria:

1. Significant deficits or limitations in intellectual functioning (often measured by an IQ of less than 70-75)
2. Significant deficits or limitations in adaptive behavior (the collection of conceptual, social, and practical skills learned and used to live, work, and play in the community)
3. The onset of limitations is during childhood (before age 18 or 22)

The aforementioned diagnostic definition would be referred to as *intellectual disability* under the medical model and as **intellectual impairment** under the social model of disability. The medical model emphasizes the individual, particularly in comparison to the "typically developing" child or arbitrary statistical cutoff points (Shakespeare, 2013). Thus, intellectual disability becomes an embodied problem that debases a person compared to a societal norm. In contrast, the social model evaluates the way society is structured, how this hinders societal engagement (including sport participation), and the supports and services essential to increase such engagement. Through this lens, intellectual impairment refers to the functional limitations an individual might experience due to a medical condition, and intellectual disability refers to the interaction between people living with impairments and a disabling world—that is, an environment and society filled with structural, cultural, and social barriers amplifies the existing impairment. These barriers extend to sport contexts and thereby individuals with intellectual impairments do not have equal opportunity to participate in mainstream and disability-specific activities (United Nations, 2006).

> *Intellectual impairment* refers to the functional limitations an individual might experience due to a medical condition, and *intellectual disability* refers to the interaction between people living with impairments and a disabling world.

Interestingly, while both institutions draw from the same diagnostic definition to contextualize their participants (Avant, 2022), Special Olympics tends to use the phrase *intellectual disability* and Virtus the phrase *intellectual impairment*. What does this mean? Does it imply that one identifies more with the medical or social model of disability? In consideration of their vision, mission, and values, it can be concluded that both movements side with the social model or a combination of both models (i.e., the ICF Framework; World Health Organization, n.d.). These organizations work to eradicate the physical, attitudinal, and sport-specific barriers that exclude individuals with intellectual disabilities from sport participation by providing a spectrum of opportunities at a recreational, developmental, and high-performance levels. Therefore, despite their opposing use of language, both Special Olympics and the Paralympics are aware of the personal and environmental factors that contribute to contextualizing intellectual disability (in sport).

Etiology and Classification of Intellectual Disability

Critical to understanding the athlete population each sport organization serves is considering the **classification** (severity) and **etiology** (cause) of intellectual disability. The cause of intellectual disability is often linked to prenatal, perinatal, and postnatal developmental stages, such as exposure to environmental factors (e.g., toxic substances, malnutrition, brain infections, or trauma) and genetic conditions (e.g., Down syndrome, fragile X syndrome, or PKU). For a majority, the cause of intellectual disability is unknown (Boat et al., 2015). Many individuals with moderate and severe intellectual disabilities also experience other cognitive (e.g., autism and ADHD), sensory (e.g., visual and hearing loss), and physical (e.g., epilepsy, cerebral palsy, motor disorders) impairments. While Special Olympics athletes are more representative of the general intellectual disability population, Paralympic athletes tend to be a distinct group with mild intellectual impairments (higher IQ) and without accompanying metabolic or physical conditions that reduce potential in athletic performance.

If defining intellectual *disability* gives consideration to societal and environmental barriers (as proclaimed by the social model), then it is important to recognize the role of such barriers in the etiology of intellectual disability. While both Special Olympics and Virtus use the three-pronged definition the AAIDD and DSM-5 provide, understanding the nuances surrounding cultural variations in the epidemiology and diagnosis of intellectual disability is critical for providing equitable opportunities. For example, spiritual or religious beliefs in some nations attribute the cause of disability to personal wrongdoing or misfortune, perpetuating stigma and shame (Burns, 2018). These nations will most likely have different ideas about inclusion and access to sport for people with intellectual disabilities. Varying cultural conceptions about disability will therefore affect the function of service structures within those regions (Burns, 2018). This is evident within Western understanding of intellectual disabilities as well. The shift from DSM-4 to DSM-5 classification (see table 8.1) allowed for a more comprehensive view of intellectual disabilities. DSM-5 classification abandoned specific IQ scores as a diagnostic criterion and focused on the skills a person had for independent living. Releasing a person from an IQ score frees them from the ceiling of expectations associated with the given number, thereby changing the way sport is provided.

Characteristics of Intellectual Disability and Sport Participation

Similar to etiology and classification, the characteristics and lived experience of disability can be vastly different from person to person. No matter the diagnosis—even if the label of intellectual disability is consistent—assumptions or generalizations cannot (and should not) be made about an individual's ability or limitations. The Dear Colleague Letter (Department of Education, 2013), which outlines the responsibilities of schools in the United States to include students with disabilities in extracurricular athletics under the Rehabilitation Act of 1973, states it this way:

> A school district may not operate its program or activity on the basis of generalizations, assumptions, prejudices, or stereotypes about disability generally, or specific disabilities in particular. A school district also may not rely on generalizations about what students with a type of disability are capable of—one student with a certain type of disability may not be able to play a certain type of sport, but another student with the same disability may be able to play that sport. (p. 5)

In sport, as with any context, it is important to understand the individual's abilities, support needs, and goals they wish to achieve. Table 8.1 provides a starting point for variations in classification and the

TABLE 8.1 Classifying Intellectual Disability

Classification of severity	Approximate prevalence by classification	DSM-4 criteria (based on IQ scores)	DSM-5 criteria (based on severity of adaptive functioning)	AAIDD (based on intensity of supports needed)
Mild	85%	IQ 50-69	Can live independently with minimal supports (e.g., reminders or help with life decisions)	Intermittent support: during times of transition, uncertainty, or stress
Moderate	10%	IQ 36-49	Independence with moderate supports (e.g., group homes); more support for social cues, social judgment, and social decisions	Limited support: to enhance adaptive functioning (conceptual, social, and practical skills)
Severe	3.5%	IQ 20-35	Self-care requires daily assistance and safety supervision; basic communication skills	Extensive support: daily support for self-care and individual functioning
Profound	1.5%	IQ <20	Usually 24-hour care and support are needed; co-occurring sensory and/or physical impairments	Pervasive support: intensive daily supports for self-care, health, and safety

Adapted by permission from National Academies of Sciences, Engineering, and Medicine, *Mental Disorders and Disabilities Among Low-Income Children,* edited by T.F. Boat and J.T. Wu (Washington, DC: The National Academies Press, 2015), 171, permission conveyed through Copyright Clearance Center, Inc.

support levels toward independent living. Keeping an individualized approach in mind, the following section considers some example characteristics that individuals with intellectual disabilities might experience in relation to their participation in sport.

Intellectual Functioning and Sport Participation

Intellectual functioning, or intelligence, refers to an individual's general mental capacity. **Cognitive skills** include learning, reasoning, problem solving, planning, inhibitory control, and selective and sustained attention, among others—all of which can affect the sport participation of individuals with intellectual disabilities, whether mild

or severe (Van Biesen et al., 2021). Certain sports require **open skills**, or activities that are less predictable and demand quick decision making by the athlete. In basketball, a player must decide to pass, dribble, or shoot based on the decisions of teammates and opponents. This is in contrast to **closed skill** activities, where the tasks and environment are more controlled, thus requiring a lighter cognitive load (Burns, 2015). At least in theory, the 100-yard dash is performed the same way from start to finish, though other confounding variables can influence performance, such as distracting spectators for an individual who struggles with selective attention. No matter the nature of the sport, several supports can help athletes develop their **sport intelligence** (Van Biesen, 2021) and sport performance. Athletes with intellectual disabilities might process and learn things slowly, so practicing high-volume repetition and combining short verbal cues with images or video demonstrations can assist with learning complex skills. Employing such strategies can benefit spectator and volunteer engagement as well (arguably for those with and without intellectual disabilities). An equitable approach to sport management will consider intellectual functioning (impairment) as well as surrounding environmental factors (disability; World Health Organization, n.d.).

> Athletes with intellectual disabilities might process and learn things slowly, so practicing high-volume repetition and combining short verbal cues with images or video demonstrations can assist with learning complex skills.

Adaptive Functioning and Sport Participation

Adaptive functioning (behavior) refers to the skills that are learned and practiced daily, including the following skills:

- Conceptual (e.g., receptive and expressive language, math and reasoning, self-direction)
- Social (e.g., empathy, self-esteem, interpersonal skills, social awareness, responsibility)
- Practical (e.g., personal care, occupational skills, managing money and schedules, using transportation, safety)

This collection of skills has a strong correlational (not causal) relationship with intelligence (Tassé et al., 2016) and determines independence in society as it is currently structured, which includes participation in sport. The range of skills varies considerably among people with intellectual disabilities, so the support needed will vary considerably

to elevate their participation in sport. Many people with intellectual disabilities experience difficulties with self-regulation. They may struggle coping with and appropriately responding to social situations or changing environments (Noel, 2018). When autism spectrum disorder (ASD) is present with intellectual disabilities, challenges with self-regulation may be exacerbated. Individuals with ASD often have unique (hyper or hypo) sensitivities to sensory input (e.g., lights, music, fabric) as well as communication difficulties that prevent them from expressing their needs.

The social and emotional challenges someone might experience should not exclude them from sport participation. Continuing with the example of self-regulation, several accommodations can be made to ensure meaningful engagement. Transitioning from the routine of training to the newness of competition can be exciting, but the commotion it brings can also be overwhelming and overstimulating. Clearly defining expectations or gradual exposure of a competition experience, including the schedule and environment, can help athletes prepare for change. Providing quiet spaces in venues during competition can help athletes decompress by reducing or managing sensory overload. Sport events (training and competition) can also accommodate every athlete's voice, even if they are "nonverbal," by using an interpreter, sign language, or alternative communication devices. In other words, sport design and management can be more inclusive when professionals reach beyond traditional practices and procedures.

Adaptive functioning (specifically **practical skills**) may also be influenced by motor disorders or physical disabilities associated with intellectual disabilities. Each athlete with intellectual disabilities can present a combination of comorbidities of their own, with different degrees of severity, that can affect sport participation. Down syndrome, for example, the most commonly known cause of intellectual disability, is accompanied by a myriad of metabolic and physical conditions—such as hypotonia (low muscle tone), reduced oxygen uptake ($\dot{V}O_2$max), hypothyroidism, and cardiorespiratory issues—that influence motor development, skill acquisition, and high-level athletic performance (Seron & Greguol, 2014; Moreau, 2021). Therefore, athletes with Down syndrome, and others with multiple disabilities, are more likely to participate in Special Olympics than Paralympic sport. Overall, effective sport management and delivery for this population should consider cognitive, social, emotional, and physical dimensions of the individual, not just their disability identifier.

> The social and emotional challenges someone might experience should not exclude them from sport participation.

Intellectual Disability and Special Olympics

The main differences between the Special Olympics and Paralympics have already been introduced. This section takes a closer look at how the Special Olympics strives to promote social inclusion through sport. It starts by examining the events that ignited change before examining the current structure of governance and operations that continue the movement forward.

Historical Context

Understanding the historical context and evolution of sport organizations is critical to successful sport management. There is always a story before the story (e.g., watch the movie *Crip Camp* about the disability rights movement), and that prequel usually reveals the trajectory, whether positive or negative, of an organization or movement. This section introduces Special Olympics through its mission statement, then explores why and how that mission started by looking at a brief chronology what led to the creation of the organization.

Special Olympics is the world's largest organization dedicated to promoting respect, inclusion, and acceptance of people with intellectual disabilities. Its mission is to provide year-round sports training and athletic competition in a variety of Olympic-type sports for children and adults with intellectual disabilities, giving them continuing opportunities to develop physical fitness, demonstrate courage, experience joy, and share their gifts, skills and friendship with their families, other Special Olympics athletes, and the community (Special Olympics, n.d.l; Special Olympics, n.d.u).

Research Drives Action

Before the 1970s, children and adults living with intellectual disabilities were misunderstood. They were excluded from all aspects of life, hidden away in homes or institutions, because no one imagined they could acquire the knowledge and skills to become contributing members of society. At the time, no one imagined that sport and physical activity could be of therapeutic value to further their development and belonging in the world. For decades, children and adults with intellectual disabilities were a neglected population, and their families were burdened by shame (Special Olympics, n.d.x).

The understanding for intellectual disabilities slowly began to evolve after a call for research in the 1950s and 1960s. The Joseph P. Kennedy, Jr. Foundation was established in 1946, one of the first of its kind to focus efforts on the care and support of people with intellectual disabilities. In following years, the foundation advocated for research about this population, starting with the causes of intellectual disabilities. Urgency around the need for knowledge emanated from Eunice Kennedy Shriver. Originally a trustee of the Joseph P. Kennedy, Jr. Foundation and then named the director in 1957, Shriver was a potent force in driving social change. When her brother, John F. Kennedy, was elected president of the United States in 1960, she urged him to make intellectual disabilities a priority. Then she helped create the National Institute of Child Health and Human Development, which was officially signed into legislation by President Kennedy on October 17, 1962 (Special Olympics, n.d.m). Research then expanded and included an emphasis on families and maternal health as well as training teachers and professionals about the development of intellectual disabilities.

A growing body of research demonstrated the benefits of physical activity for people with intellectual disabilities, namely that participation in physical activity and fitness led to greater opportunity for participation in society. This was critical for sport development. In 1964, the Joseph P. Kennedy, Jr. Foundation sponsored a two-day conference on "Developing Special Recreation Programs for the Retarded" that launched even greater exploration regarding the status and development of different physical activity opportunities for people with intellectual disabilities (American Association for Health, Physical Education and Recreation and National Recreation and Park Association, 1968). With the support of organizations like American Association for Health, Physical Education, and Recreation (AAHPER), work toward establishing year-round fitness and recreation programming began. This included community sport programming and (adapted) physical education in schools.

Summer Camp Experiment

Eunice Kennedy Shriver was not just a powerful political voice but also an active pioneer in advancing opportunities for sport and recreation for people with intellectual disabilities. The first Camp Shriver was held after a woman in Bethesda, Maryland, brought to Shriver's attention the absence of summer camp programs for her child with an intellectual disability. In June 1962, Shriver opened her backyard as a summer camp for children with intellectual disabilities. Through sport and play, her vision was to focus on what these children could do and not dwell on what they could not do. She insisted that an essential aspect of camp was the interaction of children with and without intellectual disabilities. With a goal of one-on-one instruction, the camp recruited high school and college students to volunteer as counselors. However tentative at first, counselors quickly learned that campers with intellectual disabilities were not difficult or unteachable. They were more than their ascribed stereotypes; in fact, they were children just wanting to have fun, like every other child (Special Olympics, n.d.c).

The summer camp experiment was an instant success. Shriver hosted her backyard camp annually, and Camp Shriver served as the catalyst for similar summer camp opportunities in surrounding areas. Creating opportunities for sport and recreation began to transform lives of people with intellectual disabilities as well as public perceptions. In fact, the positive aftermath of Camp Shriver may have prompted Eunice Kennedy Shriver to embrace her own vulnerability. About three months after the first summer camp experience, in September 1962, the Kennedy family made their first public acknowledgment that their sister, Rosemary, had an intellectual disability (Special Olympics, n.d.c). The article titled "Hope for the Retarded" appeared in the *Saturday Evening Post* and became pivotal in changing attitudes toward people with intellectual disabilities, convincing parents and the public that there should be no shame or guilt in difference (Shriver, 1962). In a position of influence, Eunice Kennedy Shriver used her public platform to address at full force the injustices faced by people with intellectual disabilities.

> In a position of influence, Eunice Kennedy Shriver used her public platform to address at full force the injustices faced by people with intellectual disabilities.

1968 Games: The Tipping Point

By 1966, research had demonstrated the importance of sport and recreation for people with intellectual disabilities, and year-round community and school programming was in development to deliver those benefits. One early success story of year-round programming was the Special Recreation Program (as it was then called) of the Chicago Park

District. The program's initial source of funding was a US$10,000 grant from the Joseph P. Kennedy, Jr. Foundation that allowed it to expand into 10 city parks. Encouraged by early success, the Chicago Park District began to plan a citywide track meet in 1967. Eunice Kennedy Shriver, however, asked leaders to expand their scope, for her next aspiration was for multisport, nationwide sports contests (Special Olympics, n.d.x). Such an event was implemented the following year.

The first International Special Olympics Summer Games was a one-day event held on July 20, 1968. The Games were a joint venture between the Joseph P. Kennedy, Jr. Foundation and the Chicago Park District, with the goal of publicly showcasing ability, not disability, through athletic competition. To do so, organizers of the Games received crucial support from the local government, labor unions, and volunteers. More than 1,000 athletes from the United States and Canada joined together on Soldier Field in Chicago to compete in more than 200 events, including skill-based activities and individual and team sports. The stands were virtually empty, similar to Camp Shriver, but the volunteers were plentiful. The volunteers provided support and coaching for the athletes as well as managing the athletic events. It was the first time many athletes heard applause, but it would not be their last. Inspired, Shriver pledged that more Games would be held in 1970 and every two years after. Her statement of hope at the opening of the Games would now have the chance to ring true for decades to come through the Special Olympics motto: "Let me win, but if I cannot win, let me be brave in the attempt" (Special Olympics, n.d.x; Section A New Dawn; para. 13).

Growth and Dedication to Inclusion

It only took one Games to ignite decades of empowerment for people with intellectual disabilities. Just a few months after the first Chicago Summer Games, the Special Olympics formally incorporated in December 1968 (Special Olympics, Inc.), with a seven-member board of directors. In the months and years that followed, sport and recreation programs expanded across the United States and international borders.

Through this historical context, we see that the Special Olympics gained a global foothold by staying true to its mission and attaining public and private financial and organizational support along the way. The core of the Special Olympics is to use the transformative power of sport to include people with intellectual disabilities in their communities and focus on what athletes can do rather than what they cannot do. Athletes find confidence in their abilities, and the world is exposed to a greater sense of human talent and potential. Figure 8.1 shows milestones in Special Olympics history.

Governance and Support

Special Olympics International (SOI) is the governing body of the global Special Olympics movement. It is responsible for implementing nonprofit governance practices that uplift all Special Olympics Programs (capital "P" intentional) as well as providing technical assistance to each of the seven Special Olympics regions across the globe. Special Olympics North America (SONA) is one such region and helps implement SOI policies and initiatives by supporting each accredited program. In the United States, Special Olympics–accredited programs are representative of all 50 states—for example, Special Olympics Virginia (SOVA) and Special Olympics Minnesota (SOMN). Each program is a nonprofit 501(c)(3) charitable organization responsible for following rules established by SOI in its delivery of services, the provision of sport training and competition for people with intellectual disabilities. Many accredited programs, including those in the United States, are divided into smaller geographic regions called subprograms (or areas). Subprograms have an active volunteer management team to assist with local program operations, which are the grassroots level of the movement. Local programs are the direct service unit for athletes, families, and the public to provide training and competition opportunities while

December 1971	Special Olympics is the only organization authorized by the U.S. Olympic Committee to use the name *Olympics* in the United States.
February 1977	The first International Special Olympics Winter Games are held in Steamboat Springs, Colorado. CBS, ABC, and NBC television networks covered the Games.
August 1979	The stands are no longer vacant. In fact, the Games attracted high-profile attention with boxing legend Muhammad Ali being a prominent supporter.
1986	The United Nations declares 1986 the International Year of Special Olympics.
Summer 1987	The first prime time broadcast of a Special Olympics event on a major television network (ABC) are the Summer Games in Indiana.
February 1988	Special Olympics are officially recognized by the International Olympic Committee (IOC), although the Games are not held in conjunction with the Olympic year and aims.
March 1993	Austria hosts the first Winter Games held outside the United States. A head of state takes part in the opening ceremony for the first time.
July 1995	During the World Games in Connecticut, new initiatives to promote inclusion and health made their debut, including Healthy Athletes. Also, people with intellectual disabilities serve as certified officials for the first time.
January 1997	Healthy Athletes becomes an official Special Olympics initiative.
May 2000	Athletes from every region come together to discuss the future of the Special Olympics movement in the first-ever Global Athlete Congress.
June 2003	Ireland hosts the first Summer Games held outside the United States.
October 2004	The Special Olympics Sport and Empowerment Act is signed by President George W. Bush, marking the first time Special Olympics secured legislative support. The Act pledged US$15 million every year for five years to encourage greater respect for people with Global Athlete Congress through Special Olympics Programs.
January 2013	The first Special Olympics Global Development Summit is held as part of the Winter Games in Pyeongchang. Government officials, human rights activists, and sports and business leaders explore ways to "end the cycle of poverty and exclusion for people with intellectual disabilities."
September 2013	Disney and ESPN partner with Special Olympics to support social inclusion through Unified Sports programming. They provide support with a multimillion-dollar financial and in-kind investment.
July 2015	The B. Thomas Golisano Foundation partners with Special Olympics to expand the impact of global health initiatives. They provide support with a US$25 million gift, which is in addition to a previous US$12 million gift made by Tom Golisano in 2012.
As of 2022	More than 5 million Special Olympics athletes representing more than 170 countries train and compete in 32 Olympic-type sports across 100,000 events each year.

FIGURE 8.1 Key events and milestones in Special Olympics history.

Source: Special Olympics, (n.d.x, n.d.y, n.d.z, n.d.aa., n.d.bb., n.d.cc., n.d.dd).

creating inclusive communities (Special Olympics, 2019).

The IOC officially recognized SOI through a Protocol of Agreement signed on February 15, 1988. This agreement indicates it is the solemn duty and responsibility of SOI and its constituents to uphold ideals of the Olympic movement and guard the word *Olympics* from exploitation. To do so, the Protocol of Agreement also clarified the role of Special Olympics in setting itself apart from the Olympics. The license the IOC granted to the SOI does not imply any material or financial obligation, and SOI and programs are prohibited to use the Olympic logo, emblem, motto, flag, or anthem (International Paralympic Committee and Special Olympics International, 1988). This is partly why SOI sets up an Accreditation License Agreement with its programs to ensure the rights and obligations of accredited programs under the Special Olympics banner (see Article 6 of Special Olympics governance to learn more about the accreditation process; Special Olympics, n.d.a). Overall, the Special Olympics brand is to promote social inclusion of people with intellectual disabilities through sport, and every layer of the organization takes on the same name and mission from across the globe.

Leadership and Volunteers

SOI is governed by a volunteer board of directors, as is typical of most nonprofits. SOI board members are business and sport leaders, professional athletes, educators, and experts in intellectual disabilities from around the world. They are responsible for international policy, high-level strategy, and the accountability of the organization. Ongoing growth and development of the organization is supported by a global senior management team as well as the managing directors that head the seven Special Olympics regions: Africa, Asia Pacific, East Asia, Europe/Eurasia, Latin America, Middle East/North Africa, and North America. In addition, one athlete from each region comprises the Global Athlete Leadership Council to provide athlete-centric guidance to the board and management teams (Special Olympics, n.d.j).

Volunteers must also be recognized as essential leadership in delivering the Special Olympics mission. Their commitments can range greatly; they are Games and event organizers, fundraisers, managers, health care providers, coaches, trainers, officials, unified partners, and fans. Although volunteers may be embedded within the work of every organization level, they are more often the direct service for athletes and families to provide sport opportunities (see figure 8.2). Hence, volunteers are stakeholders most positively influenced by direct contact with athletes who have intellectual disabilities (Li & Wu, 2019).

Competition and Games

The core of the Special Olympics mission statement is to provide year-round sport opportunities to strengthen personal well-being as well as inclusive communities. This section breaks down how the organization

Global Ambassadors

All volunteers are essential for successful programming and development. However, celebrity support helps raise the profile of Special Olympics and its athletes. Global ambassadors are international icons that lend their time, talent, and resources to support the Special Olympics mission. A few names that have identified themselves as global ambassadors include Apolo Anton Ohno (Olympic speed skater), Michael Phelps (Olympic swimmer), Michelle Kwan (Olympic figure skater), Vanessa Williams (singer and Broadway performer), Chris Pratt (actor and producer), and Lauren Potter (actor and advocate with Down syndrome). For a full list of global ambassadors, visit www.specialolympics.org/about/ambassadors/.

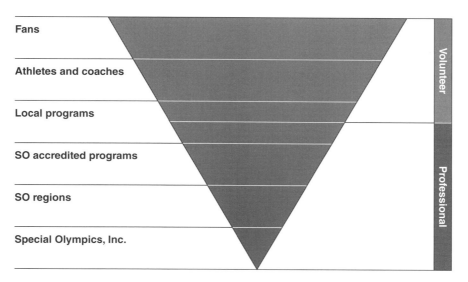

FIGURE 8.2 Special Olympics governance.
Reprinted by permission from Special Olympics North America Local Program Guide (2019), 9.

delivers sport to do so. Some aspects of Special Olympics sport management correspond to the Paralympics (e.g., athlete development and eligibility) but with unique intention.

Philosophy and Goal

"Special Olympics is founded on the belief that people with ID can—with proper instruction and encouragement—learn, enjoy, and benefit from participation in individual and team sports" (Special Olympics, 2019, p. 14). Special Olympics believes that consistent training and competition among those of equal abilities is essential for helping athletes reach their personal best on and off the field. Special Olympics also believes and has demonstrated that the power of sport—both through participation and observation—strengthens individuals, families, and communities around the world (Asunta et al., 2022; McConkey & Meneke, 2020). Therefore, the ultimate goal of Special Olympics is to continue increasing awareness of intellectual disability, ability, and inclusion through sport, so individuals with intellectual disabilities can use their skills and talents as productive and respected members of society.

Sports

Special Olympics offers year-round training and competition for individuals with intellectual disabilities through more than 30 Olympic-style individual and team sports. Each local program determines the sports and seasons provided in their regions or areas and trains volunteer coaches and officials to deliver sport-specific programming. Unlike the Paralympics and Olympics, all sports and programs are under the umbrella of Special Olympics. Thus, the rules and regulations of each sport and corresponding events can be found in one place (see Special Olympics, n.d.r) and are adapted to meet the ability levels of athletes with intellectual disabilities. Rules and regulations may be modified as well as the type of opportunity. Basketball team competition rules are based on those published by the International Basketball Federation (FIBA) yet can be modified if deemed appropriate by the Special Olympics Program to promote meaningful participation. The length of the game or shot clock, for instance, can be adjusted at the discretion of the competition manager (Special Olympics, n.d.b). If the traditional sport (e.g., 5-on-5 team competition) is not appropriate for athletes, Special Olympics provides other avenues for meaningful participation. Continuing with the example of basketball, four variations of the sport are outlined in the rulebook: speed dribble, individual skills, team skills, and 3-on-3 competition. Despite these wide-ranging adaptations, an athlete with a severe or profound intellectual disability (often accompanied by other motor and sensory disabilities) may not be able to participate competitively. As a part of their sports repertoire, Special Olympics created the Motor Activity Training Program (MATP) to provide sport-specific, noncompetitive activities based on the functional abilities of the athlete (Special Olympics, n.d.k).

Unified Sports has become an integral initiative of the movement. First pioneered in the 1980s, Unified Sports joins approximately equal numbers of teammates with and without intellectual disabilities on the same team. The underlying principle is simple: Having sport in common paves the way to friendship and understanding. There are three Unified Sports Models—competitive, player development, and recreation (Special Olympics, 2012b)—all of which must abide by the principle of meaningful involvement, which "ensures that every player is given an opportunity to contribute to the success of his or her team through their unique skills and qualities" (Special Olympics, 2012, para. 1). Unified Sports has attracted several high-profile professional sports organizations (e.g., ESPN, Major League Soccer, National Federation of High Schools) that have helped support the expansion of the program and increase the impact of social inclusion (Special Olympics, n.d.t).

Special Olympics Young Athletes is another initiative driving social inclusion. For all children ages 2 to 7, Young Athletes is an early childhood play program focused on fun ways to advance in core developmental milestones. Children learn basic sport skills, healthy habits, and **social skills**. The program provides the building blocks for children to become "physically literate" individuals (Special Olympics, n.d.f). Not only that, but Young Athletes nurtures understanding and acceptance at an early age.

Athlete and Coach Development Models

Congruent with most sport federations and national governing bodies, Special Olympics has established guidelines for helping athletes reach their goals—whether fun, fitness, or high performance—and equipping coaches to help them do so. The athlete development model (ADM) is a support plan based on a progression from sport fundamentals, learning to train, training to compete, to recreational activities (maintaining a healthy lifestyle). The model recognizes that athletes will move in and out of stages at their own pace to reach their own personal bests. Separate but related, the coach development model (CDM) provides a framework for training quality and effective coaches. The three main pillars of the model are: coach recruitment, coach education, and coach retention (Special Olympics, n.d.e). Overall, the ADM and CDM are meant to unlock success at every level for every individual.

Sport Eligibility

Participation in Special Olympics is open to every person with an intellectual disability who is at least 8 years old (Special Olympics, n.d.p). To be eligible, a person is considered to have an intellectual disability if that person satisfies any one of three requirements:

- The person has been identified as having an intellectual disability by an agency or professional.
- The person has a cognitive delay as determined by a standardized or reliable measure, such as the IQ test.
- The person has a closely related cognitive developmental disability affecting their general learning and adaptive functioning.

There are no criteria on the severity of the intellectual disability or whether the person has other physical, sensory, learning, or mental impairments. While Young Athletes services children ages 2 to 7, there is no maximum age limitation after age 8. Accredited programs may request departure to the rule if there are extenuating circumstances, but SOI has final authority in determining any exception. The one eligibility caveat is the participation of Unified Sports Partners (individuals without disabilities) who satisfy requirements for class A volunteers and

Athletes With Intellectual Impairments

- **Loretta Claiborne** is a multisport Special Olympics athlete whose testimony shows how sport begets possibility despite discrimination and ableism. Learn more about and from Loretta by watching her TED Talk (2012) "Let's Talk About Intellectual Disabilities" and visiting her website, www.lorettaclaiborne.com.

- **Chris Nikic** was the first athlete with Down syndrome to finish a full Ironman, which he accomplished in 2021. Learn more about his "1% Better" challenge and six-point strategy for reaching his (and your) potential at www.chrisnikic.com.

Criticism of Special Olympics

The organizational effectiveness of Special Olympics has not gone without scrutiny. Its mission of inclusion has its skeptics. Simplican and colleagues (2015) defines **social inclusion** as the interaction between two domains: interpersonal relationships and community participation. Although Special Olympics strives to provide inclusive programs, its efforts may fall short of genuine outcomes. For example, Unified Sports joins players with and without intellectual disabilities in training and competition. By setting, this is inclusive. It is reasonable to assume that an integrated sport setting requires and builds positive interpersonal relationships. It is not known to what extent this carries over to community participation. Research is sparse about the impact of Unified Sports compared to disability-specific programs in promoting social inclusion (McConkey & Menke, 2020).

Another Unified initiative that has been criticized is Unified Physical Education (UPE). UPE provides a school-based opportunity for students with and without disabilities to come together in the context of physical education; however, there is a lack of research appraising its value. Lieberman and Houston-Wilson (2018) argue that using a different identifier for physical education (PE), in this case *Unified* PE, suggests that general physical education is not or cannot be inclusive. In other words, creating a separate program reinforces the idea that students with intellectual disabilities cannot participate in general physical education but rather need "special" attention to promote community inclusion.

The use of volunteers without disabilities has also been criticized in evaluation of social inclusion. Specifically, roles taken by single-event volunteers do not allow for interpersonal relationships. Short one-time interactions with athletes rarely lead to the same long-lasting connections needed for community inclusion (McConkey et al., 2020). One such example is when people volunteer to cheer. Celebratory hugs and applause are not unusual to competition, but when someone is assigned to this task, it can reinforce negative stereotyping by "the infantilization or promotion of childlike perceptions of adults with intellectual disabilities" (Foote & Collins, 2011, p. 291).

Further, McConkey and colleagues (2020) found that event volunteers were unaware of other Special Olympics health and inclusion initiatives and even confused the Special Olympics with the Paralympics. A lack of familiarity or understanding about Special Olympics and its athletes more likely perpetuates existing prejudice. Therefore, while pivotal to the management of Special Olympics programming, uninformed volunteers may be disruptive to the greater mission. If inclusion is about acceptance and belonging through interpersonal relationships and community involvement, then a Unified (integrated) placement will not be enough to move the needle. Special Olympics may need to rethink how volunteers are recruited, trained, or used to reach its goal of inclusion.

comply to other standards set forth by the program (Special Olympics, n.d.p; Special Olympics, 2012a).

Divisioning

Whether a personal best or gold medal, athletes of all ability levels are encouraged to participate and compete, and each is recognized for their performance. This is the fundamental difference between Special Olympics and other sport organizations. Special Olympics believes all athletes should have an equal chance of succeeding when they enter the competitive arena. To ensure equitable opportunity, athletes are grouped with others of similar age, gender, and—most importantly—competitive ability. Special Olympics calls this competition-level matching divisioning (Special Olympics, n.d.g).

Determining Special Olympics divisioning is a two-stage process (not too far removed from the Paralympic classification protocol). The first stage involves sport-specific technical assessment. Depending on the sport, coaches submit times, distances, individual, or team skills assessments. The second stage involves observation of an athlete or team's ability to perform in competition. Athletes are then grouped into equitable and competitive divisions based on age, gender, and ability for meaningful competition. Although not an absolute rule, divisioning is guided by a measure of 15%: There should be no more than 15% variance between the highest and lowest scores within any division (Special Olympics, n.d.g; Special Olympics, n.d.h). This rule applies to local, regional, national, and international competitions. Again, divisioning is a fundamental component of competition that sets Special Olympics apart from other sport organizations, including the Paralympics.

International and National Competitions

Special Olympics Programs host year-round local training and competitions for their athletes, undoubtedly essential for grassroots movement of inclusion. However, since the first Special Olympics International Games in 1968, the World Games have become the flagship event for demonstrating acceptance, understanding, and unity. Nationally, though more recent, the same is true of the USA Games. These global and national Games have a social and emotional impact on athletes and their families as well as coaches, volunteers, and other supporters from all parts of the world (Special Olympics, n.d.v; Werner, 2015). Their impact is heightened because of the high-profile attention they receive from sponsors and individual "ambassadors"—decorated athletes and celebrities with limitless awards and accolades. The 2022 Orlando USA Games, for instance, were sponsored by companies such as Jersey Mike's, Disney, and ESPN, with a roster of ambassadors including Tyra Banks, Mark Cuban, Ellen DeGeneres, Lin-Manuel Miranda, and at least 40 more (Special Olympics USA Games, n.d.). Similar to the Olympic and Paralympic cycles, the Special Olympics World Games occur every two years, alternating between summer and winter events. The USA Games got their start in 2006 in Ames, Iowa, and occur every four years, currently with no winter cycle.

The Special Olympics Unified Cup has become another opportunity for international competition. The first tournament hosted 24 women's and 24 men's unified soccer teams in Chicago in July 2018. Toyota was the presenting sponsor of the 2022 Unified Cup in Detroit, Michigan, which is significant because the company has been a leading force in endorsing the athleticism of Paralympians as well. The Special Olympics Unified Cup shows athletes with and without intellectual disabilities from around the world competing together in a sport that is cherished globally.

Special Olympics competitions still employ the concept of divisioning; however, the World and USA Games cannot abide by the participation-for-all philosophy in the same way grassroots programs can. Only a limited number of athletes can represent their sport and accredited program; thus, athlete (and coach) selection requires a screening process. Unlike the Paralympics, however, athletes are not selected purely on merit because characteristics regarding their intellectual and adaptive functioning need to be considered. To be nominated, the athlete must have won a gold, silver, or bronze medal in at least one event in their sport (remember that divisioning still applies) and adjust to new circumstances beyond their typical routine, such as diet, coach, travel, and long days, as well as the training and competition schedule. Eligible athletes and Unified partners are then entered into their program-specific random selection draw for the Special Olympics USA Delegation (Special Olympics, n.d.s).

Special Olympics Exceeds Sport

From the beginning, Eunice Kennedy Shriver believed that participation in sport and physical activity was an invaluable experience for individuals with disabilities. Thus, the Special Olympics were founded on the idea that sport inspires hope and confidence in oneself and unites diverse communities. Special Olympics sport has opened many other avenues for promoting health and wellness and including people with intellectual disabilities. Two high-impact efforts include inclusive health and schools programming.

> The Special Olympics were founded on the idea that sport inspires hope and confidence in oneself and unites diverse communities.

Inclusive health is a Special Olympics global strategy in collaboration with the Golisano Foundation and CDC to improve health outcomes for people with intellectual disabilities. The intent is to ensure equitable access and meaningful participation within existing health systems rather separate programs for people with intellectual disabilities (Special Olympics, n.d.d). Special Olympics continues to strengthen the capacity of its own health programming to support other health organizations, providers, and educators to do the same. Healthy Athletes is the foundational Special Olympics Program toward health equity and inclusion for people with intellectual disabilities. The program provides free health screening and health education in various physical and mental health disciplines (Chandan & Dubon, 2019). Other Special Olympics health programming efforts include Family Health Forums, Health Messengers, Health Workforce, and Fitness (Special Olympics n.d.i).

Special Olympics Unified Schools (global), Unified Champion Schools (U.S.), and college clubs embrace the ideology of Unified Sports that togetherness creates understanding through friendships. Special Olympics schools programming facilitates inclusive classroom and community experiences that promote health and wellness while combating stereotypes and negative attitudes that lead to bullying and exclusion of youth with intellectual disabilities. In the United States, Unified Champion Schools engages students in three interconnected components to achieve these outcomes: Unified Sports (individual and team sports as well as physical education), inclusive youth leadership (students with and without intellectual disabilities plan and implement advocacy and awareness events), and whole school engagement (outreach activities that involve the most the student population; Special Olympics, n.d.q; n.d.w; Yin & Belyakova, 2022).

Intellectual Impairment and the Paralympics

While this chapter focuses on the Special Olympics because of its definitive provision of sport for individuals with intellectual disabilities, it is not the sole organization that does so. At the grassroots level, several nonprofit organizations provide sport-specific inclusive programs. The Miracle League (baseball) is one example. Often the organization or team will pair "Buddy" or "Challenger" with the sport name (e.g., Little League has a Challenger Baseball Division).

Many city parks and recreation departments have adaptive recreation programs that provide year-round programming for youth and adults with disabilities. Summer camp or respite centers often provide week- or weekend-long getaways for individuals with various disabilities. Finally, some school districts have leagues for students in special education (e.g., Medford League in Virginia) that are outside the framework of Special Olympics Unified schools.

At the elite level, athletes with intellectual disabilities can compete in the Paralympics. The association is uncommon, but intellectual impairment is one of the 10 impairment types (eight physical; one vision) or one of the six disability groups that are included in the Paralympic Games. The Paralympics (Stoke Mandeville Games at the time), originally served injured World War II veterans with spinal cord injuries. As the Games expanded, other disability groups gained entry into the elite arena. Athletes with amputations and visual impairments were included for the first time in the Toronto 1976 Paralympics, and athletes with cerebral palsy in Arnhem 1980 Games. Comparatively, access into the Paralympics by athletes with intellectual disabilities was delayed. The International Association for Sport for Athletes with a Mental Handicap (INAS-FMH) was established in 1986 to include athletes with intellectual impairments in the Paralympics. The organization became a member of the International Coordinating Committee (renamed the IPC) in 1988 and had success implementing their first World Games (renamed Global Games) held in Harnosand, Sweden, in 1989 (Virtus, n.d.a). In 1992, the "Paralympic Games for Persons with a Mental Handicap" were held in Madrid, Spain, immediately following the Barcelona Paralympics program as a part of their inclusion into the overall Paralympic framework. As evident by the sparsity of literature about this event, these Madrid Games are rarely recognized as "Paralympic Games" though they were included within the same IPC contract as the Barcelona Games (World

Press, 2012). INAS-FMH became INAS-FID in 1994—the International Sports Federation for Persons with Intellectual Disability—and then two years later, a demonstration program for athletes with an intellectual impairment was included at the Atlanta 1996 Paralympics. At last, during the Sydney 2000 Games, athletes with intellectual impairments were included in the Paralympic program of athletics (track and field), swimming, men's basketball, and table tennis. However, the deception of one men's basketball team posing as athletes with intellectual impairments quickly halted this forward momentum.

Setback in Sydney

A scandal during the 2000 Sydney Paralympics had a devastating impact on athletes with intellectual impairments that can still be felt today. That year, Spain had its best showing at a Paralympic Games, finishing third overall in the medal count (Brittain, 2016). Men's basketball had won gold. The celebration was short-lived once a Spanish player outed the team for fraud. Ten of 12 players did not have an intellectual impairment but were recruited to secure a medal and subsequent funding. This news had a snowball effect because cheating was suspected in other sports as well—track and field, swimming, and table tennis. An investigation ensued. After reviewing 244 athlete registration cards, it was determined that 157 were missing primary eligibility requirements or were incomplete. Of 132 possible medals, 94 had been awarded to athletes with invalid registration cards.

Though the correlation between intentional misrepresentation and invalid registration cards was not absolute, the evidence brought forth during the investigation revealed a flawed system. This discovery led to the firing of Fernando Vicente Martin, who held numerous prominent positions at the time of allegation, including vice president of the Spanish Paralympic Committee, president of INAS-FID, and president of the

Spanish Sports Federation for the Intellectually Disabled (FEDDI). In addition, all athletes with intellectual impairments were suspended from competing in IPC events. Before athletes with intellectual impairments could rejoin IPC competition, INAS had to overhaul its eligibility and classification criteria. Burns (2018) and Van Biesen and colleagues (2021) provide more detailed information about the rigorous process the organization underwent. In short, building an evidence-based classification system that determined the impact of cognitive skills on execution of sport-specific tasks took time. It was not until 2009 that the IPC General Assembly, by a slim margin, agreed to the re-inclusion of athletes with intellectual impairments so long as the INAS research group continued refinement and development of their classification systems. The 2012 London Games were the first appearance of athletes with intellectual impairments in Paralympic competition in 12 years. Their return to sport included only three: athletics, swimming, and table tennis—not basketball.

Re-inclusion in the Paralympic Games was not an instant remedy; implications of the cheating scandal had a residual effect on INAS and its athletes. Challenges around rebuilding infrastructures, support, resources, and competition schedules for elite athletes with intellectual impairments still exist (Burns, 2018). Though some nations are capitalizing on this new market of medal potential (e.g., Australia and Russia), most nations continue to sideline athletes with intellectual impairments on the "injured reserve," whether because they lack the resources to respond (e.g., developing countries) or because they are withholding resources for winning athletes in sports already on the Paralympic program (e.g., United States). Almost ironically, competition is also currently a hindrance to growth. Competition schedules of the three sports on the Paralympic docket—athletics, swimming, and table tennis—contend between IPC events and those of their respective international sports federations. Funding and resources, which include costly classification requirements, dictate which events athletes will attend. Top athletes gravitate toward Paralympic-sanctioned events, thus having an "economic and performance impact" on the organizational development of INAS (now Virtus; Burns, 2018, p. 432).

Nevertheless, rebuilding efforts are slowly showing results. The "master list" of athletes with intellectual impairments is growing, a small increment of Paralympians included. Medal potential increased during the 2016 Rio Paralympic Games with the addition of events in swimming and athletics (Burns, 2018). Classification research and sport development continues as well, currently with sights on basketball, taekwondo, and Nordic skiing. In 2018, new eligibility groups were introduced into INAS competition to expand participation to athletes with multiple and severe impairments and autism. Finally, in 2019, INAS rebranded to become Virtus, reclaiming a foothold in the Paralympic movement to help make the invisible, visible (Virtus, n.d.a).

Virtus Governance and Games

Virtus is an international sports federation for athletes with intellectual impairments. Virtus is the recognized International Organization of Sport for people with a Disability (IOSD), by the IPC as the sole representative for athletes with intellectual impairments. (International Paralympic Committee, n.d.). Virtus and the other IOSDs (CP-ISRA, IBSA, IWAS) are the governing bodies for grassroots to elite-level athlete and sport development. In 2020, Virtus membership grew to more than 80 nations, but it has little financial means to support national organizations. Raising funds for support and development is often left to each organizational level—Virtus, national organizations, and too often athletes themselves. Athletes Without Limits is the U.S. member organization of Virtus that has taken on this responsibility and worked to integrate athletes with intellectual and developmental disabilities into mainstream and Paralympic sport (Athletes Without Limits, n.d.).

> **Virtus' mission is to promote the development of elite sport worldwide for athletes with an intellectual impairment.**

Virtus is led by a governing board and supported by subcommittees for each sport and various functional specialties (eligibility, antidoping, elections, finance, medical, and legal) as well as a team of international volunteers dedicated to the organization's mission: to drive the development of elite sport worldwide for athletes with an intellectual impairment (Virtus, n.d.a, n.d.c). Chief outputs of this mission are managing world and regional championships for Paralympic and non-Paralympic sports and hosting the Virtus Global Games. Similar to the Special Olympics World Games (possibly why the switch was made from "World" to "Global" after the 1989 INAS World Games), Virtus Global Games are the pinnacle event of elite competition for athletes with an intellectual impairment. Held every four years, in a year preceding the Paralympics, the Global Games schedule is more extensive than the three sports on the Paralympic program. Demonstration events that represent the most popular sports of the host country are also included if not already a part of the Virtus program.

The vision statement of Virtus—an inclusive world for people with intellectual impairment (Virtus, n.d.a)—harmonizes with that of the Special Olympics. Unfortunately, people with intellectual disabilities continue to be marginalized worldwide. Both organizations, however, affirm the power of sport to connect communities and change the way the world sees people with intellectual disabilities. The difference is how they use sport to achieve social change, particularly in light of the three main organizational differences: athletes, structure, and philosophy.

Virtus—IPC Eligibility and Classification

The basketball controversy in the 2000 Sydney Paralympics revealed weakness in the eligibility system for the intellectual impairment group. Until sport-specific procedures were proven valid and reliable, athletes with intellectual impairments were excluded from IPC competition. Since then, in collaboration with the IPC, a Virtus research team has been working to establish a pathway for fair competition through a revised classification system. The conceptual approach established requires resolution of two fundamental questions. The first asks: Does the athlete have an intellectual impairment? Virtus requires the athletes to provide evidence of impairment in each of the three diagnostic criteria: intellectual functioning, adaptive behavior, and age of onset. At least two panel members must independently evaluate the portfolio of evidence and concur the athlete has an eligible impairment. The second question asks: Does the intellectual impairment affect key determinants of sport performance? Each international sport federation considers three phases of evidence to determine their respective minimum impairment criteria. Athletes must undergo generic intelligence testing, sport-specific testing, and game observation (for specific procedures, see Van Biesen et al., 2021). Applying such an evidence-based support system has challenges. The conceptual framework is open to revision as knowledge emerges, particularly because the impact of intellectual impairment is influenced by multiple complexities (e.g., adaptive behavior, mental and physical comorbidities, and psychological vulnerability of the population) in the context of sport (Van Biesen et al., 2021).

Compliance with eligibility criteria allows athletes with intellectual impairments to compete in Virtus Regional and World Championships. Virtus has expanded competition to include three eligibility groups: athletes with an intellectual disability (II1), athletes with an intellectual disability and a significant other impairment (II2), and athletes with autism (II3; IQ76+; Virtus, n.d.b). Virtus II1 and II2 athletes can compete in Paralympic competition since they have an eligible impairment (as determined by international diagnostic criteria) but also have to verify the impact of their impairment on sport-specific performance. In other words, athletes with intellectual impairments must comply with eligibility and minimum impairment criteria to compete in IPC-sanctioned events. Athletes are limited to a single class structure in three sports on the Paralympic program (swimming S14/SB14; table tennis class 11; track and field T20/F20).

Summary

This chapter highlighted the similarities and differences between the Special Olympics and Paralympics in their provision of sport for athletes with intellectual disabilities. It first examined the philosophical and structural differences between the two movements within three areas: athletes, philosophy, and governance. Then the chapter contextualized intellectual disability to demonstrate how associated personal and environmental factors can affect participation in sport. While intellectual impairment affects athletic performance, it should not exclude athletes from competition. Sport management should take an equitable approach and reach beyond traditional delivery avenues. Setting this foundation was important before diving into the historical narratives and governance structure of the two international governing bodies that organize sport for athletes with intellectual disabilities—Special Olympics and Virtus. Their respective stories revealed sport management implications in how they provide competition through world and national games and particularly how these movements work toward their visions of social inclusion. With emphasis on personal best, Special Olympics currently has a more diverse catalog of sport-based programs and initiatives focused on health and inclusion. Meanwhile, Virtus dwells within the elite bounds of the Paralympic movement, though still urgently working to regain traction after its reputation was sullied by a flawed classification system. Other sport organizations may work to include individuals with intellectual disabilities but not on the same global scale; therefore, continued examination of both organizations, and greater inclusion movements, to ensure the advancement of sport development for individuals with intellectual disabilities is encouraged.

CRITICAL THINKING EXERCISES

1. Identify key stakeholder roles within the Special Olympics movement at each level of governance and participation. Why is each significant to the organization's mission? How can you become a contributing stakeholder?

2. What is the significance of the 2000 Sydney Paralympic Games? What does this tell us about the difference between the Paralympics and Special Olympics?

3. Special Olympics works to increase awareness about intellectual disability and ensure everyone is a productive and respected member of society. Identify and explain the importance of Special Olympics Programs that aim toward greater inclusion.

4. What are the similarities and differences between Special Olympics and Virtus? See how well you can elaborate on each point or explain them to a friend.

CHAPTER 9

Para-Athlete Development

Darda Sales, PhD, PLY, and Laura Misener, PhD

LEARNING OBJECTIVES

After reading this chapter, you will be able to do the following:

- Explain the principles of athlete development and identify models used in athlete development.
- Describe how the long-term development model has been applied to the development of para-athletes.
- Identify considerations that are unique to para-athlete development.
- Describe areas of para-athlete development that require further investigation.

This chapter focuses on athlete development approaches, emphasizing the long-term athlete development (LTAD) model that originated in Canada and has been adopted by many countries around the world. The model has been adapted for disability sport to support growth in opportunities as well as advancement through all levels of participation. Complex interactions remain between factors associated with athlete development and the management of the unique influences of different impairments in adaptive sport contexts. These various factors are examined in relation to developing sport systems that support adaptive athlete development.

The concept of **athlete development** has evolved during the past few decades as more importance has been placed on understanding how people go from being children on the playground to elite, high-performing athletes. Athlete development is focused on first understanding how athletes progress from initiation in sport to reaching their full potential and identifying what supports are needed to help athletes reach their full potential physically, mentally, psychologically, and emotionally. Athlete development can seem as simple as go out, play, and see where you get to, but as more is learned about what elite athletes must do and the supports that they receive to get to the top of their sport, the more it is recognized that there is a much more to it.

To assist coaches and sport administrators to better help support the development of athletes, several models for athlete development have been produced. One of the first models was proposed by Bloom (1985) and identified three key stages to athlete development:

1. Early years/initiation
2. Middle years/development
3. Late years/perfection

143

Bloom's work has been influential in most athlete development models proposed during the past 30 years. In this chapter, three athlete development models will be reviewed:

1. The long-term development model
2. The American development model
3. The foundation, transition, elite, mastery (FTEM) model

There are similarities and differences for these models, highlighting how an athlete's development experience would be influenced by the athlete development model that a coach or program implemented.

Long-Term Development Model

The **long-term development model** (LTAD model, originally known as the *long-term athlete development model*), was first proposed to identify what is "to be done at each stage of human development to give every child the best chance of engaging in lifelong, health-enhancing physical activity; and for those with the drive and talent, the best chance of athletic success" (Balyi et al., 2013, p. 1). The focus was on helping participants maximize their potential through improving the quality of physical activity and sport, and the model was meant to be a guide to the participation, training, competition, and recovery pathways in sport and physical activity from infancy through adulthood.

The LTAD model has seven stages:

1. Active Start
2. Fundamentals
3. Learn to Train
4. Train to Train
5. Train to Compete
6. Train to Win
7. Active for Life

Ages were attached to the stages, and movement through the model was linear (i.e., athletes moving from one stage to the next).

The LTAD model was built from 10 key factors:

1. Physical literacy
2. Specialization
3. Age
4. Trainability
5. Intellectual, emotional, and moral development
6. Excellence takes time
7. Periodization
8. Competition
9. System alignment and integration
10. Continuous improvement

In 2005, Sport Canada identified the LTAD model as the athlete development model of choice and mandated that to receive funding, all National Sports Organizations (NSOs) had to develop their own athlete development model based on the LTAD model. Sport for Life, an independent nonprofit nongovernment organization, oversees the ongoing evolution of the LTAD model.

In 2015, LTAD model version 2.0 was released. The most significant changes were the addition of two early stages, Awareness and First Contact, which were added to make the LTAD model more applicable to athletes with disabilities. *Awareness* recognizes that there is a lack of awareness of the benefits of physical activity and the opportunities that are available to individuals with disabilities. *First contact* emphasizes the importance of positive initial engagement in physical activity for individuals with disabilities.

The most recent version of the model was released in 2019, and with it came more changes to the model. The title of the model was changed to *long-term athlete development model* to make the model more recognizable as being useful to all physical activity and not just to competitive athletes and sport. The stages of Awareness and First Contact (renamed First Involvement) were shifted from the first two stages of the model to the side to acknowledge that Awareness and First Involvement are important throughout an individual's engagement in sport or physical activity. For the first time, the authors of the model recognized that athlete development is not always linear and that there are many different pathways through the model. Last, the 10 key factors of the model were expanded to 22 key factors that operate at three levels: personal factors, organizational factors, and system factors (see figure 9.1).

American Development Model

In the United States, several national sports organizations use the **American development model** (ADM; American Development Model, n.d.; USOC, 2016), which is based on the principles of the long-term athlete development model. USA Hockey initially developed the ADM in 2009 to assist with the retention and age-appropriate development of athletes and enhance **coach education**. Following the success of the ADM, the United States Olympic and Paralympic Committee, in collaboration with other national sports organizations, began using components of the ADM in 2014. The ADM is meant for use from "cradle to grave" to help develop all components of an athlete (technical, tactical, physical, and psychological). Through the integration of the ADM programming in all areas of training, recovery, and competition, an athlete's full potential on and off the field of play can be achieved. There are 10 guiding principles to the ADM:

1. Excellences takes time
2. Physical literacy and fundamentals
3. Building athleticism
4. Specialization and early sampling
5. Growth and individualization
6. Periodization
7. Mental, cognitive, and emotional development
8. Quality coaching
9. System alignment and integration
10. Continuous improvement

The ADM also follows the stage approach of the LTAD model and has eight stages:

1. Active Start
2. Fundamentals
3. Learn to Train
4. Train to Train
5. Learn to Compete
6. Train to Compete
7. Train to Win
8. For Life

Ages for men and women are attached to each stage. Examples of age-appropriate principles of the ADM include these:

- Adapting playing surface sizes to fit the athlete

Personal factors	Organizational factors	System factors
• Physical literacy • Quality environments • Developmental age • Sensitive periods • Predisposition • Excellence takes time • For life	• Framework • Fully embedded • Awareness and first involvement • Different activities • Appropriate specialization • Periodization • Competition • Transitions	• Collaboration • System alignment • Safe and welcoming • Diversification • Long-term development • Continuous improvement • Evidence-based

FIGURE 9.1 Principles of long-term development.

- Environments focused on fun and engagement, that are challenging while still being within the physical and mental capacity of the players
- Foundational skill as a focus of practices
- Programming designed and sequenced with a long-term development view
- Activity and skill-based games
- Games that replicate game situations and roles
- Training, recovery, and competition programming that is age appropriate
- Adapting rules to promote development

Foundation, Talent, Elite, Mastery Model

Another model that has been proposed is the FTEM model, which is an acronym for **foundations, talent, elite, mastery** (AIS, 2023). These four stages can be further broken down into 10 smaller phases. Foundations can be further broken down into F1, F2, and F3, all of which focus on the acquisition of fundamental skills, starting with basic movement skills, refining basic movement skills, and applying basic movements within the structure of sport. An individual may remain in the F3 stage, or if they are identified as having potential for high performance, they may move on to the next stages quickly.

Talent has four phases, T1, T2, T3, and T4. In T1, athletes are identified through formal and informal means of having potential for high performance in any one or more of the following areas: skill, physical, psychological, or physiological. T2 is when the talent that was identified in T1 is verified or confirmed through ongoing training and competition observations by coaches or talent scouts. It is recommended that this process take place over a matter of months (Bullock et al., 2009; Gulbin, 2001; Gulbin et al., 2013; Hoare & Warr, 2000) and that all four areas identified are observed, not just the physiological.

Once potential for high performance has been verified, an athlete moves on to T3, during which they engage in sport-specific training and seek to gain ongoing improvements in performance. This stage tends to have the largest number of athletes and is important; however, due to funding models, it puts emphasis on the latter stages of the development pathway. Important developmental components can be missed due to a lack of funding. T4 begins when an athlete has gained recognition for their sporting accomplishments through scholarships, naming to national teams, drafting into professional leagues, and other high-level athletic achievements.

The macro phase of Elite has two phases. E1 is senior elite representation (in Olympic or Paralympic sport, this would consist of an athlete representing their country at the Olympics or Paralympics), and E2 is senior elite success (in Olympic or Paralympic sport, this would consist of achieving a podium finish). Mastery is the final macro phase. In the mastery phase, athletes are successful at high-profile international competitions during several cycles (i.e., experience success at two or more Olympics or Paralympics). The framework strives to represent all three possible outcomes from sport engagement, active lifestyle, sports participation, and sport excellence. The FTEM was designed to be practical in use by sport practitioners and researchers.

One marked difference that distinguishes the FTEM from the LTAD model and ADM is that there are no age boundaries attached to any stage. While the FTEM is presented in a linear fashion, nonlinear movement through the model is recognized, meaning that an athlete can enter at any point along the model and can move through the model as need be, even skipping over phases in either direction. While there are FTEM components that could be useful to para-athletes, no writings on the model discuss the application of the model to para-athletes.

Table 9.1 shows an overview of how the LTAD, ADM, and FTEM models compare.

TABLE 9.1   **Comparison of LTAD, ADM, and FTEM Models**

	LTAD	ADM	FTEM
Stages	1. Active Start 2. Fundamentals 3. Learn to Train 4. Train to Train 5. Train to Compete 6. Train to Win 7. Active for Life Awareness and First Contact/First Involvement added later	1. Active Start 2. Fundamentals 3. Learn to Train 4. Train to Train 5. Learn to Compete 6. Train to Compete 7. Train to Win 8. For Life	Foundations (F1, F2, F3) Talent (T1, T2, T3, T4) Elite (E1, E2) Mastery
Principles	1. Physical literacy 2. Specialization 3. Age 4. Trainability 5. Intellectual, emotional, and moral development 6. Excellence takes time 7. Periodization 8. Competition 9. System alignment and integration 10. Continuous improvement	1. Excellence takes time 2. Physical literacy and fundamentals 3. Building athleticism 4. Specialization and early sampling 5. Growth and individualization 6. Periodization 7. Mental, cognitive, and emotional development 8. Quality coaching 9. System alignment and integration 10. Continuous improvement	Physical literacy Talent identification and nurturing development Elite representation and success Sustained success maximizing investment
Unique features	• Guide to the participation, training, competition, and recovery pathways in sport and physical activity, from infancy through to adulthood • Originated in Canada • Nonlinear movement is recognized • Only model specifically designed to apply for adaptive athletes • No Accidental Champions further clarifies principles for adapting the model for adaptive athletes	Used "from cradle to grave" to develop athletes technically, tactically, physically, and psychologically Ages attached to stages	No age differences in stages Nonlinear movement is recognized No current evidence for use with adaptive athletes

Application of the Long-Term Development Model to Para-Athletes

The three athlete development models are similar, but one of the most notable differences of the LTD model is how it applies to para-athletes. Specifically, the LTD model is the only one that specifies its application to para-athletes. The LTD model had three rounds of evolution, and the application of the model to para-athletes became increasingly pronounced. Version 2.0 introduced the Awareness and First Involvement stages while version 3.0 recognized the importance of Awareness and First Involvement throughout the development of para-athletes. While ages are still attached to the stages of the LTD model, written into the LTD document is the acknowledgment that movement through the model is not linear. To further support the application of the LTD model to para-athletes, a supplement to the LTD model was added titled No Accidental Champions.

The **No Accidental Champions** (NAC) document was designed to identify opportunities and challenges that individuals with impairments may experience when engaging in physical activity and sport. The document also addresses ways the needs of individuals with impairments can be accommodated by the Canadian sport system by following the LTD model.

The NAC clarifies that while the LTD model provides ages for the different stages, individuals with impairments may move through the stages at different ages based on when they acquire an impairment or when they first begin to engage in sport or physical activity. The NAC also recognizes that the pace at which an individual with an impairment moves through the LTD model is different from what is written. The stages of Awareness and First Involvement are thoroughly discussed in the NAC. The 10 key factors of the LTAD model version 2.0 are outlined in the NAC and how each factor applies to an individual with an impairment is discussed (see table 9.2).

The NAC also identifies 10 "pillars of support" that are necessary for para-athletes to experience optimal development:

1. Coaching
2. Competition
3. Funding
4. Equipment
5. Facilities
6. Training and competition partners
7. Sport science
8. Officials support
9. Athlete support
10. Talent development

Considerations for the Development of Para-Athletes

As highlighted in the NAC document, in para-athlete development, there are areas of consideration that require time and attention that either differs from or is not present when working with athletes without impairment.

Impact of Impairment

An individual can acquire an impairment at any stage or age. Impairments that a person is born with are known as **congenital impairments**. Impairments that occur later in life due to trauma, surgery, disease, or illness are **acquired impairments**. Having an impairment can affect the athlete development experience, depending on the type and severity of the impairment that may affect function. The potential effects of an impairment on function are discussed in this chapter.

Age of Acquiring Impairment

The age of impairment acquisition is important because people with congenital impairments tend to move through the stages of development in a similar timeline as individuals without impairment (Dehghansai et al., 2017). However, some with congenital impairments are not introduced to sport or

TABLE 9.2 **10 Key Factors of the Long-Term Athlete Development Model Applied to Disability Sport**

Factor	Application to individuals with impairments
Excellence takes time	The 10-year rule applies to individuals with some impairments but may vary based on impairment, sport, activity, and goals of the individual.
Physical literacy	This is ideally acquired before puberty, but due to an array of reasons, such as lack of opportunity, knowledge of coaches, and so on, this may not be possible. The nature of the impairment and use of assistive devices may also affect physical literacy as can pre-injury physical activity before acquiring an impairment.
Specialization	Adaptive sports seem to be late specialization sports. All individuals with impairments, both congenital and acquired, should be exposed to a variety of sports before specializing.
Age factor	More research is needed to understand the impact of impairments on development. Therefore, the focus should be on developmental milestones as opposed to age.
Trainability	More research is needed to determine sensitive periods for optimum trainability of adaptive athletes.
Physical, mental, cognitive, and emotional development	Focus should be on developing fair play, ethical behavior, and character building, which is the same as for mainstream athletes.
Periodization	Adaptive athletes are instructed to follow the periodization as presented in the LTD model because no research to the contrary is currently available. Para-athletes should be monitored for fatigue and recovery periods should be adjusted as needed.
Calendar planning for competition	Training to competition ratios recommended in the LTD model should be followed, although impairment type might require training volumes to be adjusted. Competition should match the adaptive athlete's stage of development. This can be difficult because there is a lack of competitive opportunities, so creativity may be needed to find developmentally appropriate opportunities.
System alignment and integration	System alignment is required for optimal athlete development.
Continuous improvement	As new research, techniques, and equipment become available, sport organizations must evaluate and implement these advancements in accordance to the LTD model.

Adapted from "No Accidental Champions," Canadian Sports Centres, https://sportforlife.ca/wp-content/uploads/2016/06/NAC _ENGLISH_SCREEN_rev2013.pdf, (2013).

physical activity until later in life due to a variety of reasons, such as a lack of awareness or opportunity in both the community and within the school system, parental focus on the medical aspects of their child's care, parental fear, and parental uncertainty about having their child engage in sport or physical activity. Those with congenital impairments also may not have the same opportunities to engage in sport or physical activity, which leads to gaps in their development of physical literacy.

Physical literacy is having the confidence, motivation, knowledge, and physical skills to take part in physical activity. There is also a social component to physical literacy. Physical literacy is a lifelong pursuit that begins with the first engagement in physical activity and the development of basic movement skills and the initiation of positive physical activity habits. Physical literacy can also play an important role in the developing skills necessary for independent living.

> Physical literacy is a lifelong pursuit that begins with the first engagement in physical activity and the development of basic movement skills and the initiation of positive physical activity habits.

Sport starts with developing fundamental physical literacy skills, but individuals with an impairment may take longer to develop them because they need to first acquire basic skills. They then can move on to more advanced sport-specific skills. People with acquired impairments may come into the para-athlete development pathway at a later stage or move through athlete development quickly, particularly if they have sound physical literacy through engagement in sport prior to acquiring their impairment (Dehghansai et al., 2017). A significant hurdle for those with acquired impairments is the acceptance of their functional abilities post-injury. Early awareness of and engagement in adaptive sport can help with the acceptance process (Ballas et al., 2022).

Engagement in adaptive sport can also help those with acquired impairments develop the skills needed for independent living.

Energy Requirements

The type of impairment can also influence an athlete's development due to the impacts on energy systems. Impairments, particularly those that have a bearing on neurology (i.e., cerebral palsy, head injury, spinal cord injury), can lead to fatigue more quickly. Training plan adjustments may also be needed depending on the demands of the sport in relation to the athlete's impairment. For example, para-athletes who use manual wheelchairs and compete in a sport that requires significant use of the upper body (i.e., wheelchair basketball, wheelchair racing, swimming) require the amount of nonsport wheelchair pushing to be taken into consideration regarding training loads and recovery. Para-athletes who are ambulatory (walk with an altered gait pattern or use a prosthesis, crutches, walker, or other mobility devices) may use more energy to move through their daily lives. Therefore, these additional energy needs will also need to be taken into consideration when designing training plans, competition plans, and schedules and arranging facility use and accommodations.

Technique, Equipment, and Sport Engagement Adjustments

The type of impairment will also affect para-athlete development and the adjustments that may be needed to sport techniques. How an athlete's body moves and functions needs to be considered throughout para-athlete development (from Active Start through to Train to Win or Active for Life). At all development stages, instructors or coaches need to be aware of not only how the para-athlete's body currently functions within the movements needed for the sport but also of the potential for the para-athlete's body to function. They then need to determine how much to push their athletes toward **optimal technique** within the sport. Optimal

ABI TRIPP

I was born with mild cerebral palsy and grew up in an active family that enjoyed sports of all kinds. As a child, I participated in house league soccer, swimming lessons, and family sports like cycling and canoeing. It did not matter that I was not particularly skilled in any of these sports; it was all about trying new things and having fun. I did a triathlon for kids in my hometown, Kingston, Ontario, in 2006. It was just by chance that I met my future coach, Vicki Keith, at the event. That is when I learned about the possibility of parasport. I began swimming competitively a year later, at six years old, after joining the Kingston Y Penguins Aquatic Club (now Kingston Y Penguins Swimming). Growing up on a team for kids with disabilities and their able-bodied siblings meant that I now had a place where I was on the same team as my big brother and could train with teammates with similar physical impairments.

Abi Tripp

I was first classified as a S10SB9SM10. I was young and still needed time to develop into my body. That classification opened the doors to competitive para-swimming. I had my first Ontario ParaSport Games opportunity in Collingwood in 2008. There, I was the youngest athlete to compete at the event, and it sparked my desire to pursue the sport of swimming. I improved quickly, making my way to Regionals, Provincials, and eventually my first Can-Ams (Nationals) in 2012, where I was classified as an S8SB8SM8. Those Can-Am Championships were my first opportunity to compete against athletes with a similar level of impairment. It gave me a better idea of what I should be working toward in my training and future competitions.

Three of my teammates competed for Canada at the Guadalajara ParaPan Am Games in 2011, their successes inspiring me to earn my place on the national team. I watched how they trained and started integrating dryland and more pool time into my daily routine. My coach, Vicki Keith, helped me set and work toward my goal to compete at the Rio 2016 Paralympic Games. I had my first national team experience at the Toronto 2015 ParaPan Am Championships. These Games accelerated my experience and understanding of myself during competitions. During the week-long competition, I got a taste of international competition and an idea of what it would take in the coming year to make the leap to the Paralympic Team. At the 2016 Olympic and Paralympic Swimming Trials in Toronto, I made all my standards and qualified for my first Paralympic Games. I lowered my best times again at the Paralympic Games, thriving in the Paralympic environment, a world where having a disability puts you in the majority and not the minority.

Now, I am a part of a city club with para-athletes integrated into the program. Every day, I am training with three other national team teammates (Alec Elliot, Aurélie Rivard, and Nicolas-Guy Turbide). In this new environment, I am surrounded by like-minded athletes, and we can share the highs and lows of our lives as athletes that have a continued desire to compete at the highest level.

technique will look different depending on the individual, their functional abilities, centers of gravity, and muscular control. For example, para-swimmers who are single-leg amputees may need to kick with their foot as close to the center of their body as possible, as opposed to having their foot in line with their hip. It can take time and trial-and-error to determine what technique will work best, and instructors and coaches must be willing to take that time while listening to the para-athlete's input to determine optimal technique.

Adjustments may also be necessary to the equipment a para-athlete uses depending on the para-athlete's impairment. The adjustments may be dictated by the sport (i.e., specific wheelchairs for wheelchair basketball or wheelchair racing, sledges and sticks for para ice hockey), but they may need additional adjustments to meet the requirements of the athlete. For example, wheelchair basketball players may need seat cushions adjusted to increase comfort.

For some para-athletes and in some parasports, additional support people may be necessary for their successful engagement and development. A para-athlete with a visual impairment may require a guide or pilot. The para-athlete and coach may be able to develop a system to assist the para-athlete to train (such as a two-way radio), but if the para-athlete is to reach higher levels of development and competition, they will need a customized plan between the coach and para-athlete. The guide for a visually impaired athlete will also need to be able compete at the same level as the para-athlete; therefore, the guide would need to commit to the same level of training as the para-athlete. This needs to be considered when designing a development and training plan for a para-athlete. Other supports that could be needed include assistance transferring onto a sport-specific piece of equipment or physical help with balance during certain movements.

Awareness

A person must first know that sport is available to them before they can begin to engage in sport. Most people with impairments learn about sport opportunities from significant others in their life (e.g., family, friends, medical professionals), so it is important that information about adaptive sport opportunities be made available to both people with an impairment and the general population. Many people with impairments are not pursuing sporting opportunities for a variety of reasons (i.e., recovery from injury, unsure of their abilities, fear), and it is not until the opportunity is presented to them or their families that they even begin to consider engaging in sport (Sales & Misener, 2021).

> **Most people with impairments learn about sport opportunities from significant others in their life (e.g., family, friends, medical professionals).**

Promotion of Programs

Programs for people with impairments need to be explicit about the services they provide, their target population group, and the accessibility of their facilities. For adaptive sports that are predominantly integrated, such as swimming, clubs need to make it clear in all their communications (i.e., website, promotional materials, newsletters) that they are an integrated environment, the impairments they can support, and the accessibility of their facilities.

Motivation and Fundamental Skill Development

Once they learn about adaptive sport opportunities, they must also have the motivation to try the sport. There can be several different reasons for an individual with an impairment to begin engagement in sport. Rehabilitation or the physical therapy benefits of physical activity and sport is a common motivator. Sport and physical activity can enhance strength and flexibility or reduce pain and discomfort. Providing options for therapy can help with adherence, which is why promoting adaptive sporting opportunities to medical professionals (i.e., doctors, physical therapists, occupational therapists) is important. Sport can be a means of meeting therapeutic goals in a fun and social environment.

Once motivation has been established, the next step is for the athlete to learn the basic skills necessary for the sport. Many people with impairments will begin in community, integrated programming. Unfortunately, due to instructors' lack of knowledge for how to appropriately adapt programs to meet the needs of individuals with impairments, these are often not successful endeavors. Therefore, para-athletes frequently turn to specialized programs or one-on-one learning programs to obtain the necessary fundamental skills.

Instructors and coaches need to be trained in a variety of teaching styles and be able to adapt their teaching methods to meet the needs of the participants to assist in a positive-first sporting experience. Resources can help instructors and coaches learn to work with para-athletes, such as resources provided by the Canadian NCCP Coaching Athletes with a Disability, but most coaching education takes place in informal, mentorship settings (Winchester et al., 2011; Winchester et al., 2013). Therefore, instructors and coaches who are new to working with para-athletes need to reach out to others with experience and seek assistance available through sport organizations and coaching associations. Para-athletes and parents are valuable resources for instructors and coaches because they can provide guidance on how best to support the para-athlete and can provide insights into their functional abilities.

> Para-athletes and parents are valuable resources because they can provide guidance on how best to support the para-athlete and can provide insights into their functional abilities.

Appropriate Specialization

Para-athletes tend to have less-developed physical literacy, which is developed through engaging in a variety of sports or physical activity and obtaining a wide range of physical skills. The idea of appropriate specialization is that athletes do not focus solely on one sport too early in their development. As identified in the NAC, adaptive sports are late-specialization sports, meaning that para-athletes should engage in a variety of sports and physical activities until later in their development. However, early specialization is common for para-athletes.

One reason is that there are few opportunities for para-athletes. There are 22 recognized summer Paralympic sports compared to the 33 recognized Summer Olympic sports. Other sports are adapted to include people with impairments, but they are not as well known. People are unaware of where to go when searching for adaptive sport opportunities without programs making it known that they are open to working with para-athletes.

First contact and first impressions are important, and para-athletes will not return if programs are not explicitly welcoming. Finally, para-athletes begin to feel pressure to show alliance to a single sport due to the low numbers of people with impairments engaging in adaptive sport.

Overall, para-athletes should be encouraged to engage in a variety of sports and physical activities until the later stages of their development to help enhance their athletic ability. Coaches, instructors, and sport administrators can assist para-athletes in engaging in a variety of sports and physical activities by offering a variety of sports or physical activities as part of their core or cross-training offerings. Alternatively, adaptive sport programs could partner with other programs to provide their para-athletes with the opportunity to engage in sports and physical activities.

Developmental Age

Approximate ages are attached to each stage in the LTD model, with athletes reaching the latter stages of the model by their late teens, although it is mentioned in the LTD model that coaches should focus on the **developmental age** of the athlete, which is especially important for para-athletes. Individuals with impairments can begin their participation in adaptive sport at any time. Para-athletes can also move through the developmental stages at varying rates of speed depending on when they come into adaptive sport and their prior sport experiences. Therefore, coaches need to be mindful of the developmental age of their athlete and individualize training plans as much as possible to meet the needs of the para-athlete. An individualized approach to training para-athletes will create appropriate training plans with a long-term development focus as well as the daily practice needs of para-athletes.

Para-athletes need their functional abilities taken into consideration when coaches are designing practice plans, especially for para-athletes training in integrated or large-group training environments. Multiple practice plans may be needed to ensure that the needs of each athlete are met. A common practice adaptation is to reduce the number of repetitions, or the distance covered in a practice when a coach does not have the necessary training or experience of working with para-athletes. This is convenient for the coach and the planning of the practice, but it may not meet the physiological needs of the para-athlete. Therefore, coaches need to make sure that all athletes are meeting the training goals of the practice, even if it means developing several practice plans.

> Coaches need to involve para-athletes in developing a training plan that meets the physical, social, psychological, and emotional needs of the para-athlete.

Coaches will also need to consider developmental age when making training group assignments. Social interactions with teammates are important at all stages of life, but coaches may need to balance developmental age with opportunities for social engagement with others of similar age. A para-athlete in their late teens is in the Fundamental stage of development, which may cater toward a younger age group, and a coach would need to find a balance for the para-athlete to receive developmentally appropriate skill training with their social needs. There are several possible solutions, including having the para-athlete train part-time with a fundamental-focused training group and part-time with a teenaged training group or the coach providing the para-athlete with one-on-one skill development training and allowing the para-athlete to engage with a teenaged training group for conditioning practices. It may be difficult to find the perfect balance between the skill development and social needs of a para-athlete, but the coach, with the involvement of the para-athlete, needs to develop a plan that works best and can be adjusted as the para-athlete's skills advance.

The developmental age of para-athletes must also be considered when clubs or other sport organizations are determining selection criteria for engagement in specialty training or competition opportunities. The use of age as criterion is common across all sports. Para-athletes who are at the appropriate developmental stage for the opportunity but are not the specified age are not given the opportunity to compete. Program designers are encouraged to focus on the physical, social, psychological, and emotional development of para-athletes and to be creative when they are designing training plans, practices, or setting participation criteria.

Competition

The LTD model states that competition is important to allow athletes to test the skills they are developing, and competition is identified as early as the Fundamental stage. Athletes must have someone of similar ability to test themselves against for fair competition to take place. The classification system was designed to group para-athletes into categories with others of similar functional ability within each adaptive sport to allow for fair competition (Tweedy et al., 2014). Many para-athletes see being classified as the launching point of their athletic careers and as a pivotal component of their development

Swimming Canada: Making Development a Priority

Swimming Canada began to make a conscious effort to address and support para-athlete development in 2017. It hired a consultant who had experience in adaptive sport as a former Paralympian, current coach, classifier, administrator, and researcher to help develop a plan to address the gaps in the para-swimmer development pathway. A comprehensive review of the current development practices, programs, and policies at all levels of sport (club, provincial sport organization, national sport organization) and building off the findings of the consultant's research into para-athlete development resulted in the establishment of a multiyear strategic plan. The first course of action was to focus the development efforts within a single province to provide proof of concept, with plans to spread key findings and areas of success from the project to other provinces when possible. Swim Ontario has the largest membership of competitive swimmers of any province in Canada, so Ontario was chosen as the province to address first.

Several key areas of the plan involve education, system alignment, engagement, and marketing. The plan implementation was delayed by the 2020 pandemic, but gains under the four pillars have been made, including online coach education sessions that focus on para-specific teachings, implementing systems to allow para-swimmers to engage in the sport throughout their lifespan from learn-to-swim to masters swimming, para-athlete development camps, and tour teams have taken place. (The phrase **para-athlete development** refers to the systematic guidance of athletes with impairments from their first involvement in sport through to high performance or being involved in sport for life.) Support has also been provided to clubs and coaches whenever needed, and an awareness and education school-based program called Pools to Schools has been launched. It involves elite para-swimmers sharing their stories and life lessons with students across the province. There is much to be excited about when it comes to para-swimmer development in Ontario, but there is much to do, and none of it would have been possible if Swimming Canada had not recognized the need to prioritize para-athlete development and take a direct approach to addressing the gaps.

as an athlete (Sales & Misener, 2021). The process for going through classification varies from one adaptive sport to another, with an array of stringency in the process. In some adaptive sports, being classified is delayed due to lack of access to qualified classifiers, lack of classification opportunities, or by classification process rules. Classification is an ongoing component of adaptive sport because athletes must be classified at least at the national and international levels. Some sports also require ongoing review of classifications.

Once para-athletes have been through the classification process and have been assigned a sport class, they can then begin engaging in competition. Athletes without impairments have daily opportunities to test themselves against others of similar abilities if they train in a group environment, but it is common for para-athletes to not have an opportunity to compete against other para-athletes until they reach higher levels of competition (i.e., regional, national, international). A lack of competition can make it difficult to keep para-athletes motivated and engaged in the sport. This is more of an obvious issue for individual and integrated sports, but even team adaptive sports can be affected if significant travel is required to find another team for competition. Para-athletes can train to increase their skills in individual sports that are integrated, and they can participate in integrated competition.

A lack of competition also poses a challenge for coaches. They must be creative and provide competitive opportunities for their para-athletes. Some possible solutions include virtual competitions or traveling to competitions where other para-athletes will be present. This would include competitions for para-athletes only. Coaches can encourage their athletes to focus on competing against themselves and their own personal best in practice times, distances, and other measures, depending on the sport.

The quality of the competition can also be a challenge because there is a lack of experienced officials in adaptive sport, particularly at the local level. The quality of officiating tends to improve, and the needs of para-athletes are more efficiently met, when para-athletes move to higher competitive levels. Clubs and regional adaptive sport organizations need to train officials on how to engage with adaptive sports and to officiate adaptive sport competitions, so the para-athlete is supported through all stages of competition.

Expedited Timelines

The LTD model is based on the concept that it takes 8 to 12 years for an athlete to reach international competition. However, several studies have indicated that adaptive sport development is significantly quicker, with para-athletes advancing from regional to international competition within three to five years (Dehghansai & Baker, 2020). This expedited timeline also affects how they move through the stages of development and is due in part to the limited numbers of competitors. Fewer competitors to compete against means that para-athletes can jump from regional to international competition in only a few years (Dehghansai & Baker, 2020). Classification can also influence movement through the competitive levels because some sport classes have fewer competitors. An athlete also can be reclassified into a sport class in which they are more competitive, influencing their movement through competitive levels.

Concerns about the speed at which para-athletes move through competitive levels include that para-athletes do not have time to obtain all the physical, psychological, social, and emotional skills necessary to effectively engage in higher levels of competitions, leading to injury and burnout (Higgs et al., 2019). Protection from injury and burnout is especially important in adaptive sport because there are limited participants, so continued engagement should be protected. Recovering from injury also can take longer and possibly have lifelong effects on para-athletes, depending on the impairment and the type of injury.

The duration of the international sporting careers for a para-athlete can be quite long, with multiple para-athletes having careers spanning more than 20 years, such as para-swimmer Trischa Zorn and para-cross-country skier Brian McKeever. Zorn is one of the most decorated Paralympians of all time, amassing 55 medals (41 gold, 9 silver, 5 bronze) as she competed in seven Paralympics during a 24-year span representing the United States. McKeever is one the most decorated Paralympic cross-country skiers of all time, winning 19 medals (16 gold, 2 silver, 1 bronze) in six Paralympics representing Canada. One possible explanation for long international careers may be the current expedited timelines of para-athletes moving through the levels of competition. Therefore, it is likely that para-athletes are going through the process of developing the physical, psychological, social, and emotional skills not at lower levels of competition as described in the LTD model but at international levels of competition. Whether this is appropriate is questionable.

Coaches have a role in the expedited timelines of para-athletes. Coaches need to decide if their para-athlete is ready to navigate higher levels of competition from a holistic perspective. They need to determine if the para-athlete is ready for the physical, psychological, emotional, and social components of elite competition. If they decide they need to slow down the advancement of their para-athletes, they will need to explain their thought process and decision to the para-athlete and potentially to representatives of PSOs or NSOs.

> **Para-athletes advance through levels of competition at an expedited rate compared to the timelines depicted in the LTD model.**

Organizational Involvement

Another area of impact on para-athlete development is the involvement of sport organizations at local, regional, and national levels. The roles of sport organization level are in the LTD model, with local clubs being responsible for Active Start, Fundamental, and Learn to Train stages. **Provincial Sport Organizations (PSOs)** are responsible for Learn to Train through Train to Compete stages, and National Sport Organizations (NSO) are responsible for the latter part of Train to Compete and Train to Win stages. In adaptive sport, the NSO is involved significantly earlier in the development of para-athletes through the NSO's governance and administration of the classification system. The initial classification level in para-swimming takes place at the late Fundamental or early Learn to Train stages (Swimming Canada, n.d.), meaning that para-swimmers begin their interaction with the NSO early in their development. The NSO mandate is focused on high performance; therefore, all interactions para-athletes have with the NSO will have this focus, even early in their development.

Another reason NSOs or National Paralympic Committees (NPCs), depending on which organization is responsible for the governance of adaptive sports, are involved with para-athletes early in their development is the limited number of para-athletes. Fewer athletes means that the NSO/NPC's best interest is to know and possibly have a role in the development of the next generation of para-athletes. NSOs are motivated to be involved in the development of para-athletes from early in their development. The outcome of the development process can have a significant impact on the future of the NSO/NPC because the success of para-athletes can influence funding and sponsorship.

Coaches and parents need to be aware of the influence of the NSO on their para-athlete's development and may need to decide if the early involvement of the NSO is in the best interest of the para-athlete.

Quality Environments

Quality environments are critically important throughout the para-athlete development experience. In the LTD model, a quality environment is a training and competition environment that is safe on multiple levels (i.e., physical, psychological, emotional, and social; Higgs et al., 2019). Being in a quality environment is important for all athletes, but para-athletes face significant barriers to quality environments. Common barriers include inaccessible facilities, unwelcoming clubs, insufficient coaching due to working with coaches who do not have experience working with para-athletes and having to fit into an able-bodied environment (Sales & Misener, 2021).

Physical safety may come to mind first when considering quality environments for para-athletes because this is the most observable safety barrier to address. Questions to consider for physical environment safety include the following:

- Are there automatic doors at the entrance to the facility?
- Does the building have ramps or elevators for access to all training areas?
- Are accessible bathrooms available (wide entrances and access features)?
- Does the building have large print and braille signage?
- Would an individual using a mobility device (i.e., wheelchair, walker, cane) be able to move around the training areas with ease?
- Is public transit available within close proximity of the training facility?
- Is accessible parking available?

Similar questions would also need to be considered for any competition facilities or accommodations.

Automatic doors at facility entrances help ensure physically safe environments.

Psychological safety for sport has been defined as "the perception that one is protected from, or unlikely to be at risk of, psychological harm in sport" (Vella et al., 2022, p. 15). Anxiety, threat, and fear of being punished, embarrassed, or marginalized are examples of psychological harm (Clark, 2020). When an environment is psychologically safe, all stakeholders (i.e., athletes, coaches, administrators) are positive, respectful, and genuine in their interactions with each other to the point where people feel that they are included and can be vulnerable and take risks without concern of ridicule (Vella et al., 2022). Many para-athletes have felt marginalized or disrespected. Therefore, clubs and coaches need to be aware of this and make a conscious effort to help para-athletes feel included and that they are an important part of the club environment.

Coaches can help para-athletes feel respected by admitting when they do not have all the answers and being willing to educate themselves through formal and informal methods. Many coaches do not have experience working with para-athletes, so they need to defer expertise to the para-athlete and their families, especially about the athlete's functional abilities. Coaches who establish clear lines of communication between the para-athlete and their families can help para-athletes feel that they are heard and respected and that what they have to say matters.

For an environment to be emotionally safe, a para-athlete needs to feel that they can express their emotions free from judgment or dismissal of their emotions. Para-athletes will often be initiated into an environment with their input welcomed. Over time, as a para-athlete continues to express their needs, they can be seen as a complainer and may feel that their input is not welcome because things are not adjusted to meet their needs, or they are not invited to discuss possible solutions. This leads the para-athlete to feel that it is not safe for them to express themselves. Giving athletes an option for providing suggestions anonymously is one way to help athletes feel safe in giving input.

Para-athletes also need to feel that their coach values their input when it comes to training planning and technique adjustments. This is important because para-athletes are the experts on their functional abilities, and they know better than anyone else what it feels like to live in their bodies, including what their bodies are and are not capable of doing. This does not mean that coaches cannot ask para-athletes to try new things or to encourage them to challenge themselves during practice. It means that coaches take the time to talk with para-athletes, give them the opportunity to provide feedback, and take what the para-athlete says into consideration.

Similar to psychological safety, an environment that is socially safe provides para-athletes with the opportunity to be respected, included, and accepted by everyone, from club administrators to the coaches to their teammates. A valuable aspect of adaptive sport is that it can provide individuals with impairments with the opportunity to interact with others who have similar life experiences, something para-athletes may not experience in other areas of their lives (i.e., school, work, social groups). For team adaptive sports, the opportunity to engage with other para-athletes is built into the format of the sport. For individual or integrated sports, opportunities to interact with other para-athletes may not naturally occur, and thought and consideration may be needed to provide para-athletes with the opportunity to engage with other para-athletes regularly. In integrated environments, being accepted by teammates may have additional challenges due to the age of para-athletes, which may not align with the typical age of the developmental needs and, therefore, training

group placement. Coaches will need to be intentional in helping all athletes feel safe and included in the group.

> **Coaches will need to be intentional in helping all athletes feel safe and included in the group.**

Another element of social safety for para-athletes is that in some instances they require training partners who can help support their participation. Athletes with visual impairments require guides in adaptive sports such as cross-country skiing, downhill skiing, and triathlon. In these instances, the para-athletes need to be partnered with a guide who matches their physicality, is willing to train to the same extent as the para-athlete, and with whom they can interact socially. For other sports, para-athletes require the assistance for physical support while engaging in sport. An example is tapping in para-swimming (a person outside the pool who taps the swimmer with a visual impairment to notify them they are close to the turn), helping transfer from one piece of equipment to another in sports that use specialized wheelchairs or stands, and assistance in boccia. Again, para-athletes can be put in vulnerable situations in which they must rely on others to facilitate their engagement in sport. Significant care must be taken in selecting the proper individuals to assist in these situations for the safety and comfort of all involved.

What's Next?

There are similarities and differences within the development experiences of para- and non-para-athletes. There is no specific para-athlete development model available for coaches and sport administrators to use for guidance as they work with para-athletes. The closest thing to a proposed para-athlete development came from Patatas and colleagues (2020), which outlined factors and stakeholders that have an influence on the para-athlete development experience at different phases of development. However, the authors did not put their findings forward as a proposed para-athlete development model.

To assist in the development of a para-athlete development model, more research is required in all areas of para-athlete development. The physiological needs of para-athletes have begun to be recognized as an area for consideration, with research into areas such as the similarities and differences of the psychological needs of adaptive sport (Dieffenback & Startler, 2012; Kenttä & Corban, 2014), the preparation needs of para-athletes (Blumenstein & Orbach, 2015), and the mindfulness of para-athletes (Lundqvist et al., 2018) having already been done. Further research is required to ensure that the physiological needs of all para-athletes, regardless of impairment, functional ability, or level of support are adequately met.

The impact of the physiological effects of impairment, whether congenital or traumatic, on athlete development experience needs to be further investigated to help coaches and sport physiologists provide para-athletes with the support they need. This will be an ongoing process because there are 10 eligible impairments currently recognized in adaptive sport. There are multiple medical diagnoses that can lead to one of the 10 eligible impairments, all of which may have a slightly different impact on a para-athlete's physiological needs within sport.

Once a para-athlete development model is presented, rigorous testing, reviews, and ongoing updates will be required to ensure that the model is meeting the needs of para-athletes. As part of the ongoing review process, para-athletes will need to be consulted throughout and their experiences will need to be considered to ensure the model is meeting the needs of para-athletes at all stages of their development.

Summary

This chapter highlighted different models of athlete development. There are numerous frameworks designed to support the trajectory of an individual who might want to move from introduction to sport participation through to performance levels of sport. A few of these frameworks address adaptations for para-athletes and have been highlighted in this chapter. The long-term development model, which was developed in Canada and adopted in other countries around the world (e.g., the United Kingdom), is one of the few that offer insights and adaptations for the specific needs of para-athletes. It recognizes that the development pathways and trajectory of sport participation may differ for individuals across the spectrum of impairments. It is important that adaptive sport is not designed as a one-size-fits-all approach, and the models discussed to date predominantly lack the nuanced approach for para-athlete development.

CRITICAL THINKING EXERCISES

1. Are athlete development models useful in the development of athletes? Why or why not?

2. What are the pros and cons of applying an athlete development model designed for nondisabled athletes to para-athletes?

3. What areas of para-athlete development require the most attention by sport organizations?

4. You have been asked to design a para-athlete development model. What four key factors would you include in the design?

CHAPTER 10

Adaptive Sports and Recreation for Military Populations

Jasmine Townsend, PhD, CTRS, FDRT, CARSS-II, and Derek Whaley, MS, CTRS, CARSS-I

> **LEARNING OBJECTIVES**
>
> After reading this chapter, you will be able to do the following:
>
> - Explain the impacts of war on the health and functioning of military service members.
> - Identify health care opportunities for military service members.
> - Discuss the military heritage of adaptive sports and recreation.
> - Describe the variety of adaptive sports and recreation opportunities for military service members.
> - Describe the characteristics of adaptive sports and recreation programs for military service members.
> - Discuss the benefits of adaptive sports and recreation opportunities for military service members.

This chapter will focus on the military population in the United States, showing the impacts of war on service members and the public health system and the typical health care options available to address common service-related health conditions. This chapter will also describe the industry of adaptive sports and recreation in the context of military populations, providing insight into how the Department of Defense, Department of Veterans Affairs, and community-based nonprofit organizations contribute to opportunities available to service members. The characteristics of these programs, as well as the benefits of participation in these programs for service members, are examined.

In 2021, the Cost of War project, an initiative of the Watson Institute for International and Public Affairs at Brown University, released a report detailing the human and financial tolls of the United States' involvement in wars since 9/11 (Bilmes, 2021). The report estimated that the 20-year war on terror cost an estimated US$8 trillion and killed more than 900,000 people around the world, mostly civilians (Brown University, 2021). More specifically, during the 20 years the United States was in Afghanistan, there were more than 800,000 troops deployed, and seven years in Iraq saw more than 1.5 million troops deployed. Figure 10.1 indicates the numbers of troops wounded or killed in action in both theaters (U.S. Department of Defense, 2022). The human capital invested in Afghanistan and Iraq is the largest single long-term cost associated with these wars and will continue to come in the form of benefits and medical care provided to troops and their dependents. This is estimated to be around US$2.2 billion to date and during the next 30 years (Bilmes, 2021). These estimates do not include the roughly 10 million veterans of pre-9/11 conflicts that are still living and receiving care, many for long-term service-related health conditions that were not addressed in a timely manner. Figure 10.2 indicates the numbers of living veterans across all generations since World War II (USAFacts, 2023).

This medical care has been, and will likely continue to be, provided primarily by two entities within the United States' health care industry. The **Military Health System (MHS)** is a federalized system of health care for approximately 9.6 million beneficiaries, including uniformed (active) service members, retirees, and their family members (Military Health System, n.d.) and is primarily intended to ensure a medically ready military force. The **Veterans Health Administration**

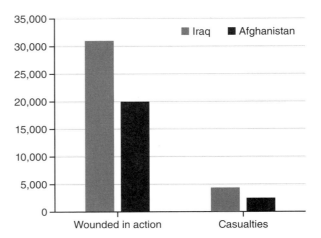

FIGURE 10.1 Raw numbers of wounded and casualties in Iraq and Afghanistan.
U.S. Department of Defense (2024).

(VHA; commonly referred to as "the VA") provides health care services to more than 9 million U.S. **veterans** (people separated from military service) and is intended to honor veterans through high-quality health care aimed at improving health and well-being following military service (U.S. Department of Veterans Affairs, 2022).

Another industry has existed parallel to the military-focused health care industry and has provided complementary support to service members. **Veteran-serving organizations (VSOs)** have existed for generations in the United States, notably the Veterans of Foreign Wars (VFW), which was established

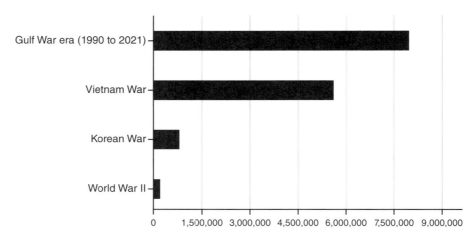

FIGURE 10.2 Living veterans in the United States as of 2021.
Data from USAFacts (2023).

in 1899, and the American Legion, which was established in 1919 (Ortiz, 2010). Historically, these organizations existed to lobby the federal government in support of veterans' issues (i.e., bonuses, pensions, and benefits), and the "Big Six" (VFW, American Legion, Disabled American Veterans, Paralyzed Veterans of America, AMVETS, and Vietnam Veterans of America) still work toward these efforts. While the lobbying power tends to be concentrated in the Big Six, there are almost 40,000 registered VSOs in the United States. (Combined Arms Institute, 2022), many of which are running smaller and less expensive operations (i.e., do not have brick-and-mortar buildings like the VFWs), are attracting a younger generation of veterans, and are focused more acutely on post-9/11 issues, like advocating for access to non-VA health care providers, among others (Steinhauer, 2019). Many of these VSOs also provide health care services intended to complement and supplement the traditional military health care options available to any generation of veterans. Regardless of where and how service members receive care, however, the need to support service members through their recovery is great and will require a variety of services to adequately address those needs. While war results in traumatic injury and death regardless of generation, the elements of these dynamics are multifaceted. This discussion is beyond the scope of this chapter; thus, while there are multiple generations of living veterans, each with unique and common experiences, this chapter will focus primarily on post-9/11 U.S. veterans.

Common Health Conditions Among Service Members and Veterans

Service-connected health conditions are complex and varied across the armed services and stem from more frequent and longer **deployments** in comparison to previous wars, as well as higher levels of exposure to combat (Bilmes, 2021). Although improvements in protective gear and emergency medical services during the **Global War on Terror** have facilitated a decrease in mortality rates, it has led to an increase in long-term health-related consequences, with approximately 40% of veterans being granted lifetime **service-connected disability ratings** by the VA (Bilmes, 2021; Church, 2009; Ciarleglio et al., 2018; Noel et al., 2011; Spelman et al., 2012). Service members have returned with impacts from injuries manifesting across multiple **health domains** (i.e., physical, psychological, social, emotional, and cognitive). Blast waves from improvised explosive devices (IEDs) are the leading cause of physical injuries, followed by occupational causes such as extreme weather conditions, poor living conditions on military installations, and environmental exposure to contaminants from burn pits or sandstorms (Church, 2009; Spelman et al., 2012).

Literature indicates that musculoskeletal, mental health or adjustment disorders, and medically unexplained symptoms (fatigue; somatic and cognitive complaints) are the most reported health conditions of returning service members (Noel et al., 2011; Spelman et al., 2012). Service members are also returning with high levels of chronic pain and comorbid mental health diagnoses such as post-traumatic stress disorder (PTSD), depression, substance abuse, and suicide risk, in addition to risk for impaired psychosocial functioning such as loss of identity and community, social isolation, unemployment and homelessness, legal problems, and marital instability. Taken as a whole, the impact of these health conditions is contributing to an increasingly large strain on the public health systems (Bilmes, 2021; Olenick et al., 2015; Spelman et al., 2012).

Veteran-Focused Treatment Options

The variety of health care systems available to service members has the capacity to offer services geared toward supporting and offering relief for the unique needs of this population segment. Services can be delivered across settings (e.g., inpatient, outpatient, **community-based**) and under the supervision of various health care professionals and community providers (e.g., primary care physicians, psychologists, **physical therapists, occupational therapists,** recreational therapists). Although services, settings, and providers may differ, at their core, treatment is viewed through the lens of functional ability and rehabilitation (Spelman et al., 2012). Best practices for treating service members are focused on an interdisciplinary team approach, which has been found to have positive effects, especially on destigmatizing and normalizing mental health conditions, which are a signature injury for post-9/11 service members (Olenick et al., 2015; Spelman et al., 2012; Tanielian & Jaycox, 2008).

Based on a battery of administered assessments and tests, veterans may be referred to any of the variety of health care services available for treatment of both physical injuries and mental health conditions that are often co-occurring and can be referred to as **polytrauma** (Pugh et al., 2014). The VA recommends **evidence-based practi**ces to serve veterans most effectively, and recent research has identified useful practices for treating PTSD, major depression, and alcohol use disorder (Hepner et al., 2018). For PTSD, these include prolonged exposure, cognitive processing therapy (CPT), eye movement desensitization and reprocessing (EMDR), cognitive behavioral therapy (CBT), brief eclectic psychotherapy, narrative exposure therapy, and written narrative exposure. For major depression, these include acceptance and commitment therapy, behavioral activation therapy, CBT, interpersonal psychotherapy, mindfulness-based therapy, and problem-solving therapy. For alcohol use disorder, these include behavioral couples therapy, CBT for substance use disorder, community reinforcement approaches, motivational enhancement therapy, and 12-step facilitation (Hepner et al., 2018; RAND Corporation, 2019).

Other treatments may also include a combination of pharmacologics and additional therapies such as massage therapy, TENS therapy (transcutaneous electrical nerve stimulation), thermal and aqua therapy, chiropractic treatment, and acupuncture (Church, 2009; Grant et al., 2015, 2017; Spelman et al., 2012). These services are primarily offered under the **medical model of care**, which uses a problem-focused approach and generally results in service providers focusing on a specific health condition, injury, or illness at a given moment with the intent to remedy that condition and without considering other contextual influences.

Alternatively, a **strengths-based approach** starts with a focus on the internal and external strengths and existing skillsets of the client rather than just the health condition. Hopes, aspirations, and values take priority in treatment, rather than symptoms and functional deficits (Hawkins et al., 2016; Heyne & Anderson, 2012). Service providers using this approach assess internal and external strengths and skillsets, set appropriate goals, use appropriate interventions and treatments, and rely on resources that promote health and the full potential of the individual (Carruthers & Hood, 2007; Hawkins et al., 2016; Heyne & Anderson, 2012; Hood & Carruthers, 2007). Recent research has argued that **nature-based and outdoor interventions** for service members align well with this strengths-based approach (Hawkins et al., 2016). Adaptive sports and recreation opportunities are another complementary and strengths-based approach

> Health services for military veterans exist across multiple settings, including inpatient, outpatient, and community-based providers. Each may use a different model of care: medical model, strengths-based approach, or nature-based and outdoor interventions.

Adaptive Sports and Recreation for Military Service Members

The term **adaptive sports and recreation** refers to "any modification of a given sport or recreation activity to accommodate the varying ability levels of an individual with a disability" (Lundberg, Taniguchi, et al., 2011, p. 206). Specialized equipment, modified rules, environments, and instruction facilitate as much independent athletic participation as possible. Organized adaptive sports opportunities originated as a treatment approach for injured World War II veterans by Dr. Ludwig Guttman of the Stoke Mandeville Hospital in England (Brittain & Green, 2012; Scholz & Chen, 2018; Slater & Meade, 2004; see chapter 4). What began in 1948 as simply rehabilitation for veterans with spinal cord injuries has grown into the modern **Paralympic Games** movement, which provides elite competition across 28 sports (22 summer sports, six winter sports as of 2020) and in parallel with the Olympic Games. Global conflicts post-9/11 have resulted in a re-emergence of the use of sport as part of the process to rebuild the physical and psychological functioning of military service members following traumatic combat experiences (Brittain & Green, 2012; Scholz & Chen, 2018). As such, opportunities for adaptive sports and recreation involvement can be found in a variety of places, including municipal parks and recreation centers, clinical settings such as hospitals and care centers, nonprofit adaptive sports organizations, and educational institutions, among others, and at introductory, recreational, and competitive levels (Lundberg, Taniguchi, et al., 2011; Mayer & Anderson, 2014). Military service members have access to adaptive sports and recreation programs through three main pathways: Department of Defense transition units, the VA, and community-based nonprofit organizations.

Department of Defense (DoD) Transition Units

Injured service personnel can engage in adaptive sports and recreation through programs in **transition units**, which are geared toward helping wounded soldiers transition back into the military force or to shift to separation from the military and to veteran status. Transition units are located at various **military installations** around the United States and across all armed services branches. Generally, service members attached to transition units are navigating complex medical care and rehabilitation and are served by a team of providers, including primary care managers; nurse case managers; and recreational, occupational, and physical therapists (U.S. Department of Defense, 2019). In addition to the standard health care received while attached to a transition unit, recovering service members can be exposed to adaptive sports and recreation activities as part of their rehabilitation. These activities may include traditional sports (e.g., wheelchair sports, track and field, sitting volleyball) and recreational and outdoor activities (e.g., fishing, hiking, horseback riding, archery; Ferrer & Davis, 2019).

As a culminating experience of both their time in the military and with the transition programs, service members can compete in the **Warrior Games**, a Paralympic Games-style athletic competition sponsored by the **Department of Defense** and for athletes in transition units who excel in their given sport and express interest in taking involvement to the next level. For those who are further committed, the Warrior Games can serve as a qualifying event for the Paralympic Games (U.S. Department of Defense, n.d.). In this way, competitive adaptive sports involvement through transition units mirrors the original efforts of Dr. Guttman at the Stoke Mandeville Hospital.

An athlete competes in recumbent cycling at the Warrior Games Challenge 2023.
MSG Mike Haley

VA Adaptive Sports

Once a service member becomes separated from the military, they can access adaptive sports and recreation through the VA's **Office of National Veterans Sports Programs and Special Events (NVSPSE)**. Through the NVSPSE, clinical experts use adaptive sports and recreation to promote health and healing and optimize independence, community engagement, well-being, and quality of life (U.S. Department of Veterans Affairs, n.d.b; therapeutic and creative arts are also part of the NVSPSE program but are beyond the focus of this chapter). Some VA hospitals also offer adaptive sports through inpatient and outpatient services facilitated by recreational, occupational, and physical therapists and aimed at addressing functional limitations in physical, psychological, social, emotional, and cognitive domains. On a nationwide level, the VA runs five annual programs that provide the largest

> Once separated from the military, a veteran has access to the VA's Office of National Veterans Sports Programs and Special Events (NVSPSE), which runs five annual programs that provide the largest offering of adaptive sport competitions and training for veterans in the United States.

ARIEL MALPHRUS BAILEY, MS, CTRS, CNA

I am a Certified Therapeutic Recreation Specialist working at Fort Stewart, Savannah, Georgia, USA. The soldiers at an Army Soldier Recovery Unit (SRU) have one mission: to heal. It is my job as a contracted certified therapeutic recreation specialist (CTRS) to provide therapeutic programs for the adaptive reconditioning program (ARP). I ensure that all activities carried out through the ARP meet the purpose and goals established by the soldier's individual comprehensive training plan in each of six functional domains: career, emotional, family, physical, social, and spiritual. These activities include adaptive sports, arts and crafts, dance, drama, music, table and board games, sports and athletics, outdoor activities, volunteer programs, and other special events. It is my job to develop and implement therapeutic programs using a systematic process of assessment, planning, implementation, and evaluation based on the needs of the SRU soldier population.

Tanner Bailey

I work on an interdisciplinary team with physical therapists, occupational therapists, nurses, social workers, and many other health professionals. One thing that excites us all is watching the soldiers participating in adaptive sports. They seem to transform in front of our eyes, going from having a lot of negative thoughts about themselves and their lives to feeling free, healthy, and capable of accomplishing things again.

During a typical week in our unit, we provide a variety of activities such as air rifle, archery, cycling, golf, rowing, sitting volleyball, swimming, track and field, and wheelchair basketball. I also have the pleasure of assisting with recruiting soldiers to participate in the Army trials with the goal of competing in the Warrior Games. As the recreational therapist, I help train recruited athletes to ensure they best represent the Army at this competition. These activities, and many others, are used not only to rehabilitate deficits in functioning (i.e., strength, flexibility, balance) but also to build on existing interests, skills, and capacities. We give the soldiers many opportunities to not only continue doing things they love but also to try new things and push themselves beyond their comfort zones. We hope that as soldiers return to their homes and communities, they will do so with leisure and recreation-based skills and interests that will lead to a long-term independent and healthy lifestyle.

---

offering of adaptive sport competitions and training for veterans in the United States (see table 10.1).

In addition to the national programs, the VA also offers the largest granting opportunity in the nation to support veterans-focused community-based adaptive sports organizations. This funding is available annually through the NVSPSE office, and from fiscal year 2017 to 2020, the VA received US$47 million in funds to distribute to veteran's service organizations, city and national municipalities, and other community groups (U.S. Department of Veterans Affairs, 2021). This funding is made available through Title VII of the **Veterans Benefits Improvement Act of 2008** (Veterans Benefits Improvement Act, 2008). Grant recipients may use the funds to support the following:

- Instruction, participation, and competition in adaptive sports
- Training and technical assistance to program administrators, coaches, recreation therapists, instructors, VA employees, and other appropriate individuals
- Coordination, U.S. Paralympic classification of athletes, athlete assessment, and sport-specific training techniques
- Program development and sports equipment, supplies, program evaluation, and other activities (U.S. Department of Veterans Affairs, 2021).

168 Introduction to Adaptive Sport and Recreation

TABLE 10.1 **National VA Adaptive Sports Events**

Event	Participants eligible	Sports available	Year started
National Veterans Wheelchair Games	Veterans with amputations, central neurological conditions, multiple sclerosis, spinal cord injury (SCI)	• Air rifle and pistol • Archery • Bowling • Disc golf • Esports • Field events • Motor rally • Pickleball • Slalom • Softball	1981
National Veterans Golden Age Games	Veterans aged 55 or older with any health condition	• Air rifle and pistol • Archery • Badminton • Basketball • Boccia • Bowling • Cornhole • Cycling • Disc golf • Horseshoes • Nineball • Pickleball • Power walking • Shuffleboard • Swimming • Table tennis • Track & field	1985
National Disabled Veterans Winter Sports Clinic	Veterans with amputations, neurological conditions, SCI, traumatic brain injury (TBI), visual impairments, and others	• Curling • Fly-fishing • Rock wall climbing • Scuba diving • Skiing (alpine and Nordic) • Sled hockey • Snowmobiling	1987
National Disabled Veterans Golf Clinic	Veterans with amputations, SCI, visual impairments, and other life-changing injuries, caregivers, VA and non-VA staff	• Golf	1994
National Veterans Summer Sports Clinic	Veterans with amputations, burns, neurological conditions, SCI, TBI/polytrauma, visual impairments	• Adaptive fitness • Adaptive sailing • Cycling • Kayaking • Surfing	2008

The NVSPSE also offers a monthly training allowance to support veterans with service-connected disabilities who are training for, selected for, or competing with the national Paralympic teams in their respective sports. These funds help offset the costs of training and align with the **VA's Vocational Rehabilitation and Employment** funding rates (U.S. Department of Veterans Affairs, n.d.a).

Community-Based Adaptive Sports

Outside of DoD and VA programs, **community-based adaptive sports and recreation** opportunities are a growing segment of the VSO industry and are heavily supported by the VA Adaptive Sport Grant mechanism. While these programs have always existed as part of a continuum of services for individuals with disabilities in general (Sable & Gravink, 2005; Zabriskie et al., 2005), the increasing needs of recovering service members has led to an increase of programs within the industry. These programs span the country, may be a part of municipal parks and recreation departments or stand-alone organizations, and offer access to adaptive sports and recreation in communities where VA-specific services may not exist. In many cases, VAs will partner with community-based adaptive sports programs to offer services to veterans that the VA cannot offer on their own (Mulhollon & Casey, 2016). These partnerships provide a continuum of services that facilitate lifelong involvement in sport and

Veterans from the Higher Ground veterans program learn to surf.
Higher Ground

Systematic Process of Adaptive Sports and Recreation Service Provision

Qualified adaptive sports and recreation service providers should begin work with their clients by assessing functional abilities across relevant domains (i.e., physical, social, emotional, psychological, cognitive). This information should be gathered using standardized and validated assessments and be used to plan appropriate activities for participants based on identified goals and needs. When implementing these activities, consider the various modifications and accommodations that people may need. Activities should occur in safe environments with trained staff focused on ensuring positive experiences and preventing injury or reinjury. Activities may be implemented as one-time events or ongoing, repeated opportunities. Progress toward goals should be evaluated consistently throughout participation in programs (formative and summative evaluation). This approach is a strengths-based approach to adaptive sports and recreation service delivery and is commonly used by certified therapeutic recreational specialists (CTRS).

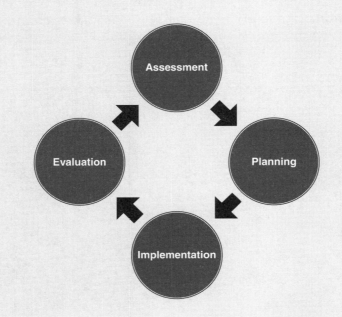

recreation activities outside of treatment settings, although many community-based adaptive sports and recreation programs also offer therapeutic services with the help of **Certified Therapeutic Recreation Specialists (CTRSs)** (see Sable & Gravink, 2005; Thompson et al., 2016; Wilder et al., 2011). Military-focused community-based adaptive sports and recreation programs may have a unique combination of program characteristics that contribute to the successes of these programs in serving the military community. Unfortunately, limited research has explored these program characteristics in a systematic way. Thus, the discussion of military-focused adaptive sports and recreation program characteristics is based on descriptive information available from program websites as well as professional expertise concerning sports and recreation program design in general and specific to adaptive sports and recreation.

Characteristics of Community-Based Adaptive Sports and Recreation Programs

Research has indicated that intentionally designed programs and experiences are highly desired for participants, customers, and consumers and have the potential to result in impactful experiences that may be memorable, meaningful, or transformative (Lundberg et al., 2021). This can be true of sports and recreation programs, yet limited research has explored the design of adaptive sports and recreation programs. Whaley et al. (2021) provide a general description of characteristics of adaptive sports and recreation programs, classifying characteristics as either intrapersonal ("I feel like I developed an enhanced or positive self-identity") or structural ("Programs were individualized to meet my goals"). The authors indicated that "programs that instill a sense of accomplishment and control over one's life, challenge participants beyond what they thought they were capable of doing and offer something new and exciting have the greatest impact" (Whaley et al., 2021, p. 2). It was unclear if the adaptive sports and recreation programs described in this study were specific to service members, yet it is likely that service members did participate in these programs since many community-based programs serve both civilian and military populations alike.

The literature surrounding the development of adaptive sports and recreation programs is sparse, especially for military-focused programs, but available information was used to develop characteristics of these programs. DoD transition units and VA hospitals do not advertise their services online in the ways that nonprofit organizations or municipal parks and recreation facilities do, so the ability to describe the characteristics of those programs is limited. However, many of those programs partner with community-based programs to offer adaptive sports and recreation services, so the information presented is based on what is known about community-based adaptive sports and recreation programs. From a broad perspective, military-focused community-based adaptive sports and recreation programs have these characteristics:

- They rely more heavily on nature-based or outdoor adventure activities (equine-assisted services, fly-fishing, hiking, skiing, water sports, etc.) and may tap into elements of novelty, risk, and challenge that are desirable among service members.

- They are often owned or operated by members of the military community (veterans and their family members), which may provide a sense of familiar language, beliefs, rituals, and humor that are specific to military culture and offer opportunities for unity, shared experience, reassurance, normalization of experiences, and rekindling of lost elements of military identity.

- They employ both therapeutic and nontherapeutic staff to facilitate activities, which gives service members a choice about what type of experience they want to have. Some programs may help them work on functional challenges they are experiencing, while others may provide recreational activities that are enjoyable or diversional.

- The activities are physically active in nature.

- There are opportunities for healthy social engagement (i.e., alcohol-free), often with other service members and their families.

- They provide one-time experiences, daily opportunities for engagement, or retreat-style (i.e., for one week) experiences. The array of experience lengths allows service members to choose program structures that fit within the schedules of their lives.

- They provide both recreational and competitive opportunities and facilitate the development of higher levels of commitment, if desired.

- Some programs provide activities to just the service member, while others include their significant others, or another supporter (i.e., battle buddy). A small number provide services to the entire family.

- Some programs serve specific generations of veterans (i.e., post-9/11 only), while others serve veterans of any generation.

- Some programs focus on specific health conditions (i.e., surfing for individuals with amputations), while others serve veterans with any condition.

Regardless of these characteristics, a vital feature of any military-focused adaptive sports and recreation program is the cultural competence of the staff members. **Cultural competence** is "loosely defined as the ability to understand, appreciate and interact with people from cultures or belief systems different from one's own" (DeAngelis, 2015, p. 1). Military cultural competence has been identified as a critical part of providing care to service members and their families (Meyer & Wynn, 2018), and with so many seeking care outside of typical military-focused health care avenues (Kuehn, 2009; QB Medical, 2021), the need for cultural competence

among community-based adaptive sports and recreation service providers is high. While most service members will experience a smooth transition from military service to civilian life, some will experience challenges (Cooper et al., 2018). Adaptive sports and recreation service providers must be educated about these dynamics and prepared with strategies to help service members successfully navigate their experiences in the programs and gain the benefits everyone desires.

Benefits of Adaptive Sports for Military Populations

There is a well-established and continuously growing body of literature that illustrates the benefits of physical activity for the health of the general population. Physical activity has been proven to help prevent and treat health conditions such as heart disease, stroke, diabetes, breast and colon cancer, hypertension, overweight and obesity and can improve mental health, quality of life, and well-being (World Health Organization, 2018). Individuals with disabilities are at much greater risk of incurring serious health problems associated with physical inactivity; thus, there is a sense of urgency in promoting physical activity for this population segment (Rimmer & Marques, 2012). The benefits of physical activity and risks of physical inactivity are no different for service members with disabilities; however, the unique nature of military service and resultant health conditions may further complicate those risks. In addition to visible and invisible health conditions (e.g., spinal cord injuries, PTSD), challenges to reintegration such as alienation, boredom, bitterness, difficult relationships, and poor mental health may all contribute to decreased involvement in physical activity (Lundberg, Bennett, & Smith, 2011). Service members are more successful

> Oftentimes adaptive sports and recreation programs for veterans tend to have elements of high risk and skill, giving the veteran moments that get back to the natural and healthy high that they previously experienced while in the armed forces.

in integrating when they are involved in their community, have peer-support networks, and can access community resources, and adaptive sports and recreation programs can facilitate opportunities for such benefits to accrue. A summary of the evidence-based benefits of physical activity across functional life domains as facilitated through adaptive sports and recreation involvement for military service members can be found in table 10.2.

> The benefits of adaptive sports and recreation participation for service members extend well beyond just the physical aspects of participating in sport and include social, emotional, psychological, cognitive, occupational, and general quality of life benefits, among many others.

TABLE 10.2 **Evidence-Based Benefits of Adaptive Sports for Military Service Members**

Domain	Outcomes
Physical	Increased and improved: • Balance • Cardiorespiratory fitness • Coordination • Health-related quality of life (HRQol) • Physical fitness • Stamina • Strength • Satisfaction with health • Weight loss
Social	Increased and improved: • Perceptions of social support • Shared experience of injury, illness, and recovery • Shared experience of military culture • Social connections and relatedness • Social functioning • Value of family and partners
Emotional	Increased and improved: • Competitive drive • Independence • Marital satisfaction • Motivation • Positive and negative affect • Satisfaction with life • Self-acceptance • Vigor Reductions in: • Total mood disturbances (tension, depression, anger) • Negative influence/perceptions of stigma

>*continued*

TABLE 10.2 *>continued*

Domain	Outcomes
Psychological	Increased and improved: • Ability • Adjustment to self-image • Competence • Determination, inner strength • General mental health • Mental alertness • Mood • Perceived stress • Resilience • Seeing beyond injury • Self-efficacy, self-esteem • Self-determination (competence, autonomy, relatedness) • Self-perception, identity, and self-concept • Sense of achievement or accomplishment • Sports competence Reductions in: • Symptoms of PTSD, depression, and anxiety
Cognitive	Increased and improved: • Attentiveness • Communication and interaction • Social awareness and knowledge of disability
Other	Increased and improved: • Ability to experience time "in the present" • Athletic identity • Community integration • Daily functioning (self-care, employment, education) • Employment • Feeling of respite from exhausting mental health symptoms (e.g., PTSD) • Leisure satisfaction • Motivation for living • Positive social comparison • Quality of life (environmental and psychological) • Reconnection to previous interests • Satisfaction with happiness • Sense of purpose and meaning in life • Sleep • Subjective well-being

Summary

Adaptive sports and recreation programs for military service members are a growing and important segment of both the recreation and health care industries. These programs provide access to health care outside of traditional medical settings and contribute to long-term, independent healthy functioning in homes and communities. Given the ongoing need to support military service members (and their families) in their transition and recovery, adaptive sports and recreation programs can contribute to these efforts in many ways. Opportunities are diverse and exist across a spectrum of industries designed to provide care, support, and transition to service members in various stages of career and life. Research is continuously shedding light on these programs and indicates positive outcomes from participation, but more work is needed to fully understand the processes by which these health outcomes are produced (i.e., what programs and activities produced which outcomes). In doing so, adaptive sports and recreation can be cemented as a useful complementary health care approach to working with injured or ill military service members.

CRITICAL THINKING EXERCISES

1. Research and discuss: What adaptive sports opportunities do veterans in your community or state have access to? Research municipal parks and recreation or adaptive sports nonprofits. What are the demographics (disabilities served, inpatient or outpatient, service providers, etc.) and characteristics (type of sports and recreation, segregated or inclusive, recreational, or competitive, etc.) of these programs?

2. Compare and contrast the medical model and strength-based approaches discussed in the chapter. Evaluate the advantages and disadvantages of each approach in the context of adaptive sports for veterans.

3. Identify and define three key concepts related to adaptive sports and veterans discussed in the chapter. Explain their significance and how they contribute to the overall well-being of veterans.

4. Reflect on your perspectives regarding the role of adaptive sports in supporting veterans. Consider how your views align or differ from the perspectives presented in the chapter. Discuss any assumptions or biases you might have.

CHAPTER 11

Adaptive Youth Sports

Anthony G. Delli Paoli, PhD, and Javier Robles, JD

LEARNING OBJECTIVES

After reading this chapter, you will be able to do the following:
- Explain the differences among adaptive youth sport contexts.
- Describe the barriers to participation for youth athletes with disabilities.
- Describe the solutions to overcoming the barriers to participation.
- Describe strategies for coaches to work with youth athletes with disabilities.

Adaptive youth sports have seen a considerable expansion in recent years, offering a more inclusive sporting experience for those with physical and intellectual disabilities. Through the integration of adaptive rules and equipment, people of all abilities can participate in a range of sports, from running and swimming to basketball and soccer. Despite this progress, significant challenges remain, including the lack of resources to support adaptive youth sport programs and the need for heightened public awareness to ensure greater inclusion for all youth. This chapter provides an overview of the current adaptive youth sport context and examines the opportunities and challenges that have emerged in recent years.

Adaptive Youth Sports Settings

Youth sports are sport programs for children and youth typically between ages 7 and 18. There are designated coaches, organized practices, and scheduled competitions organized by adults (Gould, 1982). Youth sports in the United States serve roughly 50% of children ages 6 to 17. Unfortunately, children with special needs participate at lower rates than their peers without special needs (CAGMI, 2023). A category of youth sports that specifically serves individuals with special needs is adaptive youth sport. **Adaptive youth sports** refer to youth sport that is modified or created for individuals with disabilities (American Association of Adapted Sports Programs, 2023).

Most adaptive youth sport opportunities occur in the *community setting* via public recreation (i.e., city and county recreation) and local sport organization chapters. For example, Move United's mission is to provide national leadership and opportunities for people with disabilities to develop independence, confidence, and fitness through participation in community sports, including competition, recreation, and educational programs. They offer 70 different adaptive sports representing 200 community

177

organization in the United States and serve more than 100,000 participants.

Another setting is school, where students can participate in *intrascholastic programs*, where they can participate with students from one's own school, and *interscholastic programs*, where they can participate and compete against students from other schools. Some individuals with disabilities may participate in parallel competitions with teammates who do not have a disability on the school's team, whereas other schools may have separate adaptive sport programs only for individuals with disabilities. In parallel adaptive youth sport, athletes with and without disabilities train and compete together, thus promoting teamwork and camaraderie. The team practices together, following adaptive rules and using modified equipment when necessary. During games, they compete against other schools in their district, fostering a sense of healthy competition and providing an inclusive environment for all participants.

> Adaptive youth sports occur in community, intrascholastic, and interscholastic settings.

In addition to the settings for adaptive sport, participation is influenced by a range of interconnected factors. One way to understand the complexity of sport participation is the youth sport system. The **youth sport system** is the set of the interdependent persons and contexts that influence and are influenced by an athlete in youth sport (Dorsch et al., 2020). This system shows how parents, siblings, peers, and coaches as well as teams, organizations, and communities influence and are influenced by youth sport athletes.

Parents in youth sport support athletes in adaptive youth sport. They are typically the primary caregivers who transport their youth athletes to and from practices and games. Parents of children with disabilities generally value the benefits of physical activity and recognize the associated benefits of physical activity participation. However, parents face obstacles such as a lack of regular programming, equipment, and training needed to support the participation of their youth athlete (Columna et al., 2020). Parents and their youth athletes do not exist in isolation because parents may have to balance the sport commitments of more than one child, highlighting the diversity of influence on a youth's sport experiences. When coaches and administrators do get to know families by communicating with parents to understand mutual expectations and important information related to a youth athlete's disability, adaptive youth sports become most beneficial.

In addition to the family, community youth sport programs welcome athletes of all abilities and experience levels. Volunteer youth sport coaches face challenges when coaching individuals with differing skills, knowledge, and disabilities. However, administrators and coaches often lack specific information on effectively including and coaching individuals with disabilities. Collaboration among administrators, coaches, parents, and athletes is essential to overcoming challenges and implementing facilitation strategies. This aligns with understanding the community subsystem of the youth sport system. It is important to note that effective strategies for including and coaching youth athletes with and without disabilities are often similar, with differences being a matter of degree rather than qualitative distinctions. This chapter heavily draws from the perspective that these effective strategies are useful for all youth athletes.

> Effective strategies for including and coaching youth athletes with and without disabilities are often similar rather than greatly different.

JAVIER ROBLES, JD
DIRECTOR OF CENTER FOR DISABILITY SPORTS, HEALTH AND WELLNESS, RUTGERS UNIVERSITY

Nothing is more complicated than understanding what it takes to create a successful teaching environment around issues of disability, sport, exercise, and inclusion. This is true if your audience is coaches, students, parents, or educators. There is a discomfort associated with disability issues that often prevents us from asking questions or seeking the answers we need to create success in our adaptive sports programs. As a professor and a person with a disability, I find that the answer is always to be upfront and honest, to lean into that discomfort to start a conversation. The first day of class is a little uncomfortable for my students. Many of them have not interacted face-to-face with someone in a wheelchair who is also an educator. I require my students not just to understand disability but to interact, research, and write about disability, sport, and health. I bring in speakers with various disabilities to talk from a lived experience and to answer questions about their challenges and successes. Creating an environment where uncomfortable questions are encouraged and having students interact with athletes, students, and leaders with disabilities, shows them the importance of inclusion.

Amy Bertelsen-Robles

If you want to create empathy and educate people about the importance of adaptive sports, exercise, or recreation for people with disabilities, try this:

- *Invite:* Invite people with disabilities to present to your groups. This creates a level of trust with the community and may answer questions your group may have. It also will alleviate the burden of educating and creating empathy from those athletes with disabilities in your group. A good place to start is your local independent living center or individual or group specific to adaptive sports.
- *Experience:* Organize an adaptive sports day. In my many years of teaching, I have never found a more effective tool for creating empathy than direct experience. During our adaptive sports day, we invite sports teams from track and field, wheelchair basketball, beep baseball, and many more to the university. Our students, faculty, staff, and community members are invited to participate and compete. The students in class immediately following this event have a totally new understanding of these activities. They now know the effort and hard work it takes to play.
- *Fun:* Keep it fun! It is so easy to forget that adaptive sports are supposed to be fun. They are not about disabilities or adaptive equipment but about creating an environment that is rewarding, challenging, and fun.

Adaptive Youth Sports Participation

Participating in youth sports has positive effects for all children, especially those with disabilities. Despite these benefits, children with disabilities participate at lower rates or do not participate at all compared to their typically developing peers. A range of issues are related to participating in youth sport for youth with disabilities. A challenge to resolving these issues is that they are unlikely to be resolved quickly because of their complexity. They often require many stakeholders

Introduction to Adaptive Sport and Recreation

(i.e., league directors, coaches, parents, and local and state officials) to cooperate, and that can be particularly difficult when working in youth sport. Thus, these issues may be resolved with attention focused on a limited set of issues rather than an attempt to resolve all issues collectively.

Participation Barriers

Barriers are covered more in depth in chapter 2, but it is worth revisiting a range of barriers that result in low levels of youth sport participation for individuals with disabilities. Becoming aware of these barriers and how to reduce their impact on participation is important for parents, coaches, administrators, and youth sport stakeholders to consider. Barriers include actual (e.g., cost of equipment or availability of transportation) and perceived barriers (e.g., fear of being teased). Both actual and perceived barriers are equally powerful contributors to participation. One way to better understand specific barriers is to categorize them into individual, social, environmental, and policy levels of complexity (see table 11.1).

> Both actual and perceived barriers have equally powerful influence on participation.

TABLE 11.1 **Barriers and Facilitators to Adaptive Youth Sport Participation**

	Barriers	Facilitators
Individual	Low perceived athletic competence	Improve perceived athletic competence through practice, support, and encouragement
	Poor motor skills	Motivated to be fit and healthy
	Fear of being teased or injured	Possess adequate skills to play
	Equipment costs	Fun and enjoyment
	Pain	
	Worsening of symptoms	
Social	No friends	Family encouragement, support
	Lack of parental support	Peer encouragement, support, and modeling
	No time for other activities	Appropriate facilities and program offerings
	Uninformed coaches	Trained staff and coaches
	Negative disability perceptions from others	
Environmental	Distance to playing facilities	
	Lack of programs	Trained administrations and stakeholders
Policy	Fear of liability	Information and awareness

Individual barriers occur within the youth athlete. Actual barriers are a lack of physical skills needed to play the sport and the cost of specialized equipment to make a modification. The cost of specialized equipment can vary depending on several factors, such as the type of sport, the competition level, the location, and the specific needs of the individual. For example, adaptive equipment, such as modified bicycles or wheelchairs, can be costly, with some specialized equipment costing several thousand dollars. The cost is often associated with the customization needed to provide a good fit for each player; for example, runners with amputations may use tailored prosthetics to allow them to compete safely and comfortably. A point worth considering is that some specialized equipment can be adjusted as athletes grow, whereas other equipment needs to be replaced with something new and customized each year. This can be prohibitively expensive for families to maintain.

Other individual barriers may be related to disability itself, thereby limiting participation in sports. For example, movements required to play a particular sport may worsen pain or exacerbate symptoms. Some athletes may avoid sports where there is a risk for pain or existing symptoms of a disability to worsen. These actual physical barriers also occur with perceived barriers regarding a child's fear of being teased or injured and lack of confidence in their athletic ability compared to teammates. **Perceived athletic competence**—an individual's perception of their athletic ability—is one of the strongest psychological predictors of participation and continuation in sport (Balish et al., 2014). Efforts aimed at improving a child's athletic competence are worthwhile to consider for overcoming perceptual individual barriers to participation.

Social barriers exist because of others in proximity to a youth athlete. For instance, parental actions such as not registering a child for sport because of safety concerns, no time for other activities, and a lack of parental support or encouragement are all barriers to participation (Shields et al., 2012). Although

> Youth with greater sport skills generally make it to more competitive (i.e., travel) teams and are more likely to continue their youth sport participation than youth with lesser sport skills. How might this affect how we understand the influence of perceived athletic competence with sport participation?

most parents recognize the benefits of sport participation for children with disabilities, they recognize the challenges associated with barriers (Columna et al., 2020). Perceptions of not being liked by others, the risk of being teased by teammates, and actual friends not participating in sport are social barriers that exist outside the family. Additional social barriers include a lack of understanding from support staff or coaches about an individual child's needs and negative perceptions of a disability originating from parents of youth athletes without a disability. This is a particular area of concern for volunteer youth sport coaches. Volunteer youth coaches, who frequently lack any coaching education, face challenges when coaching youth sports, let alone providing specialized guidance for youth athletes with disabilities. Collectively, those within the social perimeter of a youth athlete can influence participation through actual and perceived social barriers.

Environmental barriers exist for playing facilities and the areas within their vicinity such as walkways, streets, and stairs. Two of the most common environmental barriers are accessibility to facilities and inadequate programming. Specific facilities that have the appropriate equipment to host adaptive youth sports are often far away from youth athletes who use those adaptations. This increases travel time to practice and games that can be an additional burden on families. Some parents may decide that adaptive youth sport participation is not worth this travel burden. Adaptive youth sport programming is also often limited in both rural areas and inner cities, where there is a lack of experienced coaches and appropriate facilities (Kleinert et al., 2007). This increases the travel burden for athletes and their families to find adaptive sport programming in other communities.

Policy-level barriers exist at the local level of a sport organization, department, or league. One of the most consequential barriers to participation is a result of league administrators' fear of liability. Note that chapter 5 covers legal aspects in greater detail. A league administrator may introduce a policy or make case-by-case decisions for youth athletes with disabilities to not participate because of a fear that the athlete will get physically hurt or that using specialized equipment may hurt others. Parents may take legal action against the league, coaches, or administrators in the event of an injury. To avoid this potential scenario, league administrators default to nonparticipation. There are federal laws in the United States that protect against these types of scenarios, and they are covered in chapter 5. Unfortunately, youth sport administrators who have limited experience working with youth with disabilities or who are unaware of these laws can still influence participation.

Participation Facilitators

Despite these barriers, youths with disabilities successfully participate in adaptive youth sport. Addressing these barriers at the individual, social, environmental, and policy levels can encourage more youth with disabilities to participate. In addition to addressing these barriers, strategies to enhance participation can often be facilitators. Many of these facilitative strategies mirror barriers and can enhance participation and enjoyment in adaptive youth sport.

Addressing issues at the individual level includes working with youth athletes to develop their perceived athletic competence. Research shows that youth with higher levels of perceived athletic competence report greater sport satisfaction and enjoyment,

experience more emotional well-being outcomes, and are less likely to drop out from youth sport than those with lower levels of perceived athletic competence (Balish et al., 2014; Donaldson & Ronan, 2006; Scarpa & Nart, 2012). It is important to note that the athletic competence of a youth athlete is strongly related to perceived and actual social acceptance (Evans & Roberts, 1987; Ommundsen et al., 2010; Weiss & Duncan, 1992). Youth with disabilities who are motivated to be fit, want to learn new skills, and possess the basic skills for playing the sport are most likely to participate (Shields et al., 2012).

At the social level, families that encourage, support, model, and create opportunities for youth athletes with disabilities are more likely to participate. Beyond the family, peers without disabilities that are involved in parallel sports programs are shown to facilitate participation and in turn help reduce negative attitudes regarding disabilities. Indeed, peers play a meaningful role in developing youth athletes' sport experience (Smith & Delli Paoli, 2017). Being with friends and being accepted by them are some of the primary reasons youth participate in sport (Weiss & Amorose, 2008). Peers can help encourage participation and effort as well as model skills. These efforts aid in increasing the athletic competence of youth athletes with disabilities and others are more likely to accept it.

These strategies are most effective under the guidance of experienced and well-trained coaches. The significance of having coaches who possess the necessary training and expertise in adaptive sports is critical for engagement and meaningful experiences in adaptive youth sport. Trained coaches can provide specialized guidance, instruction, and support to ensure the inclusion and optimal development of youth athletes with disabilities. Their understanding of the unique needs, adaptations, and strategies specific to various disabilities can greatly enhance the sports experience for these athletes. Trained coaches also can effectively collaborate with administrators, parents, and

Promoting Peer Relationships

Peers can positively influence the sport experience of individuals with disabilities to promote beneficial outcomes. Useful strategies start with giving youth athletes time and space to meaningfully interact with each other. These activities should be peer-led rather than adult-led. This puts youth athletes with disabilities at the center of their sport experience, giving them authority to make decisions. Here are strategies to promote peer relationships in adaptive youth sport:

- Setting aside time for peers to get to know one another outside of sport, such as a shared meal or a team-building exercise that involves cooperative learning
- Emphasizing athletes helping each other and praising effort
- Pairing individual athletes together where each athlete is responsible for teaching each other new skills, such as using the buddy system whereby a more experienced athlete is paired with a less-experienced athlete
- Developing team goals and how each athlete can contribute to each team goal during team meetings
- Providing training on to how to effectively communicate with empathy and understanding, fostering an inclusive and supportive environment
- Encouraging athletes to celebrate achievements so they readily identify and celebrate the accomplishments of all team members, regardless of their abilities
- Creating a culture that encourages positive reinforcement and praise for individual efforts and improvements
- Promoting inclusion through awareness events off the field by organizing community service projects or participation in events that raise awareness about disabilities, allowing athletes to interact with others outside their team and develop a broader peer-support network

Remember, building relationships takes time, so be patient and provide opportunities for youth athletes to develop connections naturally. Encourage open dialogue, empathy, and mutual respect to create an inclusive and supportive environment.

other stakeholders to implement inclusive practices and foster an environment conducive to the success and well-being of youth athletes with disabilities.

> Being with friends and social acceptance are some of the primary reasons why youth participate in sport.

Addressing issues at the environmental level to increase adaptive youth sport offerings can be challenging. This is often the experience for those who reside in rural or inner-city communities where there is a lack of adaptive sport programs. Youth sport stakeholders and their parents can work with nearby communities to pool resources and offer additional programming and sport opportunities. National nonprofit organizations also offer regional or nationwide programming, including organizations like BlazeSports, Little League Challenger Division, and Move United. These organizations have tools and strategies for finding local adaptive youth sport leagues and opportunities across the United States. The American Association of Adapted Sports Programs (AAASP) works with local and state school districts to implement adaptive sports programs for students in elementary school all the way through high school. These programs offer accessible options for those looking for adaptive youth sport opportunities and provide education training and certifications for coaching adaptive sport. This may be particularly useful to address the demand for more qualified adaptive youth sport coaches.

Educating administrators and coaches on how best to work with a child may aid in better understanding the needs of the child and what modifications may be necessary for full participation. Considering poor policy decisions by administrators that may exclude youth with disabilities, soliciting parents for information is an important strategy to aid in educating administrators and coaches. Administrators understand what can be modified and how to properly place an individual in adaptive youth sport when they work together with parents. Importantly, such restrictive policies in the United States are illegal. Several laws protect the rights of children and youth with disabilities to participate in adaptive sports. They are covered in chapter 5 and are listed here:

- The Americans with Disabilities Act of 1990 (ADA) prohibits discrimination against people with disabilities in all areas of public life, including sports programs and activities.
- Section 504 of the Rehabilitation Act prohibits discrimination against people with disabilities in programs and activities that receive federal funding, including schools and sports programs.
- The Individuals with Disabilities Education Act (IDEA) ensures that children with disabilities have access to free and appropriate public education, including extracurricular activities such as sports.
- Title IX of the Educational Amendments Act prohibits discrimination based on sex in educational programs and activities, including sports programs.
- The Assistive Technology Act provides funding and support for the development and use of assistive technology, including adaptive equipment for sports.
- The Affordable Care Act requires that insurance companies cover the cost of adaptive equipment and rehabilitation services for people with disabilities, which can help with participation in sports.

These laws provide a legal framework to ensure that youth with disabilities have equal access to sports programs and activities and that they are not discriminated against based on their disabilities. However, state laws may protect individuals with disabilities at an equal or greater extent than federal laws. Consult your state laws for specific laws addressing issues of discrimination against people with disabilities.

Summary

Community youth sport programs aim to be inclusive, welcoming participants of all abilities and experience levels. This chapter looks at adaptive youth sports and shows the barriers to participation they face. It offers strategies for overcoming these barriers. Emphasis is given to coaching and peer relationship strategies to increase participation as well as the importance of perceived athletic competence, social support, and appropriate facilities to increase engagement and participation. Putting these strategies into practice requires key stakeholders to collaborate and promote greater inclusion in youth sports for individuals with disabilities.

CRITICAL THINKING EXERCISES

1. Identify and discuss three barriers to participation for youth athletes with disabilities in adaptive youth sports. How do these barriers affect their involvement and what strategies can be implemented to address them effectively?

2. Compare and contrast the barriers and facilitators to adaptive youth sport participation. Discuss how these factors can either hinder or promote the engagement of youth athletes with disabilities in sports activities.

3. Examine the role of peer relationships in adaptive youth sports. How can positive peer interactions contribute to the participation and overall experience of youth athletes with disabilities? Provide examples and strategies for promoting positive peer relationships within adaptive sports programs.

4. Discuss the legal framework that protects the rights of youth athletes with disabilities to participate in adaptive sports. Identify key laws and regulations that ensure equal access and opportunities for individuals with disabilities. How can administrators, coaches, and parents collaborate to ensure compliance with these laws and promote inclusivity in adaptive youth sports?

CHAPTER 12

Funding Disability Sport

Michael Cottingham, PhD; Tiao Hu, MS; Don Lee, PhD; and Oluwaferanmi Okanlami, MD

CHAPTER OBJECTIVES

After reading this chapter, you will be able to do the following:

- Understand the importance of and barriers to funding disability sport.
- Break down the expenses and costs related to disability sport.
- Initiate a budget plan for a disability sport program.
- Describe different sources of funding and their unique mechanisms.

This chapter will cover different aspects of funding in disability sport programming. The first section will introduce the broad context of disability sport funding, as well as its barriers and importance. Then, the costs and expenses of disability sport programs will be outlined and compared with that of able-bodied sport. Meanwhile, the budget breakdown of a hypothetical wheelchair basketball program will be provided to offer readers a clearer understanding of categories and details when it comes to disability sport programming and to help those intending to build a new program initiate a proposed budget. Next, different sources of funding will be introduced with examples describing their unique methods and mechanisms. With this foundational knowledge, one can develop or adjust strategies accordingly for specific funding sources. Last, readers will understand the different stakeholders who influence the funding system in disability sport, as we identify varying goals across programs and personnel, as well as the potential setbacks in achieving them.

While funding is necessary to support a wide array of needs in the broader context of sport, from recreational and youth teams to elite and professional ones, it is critical to appreciate why funding is important for the individual needs of sport and its development.

Adaptive sports, which are sports that are modified or created to allow for greater inclusion such that people of differing levels of ability, including people with disabilities, may participate, is still niche. While most people get to know adaptive sport through the Paralympic Games, there is a large funding gap between Olympic and Paralympic athletes. Paralympic athletes embody the highest ideals of humanity—they challenge the boundaries set by society and aim to develop and maximize their potential as world-class athletes (United Nations, n.d.). Truth be told, all sports can contribute to economic and social development, improving health and personal growth for people of all ages and groups, promote accessibility, provide economic opportunities and generate employment, and help build a culture of peace and tolerance by bringing people together on common ground that crosses national and other boundaries to promote understanding and mutual respect. Sport itself is powerful; adaptive sport potentially more so. Promoting disability sport is promoting human rights and celebrating humanity, changing lives for people with disabilities.

With these intangible values in mind, acquiring funding for disability sports has long been a lofty endeavor for athletes and **practitioners**. Compared to able-bodied sports, disability sports face distinct challenges in promotion and sponsorship, and despite some similarities in funding techniques between the two groups, disability sports receive disproportionately inferior resources. Moreover, while the academic literature has extensively covered professional, intercollegiate, and, to a lesser extent, interscholastic sports patronage, little is known about commercialization in disability sport. There is a critical need to better understand **revenue**-generating strategies and promotion of disability sports to provide equal sporting opportunities for athletes with disabilities, to overcome the lack of sponsorship, and to eliminate cost-limiting factors linked to elite disability sport participation (Cottingham et al., 2013).

> Promoting disability sport is promoting human rights and celebrating humanity, changing lives for people with disabilities.

While any sports, adaptive or traditional, require funding of necessary expenses related to equipment or competition, participation in adaptive sports is uniquely specific in its needs and, ultimately, more costly. This is an important consideration when broaching the issue of funding and finding sponsorships for adaptive sport programs. In this chapter, we will outline the particularities that substantiate expenses of disability sport (related to equipment, travel, competition, and facilities) to help you better understand the general financial needs of adaptive sport programs. We will also describe the various forms of funding available for disability sport, such as donors, grants, and government funding. Finally, we will address challenges of promoting disability sport that, in turn, affects public perceptions as well as chances to attain financial support, reflecting broad issues and providing future considerations regarding funding for different stakeholders.

Costs and Expenses Related to Disability Sport

Before we can understand the strategies for funding adaptive sport, we must understand the expenses around disability sport participation. While there is a broad spectrum from recreational to competitive sport programs, we will limit our discussion to competitive and recreational programs. You also will be introduced to several sports that you may not be familiar with. We encourage you to review videos of these sports to gain a greater understanding of them. While many sources use the terms *cost* and *expense* interchangeably, in this chapter, *cost* refers to a price paid to acquire an asset, generally as a one-time payment, and *expense* refers to an ongoing payment made regularly.

Equipment to Participate

Many disability sports require unique equipment for participation. The need for highly specialized equipment is most pronounced in mobility-based sports for athletes with mobility impairments and less pronounced in sports that are either not intensely mobile or sports for athletes without mobility impairments. For example, boccia is a relatively stationary sport designed specifically for individuals with disabilities affecting their locomotor functions. Boccia athletes kick or throw a ball onto the court, aiming to get it closest to the "jack" ball. It requires limited modified equipment, including devices or ramps for some athletes to play the ball. Sports like goalball (for blind players) also require relatively few assistive devices: a goal system, dark masks, and a basketball court where tactile court lines can be applied. Because boccia does not require intense active mobility and goalball features participants that do not have mobility impairments, both are examples of sports with relatively nominal equipment needs.

However, most disability sports are mobility-based. These include sports such as wheelchair basketball, wheelchair rugby, powerchair soccer, and amputee divisions in track, sled hockey, and related sports. The price for even entry-level equipment in these sports can range from US$1,000 to US$8,000. At more elite levels, prices can be two to three times that amount. Many mobility-based sports require specialized equipment, and equipment for one sport has little application in any other sports contexts. For example, tennis wheelchairs are different from adaptive cycling bikes, which are different from quad rugby wheelchairs, none of which can be used interchangeably.

If a person without a disability wants to play tennis for the first time, they may buy a tennis racket and shoes. If they want to get into running, they may simply purchase a different pair of shoes. An athlete with a disability, however, needs a different type of wheelchair for each sport, each costing several thousand dollars. This means that disability sports can be cost prohibitive.

Finally, all adaptive equipment needs maintenance. From prosthetics to goalball masks to wheelchair tires and tubes, equipment

Many disability sports require unique and expensive equipment for participation.

needs to be maintained. Specialized disability sports equipment is no different, except it is less available with fewer manufacturers and consequently more expensive.

Travel

If a person without a disability wants to play tennis, they can likely find a league in their community and play with dozens of players in their area. If they want to play rugby, they can probably join a league with players within a short driving distance. For disability sport athletes, finding teams and players is more difficult because there are simply fewer teams and athletes in disability sport. This means if athletes want to compete against athletes of a similar skill or disability type, they are likely going to need to travel. Cottingham et al. (2017) noted that the average wheelchair rugby team travels to more than four tournaments a year. Many of these events require air travel for not only the athletes but also the support staff, the size of which varies by sport and athlete physiology. For example, a team of sitting volleyball players may require a small support staff, while power soccer athletes may require a support staff member for each athlete on a team. For athletes with less physiologically impactful disabilities, the team may not need any able-bodied staff, instead relying on a coach or two and maybe an equipment manager. Other sports where the athletes have more impactful disabilities may require staff to assist with getting ready to compete, transferring into sports chairs, or, with some populations, assisting with personal care.

As competitiveness increases from local to regional levels and beyond, elite teams and individual sport athletes need to travel even farther to compete against the less numerous teams and athletes spread worldwide. National and international events are more costly due to travel distance and can incur higher participation fees. From ground or air transportation requiring wheelchair accommodations to registration costs, lodging, dining, and logistics and support, participating in competitive events incurs great travel expenses, particularly in adaptive sport.

However, because travel is necessary for competition, yet expensive, most events tend to involve more teams, matches, and games over a smaller window of time than might be seen in non-parasport. For example, a team might play four wheelchair basketball games during a weekend at a 16-team tournament. Consequently, hosting an event may be more complex and often more expensive.

Hosting Competition

Even if a hosting institution avoids extensive travel costs, such as airfare or ground transportation costs for their athletes, they still carry a heavy financial burden. Many (but not all) disability sports provide transportation for athletes to and from the hotel, tournament, and competition sites. This cost can increase when specific mobility transportation is needed, such as vehicles with wheelchair lifts. Renting facilities, providing meals, paying for officials' hotel rooms, transportation, and league fees add up quickly. Hosting competitions can be exceptionally expensive. Furthermore, many leagues and associations require teams to host annual competitions as part of their membership.

Facilities

Some sports do not require a unique or expensive space. An amputee runner or para-cyclist can hit the road, much as an athlete without a disability might do. For indoor sports and sports with specialized facilities (i.e., skate parks), there may be expenses related to access. Some facilities charge a monthly fee or a flat rate for a team's usage, or they require players to hold individual memberships. These fees may be covered by a program or the athletes themselves.

Historically, many facilities, especially schools and universities, have provided access to athletes with disabilities at no cost. This is changing rapidly, however, because many public facilities must generate revenue under constrained budgets and therefore are cutting such programs or offerings. As demand for gym time increases, more programs must pay for access to train and practice.

Cost Illustration From a Hypothetical Program

To get a tangible idea of the monetary demands needed to participate in adaptive sport on a recreational level, please refer to table 12.1, which represents costs for a hypothetical Division III (a division that allows newer players and newer or lesser-developed teams to play at a developmental or recreational level) wheelchair basketball program. Exemplifying a minimal level of competitive participation, this hypothetical program hosts one annual event, attends a few tournaments per year within driving distance, and attends one event at a distance necessitating air travel. This represents the least expensive program in terms of funding. More competitive programs would require a far greater budget. Please also refer to table 12.2, which has periodic expenses for the hypothetical wheelchair basketball team.

TABLE 12.1 **Division III Wheelchair Basketball Program Operational Cost**

Category	Item	Cost (US$)	Total (US$)
Personnel	Coach wages, practice	2 coaches × 312 hours × $20 per hour	$12,480
	Coach wages, tournaments	2 coaches × 17 days × 8 hours × $20 per hour	$5,440
Equipment	Tires	36 tires × $45 each	$540
	Tubes	36 tires × $10 each	$360
	Spokes		$50
Practices	Gym space rental	40 weeks × 6 hours × $30 per hour	$7,200
Driving tournaments	Gas reimbursed for players	6 vehicles × 200 miles × $0.60 per mile × (3) tournaments	$216
	Hotel	7 rooms × $130 per room × 3 nights × 3 tournaments	$8,190

>continued

192 Introduction to Adaptive Sport and Recreation

TABLE 12.1 >continued

Category	Item	Cost (US$)	Total (US$)
	Registration	$300 per tournament × 3 tournaments	$900
	Van (to transport vans) rental	$154 per day × 4 days × 3 tournaments	$1,848
	Gas for van	$0.18 per mile × 200 miles × (3) tournaments	$108
Airfare for national tournament	Airplane tickets	14 × $350	$4,200
	Registration		$500
	Van rental	$154 per day × 4 vans × 4 days	$2,464
	Gas for vans	$.18 per mile × 500 miles × 4 vans	$360
	Hotel	7 rooms × $130 per room × 3 nights × 3 tournaments	$8,190
Hosting a tournament	Officials' pay	$110 per day × 4 days	$440
	Officials' hotel	$130 per night × 3 nights	$4,390
	Officials' meals	$40 per day × 4 days	$160
	Rental court space	$30 per hour 12 games × 2 hours per game	$720
	Trophies		$50
Annual Total			$58,806

TABLE 12.2 Division III Wheelchair Basketball Budget Periodic Expenses

Item	Cost (US$)	Total (US$)	Frequency
Sport wheelchair	$4,000 per chair × 12 chairs	$48,000	Once every 5-8 years
Basketballs	$20 each × (10) basketballs	$200	Once every 5-10 years

Sources of Funding

As the hypothetical program shows, when considering equipment, facilities, travel, and other extraneous costs related to adaptive sports, expenses are often the primary barrier for people with disabilities wanting to start or deepen their involvement in an athletic program. To overcome such barriers, various **funding sources** must be attained. Many different funding opportunities help cover costs and expenses of adaptive sport, although each type of funding has its advantages and disadvantages. Several funding strategies and models will be described, from private donors to governmental funding sources and endowments.

Donors

Cottingham and colleagues (2017) discovered that the most common source of funding for wheelchair sports programs was individual **donors**. For example, the University of Alabama received a single US$3 million gift commitment to help build its training and competition facilities for adaptive athletics. These donors generally receive a tax deduction, and their money can be used for whatever a program needs. Fundraising research generally identifies an **80/20 model** (Rodd, 1996): 80% of a program's funding comes from 20% of its donors and 20% of its funding comes from 80% of its donors. In short, large donors provide the bulk of funding. This 80/20 model may seem even more dramatic with smaller programs who rely primarily on a single donor.

Acquiring donations from individual donors can be effective because a donor might be motivated by personal impact. In fact, donors often make commitments where they have prior cultivated relationships (Drollinger, 2018). This presents a challenge for adaptive sports, where many programs are managed by athletes and individuals with disabilities as opposed to well- known promoters or organizations. This issue of lacking formally trained managers or sport promoters to run adaptive sport programs will be discussed in further detail in this chapter. The need for donors is clear because individuals with disabilities are an economically disadvantaged group.

> In the 80/20 fundraising model, 80% of a program's funding comes from 20% of its donors and 20% of its funding comes from 80% of its donors.

Page et al. (2001) note that individuals with disabilities are often stuck in an economic "ghetto." While athletes with disabilities often achieve a more stable socioeconomic status compared to those who did not participate in sport (Lastuka & Cottingham, 2016), they likely do not have the relationships to leverage larger donations. Once a program begins a new relationship with a donor (in of itself a great accomplishment), these relationships may be cultivated for years before enough trust and rapport is developed for donors to increase their commitments and support of disability sport programs.

Therefore, many programs will elect to leave the 80/20 model in hopes of a groundswell of smaller donations. However, funding a program in US$10 and US$20 commitments can be exhausting and can be a strain on social circles if they are targeted too frequently. The limited research on this topic from Cottingham et al. (2017) notes that long-standing programs seem to rely on a small number of donors to make up the majority of their donation funding.

Fundraisers

Apart from seeking donors, a **fundraiser** is a traditional way to help alleviate costs related to adaptive sport. Fundraisers vary dramatically in size and scope. Smaller, less-established programs use systems such as popcorn sale fundraisers, GoFundMe programs, and car wash–type events. On the other end of the spectrum, programs with more resources may hold far more sophisticated events, such as silent auctions, 5K road races, or golf tournaments to generate external funding. Finally, some programs provide experiential fundraisers, such as having individuals participate in an adaptive event like wheelchair tennis or wheelchair rugby.

This experiential form of fundraising may be valuable because it allows for initial fundraising and provides a tactile experience to encourage fundraiser participants to potentially become longtime donors. In other words, allowing someone to try wheelchair basketball with wheelchair basketball players may provide an influential experience that fosters respect and admiration for the athletes. This would create greater legitimacy for athletic accomplishments and allow donors to see a future financial commitment as an investment in adaptive sports rather than just a charitable gift.

While connections and social capital are likely not as necessary for a fundraiser, fundraisers involve other risks. It is unlikely that an organization would lose money on trying to acquire donors unless this effort were coupled with an event. A fundraiser likely costs more, both in terms of time and money. Hosting a 5K road race can be profitable under the right conditions, but there are up-front costs such as insurance, police, medical personnel, water stations, officials, marketing, and city permits to consider. Hosting a basketball tournament where people are invited to compete in wheelchairs may still involve expenses such as facility rentals, officials, and sport jerseys. It is worth noting that time is also a serious commitment. A program could mean the organizers pour numerous hours into a fundraiser meal or event that only ends up generating a disproportionately small amount of capital. While even a few hundred dollars may be valuable to the team, when considering any fundraisers it is important to determine if the time commitment exceeds the value of monetary return.

Sponsors

Another method besides traditional fundraising and seeking donors is **sponsorship**. The *Oxford Dictionary* (n.d.) defines a sponsor as "an individual or organization that pays some or all of the costs involved in staging a sporting or artistic event in return for advertising." Sponsorship can manifest in different ways, such as sponsoring an event, an organization, a team, or a specific athlete.

A sponsor in disability sport may be **in-kind**, in which it gives product or goods instead of direct monetary funding. Examples of this include a wheelchair manufacturing company giving sports wheelchairs to a team, an airline providing free tickets, or a company donating modified vans for a power soccer program to use as they travel to competitions. In-kind donations are beneficial for funders because they allow them to donate products and services, which may be less of an outright expense for them than direct financial commitments. It also allows their product to be visibly promoted because the athletes use the items they donate.

It is more common for companies to be asked to sponsor events or programs through direct financial commitments. In return, they may receive a tax deduction, promotional visibility, or both. Broadly speaking, financial sponsorships come in two forms. The first are companies that directly target and serve people with disabilities or athletes with disabilities. The reader can go to the websites of any disability sport governing body, and they will see sponsors such as urological supply companies, medical supply companies, and sports wheelchair producers. These companies need access to specific consumers, so their sponsorship is strategic. When they sponsor these events, they gain direct access to participants through displays at competitions, but they also develop goodwill with athletes who see these companies investing in a sport they value. In these situations, the leagues or programs will often take responsibility for promoting the sponsorship.

A second type of sponsorship involves companies that do not have a direct connection to disability. These sponsorships may consist of mainstream companies such as Toyota, who has made commitments to both the United States Olympic and Paralympic Committee and the National Wheelchair Basketball Association, or companies such as Google and Amazon, who have made commitments to Oscar Mike, a veterans-only wheelchair rugby program. These commitments can be categorized as a sponsorship investment to generate revenue. As sponsorships, they are often developed with a focus on diversity, equity, and inclusion, brand image, and awareness.

Corporate sponsors want to publicly demonstrate their investment in sponsoring different athletes. When these sponsorships take place, the corporation takes the primary role of sponsorship promoter. In this way, corporations may promote athletes with disabilities alongside athletes without disabilities or as part of a larger campaign of sport promotions. Practitioners must ensure disability sport is promoted in an appropriate and nonpatronizing way, and this is often a collaborative effort between the sponsors and

the sponsored organizations upon activating the sponsorship.

> **Practitioners must ensure disability sport is promoted in an appropriate and nonpatronizing way, and this is often a collaborative effort between the sponsors and the sponsored organizations upon activating the sponsorship.**

Charity Models of Funding

While corporations without direct connection to disability may benefit from logo visibility on marketing or event displays as well as improved corporate image, some sponsors do not see funding disability sport as an investment. Instead, it is seen as a form of corporate social responsibility (or simply stated, a charity) to donate dollars and help communities without expecting those funds to generate a direct return or increase their consumer base in any significant way.

Many disability sport programs frame their fund-seeking efforts as charity-based, and they operate as nonprofit organizations to accept nontaxable donations. The benefit of operating as a nonprofit is that the organization avoids paying taxes on donations received, and the donor or sponsor may also be eligible for tax deductions, creating more incentive for them to contribute. Moreover, nonprofit organizations in the United States have a primary legal requirement to spend resources into their mission and need not be small or limited in scope. In fact, major billion-dollar operations such as the United States Tennis Association are nonprofit organizations. For a nonprofit entity, the charity model can be effective in attracting donors who may be incentivized by tax relief as well as publicity to show that their company values giving back to the community.

When considering charitable donations, however, it is important to know how to attract donors and inform them of the positive impacts of a program. This can be done in two different ways. The first is by sharing studies that highlight the benefits of adaptive sport programming to individuals and communities in general, while the second involves conducting first-hand research internally to produce results showing direct impacts specific to the program itself.

If an organization chooses to focus on the former, numerous studies show the overarching benefits of disability sport programming, including increased employment levels, lowered depression, increased independence, lowered substance abuse, and positive impacts on self-autonomy and socialization.

These benefits have been studied both qualitatively and quantitatively and can be effective at informing donors and granting bodies of the importance of similar programming. For example, a donor or granting body who is motivated by economic stimulation might be excited to know that employment rates among individuals with disabilities can increase from 18% to 68% after getting involved in sport (Latsuka, Cottingham, et al., 2016), while others might be motivated by the research showing that competitive wheelchair rugby players have lower stress and depression (Silveira et al., 2017). These studies are available through academic journals, and many can be found for free on Google Scholar. Practitioners also may be able to contact **academics** who can provide the findings or help make them more digestible. Donors and granting organizations are often swayed by data and a clear, measurable program impact.

A second option is for practitioners to produce findings on their own programs. This can be done with an informal researcher. The data that donors may want to see does not have to reach the same level of rigor that academic journals require. Researchers can collect data on numbers of participants and frequency of practices, then create basic scales that measure quality of life over time and conduct informal interviews. This research is valuable in that it can help demonstrate measurable, specific program benefits to potential donors; moreover, it can help programs evaluate their internal strengths and opportunities for improvement.

> Informal research can help demonstrate measurable, specific program benefits to potential donors; moreover, it can help programs evaluate their internal strengths and opportunities for improvement.

Larger programs and organizations may choose to partner with academic researchers to document the impacts of their programs. University professors may be willing to support research, and the process should be a collaborative one. The faculty member(s) may ask the organizational partner to fund the research or ask for permission to publish the findings as part of the contractual agreement. Again, this relationship should benefit both partners.

Sponsorship Models of Funding

Some disability sport programs are elite, professional, and not charity models in the traditional sense. The sponsors will still gain credibility for sponsorship, but they can sponsor disability sport teams and athletes in the same way that they might sponsor a team or athlete without a disability. Disability sport fans may not provide the numbers a sponsor needs to create a viable return on investment. Cottingham and colleagues (2013) found that disability sport practitioners believe that sponsors are best served when they promote the athletes with disabilities with their brands rather than expecting the athletes to exclusively promote the product.

Perhaps the best example of this is Nike's FlyEase product line. Nike developed a shoe for athletes with disabilities that would allow individuals without significant hand dexterity to independently put their shoes on. Nike has partnered with Challenged Athletes Foundation to provide every athlete receiving a grant with a pair of FlyEase. Through this effort, they can get thousands of athletes with disabilities using FlyEase and wearing their products publicly. Of course, Nike wants to sell their products to individuals with disabilities, but they also know that seeing athletes with disabilities using Nike products will improve the standing of the brand to anyone that athlete interacts with, showing that Nike values diversity, equity, and inclusion.

While charitable contributions are tax deductible, true sponsorship commitments are not. If the funder is receiving advertisements and promotional benefits, at least a portion of funding cannot be deducted from the sponsors' taxes. Still, as disability sport programs and athletes push for greater legitimacy, there are efforts to move from a charitable model to sponsorship. Some disability sport sponsorship will always be charitable, in the same way that Little League teams are often seen as charitable commitments. The key is that elite disability sport moves increasingly toward sponsorship commitments.

Grants

In this chapter, a **grant** will be defined as a financial award from a governmental entity, foundation, or similar organization to a disability sport program or athletes, typically through a competitive application process. Gifts and sponsorships often allow for flexible spending. This money can be used for whatever a program or athlete may need. Grants are typically focused and require a formula that includes justification, a budget, clearly defined outcomes, a timeline, and a means to report the project's effectiveness. There is often little deviation from the project proposal, and budget constraints allow for specific financial commitments.

> Grants typically require a specific formula that includes justification, a budget, clearly defined outcomes, a timeline, and a means to report the effectiveness of the project.

Grants may be focused on specific sports, specific goals, or regions. We will provide some examples to better understand the course and scope of different grants. The first type of grant we will exemplify is that provided by governing bodies. At the time of writing, the United States Tennis Association's Wheelchair Tennis Grassroots Grant funds programs for between US$2,000 and US$5,000 to support developmental wheelchair tennis programs. The grant requires the applicant to show how many athletes are affected, how the funds can be used, the demographics of participants, and the ongoing mechanism to track participation. Similarly, the United States Wheelchair Rugby Association provides support for wheelchair rugby teams to host clinics for players, classifiers, and referees through their clinic grant. These grants are typically funded up to US$1,500, and applicants must simply demonstrate needs and benefits.

In contrast, some granting organizations such as the Christopher & Dana Reeves Foundation and the Craig H. Neilsen Foundation provide larger grants that can be used to promote physical activity and sport programming. These grants can range from US$10,000 to more than US$100,000 for some programs. The application is more involved, as is the evaluation process. These funding agencies may limit spending on expenses like salary or travel, instead focusing on expenses such as events or equipment.

However, some organizations elect to provide direct support to athletes rather than programs. Challenged Athletes Foundation provides direct financial support to recreational and elite athletes with disabilities. They will support competition or equipment expenses, but the athlete has to provide receipts. The Kelly Brush Foundation provides funds for adaptive equipment specifically for athletes with spinal cord injuries. In both contexts, grants include required financial and medical documentation and statements from the athlete and a coach.

All of the aforementioned grants are focused on adaptive programming. There are other grants that focus on specific geographic regions where disability sport exists or target demographics that include athletes with disabilities. Examples of this might be a grant that focuses on programming in the Rocky Mountains or grants that target youth programs. In either case, a ski program could apply for funding from a professional sports team in that same geographic region that has a commitment to supporting local programming. A youth wheelchair basketball program might apply for youth program funding from an organization that has provided historical support for basketball or adaptive sport opportunities. The greatest challenge is that when applying for these "mainstream" funding sources, the applicant must provide unique justification. For example, the expenses of disability sport are so much greater than non-adaptive sport that a grant that serves 30 wheelchair basketball players might also serve 500 children at a local recreation facility. There are justifications on how and why disability sport as a **return on investment** can be far greater than funding able-bodied sport, but that argument is important when individuals apply for non-adaptive-sport-focused grants.

Governmental Funding

The United States is one of the few major countries in the world that does not have a ministry of sport. In other countries, these ministries of sport provide direct governmental funding to support competitive disability sport and, in many cases, more recreational and developmental programs. Programs may have regulations to follow to receive this funding, but in exchange they may receive a commitment of sustainability.

In the United States, there are some limited governmental funding sources for disability sport, from local to state to federal levels. Federal funding is the most limited. There are some applied grants offered through the National Institute on Disability, Independent Living, and Rehabilitation Research (NIDLRR). NIDLRR funding is competitive and narrow in scope but is relatively robust.

Some state-level agencies have limited grants for programming, but these resources can be piecemeal. We would encourage the reader to reach out to state offices of health and rehabilitation and state agencies on disability to determine what resources may be available. Most additional funding is locally available and may be available through parks and recreation departments. Often, there are partnerships between local programs and parks departments where free facility use, staffing support, or even equipment can be made available to community partnerships.

Endowments

The aforementioned funding sources represent receiving money to spend it, but **endowments** are unique funding mechanisms that can provide sustainable funds. Rather than functioning off the money you collect, the total amount provided by a donor through an endowment is fully invested and produces investment income for needed resources. Typically, an endowment can be described as an aggregate of assets invested by an institution to support a program continually over time. For example, many endowments produce about 4% a year. If an organization had a US$1 million endowment, then that would produce, on average, US$40,000 annually and support the needed organization. This money would be used to benefit the organization, while the US$1 million remained intact.

The benefit of an endowment is that it grants funding in perpetuity; it establishes a sustainable means for funding that should always continue. The primary limitation is that the cost to establish a meaningful endowment is simply beyond most programs' reach. While it lasts forever, it only provides

MICHAEL KLONOWSKI

Michael Klonowski has led an effective and dynamic career in wheelchair rugby. He is a physical therapist by training, and he began coaching the sport more than 10 years ago. He quickly rose as a skilled coach and moreover, serving the United States Wheelchair Rugby Association (USWRA) as the secretary of the board. Klonowski became the first executive director of the USWRA. The league was consistently funded by a few steady sponsors and team registration fees at the time of hiring. The position of executive director has allowed the league to explore growth, seek additional funds, and use funds to support forming teams, training opportunities, and an increasing number of certified referees and classifiers.

Michael Klonowski

Klonowski specifies that one of the greatest funding challenges is selling a product that portrays a wide spectrum of investment and skill. This catch-all approach can be challenging to brand the league as elite, competitive, or recreational and rehabilitative. The USWRA represents a variety of teams, from elite national and international contenders to recreational programs, the latter of which requires only game attendance to qualify for team inclusion. The USWRA has teams across the country, in urban and rural areas, and the sport is both competitive and rehabilitative. Packing that vision as a league that serves all the needs of its participants has been both a challenge and an opportunity in Klonowski's early tenure. He described the league as "hard to explain to a potential sponsor, but easy to fall in love with when you see it play out."

Yet, Klonowski is aware that donors and sponsors are often attracted to the inspirational sell. His personal approach is to reframe the inspiration from a viewer narrative to a peer process. He explains, "This sport is about people helping each other. It is about athletes creating a chance to grow and change in a community. It is not about giving money to these poor individuals with disabilities." Klonowski emphasizes the USWRA brand cannot be characterized or motivated by pity but by education for players, spectators, and funders.

Klonowski added the USWRA is understaffed, as are many disability sports programs, and the day-to-day operations can be a "grind." The league has committed volunteers, but he is a paid staff of one. "It takes time to network. Donors slowly increase commitments, so early in my tenure I have focused on grants, and we are targeting two fundraisers," Klonowski said. Foundations might provide short-term funding, but efforts must also be made to transition to more sustainable fundraising. "Hosting a fundraising golf event is not just collecting fees from people playing golf; you have to pull in sponsors, build contacts, set up raffles or silent auctions. These sorts of events do not make much in their first year but, within a few years they can become the backbone of your funding mix," he added.

In this way, sustainable funding may be achieved as trust is established with sponsors after years of fostering a relationship over a series of events, rather than a single event or fundraiser. As trust is built, Klonowski explains the significance of the sponsor's supporting role in shaping the USWRA brand. "It's important to connect with the people you represent. You have to make sure to make space for them. Then, you have to really believe in the product you are building together . . . then you have to sell it," he said.

Klonowski added, "It is hard to get a $100,000 commitment from an organization on a cold call, but if they give you $5,000 or $10,000, and you show them you do something special with it, they can buy into your mission and your product." Klonowski's approach for seeking both short-term and sustained investments is "working quickly to take the path of least resistance, going after money efficiently, quickly, and ethically."

roughly 4% of its value each year. Thus, many donors and program directors prefer to avoid endowments so they can access resources sooner, even if they will eventually exhaust them. Still, for the largest and most established programs, like the University of Arizona's Adaptive Athletics program, an endowment is a viable way to develop a long-term legacy.

Collegiate Programs

While collegiate programs are only a small percentage of adaptive sports programs in the United States, they represent the most direct pipeline to Paralympic-level development for wheelchair tennis, wheelchair basketball, and ambulatory and wheelchair track. Shapiro and colleagues (2020) note that there are significant intramural disability sport programs at the college level, but these programs do not compete outside the university and have minimal costs, so this section will focus on competitive collegiate programs. Their funding paths and needs are somewhat unique compared to community-based programs, and such unique needs will be outlined here.

Siegfried and colleagues (2021) found that disability sport programs existed in campus silos from recreational sports to disability service departments and academic departments. Siegfried's research further identified that the largest of these programs can run in excess of US$500,000. Still, these university divisions may only partially financially support collegiate disability sport, if at all. For example, institutions may fund staff but not operating budgets outside of personnel, or they may fund scholarships but not travel. Some institutions like the University of Texas at Arlington receive a significant portion of its operating budget through student fees. Programs like the University of Houston fully fundraise their operations budget directly, while the Edinboro University of Pennsylvania funds its program through college athletics.

These strategies can be piecemeal, and there is no one-size-fits-all approach.

Finances are still the greatest limiting factor. The primary barriers college wheelchair basketball programs often face are funding for scholarships and tuition waivers, travel funding, and quality facilities (Pate & Bragale, 2019).

A common misconception is that universities approach funding under a single umbrella. For example, a university functions top-down with a connected budget. In this way, basketball courts can be provided, scholarships can be awarded, and funds can be made available for travel, all in a cohesive mechanism. The recreation center likely has one budget that may charge for daily practices. The director would have to provide free court time, or the recreation center would have to be compensated for court time. Its budget is separate from other aspects of the university, and entities within universities often pay each other. Likewise, a department would have to absorb or fund the expenses of scholarships. These could be out-of-state or full tuition waivers, but an institutional entity will have to document and "pay" for that expense—for example, student services. Hiring a coach may take place through a different department (e.g., a department for accommodations and services for students with disabilities), who must pay for, manage, and supervise that employee. In short, many different institutional entities may have to coordinate or be lobbied separately to fund a program.

Many programs receive institutional funding, but they are responsible for extensive external revenue generation (Shapiro et al., 2020; Seigfried, 2021). Even well-funded programs like the University of Alabama must make strategic choices, such as hiring an assistant coach or offering more scholarships. Table 12.3 shows a hypothetical budget for an ambitious single-gender wheelchair basketball team. It is worth noting that many institutions provide support to collegiate adaptive sports in part, such as covering staffing and scholarships. However, they may not cover all expenses, and collegiate programs may have to use the same strategies noted in this chapter.

TABLE 12.3 Collegiate Wheelchair Basketball Program Budget

Category	Item	Cost	Total
Personnel	Head coach		$70,000
	Assistant coach		$35,000
	Graduate assistant (tuition)		$30,000
	Graduate assistant (stipend)	$1,500 per month × 12 months	$18,000
	Tutoring	$11 per hour × 80 hours a week × 30 weeks in an academic year	$26,400
	Athletic trainer	$25 per hour × 20 hours a week × 30 weeks	$15,000
	Strength and conditioning coach	$22 per hour × 20 hours a week × 30 weeks	$13,200
College-related expenses	Athlete scholarships	$22,698 per year × 12 athletes	$272,376
	Housing	$11,140 per year × 12 athletes	$133,680
	Meal plans	$4,500 per year × 12 athletes	$54,000
	Book expenses	$1,050 per year × 12 athletes	$12,600
	Student insurance	$2,000 per year × 12 athletes	$24,000
Maintenance	Tires	$45 per pair × 30 pairs of tires	$1,350
	Tubes	$10 × 60 tubes	$600
	Spokes	$10 × 140 spokes	$140

>continued

TABLE 12.3 *>continued*

Category	Item	Cost	Total
Practice	Court rental	$30 per hour × 4 courts × 15 hours per week × 30 weeks	$54,000
Hosting a tournament	Officials' pay	$110 per day × 4 days	$440
	Officials' hotel	$130 per night × 3 nights	$4,390
	Officials' meals	$40 per day × 4 days	$160
	Rental court space	$30 per hour 12 games × 2 hours per game	$720
	Trophies		$50
Travel	Bus rental	$1,425 per day × 4 days × 6 tournaments	$34,200
	Hotel	$130 per night × 8 rooms × 3 nights × 6 tournaments	$18,720
	Meals	$40 per day × 4 days × 17 people × 6 tournaments	$16,320
Grand total	-	-	$835,346

Funding Personnel: Disability Sport Promoters

Collegiate programs may benefit slightly from an additional funding source through the university, but funding the exaggerated expenses related to adaptive athletics remains a challenge. Practitioners must find various sources of income to stay afloat. From donors to sponsors, grants, endowments, and gov-ernmental aid, adaptive sport has survived and grown with the financial help of com-munities and organizations. Reaching out to such benefactors, however—and managing disability sports overall, for that matter—has historically been in the hands of practitioners who may not have had training in market-ing, fundraising, or promotion. With the high costs of competing in adaptive sports, continued and reliable funding through relationships, sponsorships, and external support remains a critical component for existing programs to progress.

A cursory review of websites for disability sport governing bodies shows that only minimal staff are committed to fundraising. The largest associations such as the National Wheelchair Basketball Association, Move United, and the United States Wheelchair Rugby Association have a single paid employee dedicated to funding and brand management. Only the largest organizations and ones with able-bodied relationships in the United States—such as the United States Tennis Association and the United States Olympic and Paralympic Committee—have highly sophisticated and reliable staff that are able to address funding and brand management.

That is not to say that regional and local program directors do not have fundraisers and people managing promotion, branding, and sponsorships; rather, it is an additional part of their jobs. Often, these responsibilities are secondary to more immediate demands. The limited research on disability sport promoters suggests that they may not have educational training and are learning to promote on the job (Cottingham et al., 2013; Siegfried et al., 2021; Williams et al., 2022). These limitations cause great stress on program directors and athletes, who are always feeling that financial pinch (Pate & Bragale, 2019). Consequently, someone may have to coach, organize programs, manage contacts with the city or community, and recruit and operate programs in rehabilitation centers, all while making sure an organization is financially viable.

One of the greatest challenges for disability sport promoters is determining how to frame disability sport. Some evidence says that selling disability by way of athletes overcoming their disability will increase spectatorship (Chatfield & Cottingham, 2017; Yamashita & Muneda, 2019). This is often called using a supercrip narrative (Sterba et al., 2022) in which athletes are depicted as inspirational role models who have overcome a physical disability and its accompanying challenges. Athletes with disabilities generally reject the supercrip narrative because it tends to objectify the person, reducing them to solely an object of inspiration and potentially perpetuating the unfortunate assumption that physical disability must be associated with a pitiful or difficult life in which accomplishing even simple or elementary tasks can be seen as heroic merely due to the presence of disability (Hardin & Hardin, 2004; Kama, 2004). More recent research indicates understanding inspiration and athleticism prevalent in sport results in media attention and funding (Cottingham et al., 2021).

Considering these underlying implications and perceptions, promoting disability sport is not as simple as it might seem. First, limited research seems to indicate that athletes with more affecting disabilities are more difficult for spectators to process (Cottingham et al., 2021). Second, research shows us that disability sport spectators simply process disability sport differently (Cottingham et al., 2023; Wann & Cottingham, 2015). They can see the same shots made and missed in a basketball game but process the game differently.

This is not to say exposure to disability sport is inherently bad. While problematic framings or inappropriate media portrayals of disability sport surely exist, exposure to disability sport breaks down barriers and removes stigmas (Bartsch et al., 2018; Matson-Barkat et al., 2022; Hu, Cottingham, et al., 2023). Furthermore, disability sport spectators are not only comprised of people with disabilities, with about half not having a disability or a friend or family member with a disability (Cottingham at al., 2014; Yamashita & Muneda, 2019). Disability sport spectators have high education levels and are affluent (Cottingham et al., 2012; Kim et al., 2022). The greatest issue is that the fan base is simply too small, and promoters must decide how to frame the sport to attract more viewers without objectifying the participants.

Given this challenge, disability sport promoters and practitioners have challenges. With little support in marketing training or expertise, they must navigate through the world of fundraising and corporate sponsorships, grants, and endowments to ensure the financial survival of their sport. This may entail not only initial pitches to acquire new sponsors, but years of fostering trust relationships within partnerships to grow sponsorships. Yet, the benefits overall for athletes and adaptive sports are undeniable. Adaptive sports increase social and economic opportunities for athletes, and showing support for their programs through corporate social responsibility elevates a company brand with positive image and publicity. These statements are supported by academics of the industry, whose continued research of the adaptive sports and sports marketing industries provide invaluable insights on media, funding, or athletics that help practitioners make the best decisions in their sport and programs. Sport practitioners rely on academic findings to indicate what works in support of their programs, considering perspectives of not only athletes with disabilities but also spectators and those with limited exposure to or understanding of disability sport.

Future Trends in Disability Sport Funding

With the increase in participation in disability sport, the progress of the Paralympic movement, and the recognized legitimacy of the sport and social media contributions, we see a positive trend for funding disability sport. More athletes appear on billboards and in commercials and are promoted with household brands. More brands commit to activate the partnership (Hu, Siegfried, et al., 2023). With the 2028 Los Angeles Olympic and Paralympic Games approaching, we expect more funding in disability sport and diversification. As public awareness of diversity in sport continues to gain traction, the recognition of disability has become more prominent. Corporate entities are placing significant value on corporate social responsibility and are investing more resources with athletes with disabilities.

Summary

Adaptive sport offers a host of benefits to its players, from recreational to elite competition. More than that, it promotes human rights and inclusion in society. Funding disability sport is important, because it not only covers the heightened expenses of disability sporting equipment, travel, competitive events, and facilities but also further promotes and develops a sport that has always had to fight for equal rights and resources compared to its able-bodied counterparts. Funding sources come in a variety of methods and mechanisms that are categorized broadly as donations and sponsorships. These can and should be fostered in relationships that will ultimately result in sustained, reliable, and perpetual funding for an organization. Finally, special considerations must consider stakeholders such as program directors, personnel, and the media, because disability sport continues to struggle with appropriate media portrayals (Hu, Cottingham, et al., 2023), and the burden of self-promotion without the expert help of agents or educated marketers.

CRITICAL THINKING EXERCISES

Los Angeles won the bid to host the 2028 Olympic and Paralympic Games. If you are a member of the United States Olympic and Paralympic Committee and in charge of marketing, you would brainstorm with your team to initiate a marketing strategy plan for promoting Paralympic Games and disability sport in general during the promotional period.

1. List all funding sources to maximize the revenue and impact of the Games.
2. List possible sponsors and reasoning.
3. List sponsorship package selling points.
4. Conduct mock negotiation with potential sponsors, with your understanding of the sponsors' needs in mind.

CASE STUDY

University of Alabama Adapted Athletics

Margaret Stran, PhD, and Brent Hardin, PhD

When I started playing wheelchair basketball in 1991, one college offered women's wheelchair basketball: the University of Illinois at Urbana-Champaign (UIUC). By 2003, when Dr. Brent Hardin and I started the University of Alabama Adapted Athletics (UAAA) program, two colleges had women's wheelchair basketball teams: UIUC and University of Arizona. There are many reasons gender inequity exists in adapted sports, but we will not explore that topic here but will say this: We believed that starting with a women's team sent a strong message about gender equity and the status of women. Plus, I am a woman, and that gave us another player our first year, so that was an easy call.

The main mission of UAAA is to provide the student-athletes with the same or proportionate experiences as other varsity athletes on campus. That focus drives our decisions and helps push for greater equity for the student-athletes.

> The main mission of UAAA is to provide the student-athletes with the same or proportionate experiences as other varsity athletes on campus. That focus drives our decisions and helps push for greater equity for the student-athletes.

This mission is why we have pushed to have full-time head and assistant coaches, a strength and conditioning coach, an athletic trainer, and event and social media coordinators. The program needs personnel who are paid to put the student-athletes' needs first to make it comparable to varsity athletics. It's also why the program has the Stran-Hardin Arena and the Parker-Haun Tennis Facility, the only two facilities on a college campus dedicated to adapted sports (as of 2021; more on these facilities later). The UA Athletics teams have dedicated facilities, and so do the teams in UAAA.

UAAA does more than just create a high-performance sports team; it also works to enhance sport, fitness, leisure, and recreation opportunities for persons with physical disabilities. UAAA sponsors women's and men's wheelchair basketball, wheelchair tennis, and adaptive track and field teams;

Dr. Stran is the author of this case study, with Dr. Hardin serving as fact-checker; the use of *I* refers to Dr. Stran and *we* refers to them both. In addition to cofounding the University of Alabama Adapted Athletics program, Dr. Stran and Dr. Hardin married in 2003.

conducts sports camps and clinics for children with disabilities; and completes research and grant projects with a focus on adapted sport.

We are often asked what our plan was when we started and whether we envisioned all this when we began. Honestly, no. We wanted to start a women's wheelchair basketball team. That's as far as we dreamed. There are still needs to be met, and work continues to address them. There is no end in sight as the program continues to create more and better opportunities for students and community members with ambulatory disabilities.

Starting the Program

It all began with a new faculty reception at the President's Mansion on campus. The president at the time, Dr. Robert Witt, had just arrived from the University of Texas at Arlington, where they had a men's wheelchair basketball team. (In 2011, UTA added a women's wheelchair basketball team with a part-time coach. The coach became full time in 2021.) When Brent and I met Dr. Witt, we told him we planned to start a wheelchair basketball team. Because of his background, Dr. Witt did not ask questions but said, "Great, let's meet and talk about it next week." Dr. Witt's support of the program from day one opened so many doors and gave us support that we did not even know we needed. Initially, that support was not financial. Instead, we applied for and received a Christopher and Dana Reeve Quality of Life Grant of approximately US$5,000. With that, we put together a season. I still remember Brent and I being outside on the quad headed to a meeting and saying, "With $5,000, we can make it happen." We can now easily spend US$5,000 on one trip. How times have changed.

See chapter 12 for more on grants.

That first team had students, staff, and junior players. We recruited our first student, Jessica Staley, who transferred from Jacksonville State University; connected with the junior team at Lakeshore Foundation in Birmingham, Alabama; and found community members and students with ambulatory disabilities to play. There was also a student at Samford University in Birmingham, Dana Meyer, who played. There were 8 to 10 players for each tournament.

The first season, Brent and I drove to tournaments in the Southeast in two vans. We played National Wheelchair Basketball Association (NWBA) Division III men's teams who agreed to play with the women's-sized ball. The women's college teams were then in the NWBA women's division, and to qualify a team only had to play a certain number of games. We did that and headed to our first national championship tournament.

The goal was to have a team made entirely of students by the 2005-2006 season, and we accomplished that. Initially, recruiting was a challenge. We attended a junior national championship with a table set up with information about the program. People would come by, and the main comments were either "I didn't know Alabama had a women's team" or "Alabama? Where's Alabama?" Mary Allison Milford was recruited at junior nationals, was the first four-year recruit to UA, and was on the first national championship team in 2009.

Brent was a new faculty member at UA in 2003 and was hired as an assistant professor of adapted physical education in the department of kinesiology. Starting a wheelchair basketball team was not in his job description. I was a student in kinesiology, working toward a PhD in sport pedagogy, which is teaching teachers how to teach physical education. One of the things that was important to starting the team is that we had keys to the buildings. Having access to buildings is an important aspect of starting an adapted athletics program, and it can only happen if those starting the program are employees of the university. Programs that are starting out need at least one university faculty or staff member who is part of the adapted athletics program to help with access.

The first practice gym was Foster Auditorium. For those not familiar with civil rights history, Foster Auditorium is where the Stand in the Schoolhouse Door occurred. Students used to go to Foster to register for classes during the 1960s. Each department would have representatives there who would approve students' schedules and accept fees. The Stand in the Schoolhouse Door took place June 11, 1963, and Governor George Wallace literally stood in front of the door of Foster to block Vivian Malone and James Hood, two African American students, from entering. President John F. Kennedy issued an executive order to federalize the Alabama National Guard, who ordered Wallace to step aside.

In 1975, Alabama women's gymnastics was started and housed in Foster Auditorium. In 2003, Foster was a neglected gymnasium that was used mostly for storage, had no air-conditioning, and had locks on the basketball rims. Brent would climb the ladder and remove the locks while I would turn on the giant fans to move the hot, humid air around as we prepared for practice. It seemed fitting that we were in Foster, with its history of both segregation and integration, first for students of color, then for women, and finally for those with disabilities. In 2009, it was announced that Foster was to be renovated and become the home of Alabama women's volleyball. The Adapted Athletics Program moved into the student recreation center in 2005.

In 2005, there was an opening for an instructor in the department of kinesiology, and I was selected to fill that position. It also meant I was taking doctoral-level classes, teaching four classes, and playing for and coaching the women's wheelchair basketball team. Looking back, I see how much work it was, but at the time I was doing so many

Vivian Malone enters Foster Auditorium at the University of Alabama to register for classes in 1963.
Bettmann/Getty Images

things I loved that I had the energy and ability to balance everything.

A long-term goal was to start a men's wheelchair basketball team. A full-time coach was needed, someone whose actual job it was to manage the expanded program. Up to this point, Brent and I were doing everything, from coaching to driving to washing uniforms, and it was not in either of our job descriptions. Dr. Witt said something to the effect of "the thing about long-term goals is they tend to stay long term. We need to make them short term and get them done." With that, he secured the funding to hire a men's coach and changed Brent's job to include managing the adapted athletics program. The first season for men's wheelchair basketball was 2006-2007. Starting the men's team was much easier than starting the women's, given that there was a head coach who did all the recruiting and an established program already in existence. Students were eager to come to Alabama and play for the team, and the first year of the men's team had 10 full-time UA student-athletes.

Sports

UAAA has high-performance sports and emerging sports. *High-performance sports* are established sports that have full competitive seasons with high expectations for success; currently for UAAA, they are men's and women's wheelchair basketball, wheelchair tennis, and adaptive track and field. *Emerging sports* are those that have been identified as being potential high-performance sports; these sports start with a few students and have a shorter competitive season, with the plan to expand the team, season, and level of competition over a few years to become high-performance sports. UAAA offers adaptive swimming as an emerging sport.

The UAAA program started with a women's wheelchair basketball team to address the gender imbalances in collegiate wheelchair basketball and then added men's because it was the next logical step. Wheelchair tennis started in 2010. That year, there was a wheelchair basketball player, Mackenzie (Mac)

Soldan, who grew up playing wheelchair tennis and missed playing. As it happened, Miles Thompson, the men's wheelchair basketball coach at the time, was also a tennis player. Mac and Miles started hitting, then Miles started coaching Mac, and the tennis program was born. We realized this could be a new sport for us, and there was a junior league from which to recruit players, so it made sense to invest in a coach. Charlie Rivera was hired as the full-time coach. After a year, he realized his heart and expertise was in the country club setting and left the program in the capable hands of a graduate student, Evan Enquist. As head coach, Evan grew wheelchair tennis at UA and across the country. A former NCAA Division I tennis player, Evan brought the game knowledge and collegiate experience the program needed. Evan went on to work with the United States Tennis Association (USTA) growing wheelchair tennis across the United States, and Tyler McKay is the head coach at UA.

In 2011, the program received a grant from the United States Olympic and Paralympic Committee (USOPC) to start adaptive rowing. (In a reflection of how times have changed, when we applied for the grant, the name was the USOC. It is now a more inclusive name and committee.) Rowing is not as prominent as basketball and tennis, and it is more of an emerging sport; there is varied interest in it from year to year and it is not highly competitive like basketball and tennis. After trying to start rowing, we learned that you need three ingredients to add a sport: interested student-athletes, a full-time coach, and equipment. A pipeline of people participating in the sport is also helpful. Rowing had equipment and a few interested people and assistance from the head coach of the university's club team, but it was difficult for her to oversee both. Limited interest and no full-time head coach to manage the program are challenges to get the rowing team more established.

> See chapter 4 for more on the Paralympics.

In the fall of 2022 we decided we had the interest, coaching, and pipeline necessary to start adaptive track and field. We have three full-time track and field athletes and three wheelchair basketball players who participate in track and field after the basketball concludes in March. We started with standing and sitting throwing events and wheelchair track. We were not going to expand into ambulatory track, but student interest was there so we decided to embrace it. The challenge with adaptive track and field is the need for many different coaches: one main coach who oversees everything, a throwing coach, a wheelchair track coach, and a running track coach. Fortunately, we have been able to connect with community coaches who are assisting with field and ambulatory track. The growth of adaptive track and field has been astounding, and we are thrilled to see it expand. That said, we are rapidly outgrowing our current facilities and are working to fundraise for an addition to the Stran-Hardin Arena (more on this arena later).

> You need three ingredients to add a sport: interested student-athletes, a full-time coach, and equipment.

The program goal was to start two sports by 2025. First was adaptive swimming. The coach of the Crimson Tide Aquatics (CTA) team is willing to bring adaptive athletes into the existing team. CTA offers year-round swimming instruction and competition for children from elementary to high school. A new adaptive swimmer would be swimming with high school athletes, but the goal is to build this group of student-athletes so they will become a group within CTA. CTA practices at UA's Aquatic Center, so student-athletes in the adaptive swimming program use the same facilities as varsity swimming and diving. There is a junior adaptive swimming league in the area, and the coach has connections with USA Swimming. There was also interest from some high school students who were adaptive

triathletes. These elements were coalescing, and there was momentum to establish an adaptive swimming program within CTA.

The second sport was wheelchair track and road racing. For that to begin, a full-time coach would need to be hired. We aimed to apply for a grant to help with the start-up costs and to develop a plan for attending existing events to let high school students know the program was beginning and start recruiting. Starting a new sport is exciting, but knowing that we have failed in the past makes it important to get it right the first time.

For those who want to start a program, we can say from experience that it is easier to start with an individual sport rather than a team sport. If you have one tennis player, then you have a team. You need at least six for a basketball team, and six is barely enough, given injuries, eligibility, sickness, and the like. That said, it is also important to know the interests of those in the area. Do you have a junior, women's, or men's wheelchair basketball team, sitting volleyball, or wheelchair rugby team in the area? If so, starting with one of those team sports might be a great fit for your location. Harder doesn't mean impossible, and meeting the needs of those in the community is what matters. It is also important to work with your strengths. Brent and I knew wheelchair basketball, so it made sense to start there. San Diego State University started with ambulatory track because the program director knew that sport.

The governing body for the sport also matters. The USTA has wheelchair tennis as a part of its programming. Wheelchair basketball has a separate governing body. As a result, wheelchair tennis is a more inclusive sport. The same can be said for adaptive rowing, adaptive swimming, and sitting volleyball because they are simply another division of the larger body; their websites have tabs for adults, junior, and adapted or sitting. Finally, knowing the sport rules for including those without disabilities is important. Some sports, such as sitting volleyball, allow those without disabilities to fully participate at all levels within the United States.

Organization

Alabama Adapted Athletics was originally housed in the department of kinesiology. It became redundant for the program to be in there, within the College of Education. As director of the program, Brent was the same as a department head and reported to the kinesiology department head and then the dean of the College of Education. To reduce this dual reporting, in 2012, the program became a stand-alone program in the College of Education.

Other collegiate adapted athletics program are housed in athletics, recreation, Disability Services, or academic departments. This diversity is similar to the way women's sports were housed before Title IX. All adapted athletics programs should be part of varsity athletics programs, but until legislation is passed that requires inclusion of student-athletes with disabilities in athletics, programs that exist or are starting out will have to go where they are welcomed.

> See chapter 5 for more on legislation related to disability rights.

People

When starting a program, it is helpful to have a few people to do many jobs: coach, play, administer, plan, drive, wash—anything. As a program grows, however, it is essential to have many people to do each job. This is what UA varsity teams have, and that is the mission of UAAA.

As a result, each team has full-time head coaches. The program has five full-time coaches: two each for women's and men's wheelchair basketball and one for wheelchair tennis. Adaptive track and field has one main coach and two coaches on contract who are experts in field and running. Five coaches use wheelchairs or have an ambulatory disability and two are women.

It is not enough to just know the game; coaches must be students of the game, constantly learning and improving their knowledge, skills, and delivery. To continue to have an excellent product, coaches must recruit new students, something that takes time and dedication. Having a program does not mean people will show up. Coaches need to connect with potential students and let them know they have the academic standing and skill to come to UA, then follow up and make sure those promising students are successful while here.

Brent's position has evolved to the point where he is in a 12-month position and teaches one class per semester. As director of UAAA, he is charged with long-range plans, personnel management, scheduling, and providing general direction for the program. We are both asked to interact with donors and give presentations, promoting the program and expanding the circle of people who know about—and support—the program. I enjoy sharing about the program but realize that the student-athletes are the best speakers for it. The student-athletes represent their sport and the university with poise, confidence, and maturity. It is wonderful to see them share their experiences and watch people change what they think about sport and disability.

My position is currently a nine-month contract position that is focused on UAAA. This position was created in 2014. I teach three classes a semester, write grants for the program, and engage in outreach. I created and lead the leadership academy, which brings together the leaders for each team and teaches them leadership skills. I do many other tasks to keep the program moving forward, and creating change is a fulfilling job.

In addition to the coaches and Brent and I, we have the director of sports performance and director of sports medicine to keep students healthy. The director of sport performance oversees strength training, nutrition, and mental performance services. They plan and implement all the strength training sessions for the student-athletes. A registered dietitian was added to share knowledge about nutrition and act as a resource for the students and the director of sport performance. They do a nutrition overview for the incoming freshmen every year and are available for questions, meal plans, and nutritional guidance during the year for all students. The dietitian is one of a vital set of volunteers.

The director of sports medicine oversees athletic training and medical needs for the student-athletes. They provide all the athletic training services and determine when student-athletes will see the team physician, who is also the team physician for UA varsity athletics. The director of sports medicine also arranges meetings with the mental performance coaches. They are available in person for team and individual meetings twice a month and via phone anytime.

We also have a director of operations. The program hosts or attends anywhere from 30 to 40 events a year. This keeps the director of operations busy. Events range from the large, such as the annual college tournament in March, to the mundane, such as board of advisers meetings. The director of operations is invaluable and keeps everything operating and attends to the finer details of managing events. A brigade of student and booster club volunteers help ensure that the scorer's table for wheelchair basketball is well managed, the gym or tennis courts are set up, and someone is there to meet and direct attendees.

A marketing director was added in 2021 to coordinate all marketing, live streaming, and social media because having a strong social media presence is vital. This includes the website, Facebook, X (formerly known as Twitter), Instagram, and event live streams. Student workers help with these duties as well.

> See chapter 6 for more on the media and adaptive sports.

Weight room facilities at UAAA.
Craig Roderick / Bella Fiore Images

The board of advisers (BOA) is similar to any board of trustees or board of directors that organizations have. It is a group of people who have shown interest and commitment to the program. Their input, insight and leadership are valued. Started in 2019, the BOA has been key to providing a different perspective on the program. The BOA has approximately 25 members and meets quarterly.

The booster club was started from a BOA member's idea and is a group of people who support the program in a small way. Membership fees range from US$25 for students up to US$500. Benefits vary based on the level but include T-shirts and VIP receptions at events. The booster club has been a low-pressure way to raise money and create a group that follows the program. Newsletters are sent out via e-mail every few months and help keep people informed and connected. The money that is donated is used based on the booster club members' ideas, with input, and the focus for expenditure is on the student-athletes; investments have ranged from new wheelchairs, to uniforms, to celebration events.

> See chapter 12 for more on donors and sponsors.

Working in tandem with the director of operations and marketing director is the director of fan engagement. They oversee promotions, the booster club, donor relations, and fan engagement. Fan engagement is key to getting people to come to events, enjoy the experience, and return. These three staff work together to provide great experiences for athletes, fans, boosters, and donors.

The student-athletes are at the heart of the program. This program was started to provide more opportunities for female athletes with ambulatory disabilities, and it continues to expand to provide more options for a greater number of students with ambulatory disabilities. The growth of the staff, and the changing nature of my and Brent's positions, reflects the importance of meeting the student-athletes' needs.

Facilities

In 2010, a leadership council brought together student-athletes from the different teams, coaches, and administrators. The need for a dedicated space for the program arose from those meetings. That planted a seed to be on the lookout for funding and a site. Discussions started with UA construction administration and preliminary plans were developed along with a site.

Things sat on the back burner until Mike and Kathy Mouron got involved in 2016. They were involved in Lakeshore Foundation's veteran housing project and met one of the program's student-athletes. (Lakeshore Foundation is also an Olympic and Paralympic Training Site.) He discussed the program and its needs. Mike reached out to Brent to learn more about the program. A luncheon was held with Mike and Kathy and about half a dozen student-athletes; a meeting was later held with Mike and Kathy and university development officers about the building. Mike and Kathy committed to helping get the building and pledged a gift of US$4 million.

> See chapter 10 for more on adaptive sports and recreation for military populations.

It was an incredible moment and reflected how far the program had evolved. This also ensured the program was not going to go away. Once a building exists, it gets filled with people, and once that happens, it is more difficult to have it disappear. Brent and I were the program for an extended period, and we knew if we left, the program would not continue. Now, there are a plethora of positions for Adapted Athletics, and the program has a home.

Most donors sit and listen and say they will get back to you. No other donor we talked to sat in a room, listened to the program needs, and committed right then. In addition to being the largest donors, Mike and Kathy have become program supporters, and, most importantly, friends. They rarely miss a home tournament or game.

In another reflection of the generosity of the Mourons, they named the facility after Brent and me. Mike told us he was naming it in honor of Kathy, and the day of the naming ceremony was a significant event. Mike was talking about how he and Kathy bought the right to name a building, but Brent and I earned the right. Thus, the Stran-Hardin Arena came to be.

It was great to be able to have input into the design of the building and meet with the architects. A focus was a limited number of doors. Of course, people in wheelchairs can open doors, but the goal was to make the building feel open and welcoming, especially for sport wheelchairs, and thus the only real doors are to offices and bathrooms. There are few thresholds, and most are even; automatic doors allow building entry; and the floors are polished concrete. There was also an emphasis on being sure the seating area was the appropriate size. Too big and even a good crowd seems small; too small and there is no room to grow fans and encourage attendance. The seating capacity is 2,000 and is the perfect size. A full house is loud and crowded with the exact college athletic atmosphere envisioned. There is room for concessions for events, a conference room, offices, a weight room, an equipment room for wheelchair repairs and maintenance, an athletic training room, a laundry area, men's and women's locker rooms with room for 18 student-athletes in each, and a regulation-size basketball court. The bleachers include wheelchair seating in every section. There is ample seating so that wheelchair users do not have to crowd at one end of the court but can spread out with other spectators.

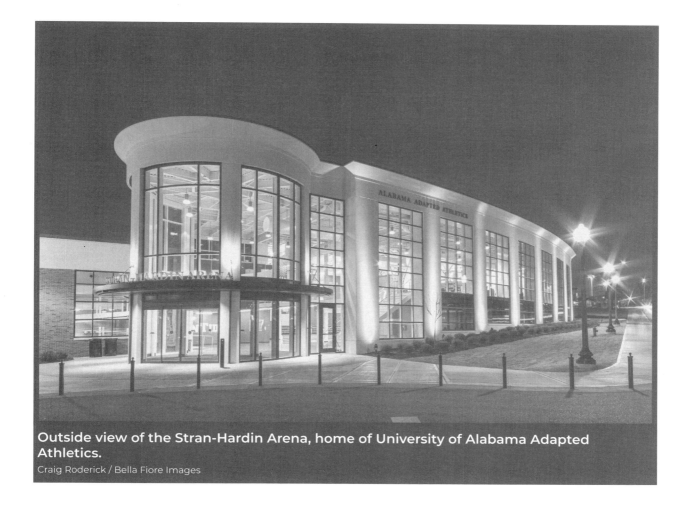

Outside view of the Stran-Hardin Arena, home of University of Alabama Adapted Athletics.
Craig Roderick / Bella Fiore Images

> See chapter 2 for more on accessible spaces.

One unique feature of the facility is the Hall of Champions. This hallway has the championship teams listed (21 as of 2023) and flags that represent all the countries of the student-athletes who have played here (i.e., Australia, Canada, England, France, Germany, India, Israel, Lithuania, New Zealand, Poland, Scotland, Spain, and the United States). It is a source of pride that students from all over the United States and the world have participated in the program. Many of these students have represented their countries in the Paralympic Games. Current and former UA athletes have been in the Paralympics since 2004. In Tokyo in 2022, there were 18 current or former athletes in the Games that participated in the program at UA.

> See chapter 7 for more on elite competition.

The upstairs or mezzanine overlooks the court. An elevator would have taken up a lot of room to be large enough to transport numerous competition wheelchairs, so a ramp was installed. It is wide enough for two sport wheelchairs to pass each other. It also doubles as a training tool, and the student-athletes do a lot of ramps. The mezzanine was intended as a study area with chairs and tables. The open concept is great—but not for studying. Most students end up studying in the conference room where they can close the door and not hear the music and noise from the weight room and buzzers and talking from the court. The upstairs is used mainly for staff meetings, a gathering space for home events for booster club members, and cardio equipment. The

Courtside view of the basketball court at Stran-Hardin Arena. The mezzanine viewing area is visible on the upper right.
Craig Roderick / Bella Fiore Images

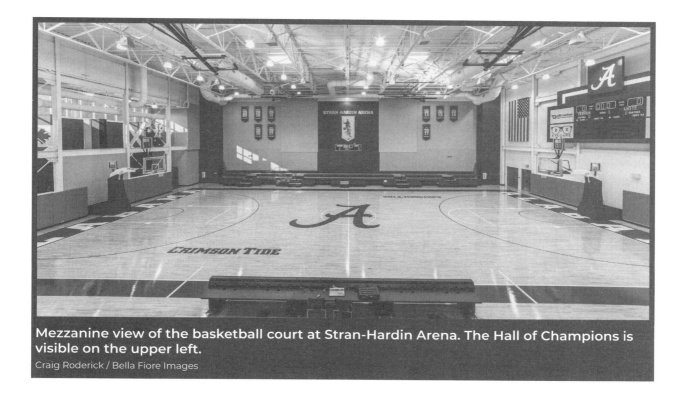

Mezzanine view of the basketball court at Stran-Hardin Arena. The Hall of Champions is visible on the upper left.
Craig Roderick / Bella Fiore Images

cardio equipment is inclusive and can be used easily by anyone from those with no leg function to those with complete leg function. Upstairs also houses a nutrition station. One of the frustrations I have as a wheelchair user is having to look through railings at events. Thus, the upstairs viewing has wire on the bottom half and glass for the top, ensuring excellent viewing.

The building is open and airy, filled with light and an athletic vibe. It is noisy and busy and reflects the passion and pride of the staff and students. The Stran-Hardin Arena opened in 2018 and was and remains the first and only facility built and designed for an adapted athletics program on a college campus.

The wheelchair tennis players had been using the recreation center tennis courts, which had no reliable water, bathrooms, storage, or court security. In fact, the wheelchair tennis storage shed was in the grass, so athletes using a tennis wheelchair could not access it. In 2019, discussions began with the UA administration about what could be built by the courts. Fundraising began, and in 2021 the Parker-Haun family committed to the building. The Parker-Haun Tennis Facility was opened in October 2021. It is a smaller version of the arena but includes all the essentials: offices, meeting space, athletic training, locker rooms and showers, national championship banners, and a porch overlooking campus.

As previously mentioned, the growth of adaptive track and field has us looking to expand the size of the arena. When we designed the arena, we did so knowing that one day we would expand. Five years later, we have the preliminary architectural design, which will add more offices, locker rooms for adaptive track and field, a quiet student lounge, a kitchen, and a dedicated cardio area.

Funding

The bulk of funding comes from the university. It does not, however, cover all expenses. To fill in the gap, we apply for two to six grants every year. Most of these grants come from foundations, rather than the federal

Inside view of Stran-Hardin Arena looking outside from the upper level.
Craig Roderick / Bella Fiore Images

Parker-Haun Tennis Facility.
Courtesy of The University of Alabama.

government, because federal funding tends to have a research component. Our focus is on creating more opportunities for student-athletes, and foundation funds tend to have a more direct impact on this group. Grants have been received from several organizations, including the Christopher and Dana Reeve Foundation, Coca-Cola Foundation, the USTA, and the Craig H. Neilsen Foundation. Student-athletes have benefited from grants from Challenged Athletes Foundation, Kelly Brush Foundation, and High Fives Foundation.

> **See chapter 12 for more on funding adapted athletics.**

We offer a tiered system of sponsorships that increases benefits as the donations increase. Some sponsors have become more like partnerships, such as Hollister Incorporated and RGK Wheelchairs. They come to our events, and we attend some of theirs. The relationship with Hollister has been rewarding because, as a urology company, they have been able to educate the students and youth campers about changes in urology products and ways to improve health. Similarly, RGK has been able to improve the quality of everyday and sport wheelchairs the students and staff use. In 2022, an agreement was signed with Crimson Tide Sports Marketing to have them take over sponsorships. This company also works with UA Athletics and does all their sponsorships. Crimson Tide Sports Marketing has a professional staff who do this full time. They are an asset to the program.

Donors help make the program, and donations are vital to providing opportunities for student-athletes. The booster club, like sponsorships, is a tiered system that allows people to select the support level that best fits their economic situation. Gifts are not restricted to the booster club but can also be directed toward an endowed scholarship or general gift funds. The booster club decides how to spend its money, with its focus on student-athlete needs. They have provided funds for uniforms, sport wheelchairs, and

championship celebrations. Three fundraisers are typically held each year for the program. One is a 3-on-3 wheelchair basketball tournament that takes place in September. This is open to anyone, and the teams are broken into groups based on experience: able-bodied teams or wheelchair teams. Another is a bowling tournament. This is another community and campus event that brings in businesses, families, and students to bowl. Finally, there is the Spring Swing, which is a wheelchair tennis tournament. There are stand-up, wheelchair, and up-down divisions. (Up-down divisions are doubles with a standing and wheelchair player on each team. This event is a staff favorite for bragging rights.)

Sport for All

The focus of the program and its activities is on the high-performance teams, but not everyone is interested in competitive sports. Thus, opportunities have been created to provide recreation options for those with disabilities on campus and in the community.

Introduction to Paralympic Sports is an activity class offered to all UA students. This class introduces students to wheelchair rugby, wheelchair basketball, wheelchair tennis, para badminton, goalball, and beep baseball (not a Paralympic sport). Approximately 20 wheelchairs are available to use with the class. These are wheelchairs that student-athletes have donated to the program after getting a new sport wheelchair from the Adapted Athletics program. The disability status of students varies, but there have been wheelchair users in class as well as those with cerebral palsy and vision loss. It is a challenge to have wheelchair users play blind sports and for those who are blind to play wheelchair sports, but it can be done.

At least one adapted physical education course is taught every semester. Most students are not physical education majors, so the focus has expanded to include physical activity. This helps those who want to become physical therapists, personal trainers, occupational therapists, doctors, and so on find meaning in the material. As part of these courses, students engage in field experiences with adults with intellectual disabilities.

One course works with the UA Crossing Points program. This is a transition program for students with intellectual disabilities who have graduated high school but, under the Individuals with Disabilities Education Act (IDEA), are still required to receive services until age 21. Crossing Points puts them on a college campus and provides job training, life skills (e.g., banking, independent living, cooking, cleaning), and recreation. The class works with students in the program who have mild to moderate intellectual disabilities. Some may be on the autism spectrum. The students enrolled in the class provide personal instruction in weight training, sports, and cardiovascular fitness. Each class section does six weeks of the field experience and spends the other weeks in the classroom. Classroom content covers disabilities such as spinal cord injuries, spina bifida, amputations and congenital limb deficiency, vision loss, hearing loss, and cerebral palsy. Guest speakers, videos, journals, and group discussions are used to help students understand disability as a diversity and a part of life.

> See chapter 8 for more on sport for athletes with intellectual disabilities and chapter 5 for more on IDEA and other legislation related to disability rights.

Another section of the course works with organizations in the community who offer day programs for adults with intellectual disabilities. These adults have moderate, profound, or severe intellectual disabilities and meet every Tuesday for a 13-week field experience. The class meets two days a week, allowing students to learn about disabilities through this field experience. Students can reflect and share what is learned in the field with the class.

In 2013, the program began offering free Crimson community wheelchair tennis clinics. The focus is to get more people in the community involved in wheelchair tennis. The clinics are offered once a week in six- to eight-week increments year-round. There is no cost, and sport wheelchairs are provided for those who do not have their own. Participants have been as young as 6 and as old as 55, ranging from beginners to experienced. Some of the players have been former wheelchair basketball players who have graduated from UA and are looking for an adapted sport that does not require nine other people to play. Some players are from the community and have never played any adapted sports before and simply want a chance to play.

To encourage campus and community experience with adapted sports, an inclusive recreation expo is held every year. Students, staff, and community members can try out wheelchair basketball, wheelchair tennis, sitting volleyball, and inclusive cardio equipment. It is a drop-in event, allowing people to try what they want as long as they want.

A wheelchair basketball camp for junior players has been offered since 2004. The camp has grown every year and includes youths ages 11 to 18. It was originally only an overnight camp, but COVID-19 protocols demanded a day camp in 2021. The success of the day camp, particularly for younger or less-mature youth, prompted a hybrid option of the traditional three-day, overnight stay at the UA residence hall and day camp. Day campers will participate in all the activities but will stay at a hotel with their parents. All youth with ambulatory disabilities need to be independent in their daily living activities, but for some, this process is slower than for others, depending on their age and abilities. The day camp allows these youth to see what they need to do to become more independent while still being around their peers in a competitive environment.

> See chapter 11 for more on sports for youth with disabilities.

The summer camp is staffed by the current full-time coaches as well as current players. They lead all basketball sessions. In addition to basketball sessions, information about nutrition, weight lifting, personal care, and wheelchair maintenance is included.

Outreach

Outreach expands the impact of the student-athletes on the community. This varies in form, but it can be on campus or in the city of Tuscaloosa. Its goals are to increase awareness about the adapted athletics program and to change the expectations of those with ambulatory disabilities. Student-athletes engage in at least four outreach activities per semester. These have ranged from reading to children with and without disabilities at the RISE Center on campus (an inclusive preschool), speaking to and or doing sport demonstrations at local schools, and serving as mentors for youth with ambulatory disabilities.

In addition to student-athletes going out in the community, community members are brought to campus to motivate and educate the student-athletes. These occur once per semester and have ranged from UA coaches such as Nick Saban, Patrick Murphy, Jenny Mainz, and Nate Oates to Regions Bank personnel talking about personal finance to Anthony Ray Hinton who shared his experiences being wrongly held on death row for 30 years. In addition to being educational, they are an opportunity for all the student-athletes to be together.

A community engagement project that I had the pleasure to be a part of was the board that started the Tuscaloosa All-Inclusive Playground Project (TAPP). This group came together to address the lack of a large inclusive playground in the city. Being part of this project was an incredible experience for me. When my son was little, I never wanted to tell him I cannot do something, so when we went to playgrounds (and we went to *all* the playgrounds in the city), I would climb with him. But none of them were accessible. The accessible, inclusive playground in Tuscaloosa, Mason's Place, was opened in 2021. It has been full of people every time I drive by (or go play). I have seen some of my coworkers there, which is exciting, because they have a wheelchair-accessible playground where they can play with their children.

Back on campus, different groups are invited to program events to increase community support and awareness of the adapted athletics program. There are more wheelchair basketball events than tennis, and because we can get people involved at halftime and between games, there is more involvement for wheelchair basketball. Promotions have included Boy Scouts night, military and police nights, Greek life nights, high school basketball teams' nights, and more. Halftime competitions are held where different groups (e.g., ROTC, law enforcement, fraternities, sororities, UA athletic teams) get in sport wheelchairs and take part in shooting and pushing games. The promotions help build a fan base and get people involved. There is a strong fan base in the city, and there is an emphasis to make the events fun for those who attend. VIP receptions are held on the mezzanine that are open to booster club members and other sponsors.

Change

I was the only student on campus in a wheelchair when I came to Alabama in 2003. When people talked about a wheelchair user, it was me. I am now one of many wheelchair users on campus. When I used to go out either on campus or in the community, people would ask me if I needed help. On campus, people now ask me if I am involved with adapted athletics. In Tuscaloosa, most people ask if I play or am involved in wheelchair sports on campus. I share this information to reflect that change can and does happen. In the almost 20 years that I have been here, there has been a cultural shift regarding ambulatory disabilities on this campus and in this city. People have been changed by the student-athletes in this program; expectations regarding a wheelchair user or an amputee have changed. They are athletes and peers, and of course they are in college, because that is what many people do after high school, regardless of the ability to walk or if you have all your limbs.

In addition to the influx of student-athletes who are at Alabama, there has been an increase in others who use wheelchairs on campus. They know there is an adapted athletics program and that the campus is both physically accessible and socially inclusive. When I came here, I had no idea this would happen, but as people are exposed to disability, it changes how they see, understand, and embrace it.

> As people are exposed to disability, it changes how they see, understand, and embrace it.

I have seen change happen—but it takes time. Many people give up because they want change to happen instantly, and they want others to quickly understand. I get it. I live with people not expecting me to be able to get out of the car on my own or being surprised that I have a job or talking to my companion because my wheelchair means that I cannot speak for myself. I have learned that while slow, change can happen. My style is not to shout but to put my head down and work. And work. And work. And eventually, results happen. I am a member of accessibility committees on campus, and for many years, I was part of an accessibility task force for the city of Tuscaloosa. I ask the student-athletes about access issues on campus and share them with the committee that can correct the problems. I have had conversations with those in UA administration about the lack of disability representation in the university—planting a seed to notice that there is a lack.

There are more than 30 student-athletes who come through the doors of the arena or the tennis facility every day who were not here 20 years ago. None of this was here. But it is now, and it will not go away. If you want to start a program, if you want to create change, then do it. Know that it will be difficult and that you will often be on your own, fighting for funds and working for hours, but it is worth it. To see students come and grow and graduate and go out in the world and forge their own path—that is change. To see alumni come and watch games and matches and be super fans—that is change. To see the university reflect the recognition of the success of this program—that is change. To read student essays about what they have learned about disability and its role in the world—that is change. And once things change, that is it. They have changed. It is easy to focus on what did not happen or what someone said that hurt, but it is more important to focus on who did help or support or listen or do. There will always be people who say you cannot create change, but those are not doing it. The people who are doing it are too busy to tell you it cannot be done. So, look for those who are working hard and making things happen and follow what they do. The results may be surprising.

> Change is hard and change is slow, but change happens.

Advice

Here are some key items to consider if you are interested in starting an adapted athletics program at a university:

1. Have someone who works at the university. You need keys to buildings and a constant presence.

2. If possible, have someone whose job it is to manage the program from the beginning.

3. To start a sport, you need three ingredients: a full-time coach, equipment, and interest. It helps if there is a junior division for the sport from which to draw student-athletes.

4. Hire good people and let them do their job.

5. If you can get in as a part of athletics, do it. That's where adapted sports belong and that is the easiest way to success. That said, if athletics will not let a new program in, get as much

support from them as possible and begin in whatever department wants an adapted athletics program.

6. Get the campus and community involved. Grow your fan base and find ways to attract people to events.

7. Apply for grants, seek donors for sponsorships and scholarships. Show the university that the money they invest for the program is returned—or exceeded—with tuition and other funds.

8. Recruit strong student-athletes and support their studies. The program will not grow if you cannot keep people in school.

9. Know your mission and make decisions based on it. Do not lose sight of the bigger picture, of who you are working for and why.

10. Know your why. Why do you get up and do what you do every day?

11. Work hard. Know change can happen but it is slow. If it takes 10,000 hours to become an expert, surely it takes at least that to create change.

12. Disability is often an overlooked diversity, but we also need to remember to include diversity in decision making. Be thoughtful about reflecting diversity beyond disability in leaders and students.

Summary

Founded in 2003, the UAAA program offers competitive wheelchair basketball, wheelchair tennis, and adaptive track and field teams. There will also be opportunities for adaptive swimming coming soon. Recreation opportunities are available for students and community members, ranging from personal fitness to Paralympic sports. UAAA is funded via the university, grants, donors, sponsorships, and booster club memberships. These funds are used to support the student-athletes as well as staff and student workers. UAAA has two facilities for its program, the Stran-Hardin Arena and the Parker-Haun Tennis Facility. For those who want to start an adapted sports program, do it. Change is slow, but it can happen. You just need to put in the work.

GLOSSARY

80/20 model—Also known as the Pareto principle or the law of the vital few, this concept suggests that roughly 80% of outcomes result from 20% of causes (Rodd, 1996). For example: 80% of a program's funding comes from 20% of its donors and 20% of its funding comes from 80% of its donors.

ableism—A form of prejudice that views disabled people as inferior, abnormal, or "less than" non-disabled people; in this able-bodied paradigm disability requires "fixing" (see chapters 1, 2, 3).

academics—Individuals who research and collect data within the disability sport community to provide relevant industry information or trends as well as suggestions or recommendations for improving issues of interest in disability sport.

acquired impairment—An impairment that develops or occurs during an individual's lifetime and is cause by illness or injury.

adaptive functioning (behavior)—Refers to the skills that are learned and practiced daily, including conceptual, social, and practical skills.

adaptive sports and recreation—An innovative health promotion program that uses sports and recreation to facilitate lifelong health, well-being, and quality of life for those of all ages and abilities living with disability in the community and beyond. Uses modifications of equipment, rules, environments, and instruction to facilitate independent engagement.

adaptive youth sports—Youth sport that is modified or created for individuals with disabilities.

American development model—Framework that is athlete-centered and coach-supported, helping all people maximize their athletic capability and use sport as a method to achieve a healthy and active lifestyle.

Americans with Disabilities Act (ADA)—Passed in 1990, the ADA is a U.S. civil rights law that prohibits discrimination against disabled people.

athlete development—The process that individuals go through to obtain and learn the necessary skills required to participate in the sport of their choosing.

athletes with high support needs (AHSN)—Those who compete within eligible sport classes in Paralympic sports and who require additional support at competitions, such as help loading a gun in shooting competitions.

athletic frame—Also called athlete-first representation; can be defined as representation that focuses on representing an athlete as an athlete first and foremost. For example, it focuses on the athlete's dedication, hard work, training, accomplishments, and feats and recognizes athletes' efforts in disability sport as competition (rather than participation).

awareness—Learning about or gaining knowledge regarding the opportunities that are available to the individual. It was also a stage added to the long-term development model in an attempt to make the model more applicable to athletes with disabilities.

barriers—Circumstances (e.g., personal, social, structural, environmental) that prevent disabled people from participating in sports or other physical activities.

Certified Therapeutic Recreation Specialists (CTRSs)—Also called recreational therapists, an allied health professional who has demonstrated competence by acquiring a specific body of knowledge and passing the National Council for Therapeutic Recreation Certification (NCTRC) exam. The CTRS employs a scope of practice based on theoretical constructs and applied methodology and addresses a wide range of disabling conditions and illnesses. In practice, CTRSs apply this critical set of competencies and skills toward the total person and the life factors that are associated with a specific disability or illness. The CTRS often serves as a member of the treatment team in concert with other health care professionals, significantly contributing to the effectiveness and efficiency of patient care and service outcomes.

classification—Athlete classification is a defining feature of parasport. It is the grouping of eligible athletes into sport classes according to how their impairment affects fundamental activities for each specific sport or discipline. This is applicable to athletes with physical disabilities as well as intellectual disabilities (see chapters 2, 4, 7, 8, 9).

closed skills—Activities where the tasks and environment are more controlled, thus requiring a lighter cognitive load.

coach education—Involves coaches' active involvement in gaining knowledge regarding the various aspects of the profession of coaching. There are formal (i.e., classes, courses, seminars) and informal (i.e., talking with other coaches, observing other coaches, mentoring) methods of coach education.

cognitive authority—A professional organization or collection of people who have the social capital to establish definitions and who are key gatekeepers in particular fields.

cognitive skills—Includes learning, reasoning, problem solving, planning, inhibitory control, selective and sustained attention, among others.

community-based adaptive sports and recreation—A critical link that can assist in bridging the gap between the treatment services provided in health care facilitates and the leisure skills, resources, and relationships that facilitate a high quality of life with family and friends in the community.

community-based—An activity that is organized and takes place locally.

comparison narrative—Focuses on stories that compare Paralympic athletes to able-bodied athletes, often with Olympic athletes who competed in a similar event, to justify or explain their athletic success.

conceptual skills—Receptive and expressive language, math and reasoning, self-direction.

congenital impairment—An impairment that is present at birth, although it may not be evident or cognized until later in life.

cultural competence—The ability to understand, appreciate, and interact with people from cultures or belief systems different from one's own.

cyborg—A hybrid body made of organism and machine.

cyborg narrative—Focuses on a Paralympic athlete's prosthetics or mobility devices as the central story rather than focusing on their athletic ability or achievements.

cycle of reintroduction—Explains the process of Paralympic athletes having to reintroduce themselves to media personnel and public every four years the Paralympic Games takes place. It highlights the lack of in-depth or critical coverage that exists for Paralympic Games.

Department of Defense—An executive branch department of the federal government charged with coordinating and supervising all agencies and functions of the government directly related to national security and the United States Armed Forces.

deployment—The movement of troops or equipment to a place or position for military action.

developmental age—An athlete's level of maturity within a sport and takes into consideration factors such as physical maturation, physical literacy, technical and tactical ability. Due to the impact of experiences in sport or physical activity, genetics and environmental variability developmental age may differ from chronological age.

direct ableism—Conscious and purposeful acts of prejudice against disabled people.

disability sport programs—Structures that provide disability sport opportunities. A program may be a single team or an entity that has multiple teams under a single organizational roof. It represents a funding structure that organizes disability sport. Some programs may offer three to five sports and multiple teams within a single sport.

disability—Any condition of the body or mind that makes it more difficult or different for the person with the condition to do certain activities (activity limitation) and interact with the world around them (participation restrictions) Within the social model this term refers to disadvantages or restrictions of activities caused by societal organizations or structures (see chapters 1 and 3).

divisioning—Special Olympics system of grouping athletes based on their gender, age, and competitive ability to ensure all athletes have an equal chance of succeeding.

donors—Individuals who voluntarily make financial contributions as a gift.

double discrimination—The discrimination women with disabilities face based on ableist and gendered stereotypes in society.

endowment—A financial account held by a nonprofit organization (e.g., university) to generate resources. The endowment creates money annually and never draws down the initial gift. Endowments are often established through donations with a primary purpose of providing long-term financial stability and support for the organization's mission or activities.

etiology—The cause of a disability or disease.

eugenics—The science of improving the population by controlling inherited qualities.

evidence-based practices—The objective, balanced, and responsible use of current research and the best available data to guide policy and practice decisions, such that outcomes for consumers are improved.

free appropriate public education (FAPE)—An educational entitlement of all students in the United States who are identified as having a disability, guaranteed by the Rehabilitation Act of 1973 and the Individuals with Disabilities Education Act (IDEA). FAPE includes both special education and related services. Special education is specially designed instruction to meet the unique needs of a child with a disability. This would include adapted physical education. Related services are the support services required to assist a child to benefit from that instruction.

FTEM (Foundational, Talent, Elite, and Mastery)—This framework is a practical tool used to help sport organizations plan and support a variety of athlete pathways. The framework recognizes that not everyone will become an elite athlete and that there are three key results from participating in sport: active lifestyle, sport participation, and sport excellence.

fundamental alteration—A change to a program, service, or activity that significantly changes the essential nature of the program, service, or activity.

funding sources—The mechanisms that organizations, individuals, or entities use to provide financial resources to support their operations.

fundraiser—Event, campaign, or activity organized for the primary goal of raising funds for charity cause.

Global War on Terror—Popularly known as the war on terror, this refers to an ongoing international military campaign launched by the U.S. government following the September 11 attacks.

grant—A financial award that includes a competitive application process. This can be provided by a government agency or nonprofit organization for a specific purpose or project.

health disparities—Preventable differences based on individual and social factors that reduce access to optimal health.

health domains—Physical health, social health, emotional health, occupational and financial health, environmental health, intellectual health, and spiritual health; these seven domains or dimensions of health are important as an integration of our sense of wellness.

ideating—Where value can be found. Innovating requires identifying a problem and exploring a solution, calling on such skills as problem solving, critical thinking, customer or user discovery, design thinking, and pitching, all of which can benefit one's career, regardless of whether that means starting a business or joining an established organization (Maurya, 2016).

impairment—A biological diagnosis on a person's body structure or function, or mental functioning.

inclusion—Subjective experience of a sense of belonging, acceptance, and value understood from the perspective of the person being included (see chapter 1). The term also refers to how diversity is leveraged to create a fair, equitable, healthy, and high-performing organization or community where all individuals are respected and feel engaged and motivated, and their contributions toward meeting organizational and societal goals are valued (O'Mara & Richter, 2014, p. 2; see chapter 2).

indirect ableism—Unconscious behavior that is not intended to cause harm but still is harmful.

individualized education program (IEP)—A plan describing the special education instructions, supports, and services a student with a disability is legally entitled to receive.

individualized inquiry—The legal requirement for an educational institution to consider the individual circumstances of a student with a disability when assessing whether the student is eligible for a reasonable modification rather than basing decisions on unfounded fear, prejudice, ignorance, or myths related to the abilities of students with disabilities.

informational frame—Focuses on educating the audience about parasport and the Paralympic movement.

in-kind—A form of donation that is not cash. For instance, it can be time, a signed jersey or donated materials.

innovation—A process by which a domain, product, or service is renewed and brought up to date by applying new processes, introducing new techniques, or establishing successful ideas to create new value. The creation of value is a defining characteristic of innovation (https://innolytics.net/what-is-innovation).

inspiration porn—The portrayal of people with disabilities as being inspirational to able-bodied people on the basis of living with a disability.

integrated setting—An educational setting where a student with a disability has equal opportunity to interact with students without disabilities.

integration—A physical space in which disabled and nondisabled people receive services together.

intellectual disabilities—A term used when an individual experiences certain limitations in cognitive functioning and skills in the medical model of disability.

intellectual functioning—Refers to an individual's general mental capacity.

intellectual impairment—A term used under the social model of disability, instead of *intellectual disability*.

International Paralympic Committee—The International Paralympic Committee (IPC) is an international nonprofit organization and the global governing body for the Paralympic movement. The IPC organizes the Summer and Winter Paralympic Games through a contractual agreement with the International Olympic Committee and the relevant Olympic host city.

intersectionality—A viewpoint for understanding how social identities do not exist independently and that different combinations of social identities result in unique situations of power or oppression (see chapters 1 and 2).

least restrictive environment—A learning environment in which a student with a disability is permitted to learn alongside their peers in the general classroom environment as much as possible.

long-term development model—A framework for the development of all people to enable peak engagement in sport and physical activity. The model has gone through three revisions since its initial release in 2005. Version 3.0 was released in 2019.

long-term development—Identifies that athlete development takes time and depicts the things an athlete needs to do at certain ages and stages.

mainstreaming—Integrating individuals with disabilities to the maximum extent appropriate. Not excluding individuals with disabilities from regular programs or requiring them to accept special services or benefits.

medical model of disability—One of several models that define how disability is portrayed or interpreted, the medical model portrays disability as a medical problem that resides in the individual as a defect in or failure of a bodily system that is abnormal and pathological (see chapter 1). Also known as the medical care model, in this biomedical approach to problems, symptoms elicited from patients are compiled. Based on these symptoms, a differential of possible diseases or illnesses is constructed (see chapter 10).

Military Health System (MHS)—A form of nationalized health care operated within the United States Department of Defense that provides health care to active duty, reserve component, and retired United States military personnel and their dependents.

military installations—A facility directly owned and operated by or for the military or one of its branches that shelters military equipment and personnel and facilitates training and operations.

multidimensional frame—Highlights a Paralympic athlete's roles outside of being an athlete such as a parent, child, friend, or employee.

National Paralympic Committee—A National Paralympic Committee (NPC) is a national constituent of the worldwide Paralympic movement. Subject to the controls of the IPC, NPCs are responsible for training and organizing the participation of athletes from their own country in the Paralympic Games. Each NPC also has a vote at the General Assembly of the IPC.

National Sports Organization (NSO)—The national body that governs a specific sport in Canada. NSOs are responsible for the management of high-performance initiatives including national-level competitions and national team selection.

nature-based and outdoor interventions—Independent or group-based activities that are undertaken in outdoor green and blue spaces.

No Accidental Champions (NAC)—A document developed by Sport for Life as a supplement to the LTD model to address factors that may be considered by those delivering sport and physical activities to individuals with impairments.

occupational therapists—A global health care profession that involves the use of assessment and intervention to develop, recover, or maintain the meaningful activities, or occupations, of individuals, groups, or communities.

Office of National Veterans Sports Programs and Special Events (NVSPSE)—Provides Veterans with opportunities for health and healing through adaptive sports and therapeutic art programs. These specialized rehabilitation events aim to optimize veterans' independence, community engagement, well-being, and quality of life.

open skills—Activities that are less predictable and demand an athlete to make a quick decision.

optimal technique—The best or most efficient or effective way of doing a physical movement or skill.

otherwise qualified—An individual who, with or without a reasonable accommodation, can perform the essential functions of the educational activity or meet the eligibility criteria for participation in the activity.

overcoming narrative—Reflects the idea that an athlete must overcome their disability (through individual and internal motivation) to achieve success. This narrative emphasizes pity from the audience rather than providing "heroic" or "superhuman" status to the athlete (like the supercrip narrative).

para-athlete development—The systematic guidance of athletes with impairments from their first involvement in sport through to high performance and/or being involved in sport for life. Para-athlete development has been stated to be similar to that of athletes without impairment development; however, there have been arguments made that this is not accurate.

Paralympic Games—The Paralympic Games are a major international sports competition for athletes with disabilities and one of the world's largest multisport events. They are split into Winter Games and Summer Games, which occur alternately every two years. Athletes from six different impairment groups compete in summer and winter sports using a classification system to ensure fair competition (see chapters 2, 4, 10).

Paralympic movement—This encompasses all athletes and officials belonging to the NPCs, the IOSDs, the International Federations, the Regional Organizations, the IPC Regional Committees, the IOSD Sports, the IPC Sports Committees, IPC Councils, IPC Standing Committees, other IPC bodies, and any other persons or organizations who agree to be.

Paralympic paradox—Coined by scholars Purdue and Howe (2012) to explain the tension that exists when covering disability sport.

Paralympic sport(s)—General reference to any sport that takes place at the Paralympic Games. The collective term for the sports events taking place at the Paralympic Games is the Paralympic program.

participating impairment groups—There are five impairment groups that are currently eligible to participate at the Paralympic Games. These are amputees and les autres, blind and visually impaired, cerebral palsied, spinal cord injuries, and intellectually disabled.

passive victim narrative—Intrinsically linked with medical understandings of disability and uses language such as "tragedy," "suffering," and "afflicted by" to describe a Paralympic athlete's disability in coverage.

perceived athletic competence—An individual's perception of their athletic ability.

person-first language—A style of wording used in reference to people with disabilities by placing emphasis on the person before the identification or disability. For example, "person with a disability" instead of "disabled person" emphasizes the individual before their characteristic.

physical literacy—Having the confidence, motivation, knowledge, and physical skills to take part in physical activity for life which is developed through engagement in a variety of physical activities.

physical therapists—Also known as physiotherapy, this is one of the allied health professions. It is provided by physical therapists who promote, maintain, or restore health through physical examination, diagnosis, prognosis, patient education, physical intervention, rehabilitation, disease prevention, and health promotion.

place of public accommodation—Any place that is open to the public where commerce is carried out and where services are provided to the general public.

polytrauma—When a person experiences injuries to multiple body parts and organ systems often, but not always, as a result of blast-related events.

practical skills—Personal care, occupational skills, managing money and schedules, using transportation, and safety.

practitioners—Individuals who work in the disability sport industry. This includes equipment managers, coaches, and other program staff. An individual may be defined as a practitioner if they are a volunteer or in a paid position, either part- or full time. Programs are staffed in many ways.

Provincial Sport Organizations (PSOs)—The body that governs a particular sport in a province and is responsible for the development of athletes, coaches, and officials.

reasonable modifications—Changes made to existing premises, policies, practices, or procedures to offer equal access and opportunity for a person with a disability.

recreational therapists—Professionals who use recreation and other activity-based interventions to address the needs of individuals with illnesses and/or disabling conditions, as a means to psychological and physical health, recovery, and well-being.

reflexive—Directed or turned on oneself. To be reflexive is to self-examine at the moment of action.

return on investment—Also known as ROI, refers to direct or indirect benefits (both can be financial or not financial) received after the organization acts. It is normally used as a metric to evaluate the profitability or efficiency of an investment relative to its cost.

revenue—Total income generated by a business effort, such as sale of goods, services, or investments.

service-connected disability ratings—A percentage assigned by the VA to a veteran's service-connected health conditions. The ratings are meant to reflect the severity of the conditions. The higher the rating percentage, the more compensation the veteran receives for the condition.

service-connected health conditions—Illnesses or injuries that are incurred or aggravated during military service.

social inclusion—The interaction between two domains: interpersonal relationships and community participation.

social model of disability—One of several models that define how disability is portrayed or interpreted, the social model has multiple interpretations but can be summarized in that society imposes disability on individuals with impairments because behaviors of those within society do not take into account people who have impairments and exclude them from various aspects of community life, which is what disables them.

social skills—Empathy, self-esteem, interpersonal skills, social awareness, and responsibility.

social-ecological model (SEM)—A framework for way of examining a problem or phenomenon at many levels (e.g., individual, organizational, policy).

Special Olympics—A global organization that supports children and adults with intellectual disabilities in health and sport.

sponsorship—An entity providing financial contribution in exchange for promotional opportunities such as endorsement from an athlete (e.g., speaking engagement, advertisement) or other benefits to the sponsoring company.

sport intelligence—The mental ability of a person to participate in sport by identifying patterns of play, knowing rules of competition, knowing sport-specific tasks, processing information related to the activity, and understanding the nature of the sport or activity.

stereotypical frame—Represents athletes' involvement in the Paralympic Games as participatory, where little attention is given to athletic accomplishments but primarily on celebrating athletes for their ability "overcome" their disability to participate in the Games. This frame encompasses the supercrip, cyborg, overcoming, passive victim, and comparison narratives.

strengths-based approach—Focus on individual strengths (including personal strengths and social and community networks) and not on their deficits. Strengths-based practice is holistic and multidisciplinary and works with the individual to promote their well-being.

supercrip—Implies a stereotyping process that requires an individual "to fight against his/her impairment" to overcome it and achieve unlikely "success" (Silva & Howe, 2012). Also called the supercrip narrative, it frames a Paralympic athlete as a hero, or superhuman-like, for being able to "overcome" their disability to achieve success.

systemic ableism—A form of ableism that includes physical barriers, laws, and practices that restrict freedom and equality for disabled people.

transition units—Provides information, tools, and training to help service members and their spouses get ready to successfully move from the military to civilian life.

Universal Design—A framework originating from architectural design with a main goal of creating physical environments and tools that are usable by as many people as possible; this can also be applied to educational and organizational contexts (Kennedy & Yun, 2019).

veteran—A person who is no longer serving in a military. A military veteran that has served directly in combat in a war is further defined as a war veteran.

Veterans Benefits Improvement Act of 2008—An act to amend title 38, United States Code, to improve and enhance compensation and pension, housing, labor and education as well as insurance benefits for veterans. It is also used for other purposes.

Veterans Health Administration (VHA, commonly referred to as "the VA")—The Veterans Health Administration is America's largest integrated health care system, providing care at 1,293 health care facilities; there are 171 medical centers and 1,112 outpatient sites of care of varying complexity (VHA outpatient clinics) that serve 9 million enrolled veterans each year.

veteran-serving organizations (VSOs)—Offer a range of services for veterans, servicemembers, dependents, and survivors. Some VSOs may provide programming for veterans in their communities, such as job fairs; others may organize events to raise money for a subset of veterans, such as housing for homeless veterans.

Virtus—World Intellectual Impairment Sport—the governing body that manages eligibility based on impairment and athlete performance.

Vocational Rehabilitation and Employment—An employment-oriented program that helps transitioning service members and veterans with service-connected disabilities and an employment handicap to prepare for, obtain, and maintain suitable employment.

Warrior Games—Created in 2010, the DoD Warrior Games introduce wounded, ill, and injured service members and veterans to Paralympic-style sports. Warrior Games showcases the resilient spirit of today's wounded, ill, or injured service members from all branches of the military.

youth sport system—The set of the interdependent persons and contexts that influence and are influenced by an athlete in youth sport.

youth sports—Sport programs for children and youth typically between ages 7 and 18 who have designated coaches, organized practices, and scheduled competitions organized by adults.

REFERENCES

CHAPTER 1

Allport, G.W. (1954). *The nature of prejudice.* Addison-Wesley.

Barton, L. (2009). Disability, physical education and sport: Some critical observations and questions. In H. Fitzgerald (Ed.), *Disability and your sport* (pp. 39-50). Routledge Publishing.

Biordi, D.L., & Nicholson, N.R. (2013). Social isolation. In I.M. Lubkin, & P.D. Larsen (Eds.), *Chronic illness: Impact and intervention* (pp. 85-115). Jones and Bartlett.

Brittain, I. (2004). Perceptions of disability and their impact upon involvement in sport for people with disabilities at all levels. *Journal of Sport & Social Issues, 28,* 429-452. https://doi.org/10.1177/0193723504268729

Cacioppo, J.T., & Patrick, W. (2008). *Loneliness: Human nature and the need for social connection.* W.W. Norton & Company.

Campbell, F.K. (2009). *Contours of ableism: Territories, objects, disability, and desire.* Palgrave Macmillan.

Dacombe, R. (2013). Sports clubs and civic inclusion: Rethinking the poverty of association. *Sport in Society, 16*(10), 1263-1278.

Darcy, S. (2012). Disability, access, and inclusion in the event industry: A call for inclusive event research. *Event Management, 16,* 259-265.

Darrow, A-A, & Hairston, M. (2016). Inspiration porn: A qualitative analysis of comments on musicians with disabilities found on international YouTube posts. *Proceedings of the 21st International Seminar of the ISME Commission on Special Music Education and Music Therapy.* International Society for Music Education.

Dovidio, J.F., Gaertner, S.L., & Kawakami, K. (2003). The contact hypothesis: The past, present, and the future. *Group Processes and Intergroup Relations, 6,* 5-21.

Fitzgerald, H. (2006). Disability and physical education. In D. Kirk, D. MacDonald, & M. O'Sullivan (Eds.), *The handbook of physical education* (pp. 752-766). Sage.

Glover, T.D. (2018). All the lonely people: Social isolation and the promise and pitfalls of leisure. *Leisure Sciences, 40*(1-2), 25-35.

Goodley, D. (2016). *Disability studies: An interdisciplinary introduction.* Sage.

Grue, J. (2016). The problem with inspiration porn: A tentative definition and provisional critique. *Disability & Society, 31,* 838-849.

Haegele, J.A., & Sutherland, S. (2015). The perspective of students with disabilities toward physical education: A review of qualitative inquiry. *Quest, 67*(3), 255-273.

Haegele, J.A. (2019). Inclusion illusion: Questioning the inclusiveness of integrated physical education. *Quest, 71*(4), 389-397. https://doi.org/10.1080/00336297.2019.1602547

Haegele, J.A., & Hodge, S.R. (2016). Disability discourse: Overview and critiques of the medical and social models. *Quest, 68*(2), 193-206. https://doi.org/10.1080/00336297.2016.1143849

Haegele, J.A., Kirk, T.N., Holland, S.K., & Zhu, X. (2021). "The rest of the time I would just stand there and look stupid": Access in integrated physical education among adults with visual impairments. *Sport, Education & Society, 26*(8), 862-874.

Harding, D.J. (2009). Violence, older peers, and the socialization of adolescent boys in disadvantaged neighborhoods. *American Sociological Review, 74*(3), 445-464.

Haslett, D., & Smith, B. (2020). Viewpoints toward disability: Conceptualizing disability in adapted physical education. In J.A. Haegele, S.R. Hodge, & D.R. Shapiro (Eds.), *Routledge handbook in adapted physical education* (pp. 48-64). Routledge.

Humpage, L. (2007). Models of disability, work and welfare in Australia. *Social Policy & Administration, 41*(3), 215-231.

International Paralympic Committee. (2006). *Paralympic School Day Manual.* Bonn, Germany: Author.

Kalymon, K., Gettinger, M., & Hanley-Maxwell, C. (2010). Middle school boys' perspectives on social relationships with peers with disabilities. *Remedial and Special Education, 31*(4), 305-316.

Liasidou, A. (2012). *Inclusive education, politics and policymaking.* Bloomsbury Publishing.

Liu, Y., Kudlacek, Y., & Jesina, O. (2010). The influence of Paralympic School Day on children's attitudes towards people with disabilities. *Acta Universitatis Palackianae Olomucensis. Gymnica, 40*(2), 63-69.

Macdonald, S.J., Deacon, L., Nixon, J., Akintola, A., Gillingham, A., Kent, J., Ellis, G., Mathews, D., Ismail, A., Sullivan, S., Dore, S., & Highmore, L. (2018) The invisible enemy: Disability, loneliness and isolation. *Disability & Society, 33*(7), 1138-1159, 10.1080/09687599.2018.1476224

Maher, A., & Coates, J. (2020). Utilizing theory to drive research in adapted physical education. In J.A. Haegele, S.R. Hodge, & D.R. Shapiro (Eds.), *Routledge handbook of adapted physical education* (pp. 81-94). Routledge.

Martin, J.J. (2019). Mastery and belonging or inspiration porn and bullying: Special populations in youth sport. *Kinesiology Review, 8*(3), 195-203.

McKay, C. (2018). The value of contact: unpacking Allport's contact theory to support inclusive education. *Palaestra, 32*(1), 21-25.

McKay, C., & Park, J.Y. (2019). The impact of Paralympic Skill Lab on college student attitudes toward inclusive sport and fitness. *International Journal of Kinesiology in Higher Education, 3*(3), 67-76. https://doi.org/10.1080/24711616.2018.1551732

McKay, C., Block, M.E., & Park, J.Y. (2015). The effect of Paralympic School Day on attitudes toward inclusion in physical education. *Adapted Physical Activity Quarterly. 32*(4), 331-348. https://doi.org/10.1123/APAQ.2015-0045

McKay, C., Haegele, J.A., & Block, M.E. (2019). Lessons learned from Paralympic School Day: Reflections from the students. *European Physical Education Review, 25*(3), 745-760. https://doi.org/10.1177/1356336X18768038

McKay, C., Haegele, J.A., & Perez-Torralba, A. (2022a). 'My perspective has changed on an entire group of people': Undergraduate student experiences with the Paralympic Skill Lab. *Sport, Education and Society, 27*(8), 946-959. https://doi.org/10.1080/13573322.2021.1949702\

McKay, C., Park, J.Y., & Haegele, J.A. (2022b). Contact theory as the theoretical basis of the Paralympic Skill Lab: A measurement of implementation fidelity. *Palaestra, 36*(3), 46-51

McManus, J., Feyes, K.J., & Saucier, D.A. (2011). Contact and knowledge as predictors of attitudes toward individuals with intellectual disabilities. *Journal of Social and Personal Relationships, 28*(5), 570-590.

Mitra, S. (2006). The capability approach and disability. *Journal of Disability Policy Studies, 16*(4), 236-247.

Panagiotou, A.K., Evaggelinou, C., Doulkeridou, A., Mouratidou, K., & Koidou, E. (2008). Attitudes of 5th and 6th grade Greek students toward the inclusion of children with disabilities in physical education classes after a Paralympic education program. *European Journal of Adapted Physical Activity, 1*(2), 31-43.

Pate, J.R., Ruihley, B.J., & Mirabito, T. (2014). Displaying disability: A content analysis of person-first language on NCAA Bowl Championship Series college athletic department websites. *Journal of Applied Sport Management, 6*(1), 1-20.

Petrie, K., Devcich, J., & Fitzgerald, H. (2018). Working toward inclusive physical education in a primary school: "Some days I just don't get it right." *Physical Education and Sport Pedagogy, 23*(4), 345-357. https://doi.org/10.1080/17408989.2018.1441391

Pettigrew, T.F. (1971). *Racially separate or together?* McGraw-Hill.

Pettigrew, T.F. (1998). Intergroup contact theory. *Annual Review of Psychology, 49*, 65-85.

Pettigrew, T.F., & Tropp, L.R. (2006). A meta-analytic test of intergroup contact theory. *Journal of Personality and Social Psychology, 90*(5), 751-783.

Reindal, S.M. (2008). A social relational model of disability: A theoretical framework for special needs education? *European Journal of Special Needs Education, 23*(2), 135-146.

Reindal, S.M. (2009). Disability, capability, and special education: Towards a capability-based theory. European *Journal of Special Needs Education, 24*(2), 155-168.

Roush, S.E., & Sharby, N. (2011). Disability reconsidered: The paradox of physical therapy. *Physical Therapy, 91*(12), 1715-1757.

Schwartz, L.K., & Simmons, J.P. (2001). Contact quality and attitudes toward the elderly. *Educational Gerontology, 27*(2), 127-137.

Sigelman, L., & Welch, S. (1993). The contact hypothesis revisited: Black-White interaction and positive racial attitudes. *Social Forces, 71*(3), 781-795. https://doi.org/10.2307/2579895

Slee, R. (2018). *Inclusive education isn't dead, it just smells funny.* Routledge.

Smith, B., Mallick, K., Monforte, J., & Foster, C. (2021). Disability, the communication of physical activity and sedentary behaviour, and ableism: A call for inclusive message. *British Journal of Sports Medicine, 55*(20), 1-5. https://doi.org/10.1136/bjsports-2020-103780

Spencer, N.L.I., Peers, D., & Eales, L. (2020). Disability language in adapted physical education: What is the story? In J.A. Haegele, S.R. Hodge, & D.R. Shapiro (Eds.), *Routledge handbook in adapted physical education* (pp. 131-144). Routledge.

Spencer-Cavaliere, N., & Rintoul, M.A. (2012). Alienation in physical education from the perspectives of children. *Journal of Teaching in Physical Education, 31,* 344-361

Spencer-Cavaliere, N., & Watkinson, E. (2010). Inclusion understood from the perspective of children with disability. *Adapted Physical Activity Quarterly, 27*(4), 275-29. https://doi.org/10.1123/apaq.27.4.275

Spencer-Cavaliere, N., Thai, J., & Kingsley, B. (2017). A part of and apart from sport: Practitioners' experiences coaching in segregated youth sport. *Social Inclusion, 5*(2), 120-129.

Stainback, W., & Stainback, S. (1996). Collaboration, support network, and community construction. In S. Stainback, & W. Stainback (Eds.), *Inclusion: A guide for educators* (pp. 223-232). Paul H. Brookes Publishing Co.

Tarvainen, M. (2021). Loneliness in life stories by people with disabilities. *Disability & Society, 36*(6), 864-882. https://doi.org/10.1080/09687599.2020.1779034

Warner, D.F., & Kelley-Moore, J. (2010). *The social context of disablement among older adults: Does marital quality matter for loneliness?* Paper presented at the National Center for Family & Research, Bowling Green, KY.

Yell, M.L. (1995). Least restrictive environment, inclusion, and students with disabilities: A legal analysis. *The Journal of Special Education, 28*(4), 389-404.

CHAPTER 2

Americans With Disabilities Act of 1990, as amended with ADA Amendments Act of 2008. (n.d.). Retrieved February 11, 2022, from www.ada.gov/pubs/adastatute08.htm.

Annamma, S.A., Connor, D., & Ferri, B. (2013). Dis/ability critical race studies (DisCrit): Theorizing at the intersections of race and dis/ability. *Race Ethnicity and Education, 16*(1), 1-31. https://doi.org/10.1080/13613324.2012.730511

Barr, M., & Shields, N. (2011). Identifying the barriers and facilitators to participation in physical activity for children with Down syndrome. *Journal of Intellectual Disability Research, 55*(11), 1020-1033. https://doi.org/10.1111/j.1365-2788.2011.01425.x.

Belcher, B.R., Berrigan, D., Dodd, K.W., Emken, B.A., Chou, C.P., & Spuijt-Metz, D. (2010). Physical activity in U.S. youth: Impact of race/ethnicity, age, gender, and weight status. *Medicine and Science in Sports and Exercise, 42*(12), 2211-2221. https://doi.org/10.1249/MSS.0b013e3181e1fba9

Berger, R.J. (2008). Disability and the dedicated wheelchair athlete: Beyond the "supercrip" critique. *Journal of Contemporary Ethnography, 37*(6), 647-678. https://doi.org/10.1177/0891241607309892

Brown, L.X.Z. (2011). *The significance of semantics: Person-first language: Why it matters.* www.autistichoya.com/2011/08/significance-of-semantics-person-first.html.

Carroll, D.D., Courtney-Long, E.A., Stevens, A.C., Sloan, M.L., Lullo, C., Visser, S.N., Fox, M.H., Armour, B.S., Campbell, V.A., Brown, D.R., & Dorn, J.M. (2014). Vital signs: Disability and physical activity—United States, 2009-2012. *Morbidity and Mortality Weekly Report, 63*(18), 407-413.

Charlton, J.I. (2000). *Nothing about us without us: Disability oppression and empowerment.* University of California Press.

Clare, E. (2012). *Exile and pride: Excerpts from "The Mountain."* https://eliclare.com/books/exile-and-pride/exile-and-pride-excerpt

Clare, E. (2013). *Notes on cure, disability, and natural worlds.* [Lecture excerpt]. https://eliclare.com/what-eli-offers/lectures/cure

Convention on the Rights of Persons with Disabilities (CRPD). (2006). www.un.org/development/desa/disabilities/convention-on-the-rights-of-persons-with-disabilities.html.

Cottingham, M., Velasco, F., Laughlin, M., & Lee, D. (2015). *Examination the size and scope of youth disability sport participation in the United States.* National Collegiate Athletic Association. 14.

Diament, M. (2021, Nov. 12). CVS drops Supreme Court case over disability community concerns. https://www.disabilityscoop.com/2021/11/12/cvs-drops-supreme-court-case-over-disability-community-concerns/29593/

Dill, B.T., & Zambrana, R. (2009). Critical thinking about inequality: An emerging lens. In *Emerging intersections: Race, class, and gender in theory, policy, and practice* (pp. 1-21). Rutgers University Press.

Fitzgerald, H. (2018). Disability and barriers to inclusion. In I. Brittain, & A. Beacom (Eds.), *The Palgrave handbook of Paralympic studies* (pp. 55-70). Palgrave Macmillan UK. https://doi.org/10.1057/978-1-137-47901-3_4

Groff, D.D.G., Lundberg, N.R., & Zabriskie, R.B. (2009). Influence of adapted sport on quality of life: Perceptions of athletes with cerebral palsy. *Disability and Rehabilitation, 31*(4), 318-326. https://doi.org/10.1080/09638280801976233

Hosking, D.L. (2008). Critical disability theory. 4th Biennial Disability Studies Conference, 17.

Howe, D. (2008). *The cultural politics of the Paralympic movement: Through an anthropological lens.* Routledge.

Hubbard, R. (1986). Eugenics and prenatal testing. *International Journal of Health Services, 16*(2), 227-242. https://doi.org/10.2190/1YKE-PHP6-H69A-YRKV

Hums, M.A., Moorman, A.M., & Wolff, E.A. (2003). The inclusion of the Paralympics in the Olympic and Amateur Sports Act: Legal and policy implications for integration of athletes with disabilities into the United States Olympic Committee and National Governing Bodies. *Journal of Sport and Social Issues, 27*(3), 261-275. https://doi.org/10.1177/0193732503255480

Iezzoni, L.I., & Freedman, V.A. (2008). Turning the disability tide: The importance of definitions. *JAMA, 299*(3), 332-334. https://doi.org/10.1001/jama.299.3.332

Invalid, S. (2017). Skin, tooth, and bone—The basis of movement is our people: A disability justice primer. *Reproductive Health Matters, 25*(50), 149-150. https://doi.org/10.1080/09688080.2017.1335999

Janus, A.L. (2009). Disability and the transition to adulthood. *Social Forces, 88*(1), 99-120. https://doi.org/10.1353/sof.0.0248

Keisch, D., & Scott, T. (2015). U.S. education reform and the maintenance of white supremacy through structural violence. *Landscapes of Violence, 3*(3). https://scholarworks.umass.edu/lov/vol3/iss3/6

Kennedy, W., & Yun, J. (2019). Universal design for learning as a curriculum development tool in physical education. *Journal of Physical Education, Recreation & Dance, 90*(6), 25-31.

Kennedy, W., Fruin, R., Lue, A., & Logan, S.W. (2021). Using ecological models of health behavior to promote health care access and physical activity engagement for persons with disabilities. *Journal of Patient Experience, 8*, 1-3. https://doi.org/10.1177/23743735211034031

Kimberlé Crenshaw on Intersectionality, More than Two Decades Later. (2017). Columbia Law School. www.law.columbia.edu/news/archive/kimberle-crenshaw-intersectionality-more-two-decades-later.

Krahn, G.L., Walker, D.K., & Correa-De-Araujo, R. (2015). Persons with disabilities as an unrecognized health disparity population. *American Journal of Public Health, 105*(S2), S198-S206. https://doi.org/10.2105/AJPH.2014.302182

Ladau, E. (2021). *Demystifying disability: What to know, what to say, and how to be an ally* (First edition.). Ten Speed Press.

Lastuka, A., & Cottingham, M. (2016). The effect of adaptive sports on employment among people with disabilities. *Disability and Rehabilitation, 38*(8), 742-748. https://doi.org/10.3109/09638288.2015.1059497

Lewis, T. (2022). *Working definition of ableism—January 2022 update.* www.talilalewis.com/1/post/2022/01/working-definition-of-ableism-january-2022-update.html

Lorenc, T., Petticrew, M., Welch, V., & Tugwell, P. (2013). What types of interventions generate inequalities? Evidence from systematic reviews. *Journal of Epidemiol Community Health, 67*(2), 190-193. https://doi.org/10.1136/jech-2012-201257

MacDonald, M. (2021). Op-ed: If the Paralympics won't model equity and inclusion, who will? *Los Angeles Times.* www.latimes.com/opinion/story/2021-08-04/paralympics-failed-to-model-equity-when-officials-excluded-becca-meyers-aide

Maroto, M., Pettinicchio, D., & Patterson, A.C. (2019). Hierarchies of categorical disadvantage: Economic insecurity at the intersection of disability, gender, and race. *Gender & Society, 33*(1), 64-93. https://doi.org/10.1177/0891243218794648

Martin Ginis, K.A., Ma, J.K., Latimer-Cheung, A.E., & Rimmer, J.H. (2016). A systematic review of review articles addressing factors related to physical activity participation among children and adults with physical disabilities. *Health Psychology Review, 10*(4), 478-494. https://doi.org/10.1080/17437199.2016.1198240

Martin, J.J. (2013). Benefits and barriers to physical activity for individuals with disabilities: A social-relational model of disability perspective. *Disability and Rehabilitation, 35*(24), 2030-2037. https://doi.org/10.3109/09638288.2013.802377

Martin, J.J. (2017). *Handbook of disability sport and exercise psychology.* Oxford University Press.

McCarty, K., Kennedy, W., Logan, S., & Levy, S. (2021). Examining the relationship between falls self-efficacy and postural sway in community-dwelling older adults. *Journal of Kinesiology & Wellness, 10*(1), 21-30.

McCarty, K., Townsend, J., & MacDonald, M. (2023). Intercollegiate sports and the need for disability equity. *PALAESTRA, 37*(2).

Meekosha, H. (1998). Body battles: Bodies, gender and disability. In *The Disability Reader: Social Science Perspectives* (pp. 163-180). Cassell.

Meekosha, H., & Shuttleworth, R. (2009). What's so "critical" about critical disability studies? *Australian Journal of Human Rights, 15*(1), 47-75. https://doi.org/10.1080/1323238X.2009.11910861

Meeks, L.M., Herzer, K., & Jain, N.R. (2018). Removing barriers and facilitating access: Increasing the number of physicians with disabilities. *Academic Medicine, 93*(4), 540-543. https://doi.org/10.1097/ACM.0000000000002112

Payan v. LACCD Explainer—Disability Rights Education & Defense Fund. (2021, December 16). https://dredf.org/2021/12/16/payan-v-laccd-explainer/

Retief, M., & Letšosa, R. (2018). Models of disability: A brief overview. HTS Teologiese Studies / *Theological Studies, 74*(1), Article 1. https://www.ajol.info/index.php/hts/article/view/177914

Rimmer, J.H., Riley, B., Wang, E., & Rauworth, A. (2005). Accessibility of health clubs for people with mobility disabilities and visual impairments. *American Journal of Public Health, 95*(11), 2022-2028.

Rimmer, J.H., Riley, B., Wang, E., Rauworth, A., & Jurkowski, J. (2004). Physical activity participation among persons with disabilities: Barriers and facilitators. *American Journal of Preventive Medicine, 26*(5), 419-425. https://doi.org/10.1016/j.amepre.2004.02.002

Ross, S.M., Schram, B., McCarty, K., Fiscella, N., Leung, W.C.W., & Lindland, K. (2021). Promoting inclusion of adults with disabilities in local fitness programs: A needs assessment. *Developmental Disabilities Network Journal, 2*(1), 8.

Saffer, H., Dave, D., Grossman, M., & Leung, L.A. (2013). Racial, ethnic, and gender differences in physical activity. *Journal of Human Capital, 7*(4), 378-410. https://doi.org/10.1086/671200

Sartorius, N. (2006). The meanings of health and its promotion. *Croatian Medical Journal, 47*(4), 662-664.

Section 504 of the Rehabilitation Act, Pub. L. No. 93-112, 29 U.S.C. (1973). www.dol.gov/agencies/oasam/centers-offices/civil-rights-center/statutes/section-504-rehabilitation-act-of-1973

Shakespeare, T. (1998). Choices and rights: Eugenics, genetics and disability equality. *Disability & Society, 13*(5), 665-681. https://doi.org/10.1080/09687599826452

Shakespeare, T., Iezzoni, L.I., & Groce, N.E. (2009). Disability and the training of health professionals. *The Lancet, 374*(9704), 1815-1816. https://doi.org/10.1016/S0140-6736(09)62050-X

Shavers, V.L., Klein, W.M.P., & Fagan, P. (2012). Research on race/ethnicity and health care discrimination: Where we are and where we need to go. *American Journal of Public Health, 102*(5), 930-932. https://doi.org/10.2105/AJPH.2012.300708

Shields, N., & Synnot, A. (2016). Perceived barriers and facilitators to participation in physical activity for children with disability: A qualitative study. *BMC Pediatrics, 16*(1), 9. https://doi.org/10.1186/s12887-016-0544-7

Siebers, T. (2008). *Disability theory.* University of Michigan Press.

Silva, C.F., & Howe, P.D. (2012). The (in) validity of supercrip representation of Paralympian athletes. *Journal of Sport and Social Issues, 36*(2), 174-194.

Smith, B., & Wightman, L. (2021). Promoting physical activity to disabled people: Messengers, messages, guidelines and communication formats. *Disability and Rehabilitation, 43*(24), 3427-3431. https://doi.org/10.1080/09638288.2019.1679896

Title IX of the Education Amendments of 1972, 20 U.S.C. § §1681 (1972). www.justice.gov/crt/title-ix-education-amendments-1972

Wagner, M., Newman, L., Cameto, R., Garza, N., & Levine, P. (2005). After high school: A first look at the postschool experiences of youth with disabilities. A report from the National Longitudinal Transition Study-2 (NLTS2). https://eric.ed.gov/?id=ED494935

Warner, D.F., & Brown, T.H. (2011). Understanding how race/ethnicity and gender define age-trajectories of disability: An intersectionality approach. *Social Science & Medicine (1982), 72*(8), 1236-1248. https://doi.org/10.1016/j.socscimed.2011.02.034

Wessel, R.D., Jones, J.A., Markle, L., & Westfall, C. (2009). Retention and graduation of students with disabilities: Facilitating student success. *Journal of Postsecondary Education and Disability, 21*(3), 116-125.

Wheelchair basketball player "wrong kind of disabled" after rule change. (2020). BBC News. www.bbc.com/news/uk-england-devon-53812366

Winnick, J., & Porretta, D.L. (2016). *Adapted physical education and sport.* Human Kinetics.

Yazicioglu, K., Yavuz, F., Goktepe, A.S., & Tan, A.K. (2012). Influence of adapted sports on quality of life and life satisfaction in sport participants and non-sport participants with physical disabilities. *Disability and Health Journal, 5*(4), 249-253. https://doi.org/10.1016/j.dhjo.2012.05.003

CHAPTER 3

Because of them we can (2019). Meet the Kenyan engineer who created gloves that turn sign language into audible speech. www.becauseofthemwecan.com/blogs/culture/meet-the-kenyan-engineer-who-created-gloves-that-turn-sign-language-into-audible-speech?

Bloomberg (2015). Bloomberg Quicktake: Original. www.youtube.com/watch?v=sk1NkWl_W2Y

Booten, M. (2018). New York City marathon builds wheelchair-accessible interactive video game. www.sporttechie.com/nyc-marathon-builds-wheelchair-accessible-interactive-video-game/?

Brown, T. (2008). Design Thinking. *Harvard Business Review*, 1.

Buhalis, D., & Darcy, S. (Eds.). (2011). *Accessible tourism: concepts and issues.* Bristol, UK: Channel View Publications.

Caciatorre, B. (2021). Degree has created the world's first deodorant for people with disabilities. www.glamour.com/story/degree-inclusive-deodorant-for-people-with-disabilities

Cassidy, T. (2022). Designers Carol Taylor and Jessie Sadler bring disability-friendly creations to runway for Australian Fashion Week. ABC News. www.abc.net.au/news/2022-05-12/disability-designs-australian-fashion-week/101059840#:~:text=%22Adapted%20clothing%22%20for%20people%20with,be%20sold%20in%20major%20stores

ComcastNBCUniversal. (2022). Sports Tech. www.comcastsportstech.com/

Darcy, S. (2017). Accessibility as a key management component of the Paralympics. In S. Darcy, S. Frawley & D. Adair (Eds.), *Managing the Paralympics* (pp. 47-90). Basingstoke, Hampshire: Palgrave Macmillan.

Darcy, S., Collins, J., & Stronach, M. (2020). Entrepreneurial spirit built of necessity for people with disability. *Sydney Morning Herald.* www.smh.com.au/business/workplace/entrepreneurial-spirit-built-of-necessity-for-people-with-disability-20201102-p56at8.html

Darcy, S., Lock, D., & Taylor, T. (2017). Enabling inclusive sport participation: Effects of disability and support needs on constraints to sport participation. *Leisure Sciences, 39*(1), 20-41. https://doi.org/10.1080/01490400.2016.1151842

Darcy, S., Maxwell, H., Edwards, M., & Almond, B. (2023). Disability inclusion in beach precincts: Beach for All Abilities—A community development approach through a social relational model of disability lens. *Sport Management Review, 26*(1) 1-23. https://doi.org/10.1080/14413523.2022.2059998

Darcy, S., McKercher, B., & Schweinsberg, S. (2020). From tourism and disability to accessible tourism: A perspective article. *Tourism Review, 75*(1) 140-144. https://doi.org/10.1108/TR-07-2019-0323

Davidson, N. (2021). 8 pieces of adaptive outdoor gear that redefine accessibility: Innovations expand opportunities for adventurers with physical disabilities. www.sierraclub-org.cdn.ampproject.org/c/s/www.sierraclub.org/sierra/2021-1-january-february/gear-guide/8-pieces-adaptive-outdoor-gear-redefine-accessibility?

DePaul, R. (2022). Presentation to Adapted Physical Activity HPED 3320, Mount Royal University, Calgary.

Dickson, T.J., Darcy, S, Johns, R., & Pentifallo, C. (2016). Inclusive by design: Transformative services and sport-event accessibility *The Service Industries Journal, 36*(11-12), 532-555. http://dx.doi.org/10.1080/02642069.2016.1255728

Dickson, T., Darcy, S., & Walker, C. (2021). A case of leveraging a mega-sport event for a sport participation and sport tourism legacy: a prospective longitudinal case study of Whistler Adaptive Sports. *Sustainability, 13*(1), 170-191. https://doi.org/https://doi.org/10.3390/su13010170

de Jong, M., Marston, N., & Roth, E. (2015). The eight essentials of innovation. www.mckinsey.com/business-functions/strategy-and-corporate-finance/our-insights/the-eight-essentials-of-innovation?

Disability:IN. (2022). The Disability Equality Index (DEI). https://disabilityin.org/what-we-do/disability-equality-index/

Faust, K. (2022). How to SCAMPER your way to innovation and creativity. https://leadx.org/articles/how-to-scamper-your-way-to-innovation-and-creativity/

Fleming, S. (2021). Nike's hands-free shoe is a step forward for inclusive clothing. www.weforum.org/agenda/2021/02/nike-hands-free-shoe-disability-inclusive-clothing?

Gallucci, N. (2018). Tommy Hilfiger unveils innovative clothing line for people with disabilities: Say hello to Tommy Adaptive. https://mashable.com/article/tommy-hilfiger-tommy-adaptive-disibility-friendly-clothing

Global Disability Innovation Hub. (2022). Who we are. www.disabilityinnovation.com/

Halpenny, M. (2020). Okanagan college students create T-Glove for quadriplegics. www.castanet.net/news/Kelowna/299397/Okanagan-College-students-create-T-Glove-for-quadriplegics

Hamilton, I. (2017). The changing tides of accessibility in gaming. www.huffingtonpost.co.uk/ian-hamilton/the-changing-tides-of-accessibility-in-gaming_b_10462956.html

Harris Prager, J. (1999).People with disabilities are next consumer niche. www.wsj.com/articles/SB945213765959569213

Hasso Plattner Institute of Design at Stanford University. (2022). Tools for taking action. https://dschool.stanford.edu/resources

Heasley, S. (2021). With disability-friendly packaging, Olay aims for greater accessibility. www.disabilityscoop.com/2021/11/09/with-disability-friendly-packaging-olay-aims-for-greater-accessibility/29584/

Huber, E. (2021). Here's what Nike's first hands-free sneaker means for people with disabilities. www.refinery29.com/en-us/2021/02/10291037/nike-go-flyease-hands-free-sneaker-adaptive-fashion

ICCSPE. (2020). How business innovation feeds into sport; innovation in a competitive environment. www.icsspe.org/content/how-business-innovation-feeds-sport

IKEA. (2022). *Vision and Business Concept.* IKEA. www.ikea.com/nl/en/this-is-ikea/about-us/vision-and-business-concept-pub9cd02291

IOC Media (2021). Worldwide Olympic partners helping to make Tokyo 2020 most innovative Olympic Games ever. www.youtube.com/watch?v=azdsuV-jHJY8

Jackson, L. (2021). It's a basic human right: the fight for adaptive fashion. www.theguardian.com/fashion/2021/feb/26/its-a-basic-human-right-the-fight-for-adaptive-fashion

Joachim, G., Schulenkorf, N., Schlenker, K., & Frawley, S. (2020). Design thinking and sport for development: Enhancing organizational innovation. *Managing Sport and Leisure, 25*(3), 175-202. https://doi.org/10.1080/23750472.2019.1611471

Joachim, G., Schulenkorf, N., Schlenker, K., Frawley, S., & Cohen, A. (2021). "No idea is a bad idea:" Exploring the nature of design thinking alignment in an Australian sport organization. *Journal of Sport Management, 35*(5), 381-394.

Jones, S. (2021). Will It Reach? | Christian Bagg and his Bowhead reach adaptive electric mountain bike. https://mpora.com/mountainbiking/will-it-reach-the-inspirational-series-from-the-inspiration-who-is-christian-bagg/

Jordan, D. (2021). Why are there more clothing lines for dogs than people with disabilities. https://metro.co.uk/2021/04/10/in-focus-there-are-more-clothing-lines-for-dogs-than-disabled-people-14376043/

Kitchin, P.J., Paramio-Salcines, J.L., Darcy, S., & Walters, G. (2022). Exploring the accessibility of sport stadia for people with disability: Towards the development of a Stadium Accessibility Scale (SAS). *Sport, Business and Management: An International*

Journal, 12(1), 93-116. https://doi.org/10.1108/SBM-05-2021-0064

MaRS (2022).Health. www.marsdd.com/our-sectors/health/

Maurya, A. (2016). The BOOTSTART Manifesto: There's never been a better time to act on your "big idea." https://blog.leanstack.com/the-bootstart-manifesto-65b41da6216

McKall, T. (2022). Christian Bagg takes on "The Longest Climb" on an MTB prototype. https://cyclingmagazine.ca/mtb/christian-bagg-bowhead-the-longest-climb/

Molon Labe (2022). The Freedom Seat—Helping passengers in wheelchairs fly in their own wheelchairs. www.youtube.com/watch?v=GG2bNDPqKlY

Munoz, R., (2021). New wheelchair prototype seat promises accessibility for in-flight travel. https://skift.com/2021/04/08/new-wheelchair-prototype-seat-promises-accessibility-for-in-flight-travel/

Network A. (2012). Adaptive snowboard reinvented: Every Third Thursday raising the bar. www.youtube.com/watch?v=brEmdlEwf4M&index=27&list=PL34695342B698FC80

Nike. (2021). This is Nike Go FlyEase. https://news.nike.com/news/nike-go-flyease-hands-free-sho

Paralympic Games. (2012). Swimming men's 100m backstroke—S6 final—London 2012 Paralympic Games. www.youtube.com/watch?v=_oXIdPoSLlE

Patterson, I, Darcy, S, and Pegg, S. (2015). Adventure recreation programming and tourism opportunities: Bringing together consumer demands and supplier understandings for people with disabilities. In *Adventure Programming and Travel for the 21st Century*, edited by R Black and K Bricker, 249-260. State College, PA: Venture Publishing.

Praxis (2022). The ideation clinic presents the 2022 Praxis Ideation Challenge. www.ideation.clinic/2022-praxis-ideation-challenge

Pro Sports Assembly (2021). From The C-Suite "Innovate for Inclusion." www.youtube.com/watch?v=MddOaP3wgMw

Purdy's (2021). Braille Box, 18 pc. www.purdys.com/braille-box-18-pc

Razzouk, R., & Shute, V. (2012). What is design thinking and why is it important? *Review of Educational Research, 82*(3): 330-348. https://doi.org/10.3102/0034654312457429

Ryan, F. (2018). Why are there more clothing lines for dogs than disabled people. https://www.theguardian.com/society/2018/jun/18/why-are-there-more-clothing-lines-for-dogs-than-disabled-people

Sabina-Aouf, R. (2019). IKEA's ThisAbles add-ons adjust furniture for people with disabilities. www.dezeen.com/2019/03/18/thisables-ikea-disabilities-furniture-design/

Shalala, A. (2015). Australia's Paralympians to benefit from more comfortable flight seating for Rio Games travel. www.abc.net.au/news/2015-09-16/measures-taken-to-improve-comfort-for-australias-paralympians/6780876

Skok, D. (2012). 6 reasons startups fail. www.forentrepreneurs.com/why-startups-fail/

Slefo, G. (2019). IKEA'S Thisables wins Cannes Lions Grand Prix for health and wellness. https://adage.com/article/special-report-cannes-lions/ikeas-thisables-wins-cannes-lions-grand-prix-health-and-wellness/2178341

Spencer, P. (2018). Accessible gaming with the Xbox adaptive controller. https://news.xbox.com/en-us/2018/05/16/xbox-adaptive-controller/

Spradlin, D. (2012). Are you solving the right problem? https://hbr.org/2012/09/are-you-solving-the-right-problem

SRI (2019). Innovation Study 2019. www.sriexecutive.com/innovation/

Stuart, R. (2022). How Christian Bagg invented a new adaptive adventure sport with the Bowhead Reach. www.mensjournal.com/sports/how-christian-bagg-invented-a-new-adaptive-adventure-sport-with-the-bowhead-reach/?

Takahashi, D. (2018). Microsoft controller makes gaming more accessible to people with disabilities. https://venturebeat.com/2018/05/16/microsoft-controller-makes-gaming-more-accessible-to-people-with-disabilities/

This Ables (2022). How did it all begin. https://thisables.com/en/about/

Tommy Hilfiger (2022). Tommy style for all. https://usa.tommy.com/en/tommy-adaptive

US EPA (2021) The Circular Economy. www.epa.gov/recyclingstrategy/what-circular-economy

Veal, A.J., & Darcy, S. (2014). *Research Methods for Sport Studies and Sport Management: A Practical Guide.* Milton Park, Abingdon, Oxam UK: Routledge.

Wainwright, O. (2014). Omniwheels and mountain trikes: Five visionary new wheelchair designs. www.theguardian.com/artanddesign/architecture-design-blog/2014/oct/09/five-new-wheelchair-designs

Wong, N. (2015). A wheelchair that might disrupt the industry. http://design-milk.com/wheelchair-might-disrupt-industry/

Zappos (2022). Functional and fashionable products to make life easier. Retrieved 2022, from www.zappos.com/e/adaptive

CHAPTER 4

Anderson, J. (2003). Turned in taxpayers: Paraplegia, rehabilitation and sport at Stoke Mandeville, 1944-56. *Journal of Contemporary History, 38*(3), 461-75.

Auxter, D., Pyfer, J., & Huettig, C. (1993). *Principles and methods of adapted physical education and recreation*. Mosby.

Bailey, S. (2008). *Athlete first: A history of the Paralympic movement*. John Wiley & Sons Ltd.

BBC. (2000). *Making sense of the categories*. BBC Sport. http://news.bbc.co.uk/sport1/hi/olympics2000/paralympics/959701.stm

Bell, D.T. (1954). Ten years physiotherapy with paraplegics. *The Cord, 6*(4), 41-43.

BOCOG. (2008). Guidelines to classification. *BOGOG*, Beijing; China, 1.

Brandmeyer, G.A., & McBee, G.F. (1986). Social status and athletic competition for the disabled athletes: The case of wheelchair road-racing. In C. Sherrill (Ed.), *Sport and disabled athletes* (pp. 181-187). Human Kinetics.

Braye, S., Gibbons, T., & Dixon, K. (2013). Disability "rights" or "wrongs"? The claims of the International Paralympic Committee, the London 2012 Paralympics and disability rights in the UK. *Sociological Research Online, 18*(3). www.socresonline.org.uk/18/3/16.html

Brittain, I. (2008). The evolution of the Paralympic Games. In R. Cashman, & S. Darcy (Eds.), *Benchmark games: The Sydney 2000 Paralympic Games* (pp. 19-34). Walla Walla Press.

Brittain, I. (2014). *From Stoke Mandeville to Sochi: A history of the Summer and Winter Paralympic Games*. Common Ground Publishing.

Brittain, I. (2016). *The Paralympic Games explained* (2nd ed.). Routledge.

Brittain, I. (2018). Key points in the history and development of the Paralympic Games. In I. Brittain, & A. Beacom (Eds.), *The Palgrave handbook of Paralympic studies* (pp. 125-150). Palgrave MacMillan.

Brittain, I. (2019). The impact of resource inequality upon participation and success at the Summer and Winter Paralympic Games. *Journal of the Nippon Foundation Paralympic Research Group, 12*(Sept), 41-67.

Brittain, I., & Hutzler, Y. (2009). A social-historical perspective on the development of sports for persons with a physical disability in Israel. *Sport in Society, 12*(8), 1075-1088.

Brittain, I., Bunds, K., & Bocarro, J. (2022). The contribution of sport in the rehabilitation process of disabled military veterans: A case study of the 2016 Invictus Games. *Journal of Global Sport Management*, doi:10.1080/24704067.2022.2031249

Cerebralpalsy.org.uk. (2022) What is cerebral palsy? www.cerebralpalsy.org.uk/cerebral-palsy.html

Connick, M.J., Beckman, E., & Tweedy, S.M. (2018). Evolution and development of best practice in Paralympic classification. In I. Brittain, & A. Beacom (Eds.), *The Palgrave handbook of Paralympic studies* (pp. 389-416). Palgrave.

Craven, Sir P. (2006). Paralympic athletes inspiring and exciting the world. Presentation at the XIXth British National Olympic Academy, Greenwich, UK on April 29, 2006.

DePauw, K.P., & Gavron, S.J. (2005). *Disability and sport* (2nd ed.), Human Kinetics.

Dunn, J.M., & Sherrill, C. (1996). Movement and its implication for individuals with disabilities. *Quest, 48*(3), 378-91.

Goodman, S. (1986). *Spirit of Stoke Mandeville: The story of Sir Ludwig Guttmann*. Collins.

Groff, G.D., Lundberg, N.R., & Zabriskie, R.B. (2009). Influence of adapted sport on quality of life: Perceptions of athletes with cerebral palsy. *Journal of Disability and Rehabilitation, 31*(4), 318-326.

Guttmann, L. (1976). *Textbook of sport for the disabled*. HM and M Publishers.

Guttmann. L. (1952). On the way to an international sports movement for the paralysed. *The Cord, 5*(3) 7-23.

International Games Stoke Mandeville (1955). *The Cord, 7*(5), 7-16.

IPC. (2019). International Paralympic Committee strategic plan 2019-2022. www.paralympic.org/publications

IPC. (2006). *Paralympic Winter Games 1976-2006: Örnsköldsvik-Torino*. RLC.

IPC. (2022a). Eligible impairment types in the Paralympic movement. www.paralympic.org/classification

IPC. (2022b). Results. www.paralympic.org/pyeongchang-2018/results

IPC. (2022c). Results. www.paralympic.org/tokyo-2020/results

Legg, D., Emes, C., Stewart, D., & Steadward, R. (2002). Historical overview of the Paralympics, Special Olympics and Deaflympics. *Palaestra, 20.1* (Winter 2002), 30-35, 56.

Legg, D., Fay, T., Wolff, E., & Hums, M. (2015). The International Olympic Committee—International Paralympic Committee relationship: Past, present and future. *Journal of Sport and Social Issues, 39*(5), 371-395.

Lockwood, R., & Lockwood, A. (2007). *Rolling back the years: A history of wheelchair sports in Western Australia*. Wheelchair Sports, WA.

McCann, C. (1996). Sports for the disabled: The evolution from rehabilitation to competitive sport. *British Journal of Sports Medicine, 30*(4), 279-80.

Merchant, W.A. (1954). The first sister of the spinal centre remembers, *The Cord, 6*(4), 51.

Misener, L., Darcy, S., Legg, D., & Gilbert, K. (2013). Beyond Olympic legacy: Understanding Paralympic legacy through a thematic analysis. *Journal of Sport Management, 27*, 329-341.

NPHT. (2022). What we do. www.paralympic.org.au/about-us/history-project/

Paralympics Australia. (2022). History project. www .paralympic.org.au/about-us/history-project/

Peers, D. (2012). Patients, athletes, freaks: Paralympism and the reproduction of disability. *Journal of Sport & Social Issues, 36*, 295-316.

Pickering, F.L. (2005). Competitive sports, disability, and problems of justice in sports. *Journal of the Philosophy of Sport, 32*, 127-132.

Purdue, D.E.J., & Howe, P.D. (2012). See the sport, not the disability: Exploring the Paralympic paradox. *Qualitative Research in Sport, Exercise and Health, 4*, 189-205.

Sainsbury, T. (1998). The Paralympic movement. Paper presented at the British Olympic Academy, Wembley Hilton Hotel, London.

Scruton, J. (1956). International Stoke Mandeville Games, *The Cord, 8*(4), 7-21.

Scruton, J. (1957). The 1957 International Stoke Mandeville Games, *The Cord, 9*(4), 7-28.

Scruton, J. (1968). History of sport for the paralysed, *The Cord, 20*(2), 14-17.

Scruton, J. (1998). *Stoke Mandeville: Road to the Paralympics*. The Peterhouse Press.

Shearman, M. (1889). *The badminton library (athletics and football)*. Longman, Green and Co.

Stoke Mandeville calling (1949). *The Cord, 2*(4), 34-35.

The 1960 International Stoke Mandeville Games for the Paralysed in Rome (1960). *The Cord, Special Edition, 14*.

USOPM. (2022). Inside the museum. https://usopm.org /plan-your-visit/inside-the-museum/

CHAPTER 5

20 U.S.C. 1412(a)(5). *Individuals with Disabilities Education Act* (IDEA)

Americans with Disabilities Act of 1990, 42 U.S.C. § 12101-12213 (1990).

Bailey v. Board of Commissioners, 427 F. Supp. 3d 806 (E.D. La. 2019).

Board of Education of Hendrick Hudson Cent. Sch. Dist, Westchester Cty. V. Rowley, 458 U.S. 176 (1982).

Caruso v. Blockbuster-Sony Music Entm't Ctr. At Waterfront, 193 F.3d 730 (3d Cir. 1999).

Clark v. Simms, 2009 U.S. Dist. LEXIS 29027 (W.D. Va. 2009).

Colker, R. (2000, July 4). ADA Title III. A fragile compromise. *Berkley Journal of Employment and Labor Law, 21*, 377.

Cooper, J., & Whittle, R. (1998). Enforcing the rights and freedoms of disabled people: The role of transnational law. *Mountbatten Journal of Legal Studies, 2*(2), 1-21.

Court of Arbitration for Sport. (2021, June 11). Media release: The Court of Arbitration for Sport (CAS) dismisses the 2nd appeal of Blake Leeper. TAS-CAS .org. www.tas-cas.org/fileadmin/user_upload/CAS _Media_Release_7930.pdf

Convention on the Rights of Persons with Disabilities. (2008a). Preamble. https://treaties.un.org/doc /Publication/CTC/Ch_IV_15.pdf

Convention on the Rights of Persons with Disabilities. (2008b). Article 30. https://treaties.un.org/doc/Publication/CTC/Ch_IV_15.pdf

Dennin v. Connecticut Interscholastic Athletic Conference, 913 F. Supp. 663 (D. Conn. 1996).

Eadens, S. (2019, April 1). After lawsuit, Wrigley includes more wheelchair seating in latest renovations. *Chicago Sun Times*. https://chicago.suntimes .com/2019/ 4/1/18482506/after-lawsuit-wrigley -includes-more-wheelchair-seating-in-latest -renovations

Feldman v. Pro Football, Inc. 579 F. Supp. 2d 697 (S.D. Md., 2008).

Gershman, D. (2008, October 29). Disabled fans cheer new handicapped seating at Michigan Stadium. *Ann Arbor News*. www.mlive.com/news/ann-arbor/index .ssf/2008/10/disabled_fans_cheer_new_handic.html

Green. (2020, March 10). Disabilities law and reasonable accommodations in sports. *NFHS.org*. www.nfhs .org/articles/disabilities-law-and-reasonable -accommodations-in-sports

Hayes, P. (2022, May 9). U.S. Tennis Association seeks to dismiss disability bias suit. *Bloomberg Law*. www .denleacarton.com/wp-content/uploads/2022/05/u -s-tennis-association-seeks-to-dismiss-disability -bias-suit-11-May-2022.pdf?x48268

Individuals with Disabilities Education Act, 20 U.S.C. § 1400 (2004).

Independent Living Resources v. Oregon Arena Corp., 982 F. Supp. 698 (D. Ore. 1997).

Jewett, A. (2022, June 29). DraftKings complaint alleges website inaccessible to visually impaired, blind. *Topclassactions.com*. https://topclassactions.com /disability-class-action-lawsuit/draftkings -complaint-alleges-website-inaccessible-to-visually -impaired-blind/

Karlik, M. (2020, April 16). Colorado soccer club settles disability discrimination claim. *ColoradoPolitics .com*. www.coloradopolitics.com/news/colorado -soccer-club-settles-disability-discrimination-claim /article_f3e3b9c4-801a-11ea-89ae-33760474cd84.html

Kempf v. Michigan High School Athletic Association, (2015, December 11). Consent Decree. Case No: 2:15-CV-14227 (E.D. Mi., 2015). https://my.mhsaa.com /portals/0/Documents/WR/sign%20language.pdf

Klein, D. (2021, January 27). Website ADA lawsuit files against Golden State Warriors. *KMT.llp*. https:// kleinmoynihan.com/website-ada-lawsuit-filed -against-golden-state-warriors/

Kramer, A. (2015, November 27). Lawsuits mount over website accessibility. *Ebglaw.com*. www.ebglaw.com/wp-content/uploads/2015/12/Stein-Joshua-ADA-Web-Accessibility-BNA.pdf

Kozlarz, J. (2019, December 10). Wrigley Field renovations under federal scrutiny for potential accessibility violations. *Chicago Curbed*. https://chicago.curbed.com/ 2019/12/10/21003390/wrigley-field-renovation-wheelchair-accessible-review-lawsuit

Landis v Wash. State Major League Baseball Stadium Pub. Facilities Dist., 403 F. Supp. 3d 907 (W.D. Wash. 2021).

Landis v. Wash. State Maj. Baseball Stadium Pub. Facilities Dist. Baseball of Seattle, Inc., 2021 U.S. App. LEXIS 26365 (9th Cir. 2021).

Miller v. California Speedway Corp., 536 F.3d 1020 (9th Cir. 2006).

Mills v. Board of Education of District of Columbia, 348 F. Supp. 866 (D. DC 1972).

National Consortium for Physical Education for Individuals with Disabilities. (2021). NCPEID's guidance for administers regarding adapted physical education service delivery. www.ncpeid.org/assets/Fall21/NCPEID%20Guidance%20Doc%20for%20Administrators.pdf

National Consortium for Physical Education for Individuals with Disabilities. (2022). 15 standards of specialized knowledge. www.ncpeid.org/apens-15-standards

Peers, D. (2018). Sport and social movements by and for disability and deaf communities: Important differences in self-determination, politicization, and activism. In I Brittain, A. Beacom (eds.), *The Palgrave Handbook of Paralympic Studies*. https://doi.org/10.1057/978-1-137-47901-3_5

PGA Tour, Inc. v. Martin, 532 U.S. 661 (2001).

Pritchard v. FHSAA, 371 F. Supp. 3d 1081 (2019).

Paralyzed Veterans of Am. V.D.C. Arena L.P., 117 F.3d 579, 326 U.S. App. D.C. 25 (D.C. Cir. 1997).

Pennsylvania Ass'n for Retarded Children v. Commonwealth of Pennsylvania, 343 F. Supp. 279 (D. Pa. 1972).

Pistorius v. International Association of Athletics Federations (IAAF), CAS 2008/A/1480 (2008).

Sandison v. Michigan High Sch. Athletic Ass'n, 64 F.3d 1026 (6th Cir. 1995).

Salsiccia v. Sharks Sports & Entertainment LLC, 2019 U.S. Dist. LEXIS 163570 (N.D. Calif. 2019).

Section 504 of the Rehabilitation Act of 1973, 29 U.S.C. § 794 (2015).

Section 504 Implementing Regulations, Title 34 C.F.R. Part 104 (1980).

Seidel, J. (2022, July 14). Chicago's U.S. attorney sues Chicago Cubs over ADA compliance in Wrigley Field renovation. *Chicago Sun Times.com*. https://chicago.suntimes.com/news/2022/7/14/23216287/chicago-cubs-wrigley-field-renovation-ada-lawsuit-wheelchair-accessibility

SHAPE America. (2018). Eligibility criteria for adapted physical education services. www.shapeamerica.org/uploads/pdfs/2018/position-statements/Eligibility-Criteria-for-Adapted-PE_rebranded_final.pdf

Stein, M.A., & Lord, J. (2008, December 8). Future prospects for the United Nations Convention on the Rights of Persons with Disabilities. *Brill Online*. https://brill.com/abstract/book/edcoll/9789004180802/Bej.9789004169715.i-320_003.xml

United Nations. (2022). UN Treaty Collection, 15. Convention on the Rights of Persons with Disabilities. https://treaties.un.org/Pages/ViewDetails.aspx?src=TREATY&mtdsg_no=IV-15&chapter=4&clang=_en

United States of America v. Ellerbe Becket, Inc., 976 F. Supp. 1262 (D. Minn. 1997).

U.S. Access Board (2003). *Guide to the ADA Accessibility Standards*. https://www.access-board.gov/ada/guides/

U.S. Department of Justices. (n.d.a). ADA Title III Technical Assistance Manual Covering Public Accommodations and Commercial Facilities. https://www.ada.gov/taman3.html

U.S. Department of Justice. (n.d.b). Accessible stadiums. www.ada.gov/sta dium.txt

U.S. Department of Justice. (1993). *ADA Title III Technical Assistance Manual Covering Public Accommodations and Commercial Facilities* (1993). www.ada.gov/taman3.html (1993 TAM)

U.S. Department of Justice. (1994). *Title III Technical Assistance Manual 1994 Supplement* www.ada.gov/taman3up.html

U.S. Department of Justice. (1996). *Accessible Stadiums*. www.ada.gov/stadium.pdf

U.S. Department of Justice. (2002, November). Settlement agreement between the USA and the Consolidated City of Indianapolis, Department of Parks and Recreation. www.justice.gov/crt/settlement-agreement-between-united-states-america-and-consolidated-city-indianapolisdepartment

U.S. Department of Justice. (2010). ADA 2010 revised requirements: Ticket sales. www.ada.gov/ticketing_2010.htm

U.S. Department of Justice. (2010, September 15). 2010 ADA Standards of Accessible Design. www.ada.gov/regs2010/2010ADAStandards/2010ADAStandards_prt.pdf

U.S. Department of Education. (2013, January 25). *Dear Colleague Letter*. www2.ed.gov/about/offices/list/ocr/letters/colleague-201301-504.html

U.S. Department of Justice. (2015, July). Frequently Asked Questions about Service Animals and the ADA, Q17. www.ada.gov/regs2010/service_animal_qa.pdf

U.S. Department of Justice. (2020, February 24). Ticket Sales. www.ada.gov/ticketing_2010.htm

U.S. Department of Justice. (2020, March). Settlement agreement between the USA and Colorado Rush Soccer Club. www.ada.gov/colorado_rush_sa.html

Weber, M.C. (2000). Disability and the law of welfare: A post-integrationist examination. *University of Illinois Law Review, 2000*, 889-956.

Weston, M.A. (2017). The international right to sport for people with disabilities. *Marquette Sports Law Review, 28*(1), 1-35. https://scholarship.law.marquette.edu/cgi/viewcontent.cgi?article=1717&context=sportslaw

Wittmer, S. (2021, July 20). CAS award in Blake Leeper case upheld (Swiss Supreme Court). *Lexology.com.* www.lexology.com/library/detail.aspx?g=ecb13538-f5ca-4d79-be07-8478d3c703d2

Wolverton, B. (2007, October 31). Education Department accuses U. of Michigan of broad violations of disabilities law in stadium changes. *Chronicle of Higher Education.* http://chronicle.com/daily/2007/10/557n.htm

Wright, P.W.D., & Wright, P.D. (2007). Special Education Law, 2nd Ed. Harbor Law Press: Hartfield, VA.

Wright, P.W.D., & Wright, P.D. (2021). Physical education for students with disabilities. Wrightslaw.com. www.wrightslaw.com/info/pe.index.html

CHAPTER 6

Barnes, C. (1994). *Disabled people in Britain and discrimination* (2nd ed.). Hurst and Co.

Beacom, A., French, L., & Kendall, S. (2016). Reframing impairment? Continuity and change in media representations of disability through the Paralympic Games. *International Journal of Sport Communication, 9*(1), 42-62. https://doi.org/10.1123/ijsc.2015-0077

Blinde, E.M., & McCallister, S.G. (1999). Women, disability, and sport and physical fitness activity: The intersection of gender and disability dynamics. *Research Quarterly for Exercise and Sport, 70*(3), 303-312. https://doi.org:10.1080/02701367.1999.10608049

Brittain, I. (2004). Perceptions of disability and their impact upon involvement in sport for people with disabilities at all levels. *Journal of Sport and Social Issues, 28*(4), 429-452. https://doi.org/10.1177/0193723504268729

Brookes, M. (2019). The Singaporean Paralympics and its media portrayal: Real sport? Men-only? *Communication & Sport, 7*(4), 446-465. https://doi.org/10.1177/2167479518784278

Brookes, M., & Khoo, S. (2021). Insider perspectives on the sustainability of the Malaysian and Singaporean Paralympic movements. *Sustainability, 13*(5557), 1-12. https://doi.org/10.3390/su13105557

Bruce, T. (2014). Us and them: The influence of discourses of nationalism on media coverage of the Paralympics. *Disability & Society, 29*(9), 1443-1459. https://doi.org/10.1080/09687599.2013.816624

CBC Media Centre. (2017, November 29). *CBC/Radio-Canada remains Canada's Paralympic network through 2020 thanks to multi-games partnership with the Canadian Paralympic Committee.* www.cbc.ca/mediacentre/press-release/cbc-radio-canada-remains-canadasparalympic-network-through-2020-thanks-to

CBC Media Centre. (2021, August 10). *CBC marks record-breaking digital audiences for Tokyo 2020, with CBC also ranking as the most-watched TV network in Canada throughout the Games.* www.cbc.ca/mediacentre/press-release/cbc-marks-record-breaking-digital-audiences-for-tokyo-2020

CBC Sports. (2021, July 19). *Here's how to watch the 3,775 hours of Olympic coverage from CBC, partners.* www.cbc.ca/sports/olympics/cbc-and-partners-to-broadcast-3775-hours-of-olympic-coverage-heres-how-to-watch-1.6108316?__vfz=medium%3Dsharebar

Channel 4. (2022, February 7). *Channel 4 announces 100% disabled presenting team for Winter Paralympics.* www.channel4.com/press/news/channel-4-announces-100-disabled-presenting-team-winter-paralympics

Cherney, J.L., & Lindemann, K. (2019). Ableism and Paralympic politics: Media stereotypes and the rhetoric of disability sport. In D.A. Grano, & M.L. Butterworth (Eds.), *Sport, Rhetoric, and Political Struggle* (pp. 143-157). Peter Lang.

Crow, L. (2014). Scroungers and superhumans: Images of disability from the Summer of 2012: A visual inquiry. *Journal of Visual Culture, 13*(2), 168-181. https://doi.org/10.1177/1470412914529109

Cumberbatch, G., & Negrine, R. (1992). *Images of disability on television.* Routledge.

Darcy, S. (2003). The politics of disability and access: The Sydney 2000 Games experience. *Disability & Society, 18*(6), 737-757.

DePauw, K.P. (1997). The (in)visibility of disability: Cultural contexts and sporting bodies. *Quest, 49*(4), 416-430. https://doi.org/10.1080/00336297.1997.10484258

Goggin, G., & Hutchins, B. (2017). Media and the Paralympics: Progress, visibility, and paradox. In S. Darcy, S. Frawley, & D. Adair (Eds.), *Managing the Paralympics* (pp. 217-239). Palgrave Macmillan UK. https://doi.org/10.1057/978-1-137-43522-4_10

Goggin, G., & Newell, C. (2000). Crippling Paralympics? Media, disability and Olympism. *Media International Australia Incorporating Culture and Policy, 97*(1), 71-83. https://doi.org/10.1177/1329878x0009700110

Golden, A. (2003). An analysis of the dissimilar coverage of the 2002 Olympics and Paralympics: Frenzied pack journalism versus the empty press room. *Disability Studies Quarterly, 23*(3/4). https://doi.org/10.18061/dsq.v23i3/4.437

Goodley, D. (2011). *Disability studies: An interdisciplinary introduction*. SAGE.

Haller, B. (2000). If they limp, they lead? News representations and the hierarchy of disability images. In D. Braithwaite, & T. Thompson (Eds.), *Handbook of Communication and People with Disabilities* (pp. 273-288). Lawrence Erlbaum Associates.

Haralambos, M., & Holborn, M. (2000). *Sociology: Themes and perspectives* (5th ed.). Collins.

Haraway, D.J. (1991). *Simians, cyborgs, and women: The reinvention of nature*. Routledge.

Hardin, M., & Hardin, B. (2005). Performance or participation. Pluralism or hegemony? Images of disability and gender in *Sports 'N Spokes* magazine. *Disability Studies Quarterly, 25*(4). https://doi.org/10.18061/dsq.v25i4.606

Hargreaves, J.A., & Hardin, B. (2009). Women wheelchair athletes: Competing against media stereotypes. *Disability Studies Quarterly, 29*(2). https://doi.org/10.18061/dsq.v29i2.920

Hartnett, A. (2000). Escaping the 'evil avenger' and the 'supercrip': Images of disability in popular television. *The Irish Communications Review, 8*, 21-29. https://doi.org/10.21427/D7271M.

Howe, P.D. (2008a). *The cultural politics of the Paralympic movement: Through an anthropological lens*. Routledge.

Howe, P.D. (2008b). From inside the newsroom: Paralympic media and the 'production' of elite disability. *International Review for the Sociology of Sport, 43*(2), 135-150. https://doi.org/10.1177/1012690208095376

Howe, P.D. (2011). Cyborg and supercrip: The Paralympics technology and the (dis)empowerment of disabled athletes. *Sociology, 45*(5), 868-882. https://doi.org/10.1177/0038038511413421

Howe, P.D., & Silva, C.F. (2017). Challenging 'normalcy': Possibilities and pitfalls of Paralympic bodies. *South African Journal for Research in Sport, Physical Education and Recreation, 39*(1-2), 191-204.

Legg, D., & Steadward, R. (2011). The Paralympic Games and 60 years of change (1948-2008): Unification and restructuring from a disability and medical model to sport-based competition. *Sport in Society, 14*(9), 1099-1115. https://doi.org/10.1080/17430437.2011.614767

Maika, M., & Danylchuk, K. (2016). Representing Paralympians: The 'other' athletes in Canadian print media coverage of London 2012. *The International Journal of the History of Sport, 33*(4), 401-417. https://doi.org/10.1080/09523367.2016.1160061

Marques, R.F.R., Gutierrez, G.L., Bettine de Almeida, M.A., Nunomura, M., & Menezes, R.P. (2014). Media approach to Paralympic sports: The view of Brazilian athletes. *Movimento: Revista Da Escola de Educação Física, 20*(3), 25. https://doi.org/10.22456/1982-8918. 41955

Misener, L. (2013). A media frames analysis of the legacy discourse for the 2010 Winter Paralympic Games. *Communication & Sport, 1*(4), 342-364. https://doi.org/10.1177/2167479512469354

NBC. (2021, September 9). *Two most-watched Paralympics telecasts on record highlight Tokyo Paralympics viewership milestones across NBC Universal*. https://nbcsportsgrouppressbox.com/2021/09/09/two-most-watched-paralympics-telecasts-on-record-highlight-tokyo-paralympics-viewership-milestones-across-nbcuniversal/

Pearson E., & Misener, L. (2022). Informing future Paralympic media approaches: The perspective of Canadian Paralympic athletes. *Communication & Sport*. https://doi.org/10.1177/21674795221103410

Pearson, E., & Misener, L. (2019). Canadian media representations of para-athletes at the 2016 Paralympic Games. *Olympika: The International Journal of Olympic Studies, 28*, 1-28.

Peers, D. (2009). (Dis)empowering Paralympic histories: Absent athletes and disabling discourses. *Disability & Society, 24*(5), 653-665. https://doi.org/10.1080/09687590903011113

Peers, D. (2012). Interrogating disability: The (de)composition of a recovering Paralympian. *Qualitative Research in Sport, Exercise and Health, 4*(2), 175-188. https://doi.org/10.1080/2159676X.2012.685101

Pullen, E., Jackson, & D., Silk, M (2022). Paralympic broadcasting and social change: An integrated mixed method approach to understanding the Paralympic audience in the UK. *Television & Media, 23*(4), 368-388. https://doi.org/10.1177/15274764211004407

Pullen, E., Jackson, D., Silk, M., & Scullion, R. (2018). Re-presenting the Paralympics: (Contested) philosophies, production practices and the hypervisibility of disability. *Media, Culture & Society, 41*(4), 465-481. https://doi.org/10.1177/0163443718799399

Purdue, D.E.J., & Howe, P.D. (2012). See the sport, not the disability: Exploring the Paralympic paradox. *Qualitative Research in Sport, Exercise and Health, 4*(2), 189-205. https://doi.org/10.1080/21596 76X.2012.685102

Quinn, N., & Yoshida, K. (2016). More than sport: Representations of ability and gender by the Canadian Broadcasting Corporation (CBC) of the 2004 Summer Paralympic Games. *Canadian Journal of Disability Studies, 5*(4), 103-129. https://doi.org/10.15353/cjds.v5i4.316

Rees, L., Robinson, P., & Shields, N. (2018). A major sporting event or an entertainment show? A content analysis of Australian television coverage of the 2016 Olympic and Paralympic Games. *Sport in Society, 21*(12), 1974-1989. https://doi.org/10.1080/1743043 7.2018.1445996

Rees, L., Robinson, P., & Shields, N. (2019). Media portrayal of elite athletes with disability—A systematic review. *Disability and Rehabilitation, 41*(4), 374-381. https://doi.org/10.1080/09638288.2017.1397775

Schell, L.A. & Rodriguez, S. (2001). Subverting bodies/ambivalent representations: Media analysis of Paralympian, Hope Lewellen. *Sociology of Sport Journal, 18*(1), 127-135. https://doi.org/10.1123/ssj.18.1.127

Silva, C.F., & Howe, P.D. (2012). The (in)validity of supercrip representation of Paralympian athletes. *Journal of Sport and Social Issues, 36*(2), 174-194. https://doi.org/10.1177/0193723511433865

Smith, B., & Bundon, A. (2018). Disability models: Explaining and understanding disability sport in different ways. In I. Brittain, & A. Beacom (Eds.), *The Palgrave Handbook of Paralympic Studies* (pp. 15-34). Palgrave Macmillan Limited.

Swartz, L., & Watermeyer, B. (2008). Cyborg anxiety: Oscar Pistorius and the boundaries of what it means to be human. *Disability and Society, 23*(2), 187-190.

Tynedal, J., & Wolbring, G. (2013). Paralympics and its athletes through the lens of the New York *Times. Sports, 1*(1), 13-36. https://doi.org/10.3390/sports1010013

United Nations (2006). *Convention on the rights of persons with disabilities.* www.un.org/esa/socdev/enable/rights/convtexte.htm

Weaving, C., & Samson, J. (2018). The naked truth: Disability, sexual objectification, and the ESPN Body Issue. *Journal of the Philosophy of Sport, 45*(1), 83-100.

Wedgwood, N. (2014). Hahn versus Guttmann: Revisiting "sports and the political movement of disabled persons." *Disability & Society, 29*(1), 129-142. https://doi.org/10.1080/09687599.2013.776488

WHO. (2023). *Disability* https://www.who.int/news-room/fact-sheets/detail/disability-and-health

CHAPTER 7

Allan, V. (2019, March 13). *Do para-athletes face abuse trying to prove their disabilities?* News Decoder. https://news-decoder.com/para-athletes-classification-abuse/

Altman, H. (2020, May 29). How Jon Stewart saved the Warrior Games from the clutches of an evildoer! *Military Times.* www.militarytimes.com/news/your-military/2020/05/29/2020-warrior-games-scrubbed-by-marine-corps-over-covid-19-concerns/

Asian Paralympic Committee. (2021a). *Asian Paralympic Committee launch new strategic plan.* https://asianparalympic.org/news-dec292019/

Asian Paralympic Committee. (2021b). *Member nations.* https://asianparalympic.org/members/

Asian Paralympic Committee. (2021c). *Our history.* https://asianparalympic.org/our-history/

Asian Paralympic Committee. (2021d). *Vision & mission.* https://asianparalympic.org/vision-mission/

BBC News. (2013, May 13). *Prince Harry starts off Warrior Games event in U.S.* www.bbc.com/news/22504970

BBC Reality Check Team. (2021, November 30). *Commonwealth: Seven things you might not know.* BBC News. www.bbc.com/news/uk-43715079

Burke, P. (2022, January 14). *Pereira appointed IOC's first head of virtual sport.* Inside the Games. https://www.insidethegames.biz/articles/1117787/pereira-ioc-head-virtual-sports

Canadian Olympic Committee. (2022). *FAQ: What are the Pan American Games?* Team Canada. https://olympic.ca/faq-what-are-the-pan-american-games/

Commonwealth Games Federation. (2020a). *David Grevemberg: Commonwealth sport—A movement in transformation.* https://thecgf.com/stories/david-grevemberg-commonwealth-sport-movement-transformation

Commonwealth Games Federation. (2020b). *Para-sport.* https://thecgf.com/our-relevance/para-sports

Commonwealth Games Federation. (2020c). *The Commonwealth Games Federation.* https://thecgf.com/about

Defense Visual Information Distribution Service. (2016). *DVIDS—2016 DoD Warrior Games.* DVIDS. www.dvidshub.net/feature/warriorgames2016

Department of Defense. (n.d.). *Warrior Games.* www.dodwarriorgames.com/about/about/#

Disability Sport. (2014). *FESPIC Games.* www.disabilitysport.org.uk/fespic-games.html

Dowdeswell, A. (2022, January 16). *Parsons offers full IPC commitment to first-ever African Para Games.* Inside the Games. www.insidethegames.biz/articles/1117469/parsons-african-paralympics-games-ipc

Dunsar Media Company Limited. (n.d.). *History of Asian Games.* Inside the Games. www.insidethegames.biz/articles/1059784/history-of-asian-games

ETH Zürich. (2021a). *CYBATHLON 2016.* CYBATHLON ETH Zürich. https://cybathlon.ethz.ch/en/projects-events/edition/cybathlon-2016

ETH Zürich. (2021b). *CYBATHLON competition.* CYBATHLON ETH Zürich. https://cybathlon.ethz.ch/en/cybathlon/competition

ETH Zürich. (2021c). *CYBATHLON disciplines.* CYBATHLON ETH Zürich. https://cybathlon.ethz.ch/en/cybathlon/disciplines

ETH Zürich. (2021d). *This is CYBATHLON.* CYBATHLON ETH Zürich. https://cybathlon.ethz.ch/en/cybathlon

ETH Zürich. (2021e). *This was the CYBATHLON 2020 Global Edition.* CYBATHLON ETH Zürich. https://cybathlon.ethz.ch/en/news/4176/this-was-the-cybathlon-2020-global-edition

ETH Zürich. (2021f, November 2). *CYBATHLON 2024: Two new disciplines and a new event format for a world without barriers.* CYBATHLON ETH Zürich. https://cybathlon.ethz.ch/en/news/5159/cybathlon-2024-zwei-neue-disziplinen-und-ein-neues-eventformat-fur-eine-welt-ohn

Forces in Mind Trust. (2020a, June 9). *Continuation of funding for Invictus Games research*. https://www.fim-trust.org/news-policy-item/continuation-of-funding-for-invictus-games-research/

Forces in Mind Trust. (2020b, September 28). *Beyond the finish line: Research insights from the Invictus Games longitudinal study*. https://s31949.pcdn.co/wp-content/uploads/INVICT1.pdf

Forces in Mind Trust. (2020c, September 28). *New research demonstrates the positive impact of participation in the Invictus Games*. www.fim-trust.org/news-policy-item/new-research-demonstrates-the-positive-impact-of-participation-in-the-invictus-games/

Herbison, J., & Latimer-Cheung, A. (2021, September 6). *After the Paralympics: New initiative to get more Canadians involved in power wheelchair sports*. The Conversation. https://theconversation.com/after-the-paralympics-new-initiative-to-get-more-canadians-involved-in-power-wheelchair-sports-167013

Indian Gaming Esports Association. (2021). *About esports—IGEA*. www.igea.gg/about-esports/

Interaction Design Foundation. (n.d.). *What is virtual reality?* The Interaction Design Foundation. www.interaction-design.org/literature/topics/virtual-reality

International Olympic Committee. (2021, August 10). *100 things to know about the Paralympic Games*. https://olympics.com/en/news/100-things-to-know-about-the-paralympic-games-tokyo-2020

International Paralympic Committee. (n.d.a). *About us*. www.paralympic.org/ipc/who-we-are

International Paralympic Committee. (n.d.b). *Governing board*. www.paralympic.org/ipc-governing-board

International Paralympic Committee. (n.d.c). *Handbook*. www.paralympic.org/ipc-handbook

International Paralympic Committee. (n.d.d). *History of the Parapan American Games*. www.paralympic.org/lima-2019/parapans-history

International Paralympic Committee. (n.d.e). *IPC Classification—Paralympic categories & how to qualify*. www.paralympic.org/classification

International Paralympic Committee. (n.d.f). *Paralympic Sports—List of Summer and Winter Para ports*. www.paralympic.org/sports

International Paralympic Committee. (n.d.g). *Paralympics history—Evolution of the Paralympic Movement*. www.paralympic.org/ipc/history

International Paralympic Committee. (2016, November 24). *Athletes with high support need—Get in touch*. www.paralympic.org/news/athletes-high-support-needs-get-touch

International Paralympic Committee. (2021, August). *IPC guide to para and IPC terminology*. Paralympic.Org. www.paralympic.org/sites/default/files/2021-08/IPC%20Guide%20to%20Para%20and%20IPC%20Terminology.pdf

International Wheelchair Basketball Federation. (n.d.). *Hanghzhou 2022 Asian Para Games*. IWBF. https://iwbf.org/event/hanghzhou-2022-asian-para-games/

Invictus Games Foundation. (2016a). *The Invictus Games Foundation*. https://invictusgamesfoundation.org/foundation/

Invictus Games Foundation. (2016b). *The Invictus Games story*. https://invictusgamesfoundation.org/foundation/story/

Invictus Games Foundation. (2018, February 15). *Uncovering the impact of participation in the Invictus Games*. https://invictusgamesfoundation.org/uncovering-the-impact-of-participation-in-the-invictus-games/

Invictus Games Foundation. (2019a). *History*. Invictus Games. https://invictusgames2020.com/en/about/history/

Invictus Games Foundation. (2019b). *Invictus Games—Invictus Games The Hague 2020*. Invictus Games. https://invictusgames2020.com/en/

Invictus Games Foundation. (2020a). *Research demonstrates the positive impact of participation in the Invictus Games*. https://invictusgamesfoundation.org/research-demonstrates-the-positive-impact-of-participation-in-the-invictus-games/

Invictus Games Foundation. (2020b, July 27). *The Invictus Games The Hague will be held from May 29 to June 5, 2021*. https://invictusgames2020.com/en/news/the-invictus-games-the-hague-will-be-held-from-may-29-to-june-5-2021/

Invictus Games Foundation. (2021a). *About us*. https://invictusgames.in.ua/en/about-us

Invictus Games Foundation. (2021b). Invictus Games Düsseldorf 2023. https://invictusgames23.de/

Invictus Games Orlando 2016. (2016). *MASI (Military Adaptive Sports Inc.)*. https://invictusgames2016.org/usa-host-2/

Invictus Games Toronto. (2017). *Venues*. www.invictusgames2017.com/venues/

Lima2019. (2019). *Parapan American Games*. www.lima2019.pe/en/lima-2019/juegos-parapanamericanos

Mackay, D. (2010, December 12). *Emotional opening ceremony for Asian para games*. Inside the Games. www.insidethegames.biz/articles/109061/emotional-opening-ceremony-for-asian-para-games

Mackay, D. (2021, March 18). *Grevemberg joins Centre for Sport and Human Rights in new role*. Inside the Games. www.insidethegames.biz/articles/1105537/grevemberg-joins-cshr-in-new-role

Military Times. (2019, July 1). If you want to be inspired, check out the Warrior Games. *Military Times*. www.militarytimes.com/news/2019/07/01/the-2019-warrior-games-drew-record-number-of-athletes-and-crowds/

NCCR Robotics. (2021). *Cybathlon*. https://nccr-robotics.ch/outreach/cybathlon/

Nelsen, M. (2021, Dec. 20). *The Saudi Arabian Olympic Committee has merged with the Paralympic Committee of Saudi Arabia to form the Saudi Olympic & Paralympic Committee. The new organization will oversee the activities of the Olympic and Paralympic movements in Saudi Arabia.* Around the Rings. www.infobae.com/aroundtherings/articles/2021/12/20/saudi-arabia-merges-olympic-and-paralympic-bodies-into-single-entity/

Nielson Sports. (2016). *Paralympics and para-sports: The rise of para-sports, the growth of the Paralympic Games and the opportunities for fans and brands.* Nielson. www.nielsen.com/wp-content/uploads/sites/3/2019/04/nielsen-sports-paralympic-report-2016.pdf

O'Mara, J., & Richter, A. (2014). *Global diversity and inclusion benchmarks: Standards for organizations around the world.* Omaraassoc. www.omaraassoc.com/pdf/GDIB_2014_Standard_A4_Version.pdf

Paris2024. (2021). *The history of the Paralympic Games.* www.paris2024.org/en/the-history-of-the-paralympic-games/

Pavitt, M. (2021, November 25). *Asian Paralympic Committee President hopes Hangzhou 2022 can boost inclusion.* Inside the Games. www.insidethegames.biz/articles/1115925/apc-president-hangzhou-2022-hopes

Pimer, D. (2019, June 21). U.S. Olympic Committee changes its name to U.S. Olympic and Paralympic Committee. *Swimming World.* www.swimmingworld-magazine.com/news/u-s-olympic-committee-changes-name-to-u-s-olympic-paralympic-committee/

Purdue, D.E., & Howe, P.D. (2013). Who's in and who is out? Legitimate bodies within the Paralympic Games. *Sociology of Sport Journal, 30*(1), 24-40. https://doi.org/10.1123/ssj.30.1.24

Ruiz, S. (2021). *Pandemic prompts cancellation of DoD's Warrior Games for 2nd year in row.* Military.Com. www.military.com/military-fitness/pandemic-prompts-cancellation-of-dods-2021-warrior-games-2nd-year-row

Sanchez, R. (2020, March 3). Dirty pool at the Paralympics: Will cheating ruin the Games? *Sports Illustrated.* www.si.com/olympics/2020/03/03/paralympiccheating

Slocum, C., Kim, S., & Blauwet, C. (2018). Women and athletes with high support needs in Paralympic sport: Progress and further opportunities for under-represented populations. In I. Brittain and A. Beacom, *The Palgrave Handbook of Paralympic Studies*, (pp. 371-388). Palgrave. https://doi.org/10.1057/978-1-137-47901-3_17

Smith, R, (2022.). Does Paralympic sport benefit the right athletes? *Ability Magazine.* https://abilitymagazine.com/does-paralympic-sport-benefit-the-right-athletes/

Taylor, D. (2017, October 31). The growth of Paralympic sport into an elite and lucrative competition means allegations of corruption and foul play have also increased. *The Guardian.* www.theguardian.com/sport/2017/oct/31/terrible-coming-age-paralympic-sport

Team Scotland. (2021). *History of the Commonwealth Games.* www.teamscotland.scot/commonwealth-games/history-of-the-commonwealth-games/

The Royal Household. (n.d.). *The Invictus Games.* www.royal.uk/invictus-games

United States Marine Corps. (2015, June 28). *2015 DoD Warrior Games.* www.marines.mil/News/Marines-TV/videoid/412754/dvpTag/basketball/

Wade, S. (2021, August 27). As athletes defy categories, Paralympics strive for fairness. *Christian Science Monitor.* www.csmonitor.com/World/2021/0827/As-athletes-defy-categories-Paralympics-strives-for-fairness

Wood, R. (2010). *History of the Commonwealth Games.* Topend Sports. www.topendsports.com/events/commonwealth-games/history.htm

World Para Athletics. (n.d.). *World Para Athletics classification & categories.* www.paralympic.org/athletics/classification

Wounded Warrior Regiment. (2010). *Inaugural Warrior Games.* Marines. www.marines.mil/portals/1/Publications/WARRIOR%20GAMES%20PT%201.pdf

Wounded Warrior Regiment. (2017). *2017 DoD Warrior Games.* www.woundedwarrior.marines.mil/2017DoDWarriorGames1/

CHAPTER 8

Asunta, P., Hasanen, E., Kiuppis, F., Rintala, P., & McConkey, R. (2022). Life is team play: Social inclusion of people with intellectual disabilities in the context of Special Olympics. *Sport in Society, 25*, 2146-2161. https://doi.org/10.1080/17430437.2022.2037565

Avant, A. (2022). *Leveling the playing field: Comparing the statutory definition of disability to disability in Special Olympics and the Paralympics* (SSRN Scholarly Paper ID 4016852). Social Science Research Network. https://doi.org/10.2139/ssrn.4016852

American Association for Health, Physical Education and Recreation and National Recreation & Park Association. (1968). *Physical education and recreation for handicapped children; Proceedings of a study conference on research and demonstration needs.* AAHPER. https://files.eric.ed.gov/fulltext/ED034345.pdf#page=49

American Psychiatric Association. (n.d.). *What is intellectual disability?* www.psychiatry.org/patients-families/intellectual-disability/what-is-intellectual-disability

Athletes Without Limits. (n.d.) *Mission.* www.athleteswithoutlimits.org/about/mission

Brittain, I. (2016). The Special Olympics, intellectual disability, and the Paralympic Games. *The Paralympic Games explained* (2nd ed., pp. 198-209). Taylor & Francis Group.

Burns, J. (2015). The impact of intellectual disabilities on elite sports performance. *International Review of Sport and Exercise Psychology, 8*, 1-17. https://doi.org/10.1080/1750984X.2015.1068830

Burns, J. (2018). Intellectual disability, Special Olympics and parasport. In A. Beacom, & I. Brittain (Eds.), *The Palgrave Handbook of Paralympic Studies* (pp. 417-437). https://doi.org/10.1057/978-1-137-47901-3_19

Chandan, P., & Dubon, M.E. (2019). Clinical considerations and resources for youth athletes with intellectual disability: A review with a focus on Special Olympics International. *Current Physical Medicine and Rehabilitation Reports, 7*(2), 116-125. https://doi.org/10.1007/s40141-019-0209-1

Foote, C.J., & Collins, B. (2011). You know, Eunice, the world will never be the same after this. *Internal Journal of Special Education, 26*(3), 11. https://files.eric.ed.gov/fulltext/EJ959020.pdf

International Paralympic Committee. (n.d.b). *About the International Paralympic Committee.* www.paralympic.org/ipc/who-we-are

International Paralympic Committee. (n.d.a). *Federations.* www.paralympic.org/ipc/federations

International Paralympic Committee and Special Olympics International. (1988). *Protocol of agreement between the International Olympic Committee and Special Olympics International.* https://media.specialolympics.org/resources/sports-essentials/sport-proclamations/MoU-International-Olympics-Committee.pdf?_ga=2.31572346.514387667.1646670865-644995323.1645023266&_gac=1.85356651.1646670865.Cj0KCQiA95aRBhCsARIsAC2xvfzz4Bjlhrq3U5eaJz_w8hFKFIFh-MB3ByPUJcp0lzRiCsQEkYsMD0IaAlAVEALw_wcB

Lieberman, L.J., & Houston-Wilson, C. (2018). Changing the name of Unified Physical Education. *Journal of Physical Education, Recreation & Dance, 89*(7), 7-8. https://doi.org/10.1080/07303084.2018.1491253

Li, C., & Wu, Y. (2019). Improving Special Olympics volunteers' self-esteem and attitudes towards individuals with intellectual disability. *Journal of Intellectual & Developmental Disability, 44*(1), 35-41. https://doi.org/10.3109/13668250.2017.1310815

McConkey, R., & Menke, S. (2020). The community inclusion of athletes with intellectual disability: A transnational study of the impact of participating in Special Olympics. *Sport in Society*, 1-10. https://doi.org/10.1080/17430437.2020.1807515

McConkey, R., Slater, P., Dubois, L., Shellard, A., & Smith, A. (2020). Engagement with Special Olympics by the general public in 17 countries worldwide. *Sport in Society, 25*(9), 1766-1777. https://doi.org/10.1080/17430437.2020.1830971

Moreau, M., Benhaddou, S., Dard, R., Tolu, S., Hamzé, R., Vialard, F., Movassat, J., & Janel, N. (2021). Metabolic diseases and Down Syndrome: How are they linked together? *Biomedicines, 9*(2), 221. https://doi.org/10.3390/biomedicines9020221

Noel, J. (2018). Recognition and treatment of mood dysregulation in adults with intellectual disability. *The Mental Health Clinician, 8*(6), 264-274. https://doi.org/10.9740/mhc.2018.11.264

Office of the High Commissioner for Human Rights (2021, January 25). *Physical activity and sports under Article 30 of the Convention on the Rights of Persons with Disabilities.* www.ohchr.org/en/calls-for-input/2021/report-physical-activity-and-sports-under-article-30-convention-rights-persons

Rosa's Law, Pub. L. No. 111-256. (2010). www.govinfo.gov/app/details/PLAW-111publ256

Shakespeare, T. (2013). *Disability Rights and Wrongs Revisited* (2nd ed.). Routledge. https://doi.org/10.4324/9781315887456

Shriver, E. (1962). Hope for retarded children. *The Saturday Evening Post*, 71-75.

Simplican, S.C., Leader, G., Kosciulek, J., & Leahy, M. (2015). Defining social inclusion of people with intellectual and developmental disabilities: An ecological model of social networks and community participation. *Research in Developmental Disabilities 38*, 18-29. https://doi:10.1016/j.ridd.2014.10.008

Special Olympics. (2012a). *Assessing players, forming Unified Sports teams and determining the best Unified Sports model.* https://media.specialolympics.org/resources/sports-essentials/unified-sports/Assessing-Players-and-Forming-Unified-Teams.pdf?_ga=2.265472207.1325296815.1646128654-1323125742.1645619447

Special Olympics. (2012b). Comparison among Unified Sports competitive, player development and recreation models. https://media.specialolympics.org/resources/sports-essentials/unified-sports/Unified-Sports-Comparison-All-Three-Models.pdf?_ga=2.258018634.1325296815.1646128654-1323125742.1645619447

Special Olympics. (2019). *North America local program guide.* https://media.specialolympics.org/sona/Resources/SONA-Local-Progam-Guide-July-2019.pdf?_ga=2.266587214.1325296815.1646128654-1323125742.1645619447

Special Olympics (n.d.a). *Article 6.* https://resources.specialolympics.org/governance/special-olympics-general-rules/article-6

Special Olympics. (n.d.b). *Basketball sport rules.* https://media.specialolympics.org/resources/sports-essentials/sport-rules/Sports-Essentials-Basketball-Rules-2020-v4.pdf?_ga=2.89245787.1325296815.1646128654-1323125742.1645619447\

Special Olympics. (n.d.c). *Camp Shriver—The beginning of a movement.* www.specialolympics.org/about/history/camp-shriver

Special Olympics. (n.d.d). *Center for inclusive health.* https://inclusivehealth.specialolympics.org/

Special Olympics. (n.d.e). *Development model for coaches and athletes.* https://resources.specialolympics.org/sports-essentials/development-model-for-coaches-and-athletes

Special Olympics. (n.d.f). Development sports implementation guide: Coaching Special Olympic athletes ages 6-12. https://media.specialolympics.org/resources/sports-essentials/developmental-sports/Developmental-Sports-Young-Athletes.pdf

Special Olympics. (n.d.g). *Divisioning.* https://resources.specialolympics.org/sports-essentials/divisioning

Special Olympics. (n.d.h). *Divisioning-fact sheet.* https://media.specialolympics.org/resources/sports-essentials/divisioning/Divisioning-Fact-Sheet.pdf?_ga=2.56674666.1325296815.1646128654-1323125742.1645619447

Special Olympics. (n.d.i). *Inclusive health.* www.specialolympics.org/our-work/inclusive-health

Special Olympics. (n.d.j). *Leadership teams.* www.specialolympics.org/about/leadership/

Special Olympics. (n.d.k). *Motor activity training program (MATP).* https://media.specialolympics.org/resources/sports-essentials/fact-sheets/FactSheet-MATP.pdf?_ga=2.104426560.1325296815.1646128654-1323125742.1645619447

Special Olympics. (n.d.l). *Our mission.* www.specialolympics.org/about/mission

Special Olympics. (n.d.m). *Out of the shadows: Events leading to the founding of Special Olympics.* www.specialolympics.org/about/history/out-of-the-shadows-events-leading-to-the-founding-of-special-olympics

Special Olympics. (n.d.n). *Rosa's Law signed into law by President Obama.* www.specialolympics.org/stories/news/rosas-law-signed-into-law-by-president-obama

Special Olympics. (n.d.o). *Special Olympics disability language guidelines.* https://media.specialolympics.org/sona/SONA-Language-Guidelines-2019.pdf?_ga=2.24790778.1325296815.1646128654-1323125742.1645619447

Special Olympics. (n.d.p). *Special Olympics official general rules.* https://media.specialolympics.org/resources/leading-a-program/general-rules/Special-Olympics-General-Rules-Amended-2015-8-17.pdf?_ga=2.90487001.299413352.1647001659-1323125742.1645619447

Special Olympics. (n.d.q). *Special Olympics Unified Champion Schools.* www.specialolympics.org/our-work/unified-champion-schools?locale=en

Special Olympics. (n.d.r). *Sports Essentials.* https://resources.specialolympics.org/sportsessentials

Special Olympics (n.d.s). Supplemental document to athlete nomination criteria. www.sotx.org/files/imported/events/scc/usa-games-advancement-criteria.pdf

Special Olympics. (n.d.t). *Unified sports.* https://resources.specialolympics.org/sports-essentials/unified-sports?locale=en

Special Olympics. (n.d.u). *What is intellectual disability?* www.specialolympics.org/about/intellectual-disabilities/what-is-intellectual-disability

Special Olympics. (n.d.v). World games. www.specialolympics.org/our-work/games-and-competition/world-games?locale=en

Special Olympics. (n.d.w). *Youth and school.* https://resources.specialolympics.org/community-building/youth-and-school?locale=en

Special Olympics.(n.d.x). *1960s: The beginning of a worldwide movement.* www.specialolympics.org/about/history/the-beginning-of-a-worldwide-movement

Special Olympics.(n.d.y). *1968 games.* www.specialolympics.org/about/history/1968-games

Special Olympics.(n.d.z). *1970s: A joyful new movement gains momentum.* www.specialolympics.org/about/history/a-joyful-new-movement-gains-momentum

Special Olympics.(n.d.aa). *1980s: Recognition and growth around the world.* www.specialolympics.org/about/history/recognition-and-growth-around-the-world

Special Olympics.(n.d.bb). *1990s: Pushing for inclusion and improved health for people with ID.* www.specialolympics.org/about/history/pushing-for-inclusion-and-improved-health-for-people-with-id

Special Olympics.(n.d.cc). *2000s: The sun never sets on the special Olympics movement.* www.specialolympics.org/about/history/the-sun-never-sets-on-the-special-olympics-movement

Special Olympics. (n.d.dd). *2010s: Building an inclusive world.* www.specialolympics.org/about/history/building-an-inclusive-world

Special Olympics USA Games. (n.d.). *Special Olympics USA Games: Orlando 2022.* NULLwww.2022specialolympicsusagames.org/

Tassé, M.J., Luckasson, R., & Schalock, R.L. (2016). The relation between intellectual functioning and adaptive behavior in the diagnosis of intellectual disability. *Intellectual and developmental disabilities, 54*(6), 381-390. https://doi.org/10.1352/1934-9556-54.6.381

United Nations. (2006). *Convention of the rights of persons with disabilities and optional protocol.* www.un.org/disabilities/documents/convention/convoptprot-e.pdf

United States Department of Education. (2013, January 25). *Dear Colleague Letter: Students with disabilities in extracurricular athletics.* www2.ed.gov/about/offices/list/ocr/letters/colleague-201301-504.pdf

Van Biesen, D., Burns, J., Mactavish, J., Van de Vliet, P., & Vanlandewijck, Y. (2021). Conceptual model of sport-specific classification for para-athletes with intellectual impairment. *Journal of Sports Sciences*, *39*(sup1), 19-29. https://doi.org/10.1080/02640414.2021.1881280

Virtus. (n.d.a). *About-Virtus*. www.virtus.sport/about-virtus

Virtus. (n.d.b). *Athlete eligibility and classification*. www.virtus.sport/applying-for-athlete-eligibilitym

Virtus. (n.d.c). *Governance and policy*. www.virtus.sport/governance-and-policy

Werner, S. (2015). Athletes', parents', and siblings' experiences from the Special Olympics World Games. *Journal of Intellectual & Developmental Disability*, *40*(2), 167-178. https://doi.org/10.3109/13668250.2015.1010148

World Health Organization. (n.d.). *International Classification of Functioning, Disability and Health (ICF)*. www.who.int/standards/classifications/international-classification-of-functioning-disability-and-health

World Health Organization. (2011). *World report on disability*. www.who.int/publications-detail-redirect/9789241564182

World Health Organization. (2021). *Disability and health*. www.who.int/teams/noncommunicable-diseases/sensory-functions-disability-and-rehabilitation/world-report-on-disability

World Press (2012, June 25). *Madrid 1992—the Paralympic Games that time forgot!* https://paralympicanorak.wordpress.com/2012/06/25/madrid-1992-the-paralympic-games-that-time-forgot/

Yin, M., Siwach, G., & Belyakova, Y. (2022). The Special Olympics Unified Champion Schools Program and high school completion. *American Educational Research Journal*, *59*(2), 315-344. https://doi.org/10.3102/00028312211032744

CHAPTER 9

American Development Model. (n.d.). *What is the American Development Model*. www.admkids.com/page/show/910488-what-is-the-american-development-model-

Australian Institute of Sport (AIS) (2023). FTEM Framework. www.ais.gov.au/ftem

Balyi, I., Way, R., & Higgs, C. (2013). *Long-term athlete development*. Human Kinetics.

Bloom, B.S. (1985). *Developing talent in young people*. Ballantine.

Blumenstein B., & Orbach I. (2015) Psychological preparation for Paralympic athletes: A preliminary study. *Adapted Physical Activity Quarterly*. 2015 Jul;32(3):241-55. https://doi: 10.1123/APAQ.2014-0235.

Bullock, N., Gulbin, J., Martin, D. T., Ross, A., Holland, T., & Marino, F. (2009). Talent identification and deliberate programming in skeleton: Ice novice to Winter Olympian in 14 months. *Journal of Sports Sciences, 27*, 397-404. https://doi.org/10.1080/02640410802549751

Clark, T. (2020). *The 4 Stages of Psychological Safety*, Oakland: Berret-Koehler Publishers, Inc.

Dehghansai, N., & Baker, J. (2020). Searching for Paralympians: Characteristics of participants attending "search" events. *Adapted Physical Activity Quarterly*, *37*(1), 129-138. https://doi.org/10.1123/apaq.2019-0071

Dehghansai, N., Lemez, S., Wattie, N., & Baker, J. (2017). A systematic review of influences on development of athletes with disabilities. *Adapted Physical Activity Quarterly*, *34*(1), 72-90. https://doi.org/10.1123/APAQ.2016-0030

Dieffenback, K.D., & Startler, T.A. (2012). More similar than different: The psychological environment of Paralympic sport. *Journal of Sport Psychology in Action*, *3*(2), 109-118. https://doi.org/10.1080/21520704.2012.683322

Gulbin , J. P. 2001 . From novice to national champion: Perspectives from the MILO Talent Search program . *Sports Coach* , 24 : 24 – 26.

Gulbin, J.P., Croser, M.J., Morley, E.J., & Weissensteiner, J.R. (2013). An integrated framework for the optimisation of sport and athlete development: A practitioner approach. *Journal of Sports Sciences*, *31*(12), 1319-1331. https://doi.org/10.1080/02640414.2013.781661

Hoare, D. G., & Warr, C. R. (2000). Talent identification and women's soccer: An australian experience. *Journal of Sports Sciences, 18*, 751-758. https://doi.org/10.1080/02640410050120122

Higgs, C., Way, R., Harber, V., Jurbala, P., Balyi, I., Carey, A., Trono, C., Mitchell, D., Grove, J., & Laing, T. (2019). 3.0 Long-term development in sport and physical activity. *Sport for Life*, 48.

Kenttä, G., & Corban, R. (2014). Psychology within the Paralympic context—Same, same or any different? *Olympic Coach*, 25(3), 15-25.

Lundqvist, C., Ståhl, L., Kenttä, G., & Thulin, U. (2018). Evaluation of a mindfulness intervention for Paralympic leaders prior to the Paralympic Games. *International Journal of Sports Science & Coaching*, 13(1), 62-71. https://doi.org/10.1177/1747954117746495

Patatas, J.M., De Bosscher, V., Derom, I., & De Rycke, J. (2020). Managing parasport: An investigation of sport policy factors and stakeholders influencing para-athletes' career pathways. *Sport Management Review*, *23(5)*, 937-951.

https://doi.org/10.1016/j.smr.2019.12.004

Sales, D., & Misener, L. (2021). Para sport development experiences: Perspectives of para swimmers and parents, *Adapted Physical Activity Quarterly*, *38(4)*, 634-660.

Swimming Canada (n.d.). Sport Classification Process - Level 2. https://swimming.ca/content/uploads/2018/02/20180215-Level-2-Classification-Process.pdf

Tweedy, S.M., Beckman, E.M., & Connick, M.J. (2014). Paralympic classification: Conceptual basis, current methods, and research update. *PM&R*, *6*(8S), S11-S17. https://doi.org/10.1016/j.pmrj.2014.04.013

Vella, S.A., Mayland, E., Schweickle, M.J., Sutcliffe, J.T., McEwan, D., & Swann, C. (2022). Psychological safety in sport: A systematic review and concept analysis. *International Review of Sport and Exercise Psychology*, 1-24. https://doi.org/10.1080/17509 84X.2022.2028306

United States Olympic Committee (USOC). (2016). American development model. https://sportforlife .ca/portfolio-item/long-term-development-in-sport -and-physical-activity-3-0/

Winchester, G., Culver, D. & Camire´, M. (2011). The learning profiles of high school teacher-coaches. Canadian Journal of Education 3(4), 216 –33.

Winchester G., Culver, D,, & Camiré M. (2013). Understanding how Ontario high school teacher-coaches learn to coach. *Physical Education Sport Pedagogy*, 18, 412–426.

CHAPTER 10

Bennett, J.L., Craig, P., Aytur, S., Thompson, C., Roscoe, H.S., & Gravink, J. (2022a). Community-based recreational therapy for veterans with behavioral health disorders: Impacts on quality of life, participation, and happiness. *Community Mental Health Journal*, 1-10. https://doi.org/10.1007/s10597-022-00962-6

Bennett, J.L., Craig, P., Aytur, S., Thompson, T., Roscoe, H.S., & Gravink, J. (2022b). Community-based recreational therapy for veterans with behavioral health disorders: Impacts on quality of life, participation, and happiness. *Community Mental Health Journal.* https://doi.org/10.1007/s10597-022-00962-6

Bennett, J.L., Lundberg, N.R., Zabriskie, R., & Eggett, D. (2014). Addressing post-traumatic stress among Iraq and Afghanistan veterans and significant others: An intervention utilizing sport and recreation. *Therapeutic Recreation Journal*, *48*(1), 74-93.

Bennett, J.L., Piatt, J.A., & van Puymbroeck, M. (2017). Outcomes of a therapeutic fly-fishing program for veterans with combat-related disabilities: A community-based rehabilitation initiative. *Community Mental Health Journal*, *53*(7), 1-10. https://doi.org/10.1007 /s10597-017-0124-9

Bennett, J.L., van Puymbroeck, M., Piatt, J.A., & Rydell, R.J. (2014). Veterans' perceptions of benefits and important program components of a therapeutic fly-fishing program. *Therapeutic Recreation Journal*, *48*(2), 169-187.

Bilmes, L.J. (2021). *The Long-Term Costs of United States Care for Veterans of the Afghanistan and Iraq Wars.* https:// jamanetwork.com/journals/jamasurgery/article -abstract/2729451

Brittain, I., & Green, S. (2012). Disability sport is going back to its roots: Rehabilitation of military personnel receiving sudden traumatic disabilities in the twenty-first century. *Qualitative Research in Sport, Exercise and Health*, *4*(2), 244-264. https://doi.org/10.1080 /2159676X.2012.685100

Brown University. (2021, September). *Costs of the 20-year war on terror: $8 trillion and 900,000 deaths.* News from Brown. www.brown.edu/news/2021-09 -01/costsofwar

Caddick, N., & Smith, B. (2014). The impact of sport and physical activity on the well-being of combat veterans: A systematic review. *Psychology of Sport and Exercise*, *15*(1), 9-18. https://doi.org/10.1016 /j.psychsport.2013.09.011

Caddick, N., & Smith, B. (2018). Exercise is medicine for mental health in military veterans: A qualitative commentary. *Qualitative Research in Sport, Exercise and Health*, *10*(4), 429-440. https://doi.org/10.1080 /2159676X.2017.1333033

Carruthers, C., & Hood, C.D. (2007). Building a life of meaning through therapeutic recreation: The leisure and well-being model, part I. *Therapeutic Recreation Journal*, *41*(4), 276-297.

Church, T.E. (2009). Returning veterans on campus with war related injuries and the long road back home. *Journal of Postsecondary Education and Disability*, *22*(1), 43-52.

Ciarleglio, M.M., Aslan, M., Proctor, S.P., Concato, J., Ko, J., Kaiser, A.P., & Vasterling, J.J. (2018). Associations of stress exposures and social support with long-term mental health outcomes among U.S. Iraq war veterans. *Behavior Therapy*, *49*(5), 653-667. https://www.sciencedirect.com/science/article/pii /S0005789418300029

Combined Arms Institute. (2022). *About: Our Story.* www.navso.org/about/our-story

Cooper, L., Caddick, N., Godier, L., Cooper, A., & Fossey, M. (2018). Transition from the military into civilian life. *Armed Forces & Society*, *44*(1), 156-177. https://doi. org/10.1177/0095327X16675965

Craig, P.J., Wilder, A., Sable, J.R., & Gravink, J. (2013). Promoting access, transition, and health: A community-based approach to managing chronic health conditions. *Annual in Therapeutic Recreation*, *21*, 45-62.

DeAngelis, T. (2015, March). *In search of cultural competence.* Monitor on Psychology. www.apa.org/ monitor/2015/03/cultural-competence

Diaz, R., Miller, E.K., Kraus, E., & Fredericson, M. (2019). *Impact of Adaptive Sports Participation on Quality of Life.* www.sportsmedarthro.com

Donaldson, D. (2016). *Wounded veterans: Reintegration through adventure-based experience: A narrative inquiry.*

Dustin, D., Bricker, N., Arave, J., Wall, W., & Wendt, G. (2011). The promise of river running as a therapeutic medium for veterans coping with post-traumatic stress disorder. *Therapeutic Recreation Journal, 45*(4), 326-340.

Ferrer, M., & Davis, R. (2019). Adapted physical activity for wounded, injured, and ill military personnel: From military to community. *Palaestra, 33*(2), 26-31.

Grant, S., Colaiaco, B., Motala, A., Shanman, R.M., Sorbero, M.E., & Hempel, S. (2017). *Needle acupuncture for post-traumatic stress disorder (PTSD): A systematic review.* www.rand.org/pubs/research_reports/RR1433.html

Grant, S., Hempel, S., Kandrack, R., Motala, A., Shanman, R.M., Booth, M., Miles, J.N.V., Dudley, W., & Sorbero, M.E. (2015). *Needle acupuncture for substance use disorders: A systematic review.* www.rand.org/pubs/research_reports/RR1030.html

Greer, M., & Vin-Raviv, N. (2019). Outdoor-based therapeutic recreation programs among military veterans with post-traumatic stress disorder: Assessing the evidence. *Military Behavioral Health, 7*(3), 286-303. https://doi.org/10.1080/21635781.2018.1543063

Greer, N., Balser, D., McKenzie, L., Nicholson, H., Senk, A., Tonkin, B., Wilt, T.J., MacDonald, R., & Rosebush, C. (2019). *Adaptive Sports for Disabled Veterans.* [Internet]. Washington (DC): Department of Veterans Affairs (US); 2019 Feb. PMID: 32181998.

Hartley, M.T., & Mapes, A.C. (2015). Resilience and sports: An innovative approach to rehabilitation counseling for veterans with spinal cord injury. *Journal of Military and Government Counseling, 172,* 2015.

Hawkins, B.L., Cory, A.L., & Crowe, B.M. (2011). Effects of participation in a Paralympic military sports camp on injured service members: Implications for therapeutic recreation. *Therapeutic Recreation Journal, 45*(4), 309-325.

Hawkins, B., Townsend, J., & Garst, B. (2016). Nature-based recreational therapy for military service members: A strengths approach. *Therapeutic Recreation Journal, 50*(1), 55-74.

Hepner, K.A., Holliday, S.B., Sousa, J., & Tanielian, T. (2018). *Training clinicians to deliver evidence-based psychotherapy: Development of the Training in Psychotherapy (TIP) tool.* www.rand.org/t/TL306

Heyne, L.A., & Anderson, L.S. (2012). Theories that support strengths-based practice in therapeutic recreation. *Therapeutic Recreation Journal, 46*(2), 106-128.

Hood, C.D., & Carruthers, C. (2007). Enhancing leisure experience and developing resources: The leisure and well-being model, part II. *Therapeutic Recreation Journal, 41*(4), 298-325.

Kay, C.W.P., & McKenna, J. (2021). The enduring well-being impacts of attending the Battle Back Multi Activity Course for the lives of recovering UK armed forces personnel. *Military Psychology.* https://doi.org/10.1080/08995605.2021.2002595

Krasny, M.E., Pace, K.H., Tidball, K.G., & Helphand, K. (2014). Nature engagement to foster resilience in military communities. *Greening in the Red Zone,* 163-180. https://doi.org/10.1007/978-90-481-9947-1_13

Kuehn, B.M. (2009). Soldier suicide rates continue to rise. *Journal of the American Medical Association, 301*(11), 1111-1113. https://doi.org/10.1001/jama.2009.342

Laferrier, J.Z., Teodorski, E., & Cooper, R.A. (2015). Investigation of the impact of sports, exercise, and recreation participation on psychosocial outcomes in a population of veterans with disabilities. *American Journal of Physical Medicine and Rehabilitation, 94*(12), 1026-1034.

Lundberg, N.R., Taniguchi, S., McCormick, B.P., & Tibbs, C. (2011). Identity negotiating: Redefining stigmatized identities through adaptive sports and recreation participation among individuals with a disability. *Journal of Leisure Research, 43*(2), 205-225. https://doi.org/10.1080/19406940.2011.627363

Lundberg, N., Bennett, J., & Smith, S. (2011). Outcomes of adaptive sports and recreation participation among veterans returning from combat with acquired disability. *Therapeutic Recreation Journal, 45*(2), 105-120.

Lundberg, N., Ward, P., Lundberg, G., Hill, B., Bown, J., Zabriskie, R., Duerden, M., & Ashby, H. (2021). Developing the Experience Impact Scale: A qualitative study using a study abroad and international internship program. *Journal of Leisure Research, 53*(2), 191-210. https://doi.org/10.1080/00222216.2021.1916798

Mayer, W.E., & Anderson, L.S. (2014). Perceptions of people with disabilities and their families about segregated and inclusive recreation involvement. *Therapeutic Recreation Journal, 48*(2), 150-168.

Meyer, E.G., & Wynn, G.H. (2018). The importance of U.S. military cultural competence. In L. Roberts & C. Warner (Eds.), *Military and Veteran Mental Health* (pp. 15-33). Springer New York. https://doi.org/10.1007/978-1-4939-7438-2_2

Military Health System. (n.d.). *About the Military Health System.* www.Health.Mil/About-MHS

Mowatt, R.A., & Bennett, J.L. (2011). War narratives: Veteran stories, PTSD effects and therapeutic fly-fishing. *Therapeutic Recreation Journal, 45*(4), 286-308.

Mulhollon, S., & Casey, J. (2016). Adaptive sports and equipment for veterans with spinal cord injuries: Community partnerships are key to a year-round adapted sports program for Milwaukee veterans. *Palaestra, 30*(4), 20-24.

Noel, P.H., Zeber, J.E., Pugh, M.J., Finley, E.P., & Parchman, M.L. (2011). A pilot survey of post-deployment health care needs in small community-based primary care clinics. *BMC Family Practice, 12,* 79.

Olenick, M., Flowers, M., & Diaz, V.J. (2015). U.S. veterans and their unique issues: Enhancing health care professional awareness. *Advances in Medical Education and Practice*, *6*, 635-639.

Ortiz, S.R. (2010). *Beyond the bonus march and GI bill: How veteran politics shaped the New Deal era*. New York University.

Peacock, S.M., McKenna, J., Carless, D., & Cooke, C. (2019). Outcomes from a one-week adapted sport and adapted adventure recovery programme for military personnel. *Sports*, *7*, 135-145.

Pugh, M.J.V., Finley, E.P., Copeland, L.A., Wang, C.P., Noel, P.H., Amuan, M.E., Parsons, H.M., Wells, M., Elizondo, B., & Pugh, J.A. (2014). *Complex Comorbidity Clusters in OEF/OIF Veterans: The Polytrauma Clinical Triad and Beyond 52*(2).

QB Medical. (2021, March). *Do veterans have access to culturally competent care?* www.qbmedical.com/blog/2020/12/24/do-veterans-have-access-to-culturally-competent-care

RAND Corporation. (2019). *Improving the Quality of Mental Health Care for Veterans: Lessons from RAND Research*. www.rand.org/pubs/research_briefs/RB10087.html

Rimmer, J.H., & Marques, A.C. (2012). Physical activity for people with disabilities. *The Lancet*, *380*(9838), 193-195. https://doi.org/10.1016/S0140-6736(12)61028-9

Rogers, S.D., Loy, D., & Brown-Bochicchio, C. (2016). Sharing a new foxhole with friends the impact of outdoor recreation on injured military. *Therapeutic Recreation Journal*, *50*(3), 213-228.

Sable, J., & Gravink, J. (2005). The PATH to community health care for people with disabilities: A community-based therapeutic recreation service. *Therapeutic Recreation Journal*, *39*(1), 78-87.

Scholz, J., & Chen, Y.T. (2018). History of adaptive and disabled rights within society, thus creating the fertile soil to grow, adaptive sports. In *Adaptive Sports Medicine* (pp. 3-19). Springer International Publishing. https://doi.org/10.1007/978-3-319-56568-2_1

Serfioti, D., & Hunt, N. (2021). Extreme sport as an intervention for physically injured military veterans: the example of competitive motorsport. *Disability and Rehabilitation*. https://doi.org/10.1080/09638288.2021.1985630

Slater, D., & Meade, M.A. (2004). Participation in recreation and sports for persons with spinal cord injury: review and recommendations. *NeuroRehabilitation*, *19*(2), 121-129.

Spelman, J.F., Hunt, S.C., Seal, K.H., & Burgo-Black, A.L. (2012). Post-deployment care for returning combat veterans. *Journal of General Internal Medicine*, *27*(9), 1200-1209.

Steinhauer, J. (2019, April). Veterans' groups compete with each other, and struggle with the V.A. *New York Times*. www.nytimes.com/2019/01/04/us/politics/veterans-service-organizations.html.

Sutton, R.J., Kay, C.W.P., McKenna, J., & Kaiseler, M. (2021). Sustained positive behaviour change of wounded, injured and sick UK military following an adaptive adventure sports and health coaching recovery course. *BMJ Military Health*, e001784. https://doi.org/10.1136/bmjmilitary-2021-001784

Tanielian, T., & Jaycox, L. (2008). *Invisible wounds of war: Psychological and cognitive injuries, their consequences, and services to assist recovery*.

Thompson, C.V., Bennett, J.L., Sable, J.R., & Gravink, J. (2016). Northeast Passage PATH(TM) Program: A strengths-based and recovery-oriented approach for veterans who experience mental health disorders. *Therapeutic Recreation Journal*, *50*(2), 138-154. https://doi.org/10.18666/TRJ-2016-V50-I2-6788

Townsend, J.A., Hawkins, B.L., Bennett, J.L., Hoffman, J., Martin, T., Sotherden, E., & Bridges, W. (2018). Preliminary long-term health outcomes associated with recreation-based health & wellness programs for injured service members. *Cogent Psychology*, *5*(1), 1-17. https://doi.org/10.1080/23311908.2018.1444330

U.S. Department of Defense. (2019). *Report to the Congressional Armed Services Committees: Section 717 of the John S. McCain National Defense Authorization Act for Fiscal Year 2019* (Public Law 115-232).

U.S. Department of Defense. (2022). *Casualty status*.

U.S. Department of Defense. (n.d.). *Warrior Games: About*. Retrieved from https://dodwarriorgames.com/about

U.S. Department of Veterans Affairs. (2021). *Report of the Office of Inspector General: Adaptive Sports Grant Management Needs Improvement*. Retrieved from https://www.oversight.gov/report/VA/Adaptive-Sports-Grants-Management-Needs-Improvement

U.S. Department of Veterans Affairs. (2022). *Veteran's Health Administration: About VHA*. www.va.gov/health/aboutvha.Asp.

U.S. Department of Veterans Affairs. (n.d.a). *Monthly training allowances: For veterans with disabilities training in Paralympic and Olympic sports*.

U.S. Department of Veterans Affairs. (n.d.b). *VHA: VA Adaptive Sports and Therapeutic Arts*. https://doi.org/10.3390/sports7060135

USAFacts. (2023). Veterans. November 27, 2023. https://usafacts.org/topics/veterans/

Vella, E.J., Milligan, B., & Bennett, J.L. (2013). Participation in outdoor recreation program predicts improved psychosocial well-being among veterans with post-traumatic stress disorder: A pilot study. *Military Medicine*, *178*(3), 254-260. https://doi.org/10.7205/milmed-d-12-00308

Veterans Benefits Improvement Act, Pub. L. No. PL 110-389 (2008). https://www.congress.gov/bill/110th-congress/senate-bill/3023?r=17

Walter, K.H., Otis, N.P., del Re, A.C., Kohen, C.B., Glassman, L.H., Ober, K.M., & Hose, M.K. (2021). The National Veterans Summer Sports Clinic: Change and duration of psychological outcomes. *Psychology of Sport and Exercise*, 55. https://doi.org/10.1016/j.psychsport.2021.101939

Whaley, D., Townsend, J., Zabriskie, R., & Entrup, N. (2021, September). Adaptive sport as transformative experiences: Findings from a pilot study. *2021 American Therapeutic Recreation Association Annual Conference Research Institute*.

Wilder, A., Craig, P.J., Sable, J.R., Gravink, J., Carr, C., & Frye, J. (2011). The PATH-Way home: Promoting access, transition, and health for veterans with disabilities. *Therapeutic Recreation Journal*, 45(4), 268-286.

World Health Organization. (2018). *Global action plan on physical activity 2018-2030: More active people for a healthier world*. World Health Organization.

Zabriskie, R.B., Lundberg, N.R., & Groff, D.G. (2005). Quality of life and identity: The benefits of a community-based therapeutic recreation and adaptive sports program. *Therapeutic Recreation Journal*, 39(3), 176-191.

CHAPTER 11

American Association of Adapted Sports Programs (2024). Off the sidelines - Into the game. https://adaptedsports.org/about-aaasp/#faqs

Balish, S.M., McLaren, C., Rainham, D., & Blanchard, C. (2014). Correlates of youth sport attrition: A review and future directions. *Psychology of Sport and Exercise*, 15, 429-439.

Columna, L., Prieto, L., Elias-Revolledo, G., & Haegele, J.A. (2020). The perspectives of parents of youth with disabilities toward physical activity: A systematic review. *Disability and Health Journal*, 13(2), 1-10. https://doi.org/10.1016/j.dhjo.2019.100851

Donaldson S.J., & Ronan K.R. (2006). The effects of sports participation on young adolescents' emotional well-being. *Adolescence*, 41(162), 369-389. PMID: 16981623.

Dorsch, T.D., Smith, A.L., Blazo, J.A., Coakley, J., Côté, J. Wagstaff, C.R.D., Warner, S., & King, M.Q. (2021). Towards an integrated understanding of the youth sport system. *Research Quarterly for Exercise and Sport*, 93(1), 105-119. https://doi.org/10.1080/02701367.2020.1810847

Evans, J., & Roberts, G.C. (1987). Physical competence and the development of children's peer relations. *Quest*, 39, 23-35.

Gould, D. (1982). Sport psychology in the 1980s: Status, direction, and challenge in youth sports research. *Journal of Sport Psychology*, 4(3), 203-218.

Kleinert, H.L., Miracle, S.A., & Sheppard Jones, K. (2007). Including students with moderate and severe disabilities in extracurricular and community recreation activities. *Teaching Exceptional Children*, 39(6). 33-38. https://doi.org/10.1177/004005990703900605

Ommundsen, Y., Gundersen, K.A., & Mjaavatn, P.E. (2010). Fourth graders' social standing with peers: A prospective study on the role of first grade physical activity, weight status, and motor proficiency. *Scandinavian Journal of Educational Research*, 54, 377-394.

Scarpa, S., & Nart, A. (2012). Influences of perceived sport competence on physical activity enjoyment in early adolescents. *Social Behavior and Personality*, 40(2), 203-204. https://doi.org/10.2224/sbp.2012.40.2.203

Shields, N., Synnot, A.J., & Barr, M. (2012). Perceived barriers and facilitators to physical activity for children with disability: A systematic review. *British Journal of Sports Medicine*, 46, 989-997.

Smith, A.L., & Delli Paoli, A.G. (2017). The influence of friends and peers in youth sport. In C. Knight, C. Hardwood, & D. Gould (Eds.), *Sport psychology for young athletes*. Routledge.

Weiss, M. R., & Amorose, A. J. (2008). Motivational orientations and sport behavior. In T. S. Horn (Ed.), *Advances in sport psychology* (3rd ed., pp. 115-155). Human Kinetics.

Weiss, M.R., & Duncan, S.C. (1992). The relationship between physical competence and peer acceptance in the context of children's sports participation. *Journal of Sport & Exercise Psychology*, 14, 177-191.

CHAPTER 12

Bartsch, A., Oliver, M.B., Nitsch, C., & Scherr, S. (2018). Inspired by the Paralympics: Effects of empathy on audience interest in para-sports and on the destigmatization of persons with disabilities. *Communication Research*, 45(4), 525-553.

Chatfield, S.L., & Cottingham II, M. (2017). Perceptions of athletes in disabled and non-disabled sport contexts: A descriptive qualitative research study. *The Qualitative Report*, 22(7), 1909-1925.

Cottingham, M., Chatfield, S., Gearity, B.T., Allen, J.T., & Hall, S.A. (2012). Using points of attachment to examine repatronage and online consumption of wheelchair rugby spectators. *International Journal of Sport Management*, 13(2), 160-172.

Cottingham, M., Carroll, M.S., Phillips, D., Karadakis, K., Gearity, B.T., & Drane, D. (2014). Development and validation of the motivation scale for disability sport consumption. *Sport Management Review*, 17(1), 49-64.

Cottingham, M., Gearity, B., & Byon, K. (2013). A qualitative examination of disability sport executives' perceptions of sport promotion and the acquisition of sponsors. *Sport Marketing Quarterly*, 22(2).

Cottingham, M., Miller, L., Mohn, R., Lee, D., & Douglas, S. (2022). Comparing consumers of different disability sports: A quantitative examination of the motives of power chair soccer and wheelchair basketball spectators. *Journal of Contemporary Athletics ISSN, 1554*, 9933.

Cottingham, M., Wann, D., Byon, K., & Hu, T. (2023). Quantifying the supercrip image: Exploring the impact of knowledge of an athlete's physical disability on spectators' impressions of performance and interest in consumption. *Journal of Sport Behavior, 46*(2).

Drollinger, T. (2018). Using active empathetic listening to build relationships with major-gift donors. *Journal of Nonprofit & Public Sector Marketing, 30*(1), 37-51.

Hardin, M.M., & Hardin, B. (2004). The supercrip in sport media: Wheelchair athletes discuss hegemony's disabled hero. *Sociology of Sport Online-SOSOL, 7*(1).

Hu, T., Cottingham, M., Shapiro, D. and Lee, D. (2023), Promote the "wow": (Mis)representation, perception and reception of media promotion on wheelchair rugby, *International Journal of Sports Marketing and Sponsorship*, 24 (3), 470-484.

Hu, T., Siegfried, N., Cho, M., & Cottingham, M. (2023). Elite athletes with disabilities marketability and branding strategies: professional agents' perspectives. European *Sport Management Quarterly, 23*(6), 1643-1665.

Kama A. (2004) Supercrips versus the pitiful handicapped: Reception of disabling images by disabled audience members. *Communications 29*(4): 447

Kim, M., Park, J., & Yoon, Y. (2022). Assessing spectator motivation for the Paralympics: the mediating role of attitude. *International Journal of Sports Marketing and Sponsorship*, (ahead-of-print).

Lastuka, A., & Cottingham, M. (2016). The effect of adaptive sports on employment among people with disabilities. *Disability and Rehabilitation, 38*(8), 742-748.

Matson-Barkat, S., Puncheva-Michelotti, P., Koetz, C., & Hennekam, S. (2022). Destigmatisation through social sharing of emotions and empowerment: The case of disabled athletes and consumers of disability sports. *Journal of Business Research, 149*, 77-84.

Oxford English Dictionary. (n.d.). Sponsor. In *Oxford English Dictionary Online*. Retrieved April 4, 2022, from www.oed.com

Page, S.J., O'Connor, E., & Peterson, K. (2001). Leaving the disability ghetto: A qualitative study of factors underlying achievement motivation among athletes with disabilities. *Journal of Sport and Social Issues, 25*(1), 40-55.

Pate, J.R., & Bragale, D. (2019). Challenges of an established amateur sport: Exploring how wheelchair basketball grows and thrives through a sport development lens. *Journal of Amateur Sport, 5*(1), 50-75.

Rodd, J. (1996). Pareto's law of income distribution or the 80/20 rule. *International Journal of Nonprofit and Voluntary Sector Marketing, 1*(1), 77-89.

Siegfried, N., Green, E.R., Swim, N., Montanaro, A., Greenwell, C., & Frederick, E.L. (2021). An examination of college adaptive sport sponsorship and the role of cause-related marketing. *Journal of Issues in Intercollegiate Athletics, 14*, 483-500.

Silveira, S.L., Ledoux, T., Cottingham, M., & Hernandez, D.C. (2017). Association among practice frequency on depression and stress among competitive U.S male wheelchair rugby athletes with tetraplegia. *Spinal Cord, 55*(10), 957-962.

Shapiro, D., Pate, J.R., & Cottingham, M. (2020). A multi-institutional review of college campus adapted intramural sports programming for college students with and without a disability. *Recreational Sports Journal, 44*(2), 109-125.

Sterba, D., Stapleton, J.N., & Kennedy, W. (2022). The supercrip athlete in media: Model of inspiration or able-bodied hegemony? *International Journal of Sport Communication, 1*, 1-5.

United Nations (n.d.). United Nations, Sports and the Paralympic Games: Promoting Human Rights, Development and the Ideals of Humanity. https://www .un.org/development/desa/disabilities/united-nations -sports-and-the-paralympic-games-promoting-human -rights-development-and-the-ideals-of-humanity .html

Wann, D.L., & Cottingham, M. (2015). The impact of team identification and knowledge of an athlete's physical disability on spectators' impressions of players. *Journal of Contemporary Athletics, 9*(3), 161.

Williams, T.L., Lozano-Sufrategui, L., & Tomasone, J.R. (2022). Stories of physical activity and disability: Exploring sport and exercise students' narrative imagination through story completion. *Qualitative Research in Sport, Exercise and Health, 14*(5), 687-705.

Yamashita, R., & Muneda, M. (2019). What motivates wheelchair basketball spectators? Analysis of moderating effects on intention to attend Tokyo 2020 Olympic Paralympic Games. *International Journal of Sport and Health Science, 17*, 217-226.

INDEX

Note: The italicized *f* and *t* following page numbers refer to figures and tables, respectively.

A

ableism
 definition of 6, 15-16
 description of 6-7, 33
 in health fields 23
 interpersonal 20-21
 intersectional view of 16
 in Paralympic Games media coverage 95-96
 in policies and practices 30
 social isolation caused by 12
 stereotypes 16
academics 196
Accessibility for Ontarians Disability Act (AODA) 66
accessibility laws, in Canada 66
Accessible Canada Act (ACA) 66
Accessible Stadiums technical assistance manual 85
acquired impairments 148
adaptive fitness space 22
adaptive functioning
 definition of 127
 sport participation and 127-128
adaptive sport and recreation
 barriers to. *See* barriers
 benefits of 172-173, 173t-174t, 204
 categorization of 20
 classification systems in 3
 in colleges 26
 collegiate programs 200, 201t-202t
 community-based 169-172
 contact theory application to 9-10
 definition of 165, 187
 development of 156
 early awareness and engagement in 150
 elite 103-119
 history of 20, 165
 inclusion in 7-9
 integrated 152
 in K-12 schools 26
 for military service members 165-174

restrictions on 3
 stakeholder-centric decision-making in 8
adaptive sport awareness programs 9-10
adaptive swimming 209
adaptive youth sports
 barriers to 180t, 180-182
 benefits of 179
 coaches for 178, 184
 facilitators of 182-184
 parental involvement in 178, 181-182
 participation in 179-184
 peer relationships 183
 in schools 178
 settings for 177-178
advocacy 41
Affordable Care Act 184
Afghanistan 162, 162f
African Para Games 119
alienation 12
Allela, Roy 35
American Association for Health, Physical Education, and Recreation (AAHPER) 129
American Association of Adapted Sports Programs (AAASP) 27, 29, 183
American Association of Intellectual and Developmental Disabilities (AAIDD) 124-125, 126t
American development model (ADM)
 description of 145-146
 features of 147t
 FETM model versus 147t
 LTAD model versus 147t
 principles of 147t
 stages of 147t
American Legion 163
Americans with Disabilities Act (ADA)
 age eligibility rules 74-75

competition rules 73
description of 22, 24, 30, 64, 184
disability as defined by 15, 70
eligibility rules 74-75
individualized inquiry 72-73
mainstreaming goal of 72
most integrated setting requirement 72, 72t
"otherwise qualified" requirement 69-70, 75
reasonable modifications requirement 70-71, 73
Section 504 of the Rehabilitation Act of 1973 and, comparison between 69-70
service animals 79-81
settlement agreements 75
sports venues regulations and guidances 76-86
ticketing policies 79, 80t
website accessibility protections 81, 86
amputees, in Paralympic Games 53
Anaheim Ducks 81
apps 86
archery 44-45, 46f
Asian Para Games 109-111, 110f
Asian Paralympic Committee (APC) 109-111
assistive devices 85-86
Assistive Technology Act 184
ataxic cerebral palsy 54
athetoid cerebral palsy 54
athlete(s). *See also* Paralympic Games athletes
 with disabilities 99
 lived experiences of 28
athlete development
 para-. *See* para-athletes/para-athletes development
 stages of 143-144
athlete development models
 American development model 145-146

252

description of 134
foundation, talent, elite, mastery model 146, 147*t*
long-term developmental model. *See* long-term development model
athlete-first representation 99-100
athletes with high support needs (AHSN) 117
Athletes Without Limits 122, 139
athletic competence 182
athletic frame 92*f*, 99-100
Australian Paralympic History Project 59-60
authority
  acceptance of social norms provided by 9
  cognitive 2-3
autism 4, 19
autism spectrum disorder (ASD) 127
auxiliary aids and services 75
Awareness stage 144

B

Badminton Library of Sports and Pastimes, The 43
Bagg, Christian 37-38
Bailey, Ariel Malphrus 167
Bailey v. Board of Commissioners 78
Banks, Tyra 136
barriers
  adaptive youth sports 180*t*, 180-182
  community 29
  description of 15
  effects of 23
  environmental 22-23, 180*t*, 181-182
  fatigue as 20, 22
  health disparities caused by 27
  individual 180*t*, 181
  International Paralympic Committee as 26
  interpersonal 27*f*, 28
  low motivation as 22
  pain as 20-22
  personal 20-22
  policy-level 180*t*, 182
  social 12, 180*t*, 181
  social isolation caused by 12
  systemic 19
basketball
  in Special Olympics 133-134
  wheelchair. *See* wheelchair basketball
Bedbrook, George 47
"Blade Runner" 93
Blauwet, Cheri 105
blind athletes, in Paralympic Games 53

Board of Education v. Rowley 68
boccia 56*t*, 108, 159, 188-189
Bowhead Reach bikes 37-38
bowling 217
braille 39
Braye, Stuart 59
bridging capital 12
British Empire Games 107
British Limbless Ex-Servicemen's Association (BLESMA) 51
Brown, Lydia X.Z. 19
business innovation 34

C

Camp Shriver 129
Canada, accessibility laws in 66
Canadian Broadcasting Company (CBC) 97-98, 101
Canadian Human Rights Commission 66
Caruso v. Blockbuster-Sony Music Entertainment Centre at the Waterfront 83
Centers for Disease Control and Prevention 122-123
cerebral palsy
  ataxic 54
  athetoid 54
  athletes with, in Paralympic Games 54
  spastic 54
Cerebral Palsy International Sports and Recreation Association (CP-ISRA) 51
Certified Therapeutic Recreation Specialists (CTRSs) 167, 170
Challenged Athletes Foundation 27, 197
Channel 4 101
charity 28
charity models of funding 195-196
Charlottesville Cardinals wheelchair basketball team 5
Chicago Park District 129-130
Christopher & Dana Reeves Foundation 197, 206
chronic fatigue 20
circular economy 34
Claiborne, Loretta 135
Clare, Eli 16
Clark v. Simms 77-78
classification(s)
  athlete, for Paralympic Games 26, 54, 117-118
  intellectual disability 125, 126*t*
  para-athlete 154
closed captioning 85
closed skills 126-127
clothing, innovations in 35-36

coach
  lack of competition effects on 155-156
  for youth athletes 178, 184
coach development model 134
coach education 145, 153
coalitions 27, 29
cognitive authority 2-3
cognitive behavioral therapy (CBT) 164
cognitive processing therapy (CPT) 164
cognitive skills 126
college, adaptive sport programs in 26, 200, 201*t*-202*t*
Comcast NBCUniversal SportsTech Accelerator 41
Comité International des Sports des Sourds (CISS) 44
common goals 9
Commonwealth Games 106-107
Commonwealth Games Federation (CGF) 106-107
community
  adaptive youth sports in 177
  coalitions in 29
  organizations in 29
community-based adaptive sports and recreation 169-172
community-based services 164
comparison narrative 94
competition
  hosting of 190
  laws and legislation that affect 73-74
  in long-term athlete development 154-156
conceptual skills 127
congenital impairments 148, 160
contact theory 9-10
continuous improvement 149*t*
Convention on the Rights of Persons with Disabilities (CRPD) 25-26, 65-66, 74, 90, 123
Cord, The 47
corporate sponsors 195
Cost of War project 161
costs and expenses
  definition of 188
  equipment 181, 188-190
  facilities 190
  hosting competition 190
  hypothetical example of 191, 191*t*-192*t*, 193*t*
  travel 190
Court of Arbitration for Sport (CAS) 73-74
Craig H. Neilsen Foundation 197
Crenshaw, Kimberlé, 22

254 INDEX

Crip Camp 128
critical disability theory 19
critical model 18-19
Cuban, Mark 136
cultural competence 172
Cybathlon 114-119, 115*f*
cyborg 93
cyborg narrative 93
cycle of reintroduction 101

D
Deaflympics 44
Dear Colleague Letter 26, 70, 125
DeGeneres, Ellen 136
de minimis standard 68
Dennin v. Connecticut Interscholastic Athletic Conference 74-75
Department of Defense transition units 165, 171
Department of Education (DOE) 67
Department of Health and Human Services 23-24
deployment 163
design thinking 40
developmental age 153-154
Diagnostic and Statistical Manual of Mental Disorders, 5th Edition (DSM-5) 124-125, 126*t*
direct ableism 6
disability
    Americans with Disabilities Act definition of 15, 70
    celebrating of 18
    Convention on the Rights of Persons with Disabilities statement on 90
    decisions influenced by orientations toward 2
    definition of 2, 64
    global prevalence of 90, 122
    health disparities and 22
    history of term 64
    impairment versus 4, 6
    innovation in. *See* innovation
    intellectual. *See* intellectual disabilities
    as intersectional experience 16
    language regarding. *See* language
    limitations associated with 2
    media representation of 90-91
    models of. *See* disability models
    negative stereotypes of 3
    prevalence of 90, 122-123
    religious discourses and 2
    Section 504 definition of 70
    "sick role" and 3
    social justice and 18
    stereotypes of 3
    television portrayals of 90-91

U.S. prevalence of 123
    youth with 182. *See also* adaptive youth sports
disability community 19
disability justice 19
disability models
    critical 18-19
    justice 18-19
    medical. *See* medical model of disability
    social 3-6, 18
    social-ecological. *See* social-ecological model
    social relational 6
disability rights
    history of 64
    international legal and policy efforts on 64-66
    laws and legislation for. *See* laws and legislation
    movement for 63-64
    person-first language and 19
    in United States 67-73
disability sport. *See also* sport(s)
    costs and expenses associated with. *See* costs and expenses
    current issues in 117-119
    framing of 203
    funding of. *See* funding
    global opportunities 119
    history of 43-44, 91
    innovation in 35. *See also* innovation
    long-term development model application to 149*t*
    mobility-based 189
    new technologies in 118-119
    physical literacy skills for 150
    promoters of 202-204
    promotion of 188
    recreational value of 58
    social reintegration value of 58-59
    spectators of 203
    World War II influences on 44-45
disability sport programs 157, 194-197, 200
disability sports games
    Asian Para Games 109-111, 110*f*
    Commonwealth Games 106-107
    Cybathlon 114-119, 115*f*
    Invictus Games 112-114
    overview of 104*t*
    Paralympic Games. *See* Paralympic Games
    Parapan American Games 66, 107-109
    Warrior Games 111-112, 112*f*
disability sports media coverage
    athlete perspectives of 98-100

competing perspectives in 96-100
    future of 100-102
    media personnel perspectives of 96-98
    Paralympic Games. *See* Paralympic Games media coverage
    quality of 98-100
    quantity of 98
    stereotypical representations in 98-100
disabled person
    inspiration porn use of 6-7, 21
    meaningful social contact for 10-11
    pain experienced by 20-22
    personal barriers of 20
    service providers' interactions with 8
    social isolation of 10, 12
    use of term 4
DisCrit 19
Disney 136
disparate impact discrimination 30
divisioning 122, 136
donors 193-194
double discrimination of female Paralympic athletes 95-96, 96*f*
Down syndrome 127-128
DraftKings 81

E
Educational Amendments Act, Title IX of 24, 184
80/20 model 193-194
Einstein, Albert 41
eligibility rules 74-75
Endeavor Games 27
endowments 198, 200
entrepreneurial mindset 41
environment
    barriers in 22-23, 180*t*, 181-182
    safety of 157-159
equal status contact 9
equipment
    costs of 181, 188-190
    innovations in 37-38
    maintenance of 189
ESPN 136
esport 36
ETH Zürich 115-116
etiology 125
eugenics 17
evidence-based practices 164
exclusion 4
exercise, low-impact 20-21
expenses. *See* costs and expenses
eye movement desensitization and reprocessing (EMDR) 164

F

Facebook 89
facilities
  costs of 190
  innovations in 38
Far East and South Pacific Games for the Disabled (FESPIC) 109
fatigue 20, 22, 150
FedEx Field 85
Feldman, Shane 85-86
Feldman v. Pro Football, Inc. 86
female Paralympic athletes
  double discrimination of 95-96, 96f
  sexualization of 96
First Contact stage 144, 153
FlyEase shoe series 36, 196-197
foundation, talent, elite, mastery (FTEM) model 146, 147t
free appropriate public education (FAPE) 24, 67-68
Freedom Seat 38
fundamental alteration defense, to reasonable modifications 71
funding
  charity models of 195-196
  future trends in 204
  overview of 187-188
  personnel involved in 202-204
  sponsorship models of 196-197
funding sources
  donors 193-194
  endowments 198, 200
  fundraisers 194
  government 198
  grants 197-198
  sponsors 194-197
fundraisers 194

G

gaming innovations 36
gender stereotypes, in Paralympic Games media coverage 95-96
global ambassadors 132
Global Disability Innovation Hub 41
global governance units 29
Global War on Terror 163
goalball 189
Golden State Warriors 81
government funding 198
grants 197-198
Grevemberg, David 107-108
guide dogs 80
Guttmann, Ludwig 44-47, 51-52, 58, 60, 91, 165

H

health disparities
  barriers as cause of 27. *See also* barriers

description of 22
  mitigation of 23-27
health domains 163
Healthy People 23
hearing impairment 85

I

ideating 34
Ideation Clinic 41
identity-first language 19
ignorance ableism 6
IKEA 35
impairment(s)
  acquired 148
  age of acquiring 148, 150
  congenital 148, 160
  disability versus 4, 6
  as diversity 4
  energy requirements based on 150
  equipment adaptations based on 152
  hearing 85
  intellectual. *See* intellectual impairment
  motivation considerations 152-153
  para-athlete development affected by 148, 150
  physiological effects of 160
  promotion of programs 152
  social model and 4
  sport engagement affected by 152
  traumatic 160
  visual. *See* visual impairment
improvised explosive devices (IEDs) 163
inclusion
  barriers to. *See* barriers
  definition of 8, 119
  integration versus 7-9
  social 135
Inclusive Fitness Coalition (IFC) 27
inclusive health 137
Independent Living Resources v. Oregon Arena Corp. 83
indirect ableism 6
individualized education plan (IEP) 67-68
individualized inquiry 72-73
Individuals With Disabilities Education Act (IDEA)
  amendment to 67
  description of 23-24, 64, 184
  free appropriate public education 24, 67-68
  history of 67
  individualized education plan 67-68
  least restrictive environment 68-69

physical education under 68-69
  school applicability of 69
  special education under 68
informal research 196
informational frames, of Paralympic Games media coverage 92f, 94
in-kind 194
innovation
  approaches to 39-41
  in biking 37
  in business 34
  in clothing 35-36
  definition of 33-34
  design thinking approach 40
  in disability 35
  in disability sport 35
  eight essentials of 34
  entrepreneurial mindset for 41
  in equipment 37-38
  in gaming 36
  in marketing 38-39
  SCAMPER approach 40
  sharing of 41
  in snowboards 37
  in sport 35
  in sporting facilities 38
  in sport marketing 38-39
  in travel and tourism 38
  in wheelchairs 37-38
innovators 35, 39
inspiration 16, 99
inspiration porn 6-7, 21
Institute for Innovation and Entrepreneurship 39-40
integration
  definition of 8
  inclusion versus 7-9
intellectual disabilities
  athletes with, in Paralympic Games 54, 138
  characteristics of 125-128
  classification of 125, 126t
  definition of 124
  Down syndrome 127-128
  etiology of 125
  history of term 123-124
  intellectual impairment versus 124
  person-first language for 123-124
  physical activity benefits for 129
  physical disabilities associated with 127
  prevalence of 123
  research regarding 128-129
  Special Olympics and 128-137
  sport participation and 125-128
intellectual functioning
  definition of 126
  sport participation and 126-128

256 INDEX

intellectual impairment
athletes with 135
definition of 124
intellectual disability versus 124
medical model and 124
International Association for Sport for Athletes with a Mental Handicap (INAS-FMH) 138
International Basketball Federation (FIBA) 133
International Coordinating Committee 138
International Council of Sport Science and Physical Education (ICSSPE) 35
International Federation of Adapted Physical Activity (IFAPA) 27
International Olympic Committee 52, 55, 91, 119, 121, 132
International Organization of Sport for People with a Disability (IOSD) 139
International Paralympic Committee (IPC)
classifications 26, 117-118
criticisms of 59
description of 10, 29, 122
eligibility criteria of 140-141
founding of 104
handbook of 104-105
history of 55, 64
IOC and 91
mission statement of 55
qualifying standards of 122
responsibilities of 105
Virtus and 140
vision of 117
International Silent Games 44
International Special Olympics Summer Games 130
International Sports Federation for Persons with Intellectual Disability (INAS-FID) 138
International Sports Organization for the Disabled (ISOD) 48, 51, 122
International Stoke Mandeville Games Committee (ISMGC) 64
International Stoke Mandeville Games Federation (ISMGF) 48
International Stoke Mandeville Wheelchair Sports Federation (ISMWSF) 48
International Wheelchair and Amputee Sports Federation (IWAS) 51
International Working Group on Sports for the Disabled 51
interpersonal ableism 20-21
interscholastic programs 178

intersectionality 6, 16, 22-23
intrascholastic programs 178
Invictus Games 112-114
Iraq 162, 162f

J
Jersey Mike's 136
Joseph P. Kennedy, Jr. Foundation 128, 130
justice model 18-19

K
Kelly Brush Foundation, The 197-198
Kennedy, John F. 128-129
Kennedy, Joseph P., Jr. 129
Klonowski, Michael 199
Kwan, Michelle 132

L
Lakeshore Foundation 27
Landis v. Wash. State Major Baseball Pub. Facilities Dist. Baseball of Seattle 85
language
identity-first 19
person-first 4, 19, 123-124
in social model of disability 4
laws and legislation. *See also specific laws or legislation*
adaptive youth sports 184
athletic participation affected by 73-75
auxiliary aids and services affected by 75
competition rules affected by 73-74
Dear Colleague Letter regarding 26, 70, 125
eligibility rules affected by 74-75
history of 64
Olympic and Amateur Sports Act 24
operating practices affected by 75
sports venues affected by 76-86
least restrictive environment 68-69
Lee, Dave 37
Leeper, Blake 74
les autres athletes, in Paralympic Games 53
long-term development 144
long-term development (LTAD) model
ADM model versus 146, 147t
competition 154-156
description of 143-145, 145t
developmental age considerations 153-154
disability sport application of 149t
expedited timelines 156
features of 147t
FETM model versus 146, 147t

organizational involvement in 157
para-athlete application of 148
principles of 145t, 147t
quality environments 157
stages of 147t
low-impact exercise 20-21
low motivation 22

M
mainstreaming 72
marginality 10
marketing innovations 38-39
MaRS 41
Martin, Casey 71-73
Martin, Fernando Vicente 138
Matheny, Johnny 35
McKeever, Brian 156
McKinsey 34
meaningful personal interactions 9
meaningful social contact 10-11
media
disability representation by 90-91
disability sport representation by 91-96
media coverage
competing perspectives in 96-100
of disability sports. *See* disability sports media coverage
of Paralympic Games. *See* Paralympic Games media coverage
media personnel 96-98
medical model of care 164
medical model of disability
assumptions in 17, 91
characteristics of 2-3
disabling condition diagnosed with 17-18
eugenics and 17
intellectual impairment under 124
social model of disability versus 4, 18
Meyers, Becca 27
Microsoft 36
Military Adaptive Sports Inc. (MASI) 114
Military Health System (MHS) 162
military installations 165
military service members. *See also veterans*
adaptive sports and recreation for 165-174
Department of Defense transition units for 165, 171
deployment of 163
health conditions among 163
overview of 161-163
statistics regarding 161-163
Miller, Robert 84
Miller v. California Speedway Corp. 84-85

Minnesota Wild 81
Miracle League 137
Miranda, Lin-Manuel 136
mobile apps 86
mobility-based disability sports 189
morale 28
most integrated setting 72, 72*t*
Motor Activity Training Program (MATP) 134
Mount Royal University's Institute for Innovation and Entrepreneurship 39-40
Move United 27, 177, 203
multidimensional frames, of Paralympic Games media coverage 92*f*, 94-95

N

National Center on Health, Physical Activity and Disability (NCHPAD) 27
National Disabled Summer Sports Clinic 168*t*
National Disabled Veterans Golf Clinic 168*t*
National Disabled Veterans Winter Sports Clinic 168*t*
national governing bodies (NGB) 29
National Institute of Child Health and Human Development 128
National Institute on Disability, Independent Living, and Rehabilitation Research (NIDLRR) 198
National Intramural and Recreational Sports Association (NIRSA) 27
National Olympic Committee 106
National Paralympic Committee (NPC) 55, 55*t*, 56*t*, 57*t*, 104, 106, 122, 157
National Paralympic Heritage Trust 60
National Sports Organizations (NSO) 144, 157
National Stoke Mandeville Games 46
National Veterans Golden Age Games 168*t*
National Veterans Sports Programs and Special Events (NVSPSE) 166-169, 168*t*
National Veterans Wheelchair Games 168*t*
National Wheelchair Basketball Association (NWBA) 29, 195, 203, 206
nature-based and outdoor interventions 164

NBC 89
negative attitudes
  ableism as cause of 12
  contact theory used to change 9-10
Netflix 89
Nike Go FlyEase shoe 36, 196-197
Nikic, Chris 135
No Accidental Champions (NAC) 148
nondisabled people
  in adaptive sport 28
  celebrating of disability by 18
  "overly helpful" 21
nonprofit 195

O

occupational therapists 164
Office of National Veterans Sports Programs and Special Events (NVSPSE) 166-169, 168*t*
Ohno, Apollo Anton 132
Olay cosmetics 39
Olympic and Amateur Sports Act 24
Olympic Council on Asia (OCA) 109
Olympic Games
  Paralympic Games and, linking of 52, 53*f*, 91, 104, 187
  Stoke Mandeville Games and 47-48, 52
open skills 126
optimal technique 150, 152
organizations
  description of 27, 29, 51
  long-term development model affected by 157
  veteran-serving 162-163
otherwise qualified 69-70, 75
overcoming narrative 93

P

pain 20-22
Pan American Games 66, 107
Para Asiad 109
para-athletes/para-athletes development
  age of acquiring impairment and 148, 150
  classification 154-156
  competition 154-156
  considerations for 148-159
  definition of 155
  developmental age 153-154
  energy requirements 150
  environmental safety for 157-159
  equipment adaptations 152
  expedited timelines 156
  factors that affect 159-160
  functional ability considerations in 154
  fundamental skills 152-153

impairment effects on 148, 150
international sporting careers 156
LTAD model application to 148
motivation 152-153
optimal technique considerations 150, 152
organizational involvement 157
physiological needs of 160
promotion of programs 152
quality environments for 157-159
specialization 153
sport engagement 152
stakeholders in 159-160
training partners 159
Paralympic, defined 52
Paralympic Games
  amputees in 53
  barrier to participation in 26-27
  benefits of 58-59
  blind athletes in 53
  Brazilian 99
  cerebral palsied athletes in 54
  chronology of 49*t*-50*t*
  cycle of reintroduction 101
  development of 51
  double discrimination of female athletes in 95-96, 96*f*
  fair competition at 54
  governance structure for 55
  Guttmann's contributions to. *See* Guttmann, Ludwig
  history of 48, 49*t*-50*t*, 59-60, 64, 91, 165
  as inclusive setting 8
  Inequality-Adjusted Human Development Index 57, 57*t*
  integrated setting versus 7
  intellectual impairment and 138
  intellectually disabled athletes in 54, 137-141
  les autres athletes in 53
  media coverage of. *See* Paralympic Games media coverage
  media personnel perspectives of 96-98
  memorabilia 59-60
  mission of 104
  Olympic Games and, linking of 52, 53*f*, 91, 104, 187
  participating impairment groups 52-54
  re-inclusion in 139
  schedule for 104*t*
  Special Olympics versus 121-122, 128, 136-137
  sport for additional impairment groups 51
  sports in 55, 56*t*
  start of 48, 49*t*-50*t*

INDEX

Paralympic Games > *continued*
Stoke Mandeville Games 45-48, 46*f*, 47*t*, 52, 58, 64, 91, 104
Summer 48, 53*f*, 55-57, 56*t*
2000 Sydney 50*t*, 52, 54, 91-93, 97-98, 108, 114, 138-140
values of 104
vision of 104
visually impaired athletes in 53
Winter 51, 55-57, 56*t*, 101
Paralympic Games athletes
athlete representation of 99-100
classification of 54, 117-118, 122
description of 105
female. *See* female Paralympic athletes
with spinal cord injuries 53
Paralympic Games media coverage
ableism in 95-96
athletic frames of 92*f*, 99
comparison narrative in 94
cyborg narrative in 93
gender stereotypes in 95-96
informational frames of 92*f*, 94
multidimensional frames of 92*f*, 94-95
overcoming narrative in 93
passive victim narrative in 93-94
stereotypical frames of 92*f*, 92-95
supercrip narrative in 92-93
Paralympic movement 104
Paralympic Paradox 97
Paralympic School Day program 10-11
Paralyzed Veterans of America v. D.C. Arena L.P. 83
Parapan American Games 66, 107-109
parasport movement 26-27, 117, 122
para-swimming 159
Pareto Principle 223
Parsons, Andrew 119
participating impairment groups 52-54
passive victim narrative 93-94
Payan v. LACCD Explainer—Disability *Rights Education & Defense Fund* 30
peer relationships 183
Peers, Danielle 59
perceived athletic competence 181
periodization 149*t*
personal barriers 20-22
person-first language 4, 19, 123-124
person with a disability 4
Phelps, Michael 132
physical education
alienation in 12
IDEA definition of 68
physical literacy 149*t*, 150, 153

physical space
inclusion as 7-8
integration as 8
value hierarchy of 9
physical therapists 164
Pistorius, Oscar 73-74, 93
place of public accommodation 76, 76*f*
policy-level barriers 180*t*, 182
polytrauma 164
post-traumatic stress disorder (PTSD) 163-164
Potter, Lauren 132
practical skills 127
practitioners 188, 202
Pratt, Chris 132
Praxis 41
prejudice
ableism as form of 6-7, 15
eugenics as form of 17
Pritchard, Thomas 75
Proctor & Gamble 38-39
Provincial Sport Organizations (PSO) 157
psychological safety 158-159
public accommodation, place of 76, 76*f*
Purdys Chocolatier 39

R

Rashed, Majid 119
reasonable accommodations 24, 26, 74
reasonable modifications 70-71, 73
recreational therapists 164, 166. *See also* Certified Therapeutic Recreation Specialists (CTRSs)
Rehabilitation Act of 1973, Section 504 of. *See* Section 504 of the Rehabilitation Act of 1973
remedial exercise 58
return on investment 198
revenue 188
Rimmer, Jim 20
Rising Phoenix 89
Robles, Javier 179
Rosa's Law 123
Rubens-Alcais, Eugène 44

S

safety
environment 157-159
psychological 158-159
social 159
Salsiccia v. Sharks Sports & Entertainment LLC 86
Sandison v. Michigan High School Athletic Association 75
SCAMPER 40

schools
adaptive athletic programs in 26
adaptive youth sports in 178
Dear College Letter provisions for 125
equitable access in 26
interscholastic programs in 178
intrascholastic programs in 178
Special Olympics programming for 137
Seattle Mariners 85
Section 504 of the Rehabilitation Act of 1973
age eligibility rules 74-75
Americans with Disabilities Act and, comparison between 69-70
description of 23, 26, 30, 64, 184
disability as defined by 70
eligibility rules 74-75
most integrated setting requirement 72, 72*t*
"otherwise qualified" requirement 69-70, 75
reasonable modifications requirement 70-71
settlement agreements 75
self-reflexivity 20
self-regulation 127
service-connected disability ratings 163
service-connected health conditions 163
sexuality 90
Shriver, Eunice Kennedy 64, 128-130, 137
"sick role" 3
Sierra Club 38
sitting volleyball 190
smartphone apps 86
Smith, Rob 118
snowboard innovations 37
social barriers 12, 181
social capital 12, 194
social-ecological model (SEM)
community level of 27*f*, 29
description of 27-28
individual level of 27*f*, 28
interpersonal level of 27*f*, 28
organizational level of 27*f*, 29
policy level of 27*f*, 30
social identities 16
social inclusion 135
social isolation
definition of 10
of disabled person 10, 12
societal barriers as cause of 4
as theory 10-12
social justice 18
social model of disability 3-6, 18

social reintegration 58-59
social relational model of disability 6
social safety 159
Social Security Disability Insurance 30
social skills 134
Sorel 36
Spanish Sports Federation for the Intellectually Disabled (FEDDI) 139
Special Olympics
  athlete development model 134
  basketball 133-134
  coach development model 134
  competitions 132-137
  core of 130
  criticism of 135
  description of 29
  disability language guidelines of 124
  divisioning in 122, 136
  eligibility for 134, 136
  global ambassadors of 132
  goal of 133
  governance of 130, 132, 133f
  history of 64, 128-130, 131f
  inclusive health strategy of 137
  intellectual disability and 128-137
  international competitions 136-137
  milestones of 131f
  mission statement of 132
  national competitions 136-137
  in 1968 129-130
  Paralympics versus 121-122, 128, 136-137
  philosophy of 133
  Protocol of Agreement for 132
  schools programming of 137
  sports of 133-134
  structure of 122
  subprograms 130
  support from 130, 132
  Virtus and 140-141
  volunteers 132
  Winter Games 136
Special Olympics International (SOI) 130, 132
Special Olympics International Games 136
Special Olympics Minnesota (SOMN) 130
Special Olympics North America (SONA) 130
Special Olympics Unified Cup 136
Special Olympics Unified Schools 137

Special Olympics Virginia (SOVA) 130
Special Olympics Young Athletes 134
Special Recreation Program 129-130
spinal cord injuries
  athletes with, in Paralympic Games 53
  pre–World War II prognosis for 44
sponsors 194-197
sponsorships 194-197
sport(s). See also disability sport; specific sport
  adaptive youth. See adaptive youth sports
  benefits of 152
  Charlottesville Cardinals wheelchair basketball team 5
  as curative factor 58
  employment rates affected by participation in 196
  environmental safety for 157
  innovation in. See innovation
  physical literacy skills for 150
  psychological safety for 158
  psychological value of 58
  quality of life benefits of 58
  reasonable modifications to 70
  recreational value of 58
  social reintegration value of 58-59
Sport Canada 144
sporting facilities innovations 38
sport intelligence 127
sport marketing innovations 38-39
sport participation
  adaptive functioning and 127-128
  intellectual disabilities and 125-128
  intellectual functioning and 126-128
sports venues
  amenities and services in, equal access to 78-86
  Americans with Disabilities Act regulations and guidances for 76-86
  assistive devices in 85-86
  closed captioning in 85
  operators of 77-78
  owners of 77-78
  as place of public accommodation 76, 76f
  repairs versus alterations in 82
  service animals in 79-81
  sightlines in, for wheelchair spaces 83-85, 84f
  wheelchair-accessible seating in 81-83, 82t

stakeholder-centric decision-making 8
Stanford University School of Design 40
stereotypes
  gender, in Paralympic Games media coverage 95-96
  in media 90
  negative 3
  supercrip 16, 21, 92-93, 99, 203
stereotypical frames
  of disability sports media coverage 98-100
  of Paralympic Games media coverage 92f, 92-95
Stoke Mandeville Games 45-48, 46f, 47t, 52, 58, 64, 91, 104
strengths-based approach 164, 170
Strike, Anne Wafula 118
summer camp experiment 129
Summer Paralympic Games 48, 53f, 55-57, 56t
supercrip/supercrip narrative 16, 21, 92-93, 99, 203
Swimming Canada 155
systemic ableism 6
systemic barriers 19

T
team morale 28
technical assistance manuals 77, 85
T-Glove 35
theory
  contact 9-10
  critical disability 19
  definition of 9
  social isolation 10-12
"ThisAbles" project 35
Title IX of the Educational Amendments Act 24, 184
T-Mobile Park 85
Tommy Adaptive 36
Tommy Hilfiger 36
tourism 38
Toyota 38, 195
trainability 149t
training partners 159
transcutaneous electrical nerve stimulation (TENS) 164
transition units 165, 171
travel
  costs of 190
  innovations in 38
Tripp, Abi 151
2000 Sydney Paralympic Games 50t, 52, 54, 91-93, 97-98, 108, 114, 138-140

U
Unified Champion Schools 137

Unified Physical Education (UPE) 135
Unified Sports 134
Unified Sports Partners 134
Unilever 38
United Nations Convention on the Rights of Persons with Disabilities (CRPD) 25-26, 65-66, 74, 90, 123
United States Department of Justice 76-77, 79, 83
United States Olympic and Paralympic Museum 60
United States Olympic Committee (USOC) 24
United States Olympic & Paralympic Committee (USOPC) 27, 106, 195, 208
United States Tennis Association (USTA) 29, 81, 195, 197, 209
United States v. Ellerbe Becket Inc. 83
United States Wheelchair Rugby Association (USWRA) 197, 199, 203
Universal Design 18
University of Alabama Adapted Athletics (UAAA)
  adaptive swimming at 209
  board of advisors 212
  booster club for 212
  change 219-220
  coursework at 217-218
  Crossing Points program 218
  emerging sports 208
  facilities at 211*f*, 212-215, 213*f*, 214*f*, 215*f*, 216*f*
  funding for 215, 217
  high-performance sports 208
  marketing director at 211
  mission of 205
  organization of 210
  Outreach 219
  people involved in 210-212
  recommendations from 220-221
  sports 208-209
  starting the program 205-208
  weight room facilities at 211*f*
  wheelchair basketball camp 218
  wheelchair track and road racing at 209
USA Games 136

V

venues. *See* sports venues
veterans. *See also* military service members
  benefits of adaptive sports for 172-173, 173*t*-174*t*
  community-based adaptive sports and recreation for 169-170
  community-based services for 164
  definition of 162
  health conditions among 163
  statistics regarding 162*f*
  treatment options for 163-165
Veterans Benefits Improvement Act of 2008 167
veteran-serving organizations (VSOs) 162-163
Veterans Health Administration (VHA)
  adaptive sports 166-169, 168*t*
  description of 162
  Office of National Veterans Sports Programs and Special Events 166-169, 168*t*
  Vocational Rehabilitation and Employment 169
Veterans of Foreign Wars (VFW) 162-163
virtual reality (VR) 118
Virtus 139-141
visual impairment
  assistive devices in sports venues for patrons with 85
  athletes with, in Paralympic Games 53
  smartphone app accessibility for patrons with 86
  sport engagement affected by 152
  training partners for 159
Vocational Rehabilitation and Employment 169
volleyball 190
volunteers 132, 135

W

Walzer, Matthew 36
Warrior Games 111-112, 112*f*, 165, 166*f*
Washington Redskins 85
weather 22
website accessibility for sports venues 81, 86
well-meaning ableism 6

WFI Stadium Inc. 85
wheelchair(s)
  cost of 189
  innovations in 37-38
  National Veterans Wheelchair Games 168*t*
  sightlines for patrons in 83-85, 84*f*
  sports venue seating requirements for 81-83, 82*t*
wheelchair basketball
  barriers to participation 26
  Charlottesville Cardinals 5
  collegiate programs 200
  hypothetical costs for 191, 191*t*-192*t*, 193*t*
  media coverage of 95
wheelchair netball 44
wheelchair polo 44
wheelchair rugby team 190
wheelchair tennis 209, 215
White supremacy 16-17
Williams, Vanessa 132
Winter Paralympic Games 51, 55-57, 56*t*, 101
World Abilitysport 51
World Bank 123
World Health Organization (WHO) 123
World Report on Disability 122
World War II 44-45, 64
Wrigley Field 82-83

X

X 89
Xbox 36

Y

youth sports
  barriers to 180*t*, 180-182
  benefits of 179
  coaches for 178, 184
  facilitators of 182-184
  parental involvement in 178, 181-182
  participation in 179-184
  peer relationships 183
  in schools 178
  settings for 177-178
youth sport system 178

Z

Zappos 36
Zorn, Trischa 156

ABOUT THE EDITORS

Robin Hardin, PhD, is a professor in the sport management program in the department of kinesiology, recreation, and sport studies at the University of Tennessee. He earned his PhD in communications from the University of Tennessee, as well as a master's degree in communications and a master's degree in sport studies. He completed his bachelor's degree in communications at East Tennessee State University. His research interests lie primarily in the areas of sport governance, holistic care of athletes, and professional development of administrators. He is the former editor of *Sport Management Education Journal* (2018 through 2021) and has served on several other editorial boards. He is a member of the North American Society for Sport Management (NASSM) and the Society of Health and Physical Educators (SHAPE America), and is a member of the official statistics staff for football, men's basketball, and women's basketball at the University of Tennessee. He is a veteran of Operation Desert Storm and retired from the Tennessee National Guard. Photo courtesy of Robin Hardin.

Joshua R. Pate, PhD, is the dean of the School of Business and Management and the program coordinator for sport management at Lees-McRae College. He earned his PhD in sport management from the University of Tennessee, as well as a master's degree in communications and a bachelor's degree in sport management. Pate's research is in disability, access, and inclusion through a sport lens. Pate has served on the editorial team of *Sport Management Education Journal* and serves on multiple editorial boards. He is a member of the North American Society for Sport Management (NASSM). He volunteered at the 2014 Sochi Paralympic Winter Games as one of 70 Paralympic News Service flash quotes reporters, with his work focused on wheelchair curling. Pate has a physical disability (cerebral palsy) and participates in recreational snow skiing, water skiing, hand cycling, and general exercise. Photo courtesy of Lees-McCrae College.

ABOUT THE CONTRIBUTORS

Laurin E. Bixby, PhD, is a research scientist at Brandeis University's Lurie Institute for Disability Policy. Bixby received her PhD in sociology and master's degree in statistics from the University of Pennsylvania. She was a Robert Wood Johnson Foundation Health Policy Research Scholar, Lex Frieden Disability Policy and Advocacy Intern at Elevance Health, and summer fellow at Mathematica Policy Research. Her work illuminates how structural ableism harms disabled people through a variety of systems, such as health care, long-term care, housing, transportation, and incarceration. Through her research, Bixby aims to inform policy and structural changes that advance disability justice and ensure the full integration of disabled people in society. Photo courtesy of Laurin Bixby.

Ian Brittain, PhD, is an associate professor in the Centre for Business in Society at Coventry University in the United Kingdom. He is an internationally recognized expert in the study of disability and Paralympic sport and has attended five summer Paralympic Games, from Sydney 2000 to Rio 2016. His research interests include historical, sociological, and sport management aspects of disability and Paralympic sport, as well as legacy and mega events, especially pertaining to the Paralympic Games. He is also an advisor to the International Wheelchair and Amputee Sport Federation. Photo courtesy of Ian Brittain.

Michael Cottingham, PhD, is an associate professor at the University of Houston and the director of the university's adaptive athletics research center and disability sport program. He has worked as a practitioner and researcher in disability sport for 25 years. He has published over 50 peer-reviewed articles and received over $1.2 million in external funding from organizations such as the National Institute on Disability, Independent Living, and Rehabilitation Research; the U.S. State Department; and the National Collegiate Athletic Association. Photo courtesy of University of Houston.

Simon Darcy, PhD, is a professor at the UTS Business School in the University of Technology–Sydney, where he is an interdisciplinary researcher, educator, and industry engagement specialist developing accessible and inclusive organizational approaches to marginalized groups. Darcy has had a long history of engaging with people with disability and brings a lived experience that enhances his academic work. His other areas of sport research involve volunteer management and understanding the social impact of sport. He has had a Linkage Projects grant from the Australian Research Council and currently has a Discovery Projects grant from ARC for his work on involving outsiders in sport. For the last decade, he has worked on disability employment and entrepreneurship through design thinking led innovation. Photo courtesy of University of Technology Sydney.

Anthony G. Delli Paoli, PhD, is an assistant professor in the department of kinesiology and health at Rutgers University and director of the university's Youth Sports Research Council. He is on the editorial board of the *Journal of Clinical Sport Psychology* and is an active member of the North American Society for the Psychology of Sport and Psychology Activity and the New Jersey Recreation and Park Association. His research was awarded the Excellence in Research Award by the *Journal of Sport and Exercise Psychology*. Photo courtesy of Rutgers, The State University of New Jersey.

Abby Fines, PhD, is an assistant professor in the kinesiology department at the University of Virginia, where she also received her doctorate. Her research interests are in the development and management of adapted sports as well as pedagogical practices used to promote inclusive opportunities. She finds that being her own experimental subject is essential for engaging students in critical reflection about disability from various perspectives. Fines has experience working alongside Paralympic and Special Olympics athletes across all levels of play and is most content witnessing the discovery and achievement of athletic potential. Photo courtesy of University of Virginia.

Justin A. Haegele, PhD, is an associate professor and director of the Center for Movement, Health, and Disability in the department of human movement sciences at Old Dominion University. His research focuses on the interdisciplinary field of adapted physical activity, with a primary interest in examining how disabled people, particularly visually impaired or blind people, experience physical activity participation. Haegele is a research fellow with the Research Council of SHAPE America, an editor for *Quest*, and an associate editor for *Adapted Physical Activity Quarterly*. Photo courtesy of Justin Haegele.

Brent Hardin, PhD, is an associate professor in the department of kinesiology and the director of the adapted athletics program at the University of Alabama. Hardin arrived at the university in 2003 as an assistant professor and soon thereafter began building the adapted athletics program with the support of cofounder Dr. Margaret Stran and University of Alabama President Robert Witt. The program started with women's wheelchair basketball in 2003 and later grew to include men's wheelchair basketball in 2006, then men's and women's wheelchair tennis in 2013; the program is set to introduce wheelchair track and adaptive swimming by 2025. What started as a small volunteer program is now home to over 30 high-performance athletes with disabilities and 13 full-time coaches and staff. The adapted athletics program at the University of Alabama is a stand-alone department and is not supported by the NCAA-affiliated athletics department on campus. Photo courtesy of University of Alabama.

Tiao Hu is a PhD candidate in sport and fitness administration at the University of Houston. She received her master's degree from the University of Georgia, where her internship with BlazeSports evoked her passion for disability sport as she saw how sport changes lives and promotes social equity. Her research focuses on promotion of disability sport and diversity within the disability sport community, and she currently has six publications. Integrating years of practice in able-bodied sport, her career goal is to use research, programming, and service in disability sport to provide equal opportunities for people with disabilities to enjoy sport and life. Photo courtesy of Tiao Hu.

Mary A. Hums, PhD, is a professor of sport administration at the University of Louisville and is a former college athletic director. In 2009, she was named an Earle F. Zeigler Lecturer, the most prestigious academic honor from the North American Society for Sport Management (NASSM). She was invited to White House events, including the 2015 White House presidential reception celebrating the 25th anniversary of the Americans with Disabilities Act. In 2014, she received the NASSM Diversity Award. In 2008, Hums was an Erasmus Mundus Visiting International Scholar at Katholische Universitat in Leuven, Belgium. In 2006, the U.S. Olympic Committee selected her to represent the United States at the International Olympic Academy in Olympia, Greece. She has worked four Paralympic Games, the Olympic Games, and the Parapan American Games. Hums coauthored Article 30.5 of the 2006 U.N. Convention on the Rights of Persons With Disabilities. She has authored over 150 refereed journal articles and book chapters and given over 200 presentations in the United States and abroad. Her advocacy writings have appeared on the websites of SportandDev, Peace and Sport, Play the Game, Mentor: the National Mentoring Partnership, and Huffington Post. Her research interests are policy development in sport organizations regarding inclusion of people with disabilities and also sport and human rights. Hums is a monogram letter winner in field hockey at the University of Notre Dame and a 1996 inductee in the Amateur Softball Association Indiana Softball Hall of Fame. Photo courtesy of Mary Hums.

Winston Kennedy, DPT, PhD, is an assistant professor at Northeastern University and has been a physical therapist since 2015. Along with his DPT, he has a master's degree in public health and a PhD in kinesiology with a concentration in adapted physical activity. Kennedy is committed to conducting research that supports the health and well-being of people with disabilities within their intersecting identities. Kennedy was a fellow in the Leadership Education in Neurodevelopmental and Other Related Disabilities fellowship program, where he earned a certificate in disability health policy. Photo courtesy of Winston Kennedy.

Don Lee, PhD, is an associate professor of sport and fitness administration in the department of health and human performance at the University of Houston (UH). Prior to joining UH in 2014, he taught for six years at both Division III and Division I schools, specializing in sport management. Lee's research focuses on sport consumer behaviors, with particular emphasis on game attendance, team merchandise purchasing, and media sports consumption. Additionally, he conducts research on measurement in sports behaviors and branding. Photo courtesy of Don Lee.

David Legg, PhD, is a professor of sport management and adapted physical activity at Mount Royal University in Calgary, Canada. As a volunteer he has been president of the Canadian Paralympic Committee and a board member for the 2015 Parapan American Games in Toronto. Legg has also served on the International Paralympic Committee's Sport Science Committee and is the past president of the International Federation of Adapted Physical Activity. More recently as a consultant, Legg worked with the Calgary Olympic Bid Corporation for the 2026 Olympic and Paralympic Games and the 2030 Commonwealth Games. Photo courtesy of Joanne Howard, Howard's Cove Photography.

Kathleen McCarty, PhD, is an assistant professor in the kinesiology department at the University of San Francisco. She is a graduate of the Health Policy Research Scholars program, funded by the Robert Wood Johnson Foundation, and the Multi-Institution Mentorship Consortium, funded by a U.S. Department of Education training grant. Her research and teaching focus on disability justice within kinesiology pedagogy, as well as a focus on adaptive sports at the collegiate level. She is passionate about how disability paradigms intersect with health, fitness, and education, and her mission is to advocate for health equity. Photo courtesy of Stephen Hew Photography, Bay Area California.

Cathy McKay, EdD, is an associate professor in the kinesiology department at James Madison University. She completed her doctoral degree at the University of Virginia and is a research fellow with the Research Council of SHAPE America. McKay's scholarly interests focus on social inclusion, changing attitudes and perspectives toward disability, and parasport education and awareness. McKay is passionate about contact theory and applying contact theory in educational settings. Photo courtesy of JMU University Marketing and Branding.

Christina Mehrtens, PhD, is an assistant professor at the University of Wisconsin–La Crosse. Her research interests are informed by her experience as the first adapted physical education teacher in a rural county of Virginia. Working with all grade levels and a variety of disabilities across the district, she implemented foundational physical education services. The experience was unfortunately a testament to the structural and societal barriers that students with disabilities face to gain equitable opportunities in physical education, recreation, and physical activity in general. Thus, her research now focuses on collaborative preservice training and professional development for school administration, physical education teachers, paraeducators, and other health practitioners to support individuals with disabilities in physical education and recreation. Photo courtesy of University of Wisconsin-La Crosse.

About the Contributors

Laura Misener, PhD, is a professor and director of the School of Kinesiology at Western University in London, Canada. Her research focuses on how sport and events can be use as instruments of social change, with an emphasis on how sport for persons with a disability can have a positive impact on community accessibility and social inclusion. Her research program is interdisciplinary and pushes the traditional boundaries of the sport management discipline to emphasize the importance of critical scholarship for innovation. She employs critical approaches to highlight inequities in systems and structures to support inclusive sport and physical activities while also offering new frameworks for best practices. Misener serves as a research and policy advisor to several disability sport organizations focused on broadening the role of sport in positive social outcomes. Photo courtesy of Michaela Devine.

Anita M. Moorman, JD, is a professor of sport administration at the University of Louisville. She teaches sport law and legal aspects of sport. She received her law degree from Southern Methodist University. Moorman is licensed to practice law in the state of Oklahoma and was admitted to practice before the U.S. Supreme Court when she served as co-counsel for nine disability sport organizations on an amicus curiae brief in the landmark case involving professional golfer Casey Martin and the PGA Tour. Photo courtesy of University of Louisville.

Oluwaferanmi Okanlami, PhD, is a physician leader at the University of Michigan and University of California–Los Angeles. His passions include medical student education and mentorship as well as providing equitable access for people with disabilities, particularly involving access to physical and emotional health and wellness through adaptive sports and fitness opportunities. In 2023, Okanlami was nominated by President Joe Biden to serve on the President's Council on Sports, Fitness & Nutrition, and he speaks around the country on topics related to diversity, equity, and inclusion, including the need for a health system that is accessible to and inclusive of both patients and providers with disabilities, and providing reasonable and appropriate accommodations for students with disabilities in higher education. Photo courtesy of Sydney Verlinde.

Erin Pearson, MA, is a PhD candidate in the School of Kinesiology at Western University in London, Canada. Her research interests include sport marketing and events, social impact and inclusion, and event leveraging. Her doctoral research examines how sport events may be leveraged using a knowledge management and transfer lens. Pearson is also a full-time faculty member in the Lawrence Kinlin School of Business at Fanshawe College in London, Canada. Her primary teaching areas are sport and event marketing, leadership, sport sponsorship, and ethics. Photo courtesy of Erin Pearson.

About the Contributors 267

Javier Robles, JD, is a teaching instructor in the department of kinesiology and health at Rutgers University and the director of their Center for Disability Sports, Health, and Wellness. He is a board member of United Spinal Association, chair of the Rutgers Adaptive Sports Day Committee, and chair of the New Jersey Disability Action Committee. He is cochair and founding member of the Rutgers University Disability Awareness Month Committee and cochair of the Rutgers University Disability Studies Minor Committee. He served as a member of the Robert Wood Johnson Foundation, National Advisory Panel on Structural Barriers to Health Committee, and guest editor for *Health Affairs* magazine's special edition on disabilities and wellness. He holds a bachelor's degree from Rutgers University and a juris doctorate from Seton Hall University. Photo courtesy of Amy Bertelsen-Robles.

Darda Sales, PhD, PLY, completed her doctoral studies at Western University, where she focused her research on adaptive athlete development, the passion for which was fueled by her experiences as a four-time Paralympian. Sales currently provides consulting services to national and provincial sport organizations looking to enhance their adaptive sport programming. In everything she does, Sales is committing to making sport at all levels more accessible to those who experience impairment. Photo courtesy of Darda Sales.

Margaret Stran, PhD, is a clinical associate professor of kinesiology and associate director of the adapted athletics program at the University of Alabama. The focus of her teaching is adapted sport and disability, while the focus of her administrative duties is grant writing and leadership development. Stran's community and outreach work is concentrated on inclusion and accessibility. Stran played and coached wheelchair basketball for 20 years. As a player, she won three national championships, a silver medal at World Championships, and bronze and silver Paralympic medals. As a coach, she helped lead her teams to three national championships and two gold medals. Photo courtesy of University of Alabama.

Jasmine Townsend, PhD, is an associate professor of recreational therapy within the department of parks, recreation, and tourism management at Clemson University and is program coordinator for the department's recreational therapy concentration. She is a Faculty Scholar in Clemson's School of Health Research. She is also the director of Clemson's adaptive sports and recreation program and the chair of the Clemson Athletic Council. Her primary research interest is investigating the outcomes of participation in recreation of all types, particularly for individuals with disabilities. Her current research focuses on the transformative nature of adaptive sport participation for individuals with physical disabilities, as well as the general health outcomes of recreational therapy.

Townsend is an associate editor for the American Therapeutic Recreation Association's annual journal, the *ATRA Annual*, as well the *Journal of Leisure Research* and other publications. Townsend's practical experience as a certified therapeutic recreation specialist and certified adaptive recreation and sport specialist includes working with youths and adults with physical, intellectual, and psychological health conditions in community adaptive sports and therapeutic recreation programs; working in wilderness and residential treatment programs for youths with behavioral and mental health conditions; and implementing international adaptive sport training programs in Indonesia, Mexico, and Thailand. She also serves on the board of directors for Project Sanctuary, a veteran-serving organization based in Colorado. Townsend lives in South Carolina with her husband, their two children, and dog. Photo courtesy of Jasmine Townsend.

Jeff M. Ward, MA, is a PhD candidate and instructor in the sport administration department at the University of Louisville. He earned his undergraduate degree and master's degree in sports management at the University of Central Arkansas. His areas of interest are athletes with disabilities and disability inclusion. He is also a military veteran, having served as a submariner on board the USS *Louisville* in Pearl Harbor, Hawaii, for three and a half years and as a hospital corpsman at Naval Station Lemoore in Lemoore, California, for five years. He took part in two major deployments in support of Operation Enduring Freedom/Operation Iraqi Freedom and Operation New Dawn. Photo courtesy of Jeff Ward.

Derek Whaley is a PhD candidate at Clemson University and is a Robert H. Brooks Sports Science Institute graduate fellow. Whaley has been the graduate teacher of record for the adaptive sports and recreation course and the recreational therapy implementation and evaluation course at Clemson University. Additionally, Whaley serves as a program director in Clemson's Adaptive Sports and Recreation Lab, which conducts ongoing adaptive sports research and implements large-scale community-based adaptive sports programs (i.e., Clemson Classic and Palmetto Games). As a certified therapeutic recreation specialist, Whaley practiced recreational therapy in behavioral health with youths and adults for 10 years in North Carolina, Montana, Wyoming, Alaska, and Michigan. He enjoys being the proud father of a son and daughter. Photo courtesy of Derek Whaley.